THE CAMPAIGN OF TRAFALGAR

The Attack at Trafalgar
From a contempory manuscript plan.

Wheather Division

1. Victory 100
2. Téméraire 98
3. Neptune 98
4. Conqueror 74
5. Leviathan 74
6. Britannia 100
7. Orion 74
8. Ajax 74
9. Spartiate 74
10. Agamemnon 64
11. Minotaur 74
12. Africa 64

Lee Division

1. Royal Sovereign 100
2. Mars 74
3. Belleisle 74
4. Tonnant 80
5. Colossus 74
6. Achille 74
7. Bellerophon 74
8. Revenge 74
9. Defiance 74
10. Thunderer 74
11. Defence 74
12. Swiftsure 74
13. Polyphemus 64
14. Dreadnought 98
15. Prince 98

Cruisers

1. Euryalus 36
2. Phœbe 36
3. Sirius 32
4. Naiad 38
5. Pickle 10
6. Entrepenant 10

THE CAMPAIGN OF
TRAFALGAR

SIR JULIAN CORBETT

NONSUCH

First published 1910
This edition 2005

Nonsuch Publishing Limited
The Mill, Brimscombe Port,
Stroud, Gloucestershire, GL5 2QG
www.nonsuch-publishing.com

British Library Cataloguing in Publication Data.
A catalogue record for this book is available from the British Library.

ISBN 1-84588-059-5

Typesetting and origination by Nonsuch Publishing Limited
Printed in Great Britain by Oaklands Book Services Limited

CONTENTS

BIOGRAPHICAL NOTE

In his 2000 Caird Medal lecture at the University of Greenwich, Professor Hattendorf, chairman of the Naval War College's Maritime History Department, stressed the debt that modern strategic thinking owes to the theorists upon whose work it is founded. There is, he states, 'an intellectual link across the entire 20th century directly to the events of the long eighteenth…' In terms of British maritime policy, foremost among these theorists is Sir Julian Stafford Corbett. Knighted in 1917 for services to the Committee of Imperial Defence, his non-traditional view of naval objectives was a direct influence on the policies of the Admiralty during the First World War. The Royal Navy acknowledge his work, in particular his theories on Command of the Sea, as being the basis for their current Maritime Strategy.

The Campaign of Trafalgar (1910) was produced with the intent of providing the first 'staff account' of the battle. Beautifully written, and possessed of a classical precision, it posits the controversial and historically accurate theory that the campaign's true importance lay, not in preventing an invasion of Britain, but in gaining control of the Mediterranean Seas; rendering Britain impregnable was, however, the reward.

Julian Corbett was born on 12 November 1854 at Imber Court, Thames Ditton, to Charles and Elizabeth. He attended Marlborough and Trinity College, Cambridge, and was awarded a first in the law tripos in 1875. Although he was called to the bar by the Middle Temple, he was not to stay within this field. His was a more literary bent, and in 1886 his first work was published, a work of fiction entitled *The Fall of Asgard; a Tale of St Olaf's Days*. Two more novels were to follow, *For God and Gold* (1887), and *Kophetua the Thirteenth* (1889).

The focus of his efforts shifted at this point from fiction towards the purely historical. In 1889 he produced a biography of Monk, which was followed quickly in 1890 by a similar work on Sir Francis Drake. He was to expand on this study with the publication of *Drake and the Tudor Navy; With a History of the Rise of England as a Maritime Power* (1898). This is considered to be his first major contribution to serious historical literature, and was widely acclaimed for the meticulous nature of its research. Corbett also revealed in this work an acute facility for analysis, an ability to draw strategic conclusions from his observations. In terms of the Anglo-Spanish war, for example, Corbett saw commerce as being the principal factor in the conflict, above the religious or political, and as the reason Spain went to war. Such a recognition of the importance of trade in international relations was to prove a key feature of his later work.

Corbett's perception of the nature of conflict was further deepened by his time as Special War Correspondent with *The Pall Mall Gazette*. It was in this capacity that he travelled with the Dongola Expedition of 1896. Together with the depth of his historical understanding, his legal and journalistic experience allowed him to bring a dramatically different insight to the study of naval strategy.

By 1898, his work had come to the attention of the Naval Records Society, its founder John Know Laughton requesting Corbett to edit *Papers Relating to the Navy during the Spanish War, 1585-1587* (1898). Corbett's association with the Society was to continue and in 1902, at their behest, he edited Sir William Slyngsbie's *Relation of the Voyage to Cadiz, 1596.*

In 1902, Captain W.J. May appointed Corbett to the post of principal lecturer on history and strategy at the newly established Naval War Course at Greenwich. His role as lecturer, as May saw it, was to elucidate those lessons of the Anglo-French Wars which might pertain to modern day conflict. Chief among these was the notion that maritime conflict, and conflict as a whole, should always be viewed in terms of a nation's overall policy. In this he was clearly influenced by Karl Von Clausewitz, and, to a lesser extent, the Swiss strategist Jomini. Clausewitz's most often quoted dictum, that 'war is merely the continuation of policy by other means', is a sentiment Corbett repeatedly echoes.

Corbett was selected to deliver the Ford Lectures at Oxford in 1903, and in 1904, he published an expansion of his War Course lectures as *England in the Mediterranean, 1603-1714*. One of the underlying themes of this work was the importance of a continual sea presence in terms of communications, a fundamental factor in his later theories on Command of the Sea.

In *England in the Seven Years' War* (1907), Corbett further expanded his contemporary theories through historical analysis. In this text, he explores the notion of 'Limited War', a concept whereby the objective of war becomes less than the total destruction of the enemy. His thinking in this regard was both original and at variance with some of his contemporaries, such as the American A.T. Mahan. He also risked running afoul of the 'Blue Water theorists' of the time, by expounding the necessity that Maritime Strategy and Land Strategy be viewed as indivisible.

The Campaign of Trafalgar (1910) was Corbett's most significant work up to this point. In this work, he examines all aspects of the campaign, rather than just the famous battle itself. He explores the intricacies of England's diplomatic negotiations, the delicate balance of her territorial arrangements in concert with her colonial concerns, and, of course, her maritime strategy. Nelson's actions in response to Admiral Villeneuve's break-out is re-examined in terms of overall policy, and the possibilities of invasion through Ireland or directly through the English Channel are interpreted within the context of realistic French ambitions.

The profound strategic and theoretical implications which Corbett derives from this study are further examined in *Some Principles of Maritime Strategy* (1911), his only non-historical work. It is a collation of all Corbett's theories, covering issues such as the holistic idea of policy and war in terms of national objective, notions of dispersal and concentration of forces, limited war, the importance of trade and communication, together with his vaunted theories on Command of the Sea.

In 1914, Corbett was awarded the Chesney Gold Medal by the Royal United Service Institute, for his editorial work on the *Private Papers of George, Second Earl Spencer* (1913), which reappraises the nature of naval administration during the Anglo-French Wars. At the outbreak of the First World War, he was to become an influential voice in the Admiralty's highest quarters, a close friend of the reformer and First Sea Lord, Baron Fisher, and is credited with having had a guiding hand in the nation's war policy.

After the war, and following his knighthood for services rendered, Corbett delivered the Creighton Lecture at King's College London in 1921. In this lecture he outlined his next project as being an examination of Napoleon and the British Navy after Trafalgar. He died on 21 September of that year, however, at Stopham, Sussex.

A dedicated historian, Corbett remains regarded as one of the deepest and most flexible thinkers in the field of naval strategic thought. His works are a current feature of maritime study and the theories, to which he gives strength through the weight of historical example, are still considered sound.

PREFACE

In the most recent bibliography of the Waterloo campaign, that prepared by Professor Oman for the *Cambridge Modern History*, there appear little short of a score of works entirely devoted to its elucidation. For the Trafalgar campaign our English language cannot boast a single one. Of the battle itself there are studies innumerable, serious, fanciful, and anecdotic; but the fact remains that, though its centenary is past and gone, no British pen has ever been set to the task of producing, from the vast store of material that exists, anything like a reasoned Staff account of the crowning chapter in the history of naval warfare. We have, it is true, Mr. Newbolt's delightful volume. *The Year of Trafalgar*; but that, although it contains the best study of the battle that has yet appeared, makes no pretence of dealing exhaustively with the policy and operations which led to it. The truth is that for all the spade work that has been devoted to it in recent years by Sir John K. Laughton, Mr. Leyland, and others, the subject has been left, so far as the Service and the public are concerned, in the same comparative darkness that enshrouds the bulk of our naval history. Nelson's share of the work has received ample justice. Indeed the campaign has scarcely ever been approached except from his standpoint. And yet till nearly the end his share was comparatively small. Until in the last month of his life, when he resumed command of the restored Mediterranean station, he had a bare dozen of the line and a score or so of cruisers under his flag, while during the year there were in commission and reserve well over a hundred of the line and four hundred cruisers.

Nor is this all. The military side of the campaign has been left in even greater obscurity than the naval. In the course of the year, besides the troops in the East and West Indies we had something like 50,000 men engaged in active overseas operations. Only a fraction of these touched Nelson, and where they did their deflecting influence on his strategy has been almost entirely ignored. Indeed it is not too much to say that the controlling fact that the campaign of 1805 was a combined campaign and not merely naval, has never been given its due importance. Still less has it been realised that it was essentially an offensive campaign, and not merely a campaign of defence against invasion. The failure to grasp these cardinal facts has clouded even Nelson's action and exposed him to criticism which he did not deserve. How much more then has it clouded the rest!

It is not that a minute study of the campaign detracts in the least from Nelson's greatness. High as such a study lifts the reputation of his colleagues, Nelson still remains the greatest of admirals. The fascination of his dazzling personality still dominates the judgment, and it is only by a severe and persistent effort of resistance that we can hope to see things in their true proportion and real meaning. If we would read the lesson aright not only must we keep Nelson's part in due subordination, but we must also continually forswear the calling of the sea and closet ourselves with Pitt and Melville, with Barham and Castlereagh. It is with them alone we may watch the inward springs at work, by which the fleets at sea were really controlled, and mark the flow of intelligence from spies and cruisers and embassies that set them in motion or stayed their action.

For such a detailed study, as most of our military campaigns but not one of our naval have received, the time has been ripened by the publication of a large proportion of the essential documents. For the diplomatic influences, which in this, as in most campaigns, provides the master-key, we have Mr Holland Rose's *Select Despatches relating to the Third Coalition against France*, 1804-5, edited for the Royal Historical Society, though, as the editor unfortunately omitted to note the dates on which the despatches were received, their connection with naval and military instructions has been impossible to trace without collation with the originals. To this collection must be added, besides the well-known correspondence of Napoleon and Talleyrand, Mons. P. Coquelle's *Napoléon et Angleterre* (1803-13), and Mons. Charles Auriol's *La France, l'Angleterre et Naples* (1803-6), both invaluable works.

For the naval side we have Mr. Leyland's *Despatches and Letters relating to the Blockade of Brest*, 1803-5, edited for the Navy Records Society, and the *Cornwallis Papers*, recently published by the Historical MSS. Commission from the collection of Mr. Cornwallis Wykeham-Martin (*Various Collections*, vol. vi. 1909). But for the most valuable published material by far we must acknowledge our debt with humility, if not with shame, to the French War Office. The monumental works of Colonel Edouard Desbrière, entitled, *Projets et tentatives de débarquement aux Îles Britanniques* (1793–1805) and *La Campaign Maritime de Trafalgar*, published under the direction of the Section Historique de l'Etat-major de 1'Armée, contain the first attempt to form a real Staff history of the campaign, and although they make no pretence of dealing adequately with the unpublished English material, they place us for the first time in a position to see the campaign as it really was. My debt to these volumes, increased as it is by Colonel Desbrière's courtesy in personally elucidating points that were obscured by faulty transcripts, is almost beyond recognition. A similar work from the Spanish side is still in progress in the *Revista de Marina* by General Galiano, a lineal descendant of a Trafalgar hero. It is useful in supplementing Colonel Desbrière's volumes, although most of the important Spanish documents were generously communicated to the French Staff by General Galiano for Colonel Desbrière's use.

Amongst manuscript sources only recently accessible, we have the *Pitt Papers*, deposited at the Public Record Office, and, still more valuable, the *Barham Papers*, which have been entrusted for publication to the Navy Records Society. To these latter I have been permitted access, and have received invaluable assistance in examining them from the editor, Sir John Laughton.

The labour of working through the mass of ship's Logs and Journals, the Admirals' and Captains' letters, and the other rich material in the Admiralty Archives, and of subsequently reducing it to narrative and critical form, has necessarily been great; but in attempting the formidable task my path has been smoothed by many ready helpers. My thanks are specially due to Captain Hudleston, R.N., for placing at my disposal his researches into the system of naval defence in home waters; to Mr. Perrin, the Admiralty Librarian, for help in every direction, and particularly in preparing the Schedule of Signals recorded as having been made at the battle of Trafalgar; and to Lieutenant Keate, R.N., for assistance in preparing the track charts from the Logs.

Of these charts, which have now been constructed for the first time, and which are the necessary basis of all strategical criticism, it must be explained that they should not be taken as absolutely correct. Except where otherwise indicated the tracks are simply plotted between noon positions, and owing to the uncertainty of longitude observations, even these positions are sometimes only approximate. This is especially the case with the smaller cruisers, whose neglected movements are not infrequently vital to a correct view of fleet operations, such as Orde's retreat from Cadiz and Nelson's final decision to chase to the West Indies. In the important case, for instance, of the *Iris*, which observed Villeneuve's final movement from Ferrol, no one on board seems to have been able to work out a longitude at all. At least none are entered in her master's log, and in running down from Ushant she made Cape Peñas instead of Ortegal, nearly a hundred miles to the westward.

In plotting the French tracks the difficulty of reaching precision has been even greater. They are primarily based on the charts given by Colonel Desbrière, but unfortunately these charts are not quite worthy of the rest of the work. They have required careful correction from the positions and courses recorded in the documents themselves. Sometimes these, too, are obviously false, especially in the case of Villeneuve's retreat from Ferrol and Cadiz; and in these cases the track shown is that actually observed and reported by our cruisers. When, as occurs in the most doubtful cases, two or more of such cruisers working independently give coinciding observations, the positions and course reported are taken as correct.

It is hoped that the movements and instructions of these cruisers, and indeed the whole system of scouting and intelligence, will be found an interesting feature of the book. Hitherto, owing to the unfortunate precedent set by James, cruiser work has usually been divorced from the major operations to which it belongs organically, and we have known little about it beyond the frigate actions that were fought. To naval officers, and indeed to all serious students of naval warfare, history so written must have a flavour of unreality that is little short of repellent. What they require is a co-ordinated account of the movements of all classes of ships engaged in each operation, and a clear knowledge of the instructions and intelligence under which it was carried out. In short, if Naval History is to establish itself as a matter of real instructional interest, students must be able to find in accounts of the old campaigns at least an indication of what they would look for in a report on manoeuvres today.

No one can approach our Naval History from this point of view, even in the tentative and imperfect manner that has been attempted in the following pages, without feeling how defective is the bulk of what we now possess. It is scarcely an exaggeration to say that the whole requires rewriting on Staff lines. But it is unlikely that so large and technical a task can ever be done adequately except by an Historical Section at the Admiralty. The need for such a Section is crying. Buried in our Naval Archives is a mass of lore, a body of matured tradition, such as no other country in the world possesses; but it lies dormant and forgotten, a wasted power of incalculable force, that might be ours behind the guns and ours alone. But to re-awaken that tradition, to make it a living thing, as it was to Barham and Cornwallis and Nelson, to render it once more the active force that gave them nerve and initiative, and that certainty of touch which seems now almost miraculous, is beyond the reach of individual effort. It needs, no less than the most technical and material parts of the naval art, a laboratory where civilian and naval experts can work side by side to supply each other's defects and ripen each other's ideas.

It has indeed been suggested that a Professorship of Naval History at a University might supply the need. But however such a chair may succeed for Military History or for forming a sound national opinion, for the practical needs of the Service it seems foredoomed to failure. What is of the sea must breathe the breath of the sea. Without it it will pine in academical speculation. In salt water the old naval tradition was born, and by salt water alone can it be nourished. Sever the work of revival from the Admiralty and you sever it from the well-spring of that intangible spirit which is our peculiar asset. It is ours alone if we choose to use it. The most perfect organisation, the most scholarly research, the most elaborate technical science, cannot supply its place. It is the product of centuries of naval warfare, and it is we who have the centuries behind us. The atmosphere they have engendered is the soul of the matter, and nowhere out of intimate touch with the fleet can its inspiration be assured.

Some day, it may be hoped, the truth may be realised. Some day, perhaps, we shall recognise the value of the force by which alone we may bend again the bow of Odysseus; and then a Historical Section will seem as indispensable a national asset as an experimental tank or a laboratory for high explosives.

J. S. C.

THE CAMPAIGN OF TRAFALGAR

CHAPTER I

Pitt's War Policy

When, in May 1804, Pitt returned to power it was with a determination to conduct the lingering war on the grand scale of his father and by his father's strenuous methods. Treasured among his papers of the time is an eloquent apostrophe urging him to rise up and take the place that had been held by William the Third, by Marlborough, and by his father: to set himself, as they had done, at the head of Europe against Europe's great oppressor, to stir the faint hearts of the Powers into united effort, and to remove from England the reproach that she had not produced a war minister since the great days of Chatham.

The people, realising how the country's strength had grown with the war, were looking to him to give expression to their rising spirit; to teach them not only how to protect themselves from invasion, but how in the consciousness of their strength to strike down their arch-enemy as they had been wont to do in old days. In this spirit he gathered up the reins, and began at once to lay his widespread plans to give the war a new and more worthy presence.

Ever since we had broken the Peace of Amiens, our attitude, in effect, had been one of defence. Napoleon's unblushing contempt for his diplomatic engagements, and his unconcealed belief that by sheer truculence he could force us out of the European system altogether, had driven Addington's peace-loving Government to declare war.[1] To wage it was another thing, and it quickly proved to be beyond their capacity. From the first they were dominated by the elaborate threat of invasion by which Napoleon seized the initiative. Seeing how weak was the army, it paralysed all hope of offensive action in Europe, and our confident enemy could make merry over a country that went to war to show that it could defend itself.

Such offensive operations as were within their resources had been purely maritime — directed against the sea-borne trade of France and her minor colonial possessions. At the outbreak of hostilities our military strength in the West Indies was considerable, for the garrisons which had been in occupation of the French islands captured in the late war had not yet returned. These were well employed in retaking St. Lucia, which had come from long experience to be regarded as the key of the naval position in the Leeward Islands. So high, indeed, did it stand as a naval position that the question of its retrocession had almost wrecked the peace which ended the Seven Years' War. But, not content with this legitimate opening, the Government, in spite of the bitter lessons of the last war, proceeded to occupy Tobago and the four Dutch settlements of Demerara, Essequibo, Berbice, and Surinam. All these sickly stations required garrisons, and the result was to demobilise a serious proportion of our slender military force, and still further to reduce the possibility of a more active policy at home.[2]

For these adventures Addington and his friends are now blamed without mercy, but candour and a reasonable knowledge of the political conditions should temper the habitual attitude of superiority which their critics are wont to adopt. To begin with, we had in any case no hope of being able to use our army in Europe with effect single-handed, and at that time we were single-handed. And in the second place, the opening moves against the Dutch colonies were, in fact, a direct blow at the object we had in view. The real cause of the war, as is now admitted on both sides, was Napoleon's shameless behaviour to the United Provinces in breach of the Treaty of Lunéville. Before the ink was well dry he had reduced Holland to the condition of a subject-ally of France. His similar behaviour in Northern Italy and Switzerland intensified the resentment his breach of faith aroused; but the virtual annexation of Holland was what made a renewal of the war inevitable. It touched our traditional policy to the quick. The menace to our position in the Narrow Seas was one we had never been willing to endure. Now our reply was a refusal to evacuate Malta as provided by the Treaty of Amiens, and so the war broke out again. It was therefore a perfectly logical opening to strike at the Dutch colonies. It was a blow that could be dealt rapidly, and was well calculated to teach any man but Napoleon the lesson he could never learn. It told him plainly that, if France could find no room for England in the councils of Europe, there would be no room for a French empire beyond the seas.

But in political effect the West Indian conquests proved of no avail, and in the actual war they counted for nothing except in one not unimportant direction. The captured islands were a hotbed of privateering, and privateering was always the chief danger to our sea-borne commerce. Long experience had shown that it could not be dealt with effectually by pelagic operations alone. Addington's policy, therefore, has at least the justification not only of having dealt a direct blow at French commerce, and therefore at her finance, but also of having adopted the most effectual method of protecting our own. And, be it remembered, it was the retention of our financial position that eventually enabled us to beat Napoleon down; it was our sole hope of securing allies: and furthermore our only possible means of offence for the moment was against French sea-borne commerce. It was a form of attack particularly embarrassing to a ruler like Napoleon, whose chief aim in consenting to a peace had been to restore his finances and his fleet. It is therefore perhaps too narrow a judgment to condemn the West Indian operations out of hand merely because they seem to sin against the principle of concentration, and were a form of war which of itself could never decide the issue. Where a maritime empire is concerned caution is required in applying the simple formulae of continental strategists. Oceanic and continental war differ widely in some of their cardinal conditions. It is not enough to apply the maxims of the one raw to the intricacies of the other, and Addington's detractors should at least indicate in what direction the troops employed could have been used more profitably than in strengthening the position of the navy and lightening its burden.[3]

Every one was quick to see that something more drastic must be done in the future, and Pitt rose to power on a wave of opinion that the hour for a change was at hand. The military forces at home had considerably increased. We began the war with a home army of little more than 50,000 regulars; by the summer of 1804 we had 87,000, besides 80,000 militia and 343,000 volunteers, or over half a million men. Pitt's first measures were directed to increasing the regular force still further; but even so, offence against such a power as Napoleon's was impossible single-handed. Only in alliance with the great military states of the continent could his father's methods be used, and simultaneously with the ripening of our striking energy alliances came in view.

It is here — in the negotiations and preliminary action for securing these alliances — that we find the key of the Trafalgar campaign. To treat it as the mere expression of the old policy of defence against invasion, which Pitt had resolved to abandon, is to seek for its meaning in vain. Yet it is on these lines the bulk of criticism runs, with the result that the real teaching has been almost entirely buried in a mass of erroneous strategical deduction. Through all this accumulation we must dig if we would recover the most precious treasure that naval experience has ever fashioned, and the first step towards recovery is to seek a simple understanding of Pitt's policy of military alliances. When Napoleon was trying to browbeat Addington's Government over their refusal to evacuate Malta — trampling on every decency of international comity — he had openly boasted that he had left England without an ally in Europe. She seemed to him helpless. In his almost crazy self-confidence he believed he could prevent the old causes producing the old effects and tread underfoot the fundamental laws which had given England her place in international politics ever since the European system had begun. Ignored by him, these laws began to reassert themselves almost immediately, and even before Pitt came back to power Russia had already made advances. Convinced by Napoleon's action in Holland, Italy, and Switzerland that he had not abandoned for a moment his ambitious dreams of European empire, she was bent on forming a defensive league to thwart his design.

It was where the danger touched her most nearly that England and England alone could give effective help. Napoleon was known to be cherishing a purpose to overrun the Ottoman Empire by way of Albania and Greece, and for this reason Russia had maintained a small squadron and a military outpost in Corfu and the Ionian Islands. We were as deeply concerned in Napoleon's design. For us Turkey was but a step on the path to India, and for this reason also we had clung, in the face of the Treaty of Amiens, to our hold on Malta. There was, moreover, another common interest at stake. It lay in Southern Italy, which Napoleon was openly threatening, and which he seemed bent on making the starting-point of his Near Eastern enterprises. Russia had taken the Kingdom of Naples under her special protection; and by a tradition as old as Cromwell, the denying of the Two Sicilies to France had become as much a dominant note of our maritime policy as the integrity of the Low Countries had been from time immemorial.

Naturally, then, the Russian overtures were well received in London, and just as Pitt came to power Woronzow, the Czar's ambassador, was able to say that a large Russian force from the Black Sea would be sent to the Ionian Islands or to Italy as circumstances might require, and that the Czar hoped his Britannic Majesty would order a corps of troops to be kept at Malta in readiness to act in conjunction with those of Russia.[4]

It is here we pick up the thread that led directly to the decision at Trafalgar. Slender as it proved to be, it is the only sure guide through the labyrinth of the campaign. The splendour and tragedy of the great day of reckoning had long cast this guiding line into obscurity. Yet, so far as human judgment can tell, without the entanglement it weaved about Napoleon the most famous naval battle in history would not have been fought. It was an effort to cut himself free from it that cost Napoleon his fleet; and unless we keep it securely between our fingers we must wander in error through the thronging movements of the year and never reach their real meaning. Let us trace the spinning of it till its strands were securely twined.

The idea that was in the Czar's mind was to form, with British assistance and above all with British subsidies, a great defensive league with Austria, Prussia, and Sweden. Whether all or any of those Powers could be induced to join was doubtful. The formation of the league must at least take much time, during which Napoleon might greatly strengthen his position. But in any event Russia and England could act together at once to bar his advance in the Mediterranean. Under the Treaty of Amiens he had agreed to evacuate the Neapolitan ports of Otranto and Taranto, in the south of Italy. But he had now reoccupied them, and from these points was not only threatening the Levant across the Adriatic, but was in a position to strike a sudden blow through Calabria at Sicily. It was vital to the situation that any such catastrophe should be prevented; and thus the idea of British troops in the Mediterranean became as it were the symbol and test of Pitt's purpose. When he pressed that the league should be offensive and for immediate action, the Czar at once reminded him that with respect to reinforcing our garrisons in the Mediterranean and assembling a corps of troops to act in Italy, Pitt had announced a delay of two or three months, not having as yet sufficient troops available for an expeditionary force. Admiral Sir John B. Warren, who was then our ambassador in Russia, immediately replied that a large part of the garrisons of Malta and Gibraltar could be spared at once and that the remainder of the British troops would soon follow if the Czar would only propose to enter into a treaty to unite the Powers into an offensive and defensive alliance.[5] Within a month Russia had decided to send an ultimatum to Napoleon demanding the evacuation of Apulia, the arrangement of the affairs of Italy, compensation to the King of Sardinia for what had been taken from him, and the evacuation of North Germany. If there were no satisfactory answer in twenty-four hours his ambassador was to leave Paris.[6] Following on this resolute step Pitt sent out Lord Granville Leveson-Gower to replace Warren in order to negotiate a regular alliance, and the special instructions he carried were first to clear up a misunderstanding that had arisen as to the British view of Russian action in Italy. Pitt wished the Russians at once to seize the passes leading into Calabria from Taranto. The Czar thought he was being urged to drive the French out of the Kingdom of Naples single-handed, and Leveson-Gower was to assure him England knew that was impossible till Austria joined. But if he attempted the lesser operation two thousand troops from Malta were ready to assist at once. The immediate British object was solely to prevent France seizing Sicily by a *coup de main* through Calabria. For without Sicily as a base of supply the position of our fleet in the Mediterranean would be very difficult to maintain.

The words in which these instructions were conveyed to Leveson-Gower by Lord Harrowby, who was then Pitt's Foreign Secretary, are worth recording and remembering, for in them lies the explanation of much naval strategy, and in particular do they afford the key of Nelson's attitude to the Neapolitan question, and the complex naval problem which it involved. The actual situation at our point of contact with Russia turned upon the command of the Mediterranean, and that depended on Nelson's power of controlling the Toulon fleet — not necessarily of blockading it, but, as he preferred to say, on "holding it in check" till it could be met and destroyed. "It would become doubtful," wrote Harrowby, in directing Gower to insist on the importance of immediate action, "whether the blockade of Toulon could be maintained as effectually as it has been hitherto [if Sicily were lost]; and in case the French fleet should escape from that port and be able to detach any considerable force to the Adriatic, the Russian Government would do well to consider the danger to which their own squadron in those seas would be exposed, and the opportunity which would be afforded to the French of making a successful attack upon Albania and the Morea."

These were exactly Nelson's ideas. He was not of course blockading Toulon closely, but endeavouring to watch the Toulon fleet in such a way that if it attempted to get to the eastward and endanger what it was his special province to defend, it would certainly be brought to action. For this purpose Gibraltar and Malta were of little use. As bases they were wrongly placed. What was wanted was one that would enable him to retain continuously the only position that was interior to either line of operation the French might adopt, whether westwards out of the Straits, or eastwards against Naples and the Levant. It was for this reason he always insisted that Sardinia and Sicily were the keys of the strategical situation.

"You will receive," Harrowby's instructions to Gower went on, "the assurances which were given by me to Count Woronzow, that exertions would be made to increase the disposal force of the garrison of Malta: and you may express a hope that a reinforcement of 5,000 or 6,000 men will have reached it in a few months. These troops will have eventual orders to act in the defence of Sicily, of Calabria, or of Turkey, as circumstances may require . . . but it seems necessary that their attention should be specially directed to the defence ... of Sicily."[7]

The despatch ended accordingly with a renewed suggestion that Russian troops should be sent at once to cooperate with the Calabrians, whom we had been supplying with arms, and to assist them to hold the passes while the British troops from Malta occupied Messina.

The new ambassador also received special instructions to press for the re-establishment of the Sardinian Kingdom in Piedmont as a barrier to France in the intended settlement of Italy. The aggrandisement of the House of Savoy, as a means of preserving the balance of power in the Mediterranean, had become a constant of British policy. The military importance of the Sardinian Kingdom was recognised universally, but in British eyes its naval value was no less; and ever since Nelson had been in command in the Mediterranean he had been pressing the strategical value of Sardinia on the Government. So soon as the new administration was fairly in the saddle he had received orders frankly endorsing his ideas, and on the very day Leveson-Gower's instructions were signed, Nelson was acknowledging the Government's directions to have a special care for Sardinia.[8]

The British proposal, which was based on separate lines of operation, did not commend itself to the Russian Government. They wanted a much larger force and joint operations in Italy itself under one commander: but in view of Napoleon's threat from Boulogne, Leveson-Gower had to say that an increase of the British force in the Mediterranean was as yet impossible.[9] Meanwhile Pitt was devoting himself with all his energy to increasing our disposal force, and was still doing his utmost not only to strengthen the regular army, but to take measures to render the home defence secure in the hands of the territorial forces.[10] Russia, after some demur, admitted the strength of the British arguments, and on the promise of 8,000 troops in a month or two, she consented to co-operate at once from Corfu with 20,000, provided the whole force was commanded by a Russian General, and that England furnished the necessary transport. To this arrangement the British Government assented, and before the end of the year Sir James Craig, who had been commanding the, Essex defence district, was ordered to prepare the necessary force for Malta.

Concurrently with the arrangement of the military convention, the negotiations for a regular alliance were proceeding, but with constant difficulties, owing to the vacillating attitude of Austria, and the mutual suspicions of all the Powers concerned. Russia could not reconcile herself to England's retention of Malta, and England suspected Russia's real aim to be the partition of the Turkish Empire. Austria was clearly more concerned with recovering the old Hapsburg possessions in North Italy than with the liberation of Europe; and as for Prussia she had obviously no end in view but the filching of Hanover. Even Sweden was only prepared to move in return for an unconscionable British subsidy that was out of all proportion to the service it was in her power to render.

To Pitt the position was galling in the extreme. For as the winter came on the situation of England greatly improved, and gave promise of freeing her arms. Her defensive system, as of old, was showing itself to be impregnable, and the fear of invasion was giving way to a fierce desire to be revenged on the man who had put her to so much alarm and expense.

The system that had been adopted was that which had so often proved its strength, and which no trick or device had ever availed to break down. Facing the army of invasion from the Texel to Havre was a swarm of sloops and gun-vessels, rendering the passage of Napoleon's flotilla impossible without battleship support. Our own flotilla was strengthened with a small battle squadron sufficient to deal with the Dutch battle squadron in the Texel, or with any small division that might escape the vigilance of our squadrons that were blockading the enemy's Atlantic ports. The whole was under the command of Lord Keith, with his headquarters in the Downs, and subsidiary bases at Yarmouth for watching the Texel and at the Nore for Dunkirk. The general plan of defence was to hold back the bulk of the defence flotilla on our own shores with coast-defence vessels, or "block-ships," as they were called, as rallying points.[11] Small advanced cruiser squadrons watched the French movements, and seized every opportunity of striking at the enemy's flotilla as it tried to concentrate in the ports of departure, Boulogne, Etaples,

Wimereux, and Ambleteuse. At the Channel Islands was an independent cruiser squadron, under Rear-Admiral Saumarez, effectually preventing the passage of transports from that direction, and barring a raid on the islands. But it also had the important function of acting as a link between Keith and the Western Squadron, by which the whole position was covered.[12] This squadron, which was in fact the main fleet, was under Cornwallis, and was holding the mouth of the Channel, and blockading Brest with extension squadrons before Rochefort and Ferrol where a French division had taken refuge.[13]

In this way, in accordance with long tradition, the fleet kept a firm hold upon the invading army — the fundamental postulate of all defence against overseas invasion — and nothing could shake it. Napoleon, it is true, believed — as others had believed before him — that it might be possible to break that hold by surprise: by the sudden intrusion of a battle squadron from a distance. Cornwallis, he assumed, could easily be evaded, for he would be held fast to Brest by the exigencies of the blockade. This belief was due to a failure to understand the function of our Western Squadron, as Norris and Anson had laid it down more than half a century before. Napoleon regarded it, as many do to this day, as a squadron blockading Brest, whereas it was in reality a squadron holding the approaches to the Channel for all purposes of home and trade defence. The blockade of Brest was incidental, as were the blockades of Rochefort and Ferrol, and in no circumstances of reasonable war risk could a serious hostile squadron enter or even approach the Channel until the Western Squadron had been brought to action and defeated. The mere confronting of that squadron with superior force had been found useless over and over again. The naval campaigns of 1779 and 1782, in particular, had proved this cardinal fact up to the hilt, and French naval opinion had grasped it almost as securely as it was held by our own Admiralty.

The actual light in which the situation was regarded by the British Government is clearly seen in the instructions which Lord Melville, Pitt's First Lord of the Admiralty, issued to Cornwallis, when in August 1804 he returned from his leave to the command of the Western Squadron. At the end of July he had come ashore for a rest from the strain of the blockade, leaving his second, Sir Charles Cotton, in command. It was only for two or three weeks. The invasion crisis appeared to be at hand, and so fully did he possess the confidence of the Admiralty and the country that neither could be easy in his absence.[14] Throughout his leave, Melville was in constant communication with him, and the instructions of August 24th were the outcome.

After reciting that the intelligence indicated immediate action by the Brest Squadron, the instructions pointed out that it might take one of two directions. The determining factor would be, whether or not the squadron sailed with a landing force. If it did not, it would mean that its object was to cover an invasion by the Grand Army. "This," the instructions say, "seems a very desperate attempt, and is likely to terminate in the destruction of their fleet, if they should be able by any unforeseen events to elude your vigilance, and thereby to make their way up Channel." So disastrous had been every previous attempt of this kind that the Admiralty did not think a repetition likely.[15] "But," they continue, "if the existing Government of France is determined to risk everything in this long-menaced attempt against this country, we are not at liberty to calculate solely on what is rational or probable, but we must likewise keep in view such contingencies as may be barely possible, and such as passion and intemperance may give rise to." Cornwallis was therefore to keep up the closest possible blockade of the enemy, and to take measures so that if by luck they escaped, he could follow and destroy them. He was further warned that if their real intention was to enter the Channel and cover the passage of the Grand Army, they would use any means in their power to mislead him. Thus accurately did the Government penetrate the inmost thoughts of Napoleon, for it was precisely on this possibility of misleading Cornwallis that his scheme was based.

The various possibilities of the case were met in the following manner. If the whole squadron escaped and Cornwallis lost touch, he was to proceed off the Lizard where he would be certain to hear if it had passed up Channel. If it had not done so, he was to take station off Cape Clear, or such other point on the Irish coast he thought advisable.

If only a section of it put to sea and it carried troops, its objective would be Ireland, and he was to detach an equal force to act as before explained. If such a detachment sailed to the southward and without troops, the object would probably be a junction with the Mediterranean fleet. If the detachment was no more than five or six ships with troops, the objective would be in the West Indies, and he was to detach thither an equivalent force.

He was also to consider the possibility that the sailing of the whole, or the greater part of the squadron, might mean raising the blockades of Rochefort and Ferrol. He was to deal with such a movement by directing the two Admirals concerned "to form a junction with their two squadrons on the north coast of Spain, or elsewhere;" and he was to give them a rendezvous for that purpose. He was also to arrange for his cruisers to bring them timely warning, and for reinforcing them from his own fleet to the extent the strength of the escaping force might demand. If either Admiral was forced by the appearance of a superior enemy to raise his blockade, he was to join the other, and they were to wait in company for the reinforcement. Directions follow for the general manner in which the blockade of Brest is to be conducted, but in spite of their minuteness they conclude with a saving clause, by which it was sought to hit the mean between tying an Admiral to the main lines of the plan of campaign and leaving him a free hand. "We are aware," it runs, "that many circumstances may occur to which these instructions are inapplicable, and for which no provision is made. In these cases you must use your discretion and judgment for your guidance, giving us the earliest information of your proceedings through our Secretary."[16]

These sagacious and comprehensive instructions cannot, of course, be regarded as purely the work of Lord Melville. They were almost certainly settled in concert with Cornwallis while he was ashore, and they reflect not only his views, but probably also those of Sir Charles Middleton, who, as Lord Barham, was to be the ultimate director of the campaign, and who, as we shall see, was even at this time unofficially the confidential adviser of the First Lord. They therefore may be taken as the highest expression of the living strategical tradition as it existed after the great maritime wars of the eighteenth century, and as such they deserve the most deferential study. Over and above the strategical exposition, it will be observed that they afford a characteristic example of the extent to which the Admiralty was accustomed to control the action of Admirals in home waters, and that they also reveal how little the Board regarded the invasion as a serious danger.

How far Napoleon ever realised the impracticability of his scheme must remain doubtful. Sometimes he said he had never intended it seriously; at others, that he only failed by bad luck and the incompetence of his Admirals. All that we can assert with safety is that no great master of war ever so fatally miscalculated the possibilities and limitations of invasion; and no great administrator ever failed so completely in organisation as Napoleon did with the arrangements for passing the sea with his Grand Army. Nothing, not even the army itself, was ever ready.[17] So glaring, indeed, was the breakdown, that wherever the Napoleonic legend is still unsullied, the only admissible explanation of the astounding confusion in which the arrangements sank ever more deeply is that so great a captain can never have intended the operation seriously.

Be that as it may, as the autumn came on, and Napoleon began to feel the toils that Pitt and the Czar were weaving round him, he let go, and was absorbed in making himself Emperor. For the winter at least the whole project was abandoned. Large sections of the flotilla were dismantled, the ports of departure were neglected, and the Channel sands began rapidly to devour the millions they had cost to make. After eighteen months of undisturbed effort, with a century of experience behind him, he had failed to solve even the initial problem of the operation; and to save his face before his disappointed country and demoralised army he faced about against Austria.

Under pressure from the Czar, her attitude to France was stiffening. She was even beginning to mass troops and form magazines at the head of the Adriatic and in the Tyrol, with intent to strike directly at the possessions Napoleon had seized in Northern Italy; and as the negotiations between England and Russia drew to a head, it looked as though she had definitely made up her mind to join the League. In Napoleon's eyes, at least, the outlook was too dangerous to be ignored. He was not prepared to face a continental coalition in British pay. To keep up the threat of a great invasion, which hitherto had served his turn so well, was no longer possible, yet by hook or by crook England must be kept quiet. The means, as he thought, were ready to his hand. Spain, as always, must be the tool of French ambition. Terrorised into opening her ports to French ships, she had for long worn her neutrality to shreds. A little increase of pressure would be enough to make her throw off the rags and appear in arms at Napoleon's side. The pressure was applied, and with the normal result. Pitt snatched up the time-honoured weapon which his father had not been permitted to employ. A blow at the rich treasure trade of Spain before declaration of war had been our regular procedure in like circumstances ever since Drake set out to strike it in 1585, and failed, "the reason best known to God." Again and again it had been used, though seldom with success, and yet we never tired. Before September was out, orders were speeding to Nelson in the Mediterranean and Cochrane before Ferrol to seize the home-coming galleons of Montevideo. A new squadron also — of which came much heart-burning — was formed under Sir John Orde to blockade Cadiz and the Andalusian coast; and in November, Commodore Moore, in command of a special cruiser squadron, had seized four treasure galleons. Spain immediately declared war, and Napoleon's new plan took shape.

Spain's declaration meant for him nominally an increase of his fleet by thirty-two of the line. It represented with the Dutch a three-power coalition, to which our navy as it stood was barely superior. But Pitt's prompt action had caught Spain unawares and unready, and the utmost Napoleon could hope was that she might have some twenty-five of the line fit for action by the spring of 1805. Till then he must do the best he could with his own. Action of some kind was imperative in order to divert the attention of the British fleet from his coasts. He could even hope to provoke in England an outcry for peace; for well within his power was a counterstroke at her colonies. Thus originated that famous movement to the West Indies — not with any idea of a crushing return upon the Channel, but simply in a desperate effort to shatter Pitt's position and to get the British fleet off his back, while he faced the threatened coalition.

In the plan of operation which he had just abandoned it had been the part of the Toulon squadron to evade Nelson, take a wide sweep round Cochrane at Ferrol, release the Rochefort squadron, and, thus reinforced, to take another wide sweep round Cornwallis at Brest and rush the Channel. Under the new scheme for colonial attack, the Toulon and Rochefort squadrons were to sail independently with a force of troops to the West Indies. There they were to recapture the Dutch islands, reinforce the French, take all they could from the British, and then return together in the spring to fall upon Cochrane, bring out the Ferrol squadron, and proceed to a French port. At the same time Ganteaume at Brest had orders to embark a third military force, and seizing the first opportunity of getting out, to operate a descent on Ireland and then to carry on north-about and liberate Marmont's corps in the Texel.

It is always difficult to say with confidence what Napoleon really intended by the tangle of schemes he spun. Knowing himself to be surrounded by traitors — even at his Council table — his only resource was to manufacture plans for their benefit which he never intended to use. In this case there can be little doubt, from all the circumstances, that Ganteaume's orders were intended for British spies in order to keep alive the threat upon the points where we were most sensitive; while those of Villeneuve and Missiessy with the Toulon and Rochefort squadrons were genuine. The idea is obvious. While a bare threat on Ireland or Scotland was sufficient for his purpose, nothing short of a real attack on the distant West Indies would avail to deflect British strategy. The whole was clearly a plan to take the place of his abortive invasion. It was designed to embarrass the British Cabinet and prevent them using their fleet and army together against him in Europe while he was cutting Austria out of the half-formed coalition.

What he saw beyond the point at which in the spring he would have the three squadrons concentrated in a home port we cannot tell. Probably he saw nothing clearly. He was too great a captain not to know that it was impossible to plan beyond the shock with Austria. The rest must depend upon the issue. In all probability his sole idea was to have his whole war strength under his hand for what was to come after. It may be also that he was beginning at last to learn the truth, which all his predecessors had reached by painful experience, that there was no way of striking England down except by a fair and successful fight for the command of the sea; and for this, with Spain ready in the spring, he could indulge at least a hope.

His faith in the steps he had taken for intimidating England is evidenced by his next move. At the end of the year urgent orders went down to Villeneuve and Missiessy to get away at once, and no sooner were the couriers gone than he made overtures to George the Third for peace, and sent to Vienna a rough demand for an explanation of the Austrian military movements. While he waited for the answers he explained his whole attitude formally to his new Council of State. By the universal testimony of his relations, his most intimate friends, and his most capable and best-informed enemies, he at this time believed he had escaped gracefully from having to attempt the invasion of England. No one who aspired to rule France could afford to ignore the old war-cry of the Republic — *Delenda est Carthago!* Austria it seemed was about to give him a pretext for escape without loss of prestige, but he had to justify to his Council the terrible cost which his pose had involved. "For two years," he said, "France has been making the greatest sacrifices that it is possible to ask of her. . . . But to be able to assemble such forces, to have 20,000 artillery horses and full equipment it was necessary to find a pretext for creating and concentrating them without giving the continental Powers cause of alarm: and this pretext was furnished by the project of a descent on England. . . . For two years I have not been able to tell you this, but that nevertheless was my sole aim. You know it now and you see the explanation of many things. But we shall not have war, and I have just opened direct negotiations with the King of England for a treaty of peace."[18]

He had scarcely made this remarkable declaration when the British answer came. His new title of Emperor was still unfledged, and all his vanity was concentrated in getting it recognised. The British answer was addressed to "The Head of the French Government"; it was signed not by the King but by the Secretary of State, and it contained a curt refusal to treat apart from the other Powers and especially Russia. It was an answer that could only arouse all that was ugly in Napoleon's character; and to make matters worse, it was followed immediately by a peaceful note from the Emperor of Austria, which snatched from his hands every pretext for attack. In the moment of his anger he found himself rudely thrust back upon his desperate enterprise — with his fleet dispersed and irrevocably engaged beyond the Atlantic, with his army sullen and demoralised, his Channel ports choked with sand, and his flotilla demobilised. His prestige and honour were more than ever bound up in the invasion, and the means at his disposal lay in more bewildering confusion. This and not escape was all his confident truculence had earned him, and there was nothing left but to pretend at least he meant to go on with it, with half the costly work to do over again.

Pitt's rough and even insolent reply, which is almost universally condemned, was exactly on a level with the way his father had dealt with Choiseul, and would have dealt with Spain. In both cases transparent chicanery was met with an almost brutal bluntness. Knowing what we do and what Pitt knew, Englishmen will easily pardon it. They will see in it the reflection of the rising spirit of the nation, the confidence in its increasing power, the high belief in its mission to awaken Europe, and the conviction, henceforth unshaken till the end, that there was no way of restoring tranquillity and freedom to the Continent till Napoleon was crushed by force of arms.

The situation was ripe for a determined stand, and negotiations for the league had proceeded so far that in loyalty we could no longer act alone. On November 6th a defensive alliance had been concluded between Russia and Austria in case of any further French advances in Germany, Italy, or the East, and both powers were arming to give it effect. Prussia was still holding back in hope of securing Hanover as the price of deserting the cause of Europe; but Sweden had consented to place England in possession of Rügen and Stralsund, so as to give her a sea base for operating in that direction in concert with Russia. The Anglo-Russian negotiations, moreover, had made so much progress that the main terms of the alliance were agreed between Pitt and Woronzow in London; and, simultaneously with the harsh rebuff to Napoleon's overtures, a formal *projet d'alliance* was forwarded to Leveson-Gower in St. Petersburg.[19]

The progress of the negotiations, however, was not unchequered. Craig's expedition continued to be for Russia the test of England's inclination and ability to carry out her part of the proposed bargain, the pledge that she was not playing the merely selfish part of turning Napoleon's efforts away from her own frontiers. A renewal of the British suggestion that troops from Malta should occupy Messina while the Russians operated in South Italy, had been received with grave suspicion; but on England's promising frankly to let her troops act under a Russian General in any part of Southern Italy the clouds were cleared. There still remained, however, the question of our retention of Malta when the final re-settlement should come. It was a point upon which, unfortunately, it was impossible for England to give way. It was for Malta she had gone to war. With the Far East looming larger and larger in her idea of empire and the discovery of Napoleon's designs on the Ottoman dominions, Malta had become the keystone of her policy as rigidly as Gibraltar had been to William the Third.

On this point the whole affair came near to wreck. In the British *projet* and draft treaty nothing had been said about Malta at all. But in St. Petersburg, where simultaneous negotiations were going on, the Czar by withholding his ratification endeavoured to force Leveson-Gower to admit a separate article on the point. The Czar's idea was to use the whole treaty as a means of forcing Napoleon by way of armed mediation to submit to the arrangement of Europe at which the treaty was aimed. Obviously if the British Government insisted on the retention of Malta the proposed mediation must fail. He therefore demanded that England should agree to evacuate the island if Napoleon insisted on it as a condition of a general peace. Leveson-Gower, who had strict instructions on the point, firmly refused to admit the addition. The Czar could not believe that Pitt, his new idol, could share the obstinacy of his envoy. He therefore referred the treaty back to London, with a positive declaration that unless the proposed terms were inserted he would decline to ratify. Pitt was aghast. There were other modifications on which he was prepared to give way, but on the question of Malta he would not budge. In his eyes it was the keystone of the whole fabric. Relations, therefore, became strained to breaking-point. To all the entreaties and protests of Woronzow, Pitt replied that France was always one of the greatest military powers that had ever been; her dominion already stretched from Cadiz to Civita Vecchia, and she was doing her utmost to make the Mediterranean a French sea. Nor was that all. The French meant to conquer the whole Ottoman Empire, and hoped to thrust the English out of India. The liberty of the Mediterranean and the independence of the Levant and Egypt demanded our retention of Malta. In a word, the security of Southern Italy, of the Ionian Islands, and of all the possessions of the Ottoman Empire, were bound up in England's being firmly set in the stronghold of the old Naval Knights. Woronzow was unmoved. Persistence in the demand, he said, would break the alliance which had just been agreed for the salvation of Europe. "It will not save Europe," Pitt broke in. "The Mediterranean, the Levant, and Egypt, will be in the power of France the moment a British squadron ceases to have for a base a good port protected by formidable fortifications. . . . So," he concluded, "whatever pain it causes us, and it is indeed great, we must give up the hope of seeing the alliance ratified, since its express condition is our renunciation of Malta. We will continue the war alone; it will be maritime."[20]

Here we have a clear exposition from Pitt's own lips of the lines upon which he hoped to fight the Trafalgar campaign and the objects it was to achieve. The war henceforth was to be for the freedom of the Mediterranean and the riparian Powers, and it was to be no longer a mere maritime war, but a war by land as well. Woronzow was as firmly persuaded as Pitt that Malta was a necessity to the British Empire; and Lord Mulgrave, who had succeeded Lord Harrowby as Secretary of State, could press the point with a clear conscience in the interest of Europe. The Czar would have had the Knights of Malta restored, but Mulgrave pointed out that the sole reason why Charles the Fifth had established them in the island was to protect Christendom against its common enemy. This they had no longer the power to do. Great Britain, as the leading naval power with no territorial ambitions on the Mediterranean shores, was their legitimate successor; for it was only as a British port and arsenal that Malta could hope to check in that quarter the progress of the present common enemy of Europe. "His Majesty," Mulgrave concluded, "in reserving to himself the possession of Malta, consults the interests of Europe in common with his own by the retention of this only exception to the national sacrifices which accompany his Majesty's great and almost unlimited exertions in the common cause." Considering not only what the other Powers were expecting for their reward, but how long England had been bearing the burden alone, and that she was agreeing to subsidise half Europe, the price she asked can scarcely be called excessive.

Such, broadly speaking, was the strained diplomatic situation when Napoleon and Pitt each developed the opening moves of their respective plans of campaign. The day the treaty was signed Villeneuve was leaving the Mediterranean, and a week later Craig sailed to all appearance straight into his arms.

For months longer the uncertainty continued, and some understanding of the complexities which the delay in the ratification entailed is necessary for any profitable study of the campaign. There seems to have been a real misunderstanding. The Czar had set his heart both on our evacuation of Malta and the reform of our Maritime War Code, and each condition he personally regarded as a *sine qua non* of the alliance. In particular, Pitt's continued insistence on the retention of Malta only confirmed his doubts as to England's disinterestedness. To our ambassador's protestations of sincerity he kept pointing to the delay in the sailing of Craig's expedition. But at last news came that it was actually on its way in the full strength that had been promised, and with instructions that were entirely satisfactory. The unratified alliance was thus partly performed, and the Czar's position became more difficult to hold. All he could now ask was that Craig should not actually commence any operations in Italy till he had concerted measures with General Lacy, who had been appointed to the supreme command at Naples.[21] This, too, was agreed. Pitt moreover ratified the whole treaty, with the exception of the added clause about Malta, and on this he even gave way a little. He was ready, if the peace of Europe were found to depend on it, to evacuate the island on certain conditions, one of which was that Minorca should be ceded to England in its stead. But this concession was only to stand if Napoleon accepted the terms of the allies at once and peacefully. As the result of successful war, England would still insist on the retention of Malta. The Czar was not immediately convinced. Still he fought for his own dream and the reform of the British Maritime Code, and eventually it was not till July — by a most unhappy delay — that his hesitation ended and the ratification was signed.[22]

In proceeding with the study of the campaign it must, therefore, be kept firmly in mind that at its outset the dominant factor in the war was still undetermined. No design or act of statesmen or of high officers must be judged apart from this controlling deflection. Neither Pitt nor the Admiralty could tell whether to design the campaign as a single-handed effort or on the great lines of co-operation with one or more of the first-class military Powers. With this caution it may be well to give at once the leading terms of the treaty, as it was eventually concluded. "By the first article Russia undertook to do her utmost to form a league of the continental Powers, and in concert with them to provide a force up to half a million men. The second declared the objects to be: to force the French to evacuate Hanover and North Germany; to establish the independence of Holland and Switzerland; to re-establish the King of Sardinia in Piedmont, and to secure the integrity of the Kingdom of Naples and the evacuation of the whole of Italy, including the island of Elba. By the third article England undertook to further the common cause with her forces by land and sea, and to provide transports for moving the allied troops as the plan of operations should require, and also to provide subsidies at the rate of a million and a quarter for every hundred thousand regular troops the allies put into the field.

Here, then, was the great new factor of the changed war policy which influenced it from the outset. The British fleet was no longer to be used merely for maritime operations. England bound herself to use it in furthering a vast continental war. Should Austria alone join the league the main active theatre for our fleet and army must be on the Italian coasts and in the Eastern Mediterranean, where Nelson had long been clamouring for military action. If Prussia joined we should be forced to act in the North Sea and the Baltic, where we already had secured a footing at Rügen and Stralsund.

The second new factor was that henceforth the war was to be what strategists call "an offensive return." It was the realisation of the spirit which Pitt had inherited from his father, and of the advice with which Dumouriez had concluded the famous project of defence, presented to the British Government about the time Pitt had come to power. "It is time," he said, "to cut the thread which holds the sword of Buonaparte suspended over England. . . . Nought is more perilous than perpetual defensive, nor offers a vaster field for attacks of all kind, whether near or remote, on the part of a foe. . . . Whither, I ask you, would this everlasting defensive warfare tend? . . . How could the Powers of Europe ever take heart anew if this system, so nearly akin to fear, were fated to endure much longer., . . . Doubtless it behoved to attain to the offensive methods through the defensive first; but if, from this year on, attack does not supersede resistance, then you will see the chances augment very speedily in favour of Buonaparte."[23]

To approach the Trafalgar campaign without these two factors clearly in view is to misconceive it from end to end. To judge it as a defensive campaign, to regard Trafalgar as having been fought purely for the security of these British Islands is to misjudge the men who designed it, and, above all, the men who fought it with such sure and lucid comprehension. For them, from first to last, the great idea was not how to avoid defeat, but how to inflict it. England had found herself again. The spirit of Marlborough and Chatham was stirring; she was striving to strike, and no longer waiting for the blow — to strike for Europe and not only for herself. To think of her as only bent on her own security is to lose the whole grandeur of the theme; to misinterpret the bold confidence with which her seamen took risks, apparently reckless. The lack of clear grasp as to how the great campaign was conceived has led lesser men in a later age to brand those strokes of genius as blunders of ignorant men. It is time such things should cease. Let us rather, in tracing the broad sweep and subtle interlocking of their moves, humbly sit at the feet of the giants who dared to make them. So may we learn what men, inspired by a living naval tradition and ripened with the maturity of long war experience, could achieve by right understanding, by instructed fearlessness of risk, and by intelligent submission to the central idea on which the great war-plan was designed.

CHAPTER II

Napoleon's First Miscarriage

The first move of the campaign was made by Missiessy from Rochefort. In response to the urgent orders to get to sea which Napoleon sent down the day his overtures for peace started for London, he embarked his troops to the number of 3,500 at the Isle of Aix. Here it was the Rochefort squadrons, owing to the shoals in the river, had always to complete for sea. To blockade the Atlantic ports securely during the winter was not regarded by the British Admiralty as a possible operation of war, but Missiessy was being watched by a detachment of the Western Squadron under Sir Thomas Graves, an officer who had distinguished himself as Nelson's second at Copenhagen. As his duties also embraced the blockade of Bordeaux to prevent stores passing northward to the invasion ports, he had to cover the ground from the Isle d'Yeu to the mouth of the Gironde, not far short of a hundred miles. To supply his squadron at sea was moreover impossible, and it so happened that just as Missiessy had his orders to sail Graves found it necessary to take his battle squadron into Quiberon Bay to water, Quiberon being the road we had always used as an advanced base for the Rochefort division ever since Hawke's great victory in 1759. Captain Patrick Campbell in the *Doris* frigate was left to keep observation. On January 8th he ran inside for a closer view, and found Missiessy busy embarking his troops and stores. Hurrying out again he met the *Felix* schooner fresh from Graves, who informed him of the Admiral's whereabouts, and Campbell sped northwards to report his news, leaving the Felix in his place.

On the 11th all was ready at Aix, the wind was easterly with thick weather and snow, and Missiessy decided to weigh in the early afternoon so as to run through the blockading line in the night. Luck and good judgment gave him a complete success. He believed indeed that he had run entirely clear, but he counted without the *Felix* who was too vigilant. Next morning she sighted the French squadron, counting one three-decker, four seventy-fours, and five cruisers. All day she shadowed them, and under cover of night left them streaming northward on a rising south-westerly wind about fifty miles south-west of Isle d'Yeu, and ran for Quiberon.

Meanwhile the *Doris*, on her way to join Graves, had also sighted the French squadron, and under a press of sail which led to severe casualties in her rigging, she had reached Quiberon, but only to find Graves had sailed. Hearing he was somewhere south-west of Belleisle, she tried to beat out again and in doing so ran on a sunken rock. All night she toiled at the pumps, and at last succeeded in mastering her leaks. Then came the *Felix* to report the enemy's position, and Campbell grew desperate. A southwesterly gale was blowing up, and he knew Graves, according to the regular practice, would bear up into the bay for refuge, and then he would be unable to move. At all hazards he must be stopped before it was too late. Scarcely able to keep his ship afloat, and with his rigging badly damaged, Campbell struggled to beat out against the rising gale. It proved beyond his power; he had to bear up and anchor, and two days later the *Doris* foundered, all hands being saved by the *Felix*. On the 16th Graves appeared. The *Felix* signalled the enemy was out, and the Admiral immediately hauled his wind, and made a great effort to turn back. But he had run too far. In the teeth of the raging gale he could not weather Belleisle, and there was nothing for it but to bear up and anchor.[1]

All this time Missiessy was struggling out of the Bay, suffering all kinds of disasters aloft, but still holding on with the utmost determination, and so got clear away. In the British fleet no one knew what to make of it. Some of his early disasters had been witnessed by the cruisers, and the general opinion was that the furious weather must have forced him back into Rochefort, or L'Orient, or even Brest. Brest indeed was believed to be his destination, and the northerly course he had been forced to take confirmed the impression. Cornwallis was not there. He had been driven by the gale to run for Plymouth, and did not return till the end of the month. Even so it was a full week before the weather permitted the three ports to be looked into, and then Missiessy was nowhere to be found. That the Rochefort squadron was bound for the West Indies entered no man's head. Who indeed would have guessed that Napoleon was throwing away the game for which he had played so high, by involving his fleet in colonial expeditions? No one out of intimate touch with the political situation could have been expected to divine the truth, and naturally enough it was at headquarters — the centre of information — that the situation was first penetrated.

But even in London, Missiessy's destination was a matter of inference. The information hovered between the West Indies and the Mediterranean. To the Cabinet the latter destination must have seemed the most probable, because it was the one they feared the most, since the negotiations with Russia for joint operations in South Italy were just taking shape. Their first precaution accordingly, on hearing of Missiessy's disappearance, was to provide for the reinforcement of Nelson, should it prove that the enemy's squadron had entered the Straits. It was done in the usual way. On February 14th, Cornwallis was ordered to send Sir Robert Calder, his third flag officer, with six of the line from the Brest blockade to relieve Cochrane off Ferrol and Cochrane was to take six — a force equal to Missiessy's — and pursue him. He was to call at Lisbon for information, and if none was to be had to speak to Orde off St. Vincent, who, since the breach with Spain, had been watching Cadiz with five of the line. If Missiessy had gone to the Mediterranean he was to follow him and join Nelson. If there was no news he was to call at Madeira, Cape Verde, and finally Barbados. There he was to take up Commodore Samuel Hood, who commanded on the Leeward Islands station. If still there was no news, he was to send three of the line to reinforce Dacres at Jamaica, but if he heard the enemy had gone to their northern base at St. Domingo he was to send six to Jamaica. In pursuance of these orders, Cochrane sailed from Ferrol on Calder's arrival at the end of February after Missiessy had been already a week at Fort de France in Martinique.[2]

In the Mediterranean Napoleon's sudden change of purpose caused the campaign to open in equal bewilderment. When Villeneuve received the urgent orders of January 2nd Nelson was cruising close before Toulon. He had appeared there on December 26th for a reconnaissance, having received information that Villeneuve was "embarking troops and preparing for some immediate expedition."[3] He was in one of the worst of his shifting moods. The *Swiftsure* had just joined with despatches that told how the most lucrative part of his command had been taken from him.[4] By tradition the Mediterranean station extended outside the Straits' mouth as far as Cape St. Vincent, covering the route of the rich Spanish-American trade. But so soon as Pitt had made up his mind to strike at Spain he determined to change the usual distribution of the fleet. The Mediterranean was so far from the centre of intelligence and especially when its commander had to fix his attention upon its eastern half, that the old arrangement could not work smartly in the new conditions. Pitt therefore sanctioned the formation of a new squadron to be called the "Spanish Squadron," under the direct control of the Admiralty. Its station was to extend from the Straits' mouth up to Finisterre, where it joined hands with the Ferrol extension of the Western Squadron. The man the Admiralty chose for this rich command was, as we have seen, Sir John Orde, Nelson's *bête noir*. He seems to have been possessed with the idea that Orde had never forgiven him for the Battle of the Nile. Orde, being his senior, had expected to command the famous detachment himself. In his disappointment he had behaved at the time with some insubordination, and Nelson seems to have believed that Orde owed him an undying grudge. Whatever may have been Orde's feelings under the smart, so far as we can judge, his sense of injury was by this time forgotten in a genuine admiration of Nelson's genius. Possibly it was this that accounted for Lord Melville's making an appointment apparently so tactless; but more probably it was because permission was at the same time given to Nelson at his own request to come home on sick leave.

But with the prospect of the French coming out, Nelson had no idea of availing himself of the permission. He remained on, unaware of the change in Orde's attitude towards him, and he would have been more than human if, situated as he was, he had not resented the pecuniary loss the new command involved. His letters indeed at this time are full of protests, somewhat suspicious in their emphasis and recurrence, that prize-money had nothing to do with his disapproval of the redistribution. Be that as it may, the fact that is of importance is clear — from first to last Nelson regarded Orde, with whom it was of the utmost importance that he should co-operate frankly, with a rooted suspicion that tended seriously to imperil the interests of the country.

In eager expectation of an action to calm his troubled spirit, Nelson remained before Toulon till January 10th, and then, leaving a couple of cruisers behind, he held away for his advanced base at Maddalena, in the north of Sardinia, just as Missiessy was coming out of Rochefort. "With respect to the French fleet," he wrote to Hugh Elliot, our representative at Naples, "I wish to God they were out." His prayer was quickly answered. On the 14th Villeneuve found the coast was clear. Two days later he tried to drive off Nelson's cruisers, and on the 17th, as Napoleon was informing his Council he had never intended to invade England, he put to sea with eleven of the line and nine cruisers. For two days the British frigates shadowed him, and then in the latitude of Ajaccio both went off to Maddalena to inform Nelson they had left the enemy standing south-south-west. Why both of them left together contrary to the usual practice is nowhere explained, but it appears to have been due to the strength and activity of Villeneuve's frigates. To Nelson it made no difference.

In his opinion there was but one thing to do. With his unsurpassed sensitiveness to the kernel of a situation and his enduring grasp of his place in a war-plan, he permitted no possibility of a diversion to influence his movements. He was there to command the Mediterranean, and the permanence of that command hung on the integrity of Sicily. We have seen how large a place it was then filling in the eyes of the Cabinet at home, how they were straining the resources of home defence to provide a force to secure it. So far as England's capacity for actively assisting the coming coalition was concerned, it was the thrust-block of the engine Pitt was constructing so laboriously. And for Nelson, too, it was no less. In common with all Europe he believed that the entire conquest of Italy was Napoleon's immediate aim. He could not dream any more than Cornwallis or Graves how confused was the game the redoubtable enemy had begun to play as he felt his grip of the situation slipping. Had Nelson been less certain than he was of the point where Napoleon's most telling stroke could be delivered, we may still doubt if he would have done otherwise than he did. For all his passion for action, for all his firm belief in the destruction of the enemy's fleet as the solvent of all difficulties, never once did he seek such a decision at the risk of laying open a vital point. Never once did he expose what it was his essential function to defend for an uncertain chance of contact with the enemy's fleet. And so he acted now.

Without a moment's hesitation, in the dead of night, and a north-westerly gale, he led his fleet through the perilous Biche Passage and sped down the eastern side of Sardinia to bar Villeneuve's way to Naples and Sicily.

The reasoning on which he formed his decision he explained to his confidant, Captain Sir Alexander Ball, Governor of Malta. Since easterly winds had prevailed for a fortnight before Villeneuve sailed, it was to be assumed he did not intend to go west. As he had steered south-south-west and obviously wished to avoid an action, it was scarcely less likely that he meant to attack either Sardinia, Naples, or Sicily. "However," he said, "I did not choose to run that risk." He had first to assure himself the enemy had gone to none of these places.[5]

Having reached the south end of Sardinia, he was faced with a heavy westerly gale that held him there till the 26th. There his cruisers began to come in, but with no news of Villeneuve's position. They could only tell that one ship at least had been disabled in the heavy weather. On this Nelson judged much as Graves had done, but with surer material. So wide and complete had been the sweep of his cruisers that their failure to locate Villeneuve, combined with the evidence of the disabled ship, assured him that one of two things had happened — either he had put back to Toulon or had passed on to attack Greece or Egypt. These two places were second only to Naples, Sardinia, and Sicily in the defensive function that had been assigned to him. Clinging, therefore, to the line he had hitherto followed, and of whose correctness he had no doubt, he held away for the Morea. There he found all quiet. Nothing had been heard of the French squadron, but there was news that the French ambassador had just been recalled from Constantinople. Egypt, then, was almost certainly Villeneuve's destination, and without an hour's delay Nelson carried on to Alexandria.

Meanwhile Villeneuve had had neither the luck nor the determination of Missiessy. With his ships encumbered with troops, he found it beyond the power of his raw crews and officers to face the gale. All was soon havoc aloft, the fleet lost cohesion, and Villeneuve, overcome with the oppression of an unlocated and redoubtable enemy, felt it madness to proceed. He consulted General Lauriston, a highly trusted staff officer of Napoleon's, who was in command of the troops, and together they decided to turn back. "Finding ourselves," he wrote to Napoleon to explain his conduct, "observed from the first night of our getting out by two English frigates, which could not fail to bring down on us the whole force of the enemy, and it being out of our power to make much sail with the ships so much maltreated, we agreed to return." This was on the 19th, and by the 21st he was safe again in Toulon, while Nelson cleared for action, was still waiting for him at the south end of Sardinia. Obviously, then, if Nelson had chosen to make a dash for Villeneuve directly he heard he was out he might have destroyed or captured the whole of the ships that were still with his flag. A less correct officer might well have done so. But for Nelson it was not good war. The chance of contact was far too uncertain to justify uncovering the point of greatest danger.[6]

To Napoleon the breakdown of his naval combination was a severe shock. He was still bent on flinging his whole fleet into colonial operations, and on January 16th the day before Villeneuve sailed, he was busy drafting a scheme for extending the attack to India. It was to be carried out by Ganteaume from Brest. With his twenty-one of the line and nine or ten cruisers and six transports, carrying altogether 15,000 troops, he was to break the blockade at a favourable moment, move down to L'Orient, where he was to pick up a ship of the line, and then to Rochefort for another and 2,000 additional troops. Thence he was to proceed to release the Ferrol squadron, which would give him five more French of the line, as many Spanish, and eight or nine cruisers. Half of them would be armed *en flûte* as transports, and would have on board a further 6,000 troops, half French and half Spanish. With this force he would proceed to Mauritius where he would find 3,000 men. He would then have an army of 23,000 French and 3,000 Spaniards, with which "indubitably," as Napoleon wrote, "they will make a terrible war on England which may bring about a final decision." Of the probable action of the British fleet there is no mention. Its silent elimination from the problem is striking. But it was characteristic of all Napoleon's naval strategy that, in sharp contrast to his military plans, he practically ignored his enemy or assumed in them an incredible simplicity.[7]

It was while Decrès, his Minister of Marine, was working out this remarkable vision that news came of Villeneuve's failure. It was also the moment when Napoleon was fuming over Pitt's rough defiance. The submission of Austria had not yet come. What was he to do? He had sent a challenge to Vienna and had failed to frighten Pitt. As the situation thus darkened, so his mind becomes almost impenetrable, and we can only grope in it by the light of the ill-considered orders he gave.

Missiessy was now beyond recall, and the first step taken was to warn him that he would be unsupported except for a few more cruisers, and that the combination with Villeneuve was cancelled. "His Majesty," Decrès informed him, "has decided that the squadron under command of Vice-Admiral Villeneuve is to have another destination. . . . Your operations, therefore, become independent, and should be directed by you in accordance with your original instructions given to meet the case of your not being able to count on the projected junction with Vice-Admiral Villeneuve." This meant he was to throw reinforcements and supplies into St. Domingo and come home. Rochefort, he was told, would probably be found open.

But what did Napoleon mean by the new destination for Villeneuve? Clearly not the invasion of England. Not a single step had yet been taken to reconstruct the shattered preparations. Even without Austria and Russia threatening him on his eastern frontier and in Italy, the invasion had passed beyond his strength, and now was the crisis of the Austrian threat. Villeneuve was told to collect his scattered squadron, and while he refitted, Lauriston was to disembark the troops, fill up his battalions to their full strength, and look out for more transports. "At the end of the month," Napoleon told him, "you will receive an order to re-embark for elsewhere, for the season is past for your former destination."

The day this enigmatic letter was written the orders for an Austrian campaign were countermanded. A pacific answer had come from Vienna, but still — not for a full month — is there any sign that Napoleon felt himself forced to return to the necessity of a direct attack on England. The French General Staff, after a profound study of the situation, suggest that he was still bent on his latest idea of attacking India, and that Villeneuve was to combine with Ganteaume. By this time he must have had his suspicions of the joint effort of Russia and England to bar his progress in the Eastern Mediterranean. What could be more characteristic of his methods than to outwit them by directing his attack by way of the Cape? It is indeed difficult to avoid the supposition that at this time he had come to regard the invasion of India as an easier matter than the invasion of England, that he was realising the truth of the paradox, which history proves up to the hilt, that in default of naval command attack over an open sea is far lest difficult than over a narrow sea. The simple reason is that over an open sea evasion of the enemy's defensive arrangements is comparatively easy, as had been proved by Hoche's attack on Ireland and his own adventure to Egypt.

Possibly, however, the whole scheme was only intended for British spies, or, if not originally so intended, was used for this purpose when it was found to be impracticable. We know, at any rate, that from this time forward for several months he was under the hallucination that he had diverted our naval effort to India.

All we can tell for certain is that, whether or not the Indian scheme was ever seriously intended, it was abandoned within a few weeks of its conception. By the end of the month, for reasons it is now impossible to fathom, he had been forced to take up the invasion again, and was preparing the way for it by a naval combination scarcely less extravagant in design than his Indian dream. Between February 29th and March 4th he issued the orders for his famous concentration in the West Indies.

To explain, so far as is possible, this startling return to his abandoned project — with the conditions far more difficult than before — let us see what was uppermost in his mind at the moment. It was undoubtedly the absorption of Northern Italy into the French Empire by forming a new Kingdom of Italy out of the revolutionary states which had arisen on the ruins of the old Sardinian, Austrian, and Genoese possessions. The main objection to this stroke of policy was that, if crudely done, it would force Austria into action and give a dangerous stimulus to the efforts of the Czar and Pitt to form their coalition. For some weeks, therefore, he had been trying to persuade one of his brothers to accept the crown of the new kingdom, and on their steadfast refusal he resolved to crown himself. Here, then, he had to face the certain irritation of Austria; and the Anglo-Russian negotiations for joint military action to prevent his further expansion in Italy were now practically complete. The obvious move, therefore, was to use the army he was compelled to keep on a war footing as a threat to England. It was the only way to prevent her putting forth such strength in the Mediterranean as would make the joint action with Russia really formidable, and encourage Austria to burn her boats.

Whether he still believed in his heart the invasion was possible we cannot tell. If he did, it can only have been by the well-known trick of his gambler's mind, that everything was possible on which he had set his desire. His star had once removed mountains; he had trusted it to make the desert flow with milk and honey, and now, perhaps, he believed it could bridge the sea.

Nothing less will explain the madness of the resumed attempt. When he first set himself to the task he put the necessary military force at 150,000 men. Since then the strength of the British army and the whole system of defence had greatly increased — in numbers, mettle, training, and organisation. Yet, even in view of the clouds that were darkening the opposite horizon, he could barely keep half that number in touch with the Channel coast. Even when, after six months' preparation, what is called the supreme moment came — when, so the legend goes, he only failed by the blunders of his Admirals — he had no more than 90,000 men in reach of his flotilla. The arrangements for embarkation and transport were even wider of the mark. The ports were choked with silt, so that many of the boats, even at high tide, were aground, and months of labour did little to get the harbours clear, except in the unimportant case of Wimereux. In Boulogne, after six months' effort, not half the units assigned to the port could get out in one tide. The flotilla itself was still unconcentrated, entirely unorganised, distributed in no relation to the various divisions of the army, and in need of formidable repairs. The idea that his organisation was such that he could embark 150,000 men in two hours, is one of the most remarkable myths of the Napoleonic legend. The utmost he ever even approached was the bare possibility, in perfect weather, of getting 90,000 afloat in from twelve to eighteen hours, but nothing like this was ever actually accomplished.[8]

Undoubtedly, what caused him to shut his eyes to all these difficulties was the brightness of the reports from Spain. Stung with the blow which England had struck before declaration, she was throwing herself into the war with unexpected ardour. All that Napoleon had dared to hope from her fleet bid fair to be fulfilled. If, ashore, his prospects were darker than before, at sea they were far more promising, and he flung all his sanguine spirit into the naval part of the venture, ignoring the rest, with which he had no heart to grapple.

The first indication of his idea that an effective concentration of his whole naval force was possible in the West Indies occurs in certain communications he made to the Spanish Government on February 19th, but it was not till the 27th that the first orders were issued. On that day were signed directions to Missiessy cancelling his last orders to return, and bidding him stay where he was till the end of June, in immediate readiness to join such forces as should appear at Martinique. On the same day Admiral Gourdon, who commanded the French squadron at Ferrol, was told to be ready to come out with such Spanish ships as were fit for sea and combine with a French squadron, which would soon appear before the port. Three days later the main orders went forward. Ganteaume at Brest was told to embark some 3,000 troops over and above those serving as marines, and to sail at the earliest possible moment with twenty-one of the line, six frigates, and two transports with victual for Gourdon's squadron. He was to make direct for Ferrol, endeavour to destroy Calder's blockading squadron, call out Gourdon by signal, and then proceed to Martinique, where he would find the Toulon and Rochefort squadrons awaiting him. There he was to reinforce the garrison with a thousand of the troops, and then, with the rest and the forty sail of the line he would have under his flag, he would operate his return to Europe without losing an instant. Off Ushant he was to attack any British force he found there and then push direct to Boulogne, where he would be expected between June 10th and July 10th. Such was the complete plan which Napoleon hoped to achieve, but alternative orders were given to meet the case of the Toulon squadron failing to appear. Ganteaume would then have twenty-five of the line, and after waiting thirty days for Villeneuve he was still to try to fight his way through to Boulogne. If, however, he found that from any adverse causes he had less than twenty-five, he was to return to Ferrol, where he would find a concentration of all the French and Spanish naval force in Europe awaiting him, and thence, without entering the port, he was to make for Boulogne as before.

On the same day went corresponding orders to Villeneuve. As Ganteaume was to bring out the Ferrol squadron so he was to relieve that of Cadiz, and to proceed with it direct to Martinique. There for forty days he was to hold his squadron in instant readiness to come out on Ganteaume's signal, for Ganteaume when he arrived would probably not anchor; and at the end of that period, if Ganteaume had not appeared, he was to land his troops in the French islands, do what harm he could to the British Colonies, and then take up a station at the Canaries upon the East India trade route. Possibly Ganteaume might meet him there, but if he did not appear in twenty days, then Villeneuve was to return to Cadiz, where he would find further orders. It will be observed that these orders made no provision for the concentration at Ferrol which Ganteaume had been told to expect if that at Martinique failed, but possibly it was Napoleon's intention to arrange for the latter when the situation was further developed.

Such was the giant stroke of genius, for so it has come to be regarded, by which, as he told Villeneuve, the destinies of the world were to be changed. What did his Admirals think of it? Their opinion is not on record. We must be content with that of their successors, given after patient and exhaustive study of the whole question.

" Two escapes," says Colonel Desbrière under sanction of the French General Staff, "two escapes from ports blockaded by a superior force; two blockades to be broken, at Cadiz and Ferrol; a junction at Martinique already indicated to the English by the despatch of Missiessy — such was the programme if we confine ourselves to the letter of the instructions. It is useless for historians to admire it. Such a plan would be unworthy both of Napoleon and his genius, if we could discover nothing deeper in it."

And what is it that is found? Little more than another device to save his face, and escape from the hopeless invasion without loss of prestige. Since the army of Boulogne must wait for the fleet, three months was the least interval that must elapse before it could think of moving, and in three months much would have happened. By that time the air would have cleared. Napoleon's course would be more sharply defined. It is pointed out on his behalf, moreover, that the plan as it stands entirely ignores the enemy, whereas Napoleon's practice and genius forbid us to believe he did not take the natural British movements into serious account. He must have known, it is urged, how great were the chances against its success. "If Ganteaume succeeded," so runs the case for the defence, "in concentrating an enormous fleet of forty-eight sail in the West Indies, a great naval battle was inevitable. It might be fought in American or in European waters, but with such adversaries as the English it was impossible to avoid it, and Napoleon knew this better than anybody. . . . But then the defeat of Ganteaume . . . it would certainly mean the end of the English expedition, but the fiasco would not be Napoleon's. On another's head would lie the responsibility for the check. . . . On the other hand, a great victory at sea — that meant the ruin of England, even without the descent being put in operation. . . . In short, the plan of March 2nd seems to be of the type which his secretary calls *thèmes à deux fins*. The worst that could come of it was the defeat in distant seas of mediocre squadrons, a defeat which would quickly be forgotten in grand victories on land. But the plan in no way solved the problem he had set himself, 'to make the descent without being master of the sea.' On the contrary, it shrinks from the solution and adjourns it till the moment when the command of the sea, having been won by force, the very question of the descent would no longer exist."[9]

Such is the most authoritative French view of Napoleon's actual intentions. Had he really grasped at last that in the face of the British fleet, and its traditional strategy, the problem of invasion over an uncommanded sea was insoluble? Was he really riding for a fall? To British ears the explanation sounds almost as fantastic as the plan. The old confusion of thought jars through the orders from end to end. While they are mainly and ostensibly directed at securing permanent command by fighting, they harp throughout on the possibility of securing temporary local command by surprise. The grip of the problem is as loose as ever, and Englishmen with judgment unoppressed by the Napoleonic legend, will rather see in it the work of a self-confident amateur in naval warfare, the blindness of a great soldier to the essential differences between land and sea strategy, and something perhaps of the exasperated despot who refused to own himself beaten.

But the grandiose plan went forward, and while half the world was in labour with it, on the English side there was scarcely a sign of movement. Nelson was hurrying back to his post from Egypt, but everywhere else the squadrons were maintaining their silent vigil; and, scarcely to be noticed beside the stupendous combination of Napoleon, was Pitt's little expedition, painfully gathering at Portsmouth, which yet was to prove the insidious drop of poison — the little sting — that was to infect Napoleon's empire with decay, and to force his hand with so tremendous a result.

CHAPTER III

Opening Of The Campaign

Of Napoleon's design the British Government had no suspicion. All there seems to have been to disturb their home defence and their effort to push forward into the Mediterranean was the possibility of another colonial raid to follow that of Missiessy. To meet this eventuality, on March 2nd an order was sent to Cornwallis, who was then in Torbay, to form a flying squadron of five of the line and complete their stores for foreign service.[1] This squadron was placed under the command of Collingwood in his three-decker, the *Dreadnought*; but Cornwallis did not detach it from his flag, and when he sailed on March 7th to resume his station he had, with ships joining on the way, a fleet of twenty-one sail, including no less than eight three-deckers. On detaching Collingwood he would still have seven three-deckers and nine others, and with this force he was to blockade Ganteaume, who had been definitely ascertained to have three large three-deckers and eighteen others. In other words, Cornwallis was expected to hold Ganteaume with sixteen of the line against twenty-one.

In modern criticisms of the campaign it is always taken for granted that this relation between the two forces placed Cornwallis in clear inferiority. Whether this was the view of our Admiralty or of Ganteaume is, however, by no means certain. The difficulty of appraising the value of battle units was in those days probably as great as it is now; but unless one can reach some idea of the standard upon which the dispositions of force were made, all attempt to appreciate the strategy of the time is idle

One point comes out clearly at once. From many indications in lists and despatches we can be sure that neither the British nor the French naval staffs were content to count numbers only. It is obvious they attached some special importance to three-deckers over and above two-deckers. Estimates of comparative force always distinguish these vessels from the rest, and in the naval correspondence of the time the reason is made quite clear. "We had seven three-deckers," wrote Nelson's chaplain just after Trafalgar, "they only three; but their ships in general very large and carrying eighty guns." "He knew," says one of Nelson's captains in the great chase to the West Indies, "that the French had no three-decked ships in their fleet, and he reckoned on the great superiority in close action of three batteries of guns over two." When Hardy, his flag-captain, came to be First Sea Lord he inaugurated a policy of large three-decked ships; and Briggs, who knew him well at the Admiralty, assures us "he attached as much importance to three-deckers and 90-gun ships as Voltaire did to big battalions" — that is, he regarded Providence as always on their side.

In France it was the same. When, at the end of March, Ganteaume was explaining to Napoleon an abortive attempt he had just made to break out of Brest and how narrowly he had escaped being attacked at anchor, he said: "The enemy had three of the line less than us; but he had eight of the first rank, while we had only three."[2] It was a plea that could not fail to appeal to Napoleon, for the highest relative appraisement of three-deckers that is known comes from his pen. Speaking of Calder's action he says: "The advantage of three three-deckers against a squadron that has none is equal to a difference of eight ships of the line, all enured to the sea and perfectly trained."[3] So extreme a view of the relative superiority of three-deckers need not be taken too literally, for Napoleon's object in writing the letter was to give the action an appearance of a victory for Villeneuve. But after all allowance made for exaggeration it confirms the high value that in both services was set upon three-deckers. This is the more remarkable because the new type of 80-gun two-deckers, both in the French and our own service, could deliver a broadside as heavy as the second-rate 98-gun three-deckers, and only one-seventeenth less than the first-rates.[4] But over and above weight of metal, three-deckers were regarded as having other advantages. "When it comes to boarding," writes Bigot de Morogues, "they dominate vessels of lower rate. The small-arm fire of large ships commands that of small ones; all the shot plunge and get home over the bulwarks." When British three-deckers came to be armed with 68-pounder carronades on the quarter-deck and forecastle this advantage of "command" became of course very great. "Finally," Morogues proceeds, "the crew can get down to board a small ship more easily than they can climb into a big one. In a heavy sea big vessels can use their lower battery more easily. If both have to close their lower ports the advantage of three-deckers will be still greater in respect of guns, for instead of three batteries against two they will have two against one. . . . Large ships, too, have greater solidity and better resistance to attack." These views still passed current in the British navy, or at least appeared verbatim in all the English text-books.[5]

To determine the actual relative value of the two types in Admiralty calculations is more difficult. Captain Mahan has called attention to a passage in one of Nelson's letters as elucidating the point. "Two [two-deckers]," he wrote, "alongside an enemy are better than three-deckers a great way off." "This remark," as Captain Mahan comments, "connotes that in current naval opinion one three-decker was better than two seventy-fours, conditions being similar."[6] Such a conclusion is perhaps more than the passage would bear if unsupported. But it is not without corroboration. For if we analyse the opposing squadrons of the campaign, we find again and again, that by counting three-deckers as two units, and seventy-fours as one unit, we get something like equality between the two squadrons. So constant and so nearly exact is this relation, at least for the more vital positions, that it is just possible this was actually the rough basis on which our Admiralty made their distribution. The idea indicated is that, having thus secured nominal equality, they trusted to the superior efficiency of our service as a whole for the necessary margin of strength. A similar basis of calculation appears to have prevailed in France. When, at the crisis of the campaign, Ganteaume was urged by Napoleon to make a dash up Channel with his twenty-one of the line, of which three only were three-deckers, he objected "on the ground that at any moment he might be confronted with thirty of the line of which twelve were three-deckers, a force," he says, "which would be almost double ours."[7]

On the question of tactical values there still remains another point to be cleared up before we can approach the campaign with any security of judgment. Modern English critics of high authority have pronounced that although the British service was richer in three-deckers, yet this apparent superiority was discounted by the fact that, ship for ship and rate for rate, French ships were superior in size and weight of metal to the British.[8] This result is arrived at by comparing the nominal broadside, or weight of "rated" guns only. But this test is misleading owing to the fact that most of the British ships now carried a formidable extra or unrated battery of heavy carronades on their quarter-decks and forecastles. Even the largest class of 24-pounder seventy-fours, such as the Mars, carried from twelve to fourteen 32-pounders, which raised the weight of the broadside at fighting range to over 1,000 lbs.[9]

As to the undoubted value of the new armament and its logical consequence, we have the opinion of that great artillerist Napoleon himself. At the crisis of the naval struggle nothing caused him more anxiety than the advantage derived by his enemy from this carronade armament. In March 1805, so great was his concern that he gave Decrès a definite order to re-arm certain types of ships including seventy-fours on the all big-gun one-calibre system. "I have several times spoken," he says, "of my project of arming ships of the line with guns of the same calibre." All light guns from 12-pounders downwards were to be abolished, and nothing but 36-pounders and 36-pound carronades retained. "I think," he says, "this carronade will have greater power than an ordinary 18-pounder. . . . When ships are firing at 600 toises (about 1,600 yards), they will not do much harm; at 300 toises this volume of 36-pound shot will smash the masts and spars." Decrès accordingly was to arm a frigate in this way, and also a seventy-four "with 36-pounders in its first battery, and 36-pound carronades in its second, and lighter carronades on the quarter-deck and forecastle. "In this war," he urges, "the English have been the first to use carronades, and everywhere they have done us great harm. We must hasten to perfect their system, for the argument is all on one side for sea service in favour of the system of large calibres, and we ought to put the calibres higher than 36 if it were not for the difficulty of handling the shot. I specially desire that you will not lose sight of an object so important. I am persuaded that a seventy-four able in this way to fire seventy-four or seventy-six guns with 36-pound shot would have an incalculable advantage over a ship armed in the ordinary way."[10] The trouble was to get carronades enough, and all through the year he kept pressing his minister on the subject. "It was with carronades," he says, "the English set the *Lorient* on fire [that is, at the battle of the Nile], and in them they have an immense advantage over us;" and a fortnight later more urgently, in answer to Decrès' difficulties in providing them: "The least that can be asked of the administrative branch is that soldiers shall fight with equal arms. It is the first duty of a minister, and nothing can excuse his not fulfilling it. Have we not disadvantage enough without that of armament? Your 'its' and 'buts' — that is no justification." Then a week later, as the crisis approaches and Ganteaume cannot move from Brest, more vehemently still: "But, for God's sake, ship me some carronades. It is only with guns you can arm ships of the line, and for ships of the line there is nothing but guns of heavy calibre." So every week comes a fresh reprimand. "The English," he writes from Genoa, as he is about to start for Boulogne, "without saying a word, have practised this method. Here's ten years we are behind their Admiralty. . . . I see no attention being paid to it." But to the end he could not get it done.[11]

It is clear then that we cannot assume that our superiority in three-deckers was neutralised by the greater size and nominal armament of the French two-deckers. However low may be our opinion of Napoleon on points of naval tactics and strategy, as an authority upon gunnery he stands in the first rank. It is entirely a question of gunnery and armament, and judging by these tests Napoleon — the man most nearly concerned and having through his excellent naval intelligence department the best means of knowing — had no doubt whatever that we had stolen a march on him and that ship for ship we had a material advantage that was not fair to his own men.

This opinion in the absence of strong rebutting evidence we are bound to accept. We must take it that there was nothing in the respective armaments to negative the basis of comparison which is to be assumed from the actual British distribution, and which is confirmed by Ganteaume and Napoleon, that one three-decker in a squadron was regarded as the equivalent of at least two two-deckers. Even the presence of the powerful French 80-gun ships will not detract from the general rule, for we too had this type of ship, and any excess the French had would be balanced by our first-rate three-deckers, while the second-rates, that is three-decked ships under 100 guns, balanced the seventy-fours.

With this rule then as a rough guide we may approach the campaign with some confidence in our ability to appraise the relative values of fleets. As March drew to an end the real campaign of Trafalgar was about to open. To appreciate the situation it must be borne in mind that it was to open not only with the first moves of Napoleon's great offensive combination, but also with the first moves of our offensive combination with Russia. By the middle of March, it will be remembered, the basis of the treaty with Russia had been settled and the British draft had gone to St. Petersburg. Without waiting for the actual conclusion of the treaty Craig's orders were issued. His force, besides 300 light dragoons, consisted of six battalions of infantry, two of which were to be dropped at Gibraltar and the rest taken on to garrison Malta, thereby setting free some 8,000 seasoned troops. Forty-five transports were ready for their reception, and for the escort two of the line, the *Queen*, a three-decker, and the *Dragon* 74, which Rear-Admiral Knight was taking out to reinforce Orde before Cadiz.

The instructions of Earl Camden, Secretary for War and the Colonies, dated March 28th, directed the expedition to proceed to Malta unless in the progress of the voyage extraordinary circumstances should make it necessary to alter the course. The document was drawn in the traditional manner of the elder Pitt, enumerating every probable objective upon which the force might be used with profit, so as to give the General the freest hand to act in accordance with circumstances as he found them. But the main purpose was kept clearly in the front. "It being of the utmost importance," they ran, "that Sicily should not fall into the hands of the French, the protection of that island is to be considered as the principal object of the expedition. In his method of procedure Craig was to be guided by Hugh Elliot our minister at Naples, who had to consider the possibility of having to act with or without the concurrence of the King of Naples. In the former case Craig was to do all in his power to assist the King to secure Sicily. If, however, the King did not ask for help and should be induced by France to close his ports to British ships, or if the French should attack the island or even be certainly known to be preparing an attack, then he was to use his utmost exertions, in concert with Lord Nelson, for the defence of Sicily, with or without the King's assent. Such was the substance of Craig's instructions — a clear enunciation of our old policy, that the key of the Mediterranean, whatever the attitude of its ruler, must not pass into French hands. Upon so much we were determined, and determined, moreover, with or without the assistance of Russia.

But further "most secret" instructions were given him in view of Russian co-operation. Here again two cases had to be considered; "first, that of an attack being made by the French upon Naples and his being called upon by Mr. Elliot or the Russian commander to assist in defending the Neapolitan dominions. Secondly, the case of the French forces being driven from Naples by the Russian army or withdrawn with a view to counteract the movements of armies which might be acting against France in the North of Italy." In either case he was authorised on application from Elliot or the Austrian or Russian commanders to use his force in Italy, if in his judgment he considered effective service could be done; and for this purpose he might place himself under General Lacy, the Russian Commander-in-chief. He was, however, to bear in mind that there might be other services which would call for the employment of his force, particularly the protection of Alexandria and Sardinia, and he was therefore not to engage so far in the continental campaign as not to be able to withdraw his force if necessary.[12]

Sir Henry Bunbury, who was Quartermaster-General to the expedition, severely criticises these instructions. "The different and unconnected objects," he writes, "to which Sir James Craig's attention was thus directed, afford us ample evidence, that the views of the Cabinet were based on no principle or sound plan of operations." But clearly they were based — soundly enough — on the uncertain diplomatic situation and on its most likely developments. They were designed in relation to our engagements with Russia, and at bottom were the expression of a determination with or without her assistance to secure the naval positions which in Nelson's view were essential to the command of the Mediterranean. Could there be any doubt that this was the connection and the principle in the mind of the Cabinet, it must be removed when we know that the day before Craig's orders were signed a copy of them was forwarded to Nelson.[13]

Besides the duty of escorting the expedition Knight's squadron was to take down the Mediterranean and East and West Indian trade — all of which went together as far as the latitude of Cape St. Vincent. To pass this vast convoy through in the face of the enemy's undefeated fleets was no light task. Craig himself had to traverse 2,500 miles of uncommanded sea in the face of five hostile squadrons, none of which were too strongly blockaded and not one of which had yet been brought to action.

The principle on which we have always conducted such operations is to provide, firstly, an escort strong enough to resist sporadic attacks from minor cruising squadrons; and secondly, powerful covering squadrons to prevent serious fleet interruption. Knight's squadron formed the escort; while the cover was provided by our various blockading squadrons. All that was required was to link them up in regular succession, and orders were now issued for the chain to be formed. Cornwallis could make sure of Brest and Calder of Ferrol. Beyond the secure coast of Portugal, Orde was directed to look out for the expedition and see it safe past Cadiz and Cartagena a certain distance up the Straits. There Nelson was to take up a position to cover its passage to Malta against any force issuing from Toulon.[14] It was a bold operation, but the risk had to be run, and how serious that risk was we shall presently see.

As the last preparations were being made and the great convoy was gathering at Spithead, Napoleon's widespread movement was ripe for execution. From every blockaded port were coming in reports that could not be mistaken. Off Ferrol Calder obtained information that the squadron was to be ready to sail on March 22nd. On the 26th Ganteaume was observed moving out of Brest harbour into the outer road. Cornwallis had just gone home on sick leave: his successor had not arrived. Sir Charles Cotton had been left in command with seventeen of the line and he immediately moved close in, for the Brest blockade, unlike that of Toulon, was always of the closest possible kind.[15] The idea of keeping the French in seems normally to have dominated that of bringing them to action, and in the present case nothing could have been more exasperating for Napoleon. His plan of campaign rested on Ganteaume's being able to get to sea without fighting. On March 24th he telegraphed to Napoleon that the enemy were in the

Iroise passage and to sail without an action was impossible. The signal stations could only count fifteen of the line and he wished to risk an action. "Success is not doubtful," he urged. "I await your Majesty's orders." "A naval victory," Napoleon replied, "in existing circumstances can lead to nothing. Keep but one end in view — to fulfil your mission. Get to sea without an action."

It was under these final orders that Ganteaume on March 26th moved outside the Goulet or Gut into the Bertheaume anchorage, which had been heavily fortified to facilitate his escape. All he required was a spell of thick weather. Next morning it came and he signalled to weigh; but just as he was making sail the fog lifted, and in the light of a glorious spring morning the signal station announced the British fleet in the offing. Cotton was standing in on a gentle northerly breeze with his whole seventeen sail. Bound by his orders, Ganteaume directed the fleet to moor where it was, and Cotton held on to within five miles of him. It was more than Ganteaume could endure. He feared an attack at anchor, another Battle of the Nile, and though, with the wind as it was, a return into Brest was impossible, he signalled to prepare to make sail. "My position, Sire," he wrote to Napoleon, "on this occasion was difficult. I found myself compelled to disobey the orders you had given me, as to risking an action of which the issue was doubtful." He had actually made the signal to cut and form battle order as convenient, when he saw Cotton tack and stand out again. "Night closing very fast," wrote Cotton, "and having previously placed Rear-Admiral Sir Thomas Graves with four sail of the line and other smaller vessels to keep sight of the enemy, I stood out with my squadron." It was a fine chance missed, a chance of at least putting the Brest squadron out of action for the campaign; but seeing Cotton was only in temporary command he can hardly be blamed for not risking the fleet in such dangerous waters and for preferring to take a more open position, where, as he said, "should they proceed to sea I have confident hopes I shall be able to intercept them." But Ganteaume made no further effort. On the third morning the wind came fresh from the south-west and he was forced to run back into Brest for safety.[16]

As the reports of these simultaneous movements reached the Admiralty their anxiety centred on Ferrol. It seemed to be indicated as the focus of the mysterious plan that was obviously in the wind. Urgent orders were accordingly sent to Gardner to get to his command at once and to reinforce Calder to the utmost of his ability. But the danger was not there. Gourdon was not to move from Ferrol till Ganteaume appeared, and in that port too all remained quiet. Only in Toulon was there any change. "Get to sea without an action," Napoleon had telegraphed to Ganteaume on the 24th. "That which is to join you has started." This was not true. Villeneuve was still in Toulon and Nelson was watching him before the port; but it was characteristic of Napoleon's handling to stimulate his Admirals with rose-coloured information. When Nelson had satisfied himself by his cast to the eastwards that the Morea and Egypt were safe, he returned in hot haste to Pula Roads in the south of Sardinia, to meet his store-ships. There he was kept by foul weather all the first week in March. Not till the 9th could he get to his rendezvous in the Gulf of Palmas, at the south-west of the island, and next day, having heard Villeneuve was again embarking his troops, he decided to take the squadron up to Toulon.[17]

At the crisis which had now come he had to act entirely on his own inspiration. Of two successive despatch vessels which had been sent him, one had been wrecked off Cadiz and the other had run into Villeneuve's fleet and been captured. He had heard nothing from home since November, and his position consequently was one of peculiar difficulty. He found at Toulon every appearance that Villeneuve was about to put to sea, but whither he could not tell. For a long time past he had believed that his resolute covering of Sicily and the Levant would sooner or later force the Toulon squadron out of .the Mediterranean. Yet he still inclined to think Egypt was their aim, and he was still bound both by his orders and his own judgment to make Sicily and Sardinia his first care. To cover both the eastward and westward lines of operation was impossible, except by lying close before Toulon, and that was a station that could not be maintained indefinitely, nor while it was maintained was there any hope of bringing Villeneuve to decisive action. Nelson therefore had to make his choice between one line and the other. That which led out of the Straits was the line of least danger; the line of greatest danger was that which led to Sicily and Naples, and this one he determined to secure. But the other was not opened without an effort to force his adversary away from it, and entrap him into an action which would solve the strategical dilemma.

On March 11th Nelson laid down the whole scheme in a "Most Secret Memorandum." The fleet rendezvous must be one that would cover Naples, Sardinia, and Sicily. Palmas was chosen. But before going there he meant to show himself off Barcelona. This was the trap. On the one hand it would prevent Villeneuve stealing down the Catalonian coast out of reach, and on the other it would tempt him to put to sea directly to the eastward where Nelson believed his real objective lay. Accordingly he suddenly disappeared from before Toulon and nothing but a couple of cruisers were to be seen.

On March 26th Villeneuve received his final orders to sail for Martinique not later than the morrow. He had just heard Nelson had been seen off Barcelona on the, 17th. "If he maintains this position," he wrote, "I shall have great difficulty in reaching the Straits." On the evening of the 30th he put to sea in the *Bucentaure* 80, with three other 80-gun ships, seven seventy-fours, eight cruisers, and over 3,000 troops. In order to give Barcelona a wide berth he laid his course to the southward intending to pass outside the Balearic Islands. Next day he found himself shadowed by the two frigates that Nelson had left on the Toulon rendezvous. In the night they disappeared. So far then all was going as Nelson wished. The trap was acting perfectly. The course Villeneuve was taking would bring him well within striking distance of Nelson's secret position. But at the last moment everything was upset by one of those incalculable chances which are inseparable from naval warfare. In the morning Villeneuve had the luck to speak to a neutral — a Ragusan merchantman — and learned from her where Nelson was. She had sighted his squadron not on the Spanish coast at all, but at Palmas. In the very hour of success the trap was sprung, and Villeneuve immediately altered his course to pass inside the Balearic Islands. It was a stroke of ill luck against which Nelson had not provided. A rigorous criticism will say that the chance of Villeneuve's getting intelligence from a neutral was one on which Nelson ought to have counted in those busy seas, and that when he left the inner Balearic channel open he should have had a cruiser there to watch it, especially as it led directly to Cartagena where a Spanish squadron lay. Whether Villeneuve was bound east or west it was a probable line for him to take. But from this counsel of perfection Nelson's schemes fell short — perhaps from lack of cruisers — and Villeneuve was able to run clear down the coast of Spain out of his ken.[18]

An acute crisis in the campaign was the result. As Villeneuve thus successfully opened the great attack, Craig at Portsmouth had just completed the embarkation of his force, and all was ready. Knight was only waiting for a wind and for the trade to assemble, and to all appearance the two hostile offensive movements were about to clash at sea and precipitate a catastrophe.

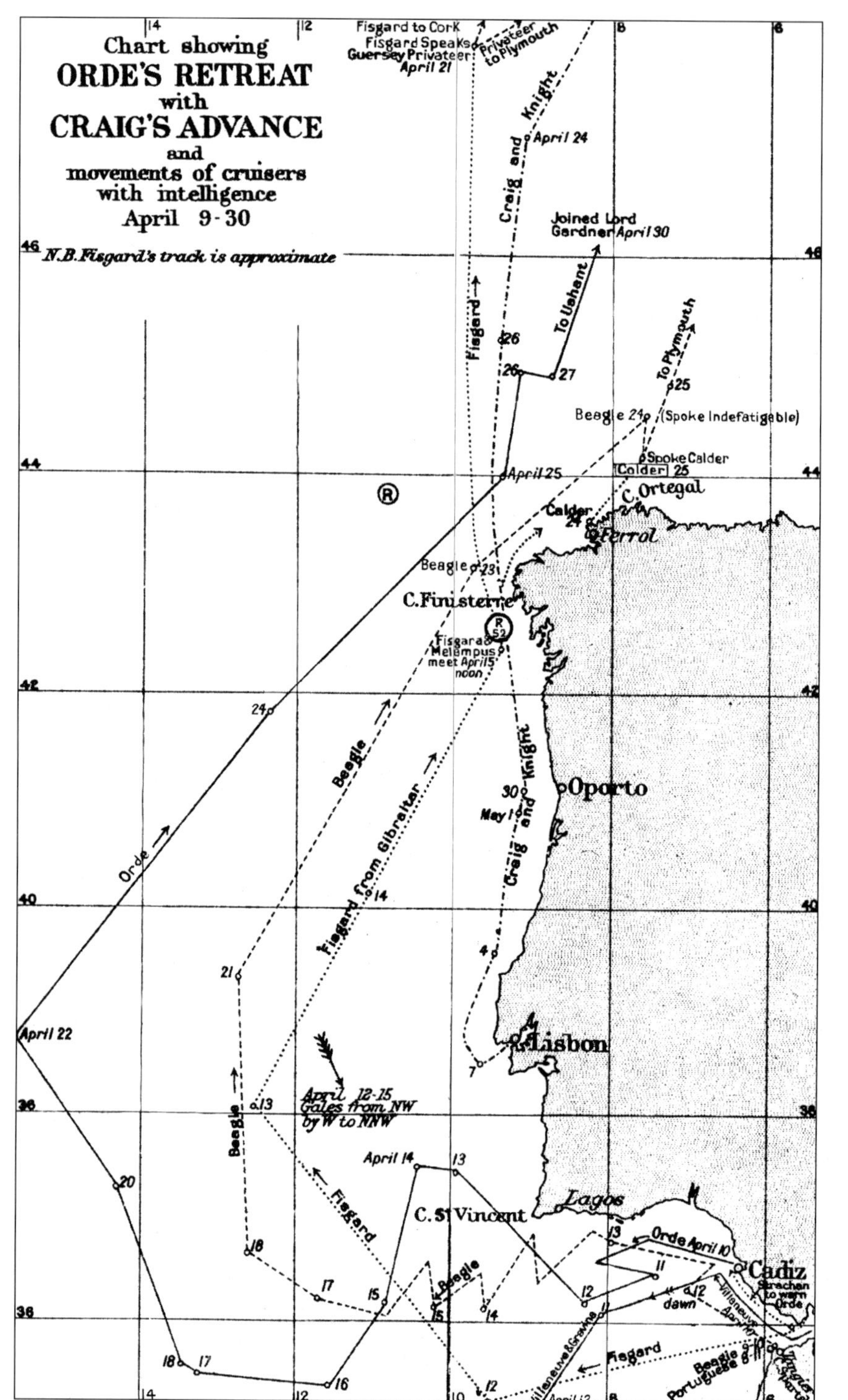

Chart showing
ORDE'S RETREAT
with
CRAIG'S ADVANCE
and
movements of cruisers
with intelligence
April 9-30
N.B. Fisgard's track is approximate
Fisgard to Cork
Fisgard Speaks Guersey Privateer April 21
Privateer to Plymouth
Craig and Knight
April 24
Joined Lord Gardner April 30
To Ushant
To Plymouth
Beagle 24 (Spoke Indefatigable)
Spoke Calder
Calder 25
April 25
C. Ortegal
Calder 24
Ferrol
Beagle 23
C. Finisterre
Fisgard & Melampus meet April 15 noon
Beagle
Fisgard from Gibraltar
Oporto
May 1
Orde
Lisbon
April 22
April 12-15 Gales from NW by W to NNW
Fisgard
April 14
C. St Vincent
Lagos
Orde April 10
Cadiz
Strachan to warn Orde
dawn
Villeneuve April 9
Villeneuve & Gravina
Portuguese
Beagle
Tangier

CHAPTER IV

Villeneuve's Evasion

As yet Villeneuve knew nothing definitely of the great combination he was to carry out. So far as he had been informed his mission lay wholly in the West Indies, where he was to operate against the English islands and reinforce those of France. All else was under sealed orders, yet he had been given a hint that there was more beyond. "The Squadron," wrote Napoleon, "with the command of which I have entrusted you is destined for an operation of an importance quite above that for which I first intended it." It was with these words that on March 22nd he prefaced his final urgent orders for Villeneuve to get to sea and pick up what Spanish ships should be found ready at Cadiz; and as the Emperor penned the orders Nelson was anchoring his battle squadron at his rendezvous in the Gulf of Palmas to watch the snare he had set.

As he lay there waiting for the word from his observing cruisers, the strain upon his high-wrought temperament grew each day more intense. He was still fretting over his false cast to Egypt, for in his absence our Levant convoy homeward-bound had been cut up by a cruiser squadron from Toulon. Both the escorting vessels had been captured, but only after so stubborn a resistance that the greater part of the convoy escaped into Gibraltar. Nelson had just heard of their being there, and knowing they would be exposed to an attack from the Algeçiras gunboats, he determined to detach Sir Richard Strachan in the *Renown* 74, which was due home for a refit, to see them clear.[1]

But anxiety for the trade was the least of his trials. As the days went by without a sign of any movement from Toulon, he began to think Villeneuve was not coming out at all "I shall remain here a few weeks longer," he wrote to his friend Sir Alexander Ball at Malta, "when, if the French do not put to sea, I think it very probable they will lay up for the summer, unless the Brest or Ferrol and Cadiz fleets should come into the Mediterranean." To Elliot he expressed the same opinion. Ill news from Naples compelled him to face the possibility of a powerful naval operation in that quarter and was turning his mind from Egypt. It will be remembered that one of Napoleon's first steps in the war had been to order General St. Cyr to reoccupy the southern Neapolitan ports which he had evacuated under the Treaty of Amiens, and Apulia ever since had been in the occupation of a corps of observation, facing the Russians at Corfu and watching the Neapolitan Court. At the first sign of Russian intervention Napoleon had reinforced it, and St. Cyr's standing orders were to march on Naples the moment the Russians moved.[2] Vague rumours of Craig's expedition had further aggravated the situation. The Neapolitans had magnified it to 20,000 men, and were arming in readiness to co-operate. This Napoleon would not endure, and St. Cyr had been instructed to demand on pain of an immediate attack not only that the mobilisation should cease, but that Elliot must be expelled. To Nelson's dismay Elliot was inclined to submit. He had just told the harassed Admiral that his object all along had been to temporise "in order to gain time for the arrival of the foreign auxiliaries, Russian and English, which have been so long promised"; and if the King asked him to retire to Sicily he probably should do so. In that case he should want a passage in the *Excellent*, the ship of the line which Nelson had been authorised to keep permanently at Naples for the safety of the Court.[3] Elliot's apparently weak attitude completed Nelson's depression. "France," he wrote to Earl Camden, "will have both Sardinia and Sicily very soon, if we do not prevent it, and Egypt besides." Then he heard that Villeneuve had embarked his troops on March 21st, and his spirits rose. He weighed to move to the southward, but squally weather compelled him to take refuge in Pula Roads. On April 3rd he weighed again, and on the following morning one of his observing cruisers ran into the fleet with news that three days since, at eight o'clock on the morning of the 31st, she had left Villeneuve some sixty miles south-by-west of Toulon, or about 300 miles from where Nelson was. He immediately moved to the westward, "as I do not believe," so he said, "the French will make Toro . . .; but I believe if they do not make Toro, they will make Galita."

Toro is a little island off the south-west extremity of Sardinia, and Galita lies off the coast of Tunis just a hundred miles to the southward. What then was apparently in his mind was that the French, instead of making the usual landfall for a voyage from Toulon to Sicily, would try to get round him by hugging the African coast, and he must cut them off. There was still, however, another cruiser to come in, before he need commit himself to any serious movement. In the afternoon she appeared, but only to say that in the night of the 31st she had completely lost touch. She had in fact been thrown out when Villeneuve changed his course in the night on the Ragusan's report of where Nelson really was. In the absence of better intelligence Nelson was forced to play for safety. He immediately decided to take up a position with his battle squadron midway between Sardinia and Galita, extending his cruisers so as to cover the whole passage from Toro to the Tunisian coast, and barring the way to Naples, Sicily, and Egypt.

With characteristic concentration of purpose he was fixing his mind firmly on his primary function. "The French," he explained to Lord Melville on April 5th, "could not pass before to-day if this be their route. I must leave as little as possible to chance, and I shall make sure they are to the eastward of me, before I risk either Sardinia, Sicily, or Naples: for they may delay their time of coming even this distance, from an expectation that I shall push for Egypt and thus leave them at liberty to act against Sardinia, Sicily, or Naples." From this clear determination to permit no lesser object to loosen his grip on the vital part of the war-plan which had been specially confided to his charge, he never swerved for one moment. For forty-eight hours he waited in the central position he had taken up, and by that time he could feel sure he had eliminated from the problem the possibility of Villeneuve's adopting the stratagem that he had suspected. Still there was another way in which it was possible for his adversary to throw his troops into Naples or Messina by evasion. He might double back from the point where Nelson's cruisers had located him and pass inside Corsica and Sardinia, either north-about or through the Straits of Bonifaccio. Till he had cleared this possibility everything else must wait. "I am in truth half-dead," he wrote to Ball on the 6th, "but what man can do to find them out shall be done. But I must not make more haste than good speed and leave Sardinia, Sicily, or Naples open for them to take should I go eastward or westward without knowing more about them." That evening to make the vital ground sure he redistributed his cruisers, and next day moved off with his battle squadron to take up the position which the new possibility demanded. This position was at the island of Ustica, some fifty miles to the northward of Palermo. His object, as he said, was "to be ready to push for Naples should they be gone there or to protect Sicily."[4] His new station he reached on the 7th, resolved not to budge from it till he was certain neither Sicily nor Naples was Villeneuve's objective. "I must be guided," he wrote hurriedly to Elliot, "on my further movements by such information as I may be able to obtain: but I shall neither go to the eastward of Sicily nor to the westward of Sardinia until I know something positive."

We are accustomed to dwell with exultation over Nelson's brilliant inspirations and his fiery action, yet surely no great commander was ever more precise for "positive information," no one more careful not to act on mere intuitions. And surely no moment glows more steadily with his real genius for war than this. In resolute singleness of purpose he had narrowed his action down to the utmost possibility of what he was certainly able to perform, and consumed as his strained spirit was with thirst for action nothing would induce him to try for more than his strength warranted or to hazard the greater danger in uncertain possibility of preventing the less. We can easily imagine what the self-restraint must have cost such a nature as his, but he did not flinch. Of all dangers the least that could befall was that Villeneuve should quit the Mediterranean and abandon its command. His duty was to secure that command. Upon that and the positions essential to it he concentrated a force which was only just equal to the task, as though he divined that upon the preservation of that command the whole of Pitt's war-plan turned — and the way out of the Straits was left absolutely open.

So while Nelson waited resolutely for the one touch of certainty that alone could start him into action, Villeneuve pursued his way unmolested — unmolested but not undisturbed. On his heels was the menace of the unlocated fleet led by the "fougueux amiral," as they called him in France. On April 7th, as Nelson was taking up his position at Ustica, he was becalmed off Cartagena. There he could see Salcedo's squadron of six of the line apparently ready for sea, and he sent in to invite them to join his flag. They were willing enough in any case to have his escort to Cadiz, if he would only wait till they sent for permission and got their powder on board. But that was more than Villeneuve dared do. In the evening an easterly breeze came up fair for a run through the Straits and away he went, leaving the Cartagena squadron isolated.

While becalmed off the port he had heard that the situation at Cadiz was unchanged. Gravina was there with fifteen of the line, but of these only seven or eight two-deckers were as yet ready for sea, and he was being watched by Orde with a somewhat inferior force of one three-decker and four others, of which three were only sixty-fours. For Orde it was therefore a critical moment. His conduct when the thunderbolt fell on him has been universally condemned and covered with contempt. To deal so with the situation is unprofitable. Let us rather see what may be learned from an exact view of his difficulties and of the way he arrived at the conclusion he did.

He was chafing even more than Nelson at the strained conditions which the division of the Mediterranean station had set up. The Admiralty, in response to Nelson's protest against his loss of prize money, had just informed Orde he would have to share a proportion of his captures with his brother Admiral. He had applied to them as to what he was to do with the treasure with which his ships were laden and this was all the answer he got. There were other sources of friction inherent in the situation which with the rest made it unendurable, and three days before Villeneuve sailed he had formally asked to be relieved.[5]

As Villeneuve left Cartagena some store-ships had joined Orde, and since the easterly wind had not reached him he was taking advantage of the calm to clear them. By midday the work was in full swing. Every ship had a transport alongside, the decks were cumbered with casks and cases, and the men were at dinner, when suddenly they saw a ship of the line running before the coming breeze under a press of sail, firing guns and making the signal for a superior enemy's fleet. It was Sir Richard Strachan in the *.Renown*. On the previous day, in pursuance of the mission on which Nelson had sent him, he had seen the homeward-bound convoy clear of Cape Spartel and the Algeçiras gunboats and privateers, and had then turned back to Gibraltar for some needful repairs. As morning broke he was off Tarifa, and so had seen Villeneuve coming out of the Straits.[6]

Instantly he went about, and accompanied by his frigate made for Orde, and had it not been for his smart warning Orde always believed he must have been destroyed.

The breeze that Strachan was bringing down had not yet reached him, but he made the signal to weigh, and prepare for action, cast off his transports with directions to retire to neutral waters at Lagos, and then did his best to form order of battle. As the breeze swelled his canvas he moved away towards Lagos under easy sail and in the larboard line of bearing — that is, in immediate readiness to form line of battle, and engage to cover the retreat of his store-ships. But Villeneuve had but one idea in his mind, and with his cruisers ahead of him he was content to make for the mouth of Cadiz Bay, without any attempt to molest Orde's deliberate movement.

It was a narrow escape, but there had been no panic or hurry, no cutting or slipping, but a thoroughly seamanlike retreat. What to do next was the difficulty. Ought he to stay where he was and wait for Nelson, ought he to go into the Straits, or ought he to go north and close on the Western Squadron? At Lagos he called Strachan to council. Strachan, who had just left Nelson and knew how much his mind had been occupied with Egypt, assured Orde that Villeneuve's escape could only be explained by Nelson's having gone again to Alexandria. Then Orde made his decision. He could not doubt that Villeneuve had come to bring out Gravina's squadron; and he had just heard the news of Ganteaume's having come out of Brest into Bertheaume Road. The indications in his opinion pointed to a great and dangerous concentration of all Napoleon's squadrons, and on this appreciation there was in his eyes but one thing to do. Strachan's cruiser the *Sophie* was ordered to Ushant immediately to warn the Admiral, and to inform him that he himself would close upon him, if, as he said, nothing occurred in the morning to prevent his doing so. "I shall make the best of my way to join Lord Gardner," he wrote to the Admiralty, "as an immediate accession of force may be of importance at this critical juncture."

In view of the charges which were made so freely by Nelson and others against him, it is important to note that it was not his whole fleet he was taking north, but only his battle squadron. The whole of his cruisers, as we shall see, were left behind with carefully framed orders for keeping touch with Villeneuve. Two days later — on April 12th — as he had seen nothing of the enemy his view of the situation was confirmed, and it became, of the utmost importance to warn the Admiralty as soon as possible. Baffling winds were still preventing him from doubling Cape St. Vincent, the *Sophie* was still in company, and he charged her with further despatches in which he developed fully the appreciation on which he was acting. "I am persuaded," he wrote to the Admiralty, "the enemy will not remain long in Cadiz, and I think the chances are great in favour of their destination being westward where by a sudden concentration of several detachments, Bonaparte may hope to gain a temporary superiority in the Channel, and availing himself of it to strike his enemy a mortal blow." Here, then, for the first time from an English pen we have a just appreciation of the real situation, and it comes from this despised officer. It was not that he did not realise the importance of the Mediterranean, but that he felt the danger was past. "Could I have brought myself," he went on, "to believe the fleet would return towards the eastwards I should not have hesitated one moment to risk passing the Straits, although left ignorant by Lord Nelson of his position and movements." With him as with Nelson it was a question of the point of greatest danger, and that he saw at the mouth of the Channel. "In bringing to England the large ships under my command," he says, "I shall afford an opportunity to dispose of them anew: by which little can be risked, and much might be gained if the enemy's blow is aimed at England or Ireland."

For the next two days he laboured round St. Vincent, and then, owing either to stress of weather or to a desire to sweep the ground he was leaving, he stood back to the south. By the 16th he had stretched down below the latitude of the Straits, and next day he began to make the usual westing for a voyage north. In all this time he had not found a trace of Villeneuve, but whatever the intention of his movement, the result left him convinced of the correctness of his appreciation.[7] He accordingly resolved to send forward the *Polyphemus*, his fastest two-decker, to communicate his final view to the Admiralty. She was charged with a despatch in which his appreciation was more fully reasoned in the light of Villeneuve's disappearance. He assured them that whatever had happened the enemy could not possibly have got ahead of him to the northward. It was true that his failure to find Villeneuve to the westward might suggest a return to the Mediterranean, but he argued with ability that the whole strategical conditions rendered that course the least likely and the least dangerous. Villeneuve, he urged, could not hope to evade Nelson twice; and even if he did pass back into the Straits reinforced from the Cadiz squadron, still it did not mean defeating Nelson. The men of the War of American Independence had too much experience of the preventive power that lay in a well-handled inferior fleet; and of his rival's tactical genius Orde had the highest opinion. "I dare believe," he wrote, "Lord Nelson will be found in condition with his twelve of the line and numerous frigates to act on the defensive without loss, and even to hang heavily on the skirts of the enemy's fleet should it attempt any material service, especially when encumbered with troops." It was so Kempenfelt had laid down the power of a naval defensive in the darkest days of the old war, and Nelson's own views to the same effect on the possibilities of retarding operations at sea are well known.

Finally, he clinches his reasoning with a last penetrating appreciation. "Besides," he says, "I am perfectly convinced that the French are too well aware of the advantage they may derive in a contest with us by having their fleets out of the Mediterranean, ever to send them back to that sea, if they can avoid it." He was absolutely right though he did not as yet know the sting that was about to be put forth, which in the end was to make it impossible for Napoleon to avoid ordering them back.

It is but bare justice, therefore, to Orde to recognise that his closing in with his battle squadron was in line with the British strategical tradition of concentration on the Western Squadron and that his decision was based on a sagacious penetration of Napoleon's war-plan. Had he made the move without taking every precaution in his power to keep touch with Villeneuve he would nevertheless have been seriously to blame. But in fact he did do everything that the means available permitted, and his first care before moving his battle squadron had been to make a thoughtful disposition of the cruisers he was leaving behind. He had already sent off a merchantman to find Nelson,[8] and before going north he despatched a cruiser to the West Indies and a cleared transport for Madeira to warn the home-coming East Indiamen. Nelson's old friend, Captain Sutton, of the *Amphion* frigate, with two sloops under him, the *Wasp* and *Beagle*, was all he had left to watch Villeneuve. Sutton was directed to take station off St. Vincent "to gain intelligence of the enemy's movements and prevent vessels bound east of the Cape from falling into the enemy's hands." If he ascertains Villeneuve has gone west, he is to direct all ships of the line he may meet to go to Ushant; if he has gone east, then they are to try to join Nelson. The *Wasp* was to observe Cadiz. The *Beagle*, which was already cruising between Capes Spartel and Trafalgar, Sutton was to keep there to hold the privateers in check, and report enemy's squadrons. But in truth she was no longer there. Unknown to Orde, she had already located the enemy, and having failed to find her chief, was then well on her way to England.[9]

With a decision founded on so well reasoned an appreciation, there seems little fault to find. It has been objected that he might better perhaps have fallen back with his battle squadron on Calder, and this indeed was what the Admiralty ordered him to do when they knew what had happened. But in view of the prevailing northerly winds, Ferrol was notoriously hard to reach. The true course for Ushant lay far to the westward, and Nelson himself was afterwards forced to take it when he in his turn closed on Cornwallis. The fact is, however, that in spite of these difficulties Orde did try to get in touch with Calder, and it was not his fault that he failed. After holding the usual course north-westward till the 22nd, he found a wind that enabled him to reach north-east, and in three days he passed near the Finisterre rendezvous. There he should have found one of Calder's cruisers, which was always stationed there, but the rendezvous was bare. The fact was the *Melampus* (Captain Poyntz) had left it just a week before. By a piece of extraordinarily smart work, to be related presently, he had got news of Villeneuve's having passed the Straits, and had gone off to warn Calder. Before he could be replaced Orde arrived. Nevertheless Orde held on till he was some fifty miles north-west of Ferrol and actually on Calder's station. Still there was no trace of him, and Orde, assuming apparently that he must have had news of Villeneuve and fallen back on Ushant, stood away north to do the same.[10]

Such are the true facts of this interesting case, and in face of them it is bare justice to revise the cruel judgment which has passed into history upon Nelson's hasty and ill-informed strictures. If Orde failed to do all that might have been done, it was mainly due to the disposition of his scanty cruisers. In the arrangement he adopted there was one important point he had failed to reckon, and that was the moral effect of Nelson's unlocated fleet on the French Admiral's nerves. Yet the omission was pardonable. He was not to guess that Villeneuve, having risked so much to join Gravina's fleet, would not dare to wait long enough to make the junction complete. Yet so it was. At eight o'clock on April 9th the French anchored outside the bay and signalled for the *Aigle*, a French seventy-four that had taken refuge there early in the war, and to Gravina and the Spaniards to come out. By ten o'clock they had begun to move, and at one o'clock Villeneuve made the signal to weigh. In his eagerness to hide his tracks from Nelson he dared not sacrifice the obscurity of a single night. After waiting less than four hours, he held away in the dark, leaving the Spaniards to straggle after him as best they could. Had Orde remained he might have captured them nearly all, but can he be blamed if he never thought such a movement possible? And yet — if he had only waited to make sure, if just for one day he had "hung heavily on their skirts," as he expected Nelson to do! But his chance was gone, and so it happened beyond all calculation before Sutton could even begin his observation, Villeneuve and Gravina were gone, and from that moment they were completely lost to British ken.

CHAPTER V

Lord Barham At Work

At home, in the centre of war direction, all was confusion. No moment could have been more inopportune for the escape of the Toulon squadron. At the end of the previous year the famous Commission for inquiring into the state of the Navy, which had been sitting since 1802, issued its Tenth Report, and public opinion was startled with irrefutable evidence that certain irregularities had been permitted with the Navy balances. Lord Melville as First Lord was of course responsible. He was moreover a bosom friend of Pitt, and the temptation for the Opposition to raise a storm was irresistible. Just as Villeneuve was approaching the Straits it burst with a formal indictment in the House of Commons. Pitt exhausted all his powers in the defence of the friend who had been serving him and the country with so much ability. So brilliant and impassioned was his effort that he was within an ace of success. In the end the motion was carried against him, but only by the Speaker's casting vote. Under the shock Pitt broke down, and as he rose to leave the House the young bloods of his party closed round like a body-guard lest his enemies should see his tears. Next day, as Orde's blockade was being broken, Melville resigned, and the Admiralty was without a head.

Fortunately there was at hand a means of preserving continuity. The veteran Sir Charles Middleton was still alive, and though just turned eighty was still full of vigour in mind and body. Throughout the War of American Independence he had been Controller, standing out through that period of inept administration as the pillar of the service, the confidant to whom all the best men afloat turned in their distress and despair. During his tenure of the office the Supply department of the Navy had been put at last in a fairly efficient state, though he himself was dissatisfied. He longed to see much further improvement, which without support from above he had not the power to effect. A few years later the power he sought was within his grasp. In 1788 Pitt, during his first administration, decided to replace Lord Howe by a civilian. The man he selected was his own inexperienced and not too capable elder brother, Lord Chatham. He had a remarkable talent, however, for smoothing business in the Cabinet, and to meet the inevitable objections to the appointment of such a man to the head of the Admiralty, Pitt decided to offer the post of First Sea Lord to Middleton. It was felt that if Chatham were given the veteran Controller for his chief professional adviser public opinion would be satisfied. Though Middleton had never flown his flag, he was recognised as a master of the naval art second only to Howe himself. "Sir Charles Middleton's name and character," wrote Grenville, "will hold out a solution." Middleton, however, in loyalty perhaps to Howe, would not lend himself to the solution and declined to serve.[1] About eighteen months later he went even further, in marking his disapproval of Lord Chatham's appointment and the way he was administering the Admiralty. Regardless of everything but the good of the service, he had laid the shortcomings of colleagues and subordinates candidly before a Committee of Inquiry. Unsupported by the Government he found his position impossible, and in February 1790 he had placed his resignation in Pitt's hands. His evidence at the Inquiry, he explained, had created so much jealousy of him in the office that in view of the delay that was going to occur in acting on its report it was impossible for him to go on. Pitt and his brother apparently tried to induce him to remain, but he was obdurate. "The motives of my resignation," he wrote to the Prime Minister a week or two later, "are by no means merely personal. I am so firmly persuaded that the present situation of the Navy Office could afford me no means of continuing any longer useful, that I flatter myself with your and Lord Chatham's candour in admitting the propriety of my resignation."[2] Later on, however — in 1794 — when the new war had broken out, he loyally came forward again and accepted a seat on the Board under Lord Chatham, with Hood, Gardner, and Affleck for his naval colleagues.

Since then he had been unemployed but not unoccupied. Melville was his near kinsman and rested on him as his confidential adviser. Wilberforce, indeed, who had found in Middleton's progressive mind one of his earliest supporters in the Slave Trade crusade, assures us that "Lord Melville's plans for the naval force of the kingdom were in fact Sir Charles's."[3] Seeing what Middleton's reputation was both in the service and the Cabinet, and that Gambier the First Sea Lord was his nephew, this is credible enough, and indeed by no other means can we account for the precision and balance with which all the best traditions of the service had been embodied in the strategy of the war.

A further reason for Pitt's insisting on the appointment was, if we may believe Wilberforce, that Melville himself had named Middleton as the best man to succeed him. But it was not without a severe struggle that the minister got his way. The King wanted Chatham again or Castlereagh or Charles Yorke, who had been Secretary for War under the last administration. Addington, from whose inadequate hands Pitt had snatched the direction of the war, had consented early in the year to join his Government, with the title of Lord Sidmouth, but characteristically he expected further reward. Now he demanded the vacant place for one of his own men. In the stress of the war on his enfeebled constitution it was more than Pitt could endure. Without a sure hand at the Admiralty he must break down. "It is inconceivable," wrote Woronzow to his Government in the midst of the political and naval crisis, "how one man can suffice for such a weight of business and fatigue; how he can keep straight in his head so many tangled and heterogeneous matters; how he can disentangle and grasp them and develop them with such singular judgment and lucidity."[4] For a fortnight Pitt hesitated under the strain. Then he informed Sidmouth that further delay was impossible and that he had submitted Middleton's name to the King. Sidmouth and his closest follower, the Earl of Buckinghamshire, who was his nominee for the place, immediately tendered their resignations. To all Pitt's other troubles was added a ministerial crisis; but he persevered, and finally, on promising Sidmouth that Middleton's appointment was to be regarded "as not for long," both the recalcitrants consented to retain office.

So the veteran was duly gazetted as First Lord. To get over the difficulty of his not being in Parliament he was raised to the peerage as Lord Barham, though the King, in giving his assent, made the remarkable stipulation that "his attending Cabinet meetings ought to be confined to subjects regarding the Navy."[5] Thus at the eleventh hour came Middleton's long-deferred chance of setting his seal on the great work to which he had devoted his strenuous life; and thus at the crying moment the country, by Pitt's firmness and sagacity, secured for her councils the man who, for ripe experience in the direction of naval war in all its breadth and detail, had not a rival in the service or in Europe. Even Charles Yorke, in spite of his disappointment in not getting the post himself, could say handsomely, "The news today is, Sir Charles Middleton is to be First Lord. I was not aware that at his advanced age his health and faculties were equal to such a post. If they are he is indisputably the fittest man that could be chosen to occupy it at the time. His abilities were always considered great, his experience is consummate, and he has few equals in application and method of business."[6] It was not, however, till the last day of April that Barham's appointment was confirmed and the crisis was at an end.

In the height of it — on the 19th — Craig and Knight had put to sea. It was high time, if any good was to come of the expedition. Already the Czar had been protesting at the delay, and Napoleon was just starting for Milan to crown himself King of Italy. Now or never was the time to act. Yet as Craig and his troops pursued their way down Channel there were flying across the Bay two cruisers with the momentous news that the Toulon fleet had passed the Straits too late to warn the Government that all had gone wrong. Villeneuve was out, no one knew where; neither Nelson nor Orde had received their orders for covering Craig's passage, and Knight had only a ninety-eight and one seventy-four to escort the expedition. It was practically in the air.

Not till a week after the expedition had sailed was the alarming truth known, and then only by the promptness and decision of a detached cruiser captain. As Villeneuve passed through the Straits, Captain Lord Mark Kerr, of the frigate *Fisgard*, was refitting in Gibraltar with half his gear ashore.[7] With prompt decision he hired a brig, put a lieutenant in command, and sent her away to find Nelson. Working all night long, while Villeneuve was hurrying away from Cadiz, he managed to put to sea early on the 10th, leaving his gear behind him, and determined to carry the news to Ireland and Ushant with the utmost possible speed.[8] Outside the Straits not a sign of the enemy was to be seen. He spoke two or three cruising privateers, but they too had not a word to tell, so mysteriously had Villeneuve disappeared. His luck was incredible, and Kerr had nothing to carry with him but the certainty that he had passed the Straits. In five days, in spite of the northwesterly winds that had baffled Orde's efforts to double Cape St. Vincent, he managed to speak to the *Melampus*, the cruiser which Calder kept stationed on the regular Finisterre rendezvous.[9] She went off to Calder and Calder sent her on to Gardner, leaving Kerr free to go straight on to warn Ireland. Calder, unlike Orde, boldly held his ground, but his case was widely different. Orde's blockade had been broken, Calder's had not, and it was obviously his duty to maintain it as long as he could. Moreover he was in no danger of being embayed and held to mercy, as Orde was in the precarious winds of the Cadiz station. By no means could a squadron coming from the south force him to action if he chose to retire. He therefore contented himself with retaining one of Gardner's cruisers to replace the *Melampus* off Finisterre; and so, secure from surprise, he held on confidently where he was.

Meanwhile Kerr hurried on for Ireland. Midway across the Bay he had the luck to meet a Guernsey privateer lugger. He ordered her into Plymouth with a despatch for the Admiralty and himself carried on for Cork, communicating his news to Gardner's outlying cruisers as he passed.[10] It was a fine performance. Few features, indeed, of these wars are more striking than the resource and decision which cruiser captains showed in spreading intelligence of this nature on their own responsibility and their own grasp of the situation.

It was through Gardner that the Admiralty first got Kerr's startling news. They had it on the 25th, just a week after Craig and Knight had sailed; and on that day were issued a series of those remarkable orders which always seemed ready for any eventuality, and which can only have proceeded from the rich store of strategical tradition that was accumulated in the brain of Middleton. By that time he knew the King had approved Pitt's choice, and doubtless he was already at work.

The first thought was for the safety of the West Indies. A raid in that quarter had long been expected, and in the eyes of the Admiralty it was Villeneuve's most likely object. Indeed, for some time Pitt had had in his possession information from the famous spy, "L'Ami," that an attack on Jamaica was in contemplation, and Missiessy's voyage had already indicated the West Indies as a danger area. Consequently Cochrane's general instructions were immediately supplemented by orders that if Villeneuve's objective were found to be Jamaica he was to join Dacres at Port Royal with his whole battle squadron. This would produce a concentration of eleven of the line, of which one was a three-decker, a force strong enough to hold in check Villeneuve and any Spanish ships that might have joined him from Cadiz, till such time as reinforcements should reach the station.

On this last point they had little cause for anxiety. The necessary reinforcements would probably reach him automatically. It was an old but now forgotten tradition which throws much light on Nelson's great movement, that in such an eventuality as had occurred the Commander-in-chief in the Mediterranean should send or follow with a proportion of his force large enough to make the British squadron in the threatened area superior to that of the enemy. Originally, indeed, it had been the practice to insert such a clause in the Mediterranean instructions. In 1704 Rooke was directed that if the Toulon fleet got out of the Straits his first duty would be to follow it and bring it to action. As late as 1756 Byng's instructions contained categorical orders on the point. Consequently it is no matter of surprise to find the Admiralty expecting that Nelson would act on the well-established tradition, and in this spirit supplementary orders were quickly framed for him.

He was told that Knight's two ships, which formed Craig's escort, were to proceed at once to Barbadoes, "if you have not already detached a number equal to the enemy." If he had done so, he was to order Knight's ships to join Orde, and Orde was to send them on with Craig's expedition; for, of course, if Villeneuve had gone west there was nothing for the expedition to fear except the weak Spanish squadron in Cartagena, which was reported not yet ready for sea. There was, moreover, no further need for Nelson to act as covering squadron in accordance with his orders of ten days before. "Their Lordships trust," the new orders ran, "you have had early intelligence of the sailing of the Toulon fleet, and that you have in consequence detached a number of ships equal to that of the enemy in pursuit." What remained of his squadron he was to send to join Orde before Cadiz, he himself of course being expected home on sick leave.[11]

Two days later, however, a misgiving as to what Nelson might do led to further precautions. It was now known that he had been in position at Maddalena about the time Villeneuve sailed, and the most natural explanation of his missing him was that once more he had gone to Egypt. The fear was, so Yorke wrote to Lord Hardwicke, "his only eye is directed eastward, and we shall find ourselves in a great scrape."[12] It was decided, therefore, to take steps to reinforce the West Indies directly from Gardner's fleet in case it should prove that Nelson had gone astray. The means already existed in the Flying Squadron, which, it will be remembered, had been formed for special service under Collingwood. The only difficulty was that Gardner's fleet was not yet up to its full strength, and the detachment would weaken it seriously. But the difficulty was faced. Besides Gardner's regular reserve there were other ships available which only required crews and fitting for sea, and with pressure they could be ready in time to replace the West Indian detachment. To this end every nerve was strained and every sacrifice made. The War Office offered its help, and the Port Admirals were informed that orders had been issued for the troops of the garrisons to assist in the work. They could apply to the Generals for the men they wanted, and they were "to use every possible exertion in getting the ships ready for sea with the utmost despatch." Cruisers were freely sacrificed to the now all-important battle strength, and at every port authority was given to draw upon any frigates that were at hand to complete the complements of the ships of the line.[13]

The Flying Squadron at this time consisted of ten of the line, and it was decided to use half of it at once. Accordingly Gardner was directed to detach Collingwood with his flagship, the *Dreadnought* 98, and four two-deckers, and to hand him sealed orders, which were to the following effect. He was to proceed with all expedition to Madeira, and without anchoring to send in for intelligence of the French fleet or of any British ships that had been seen to pass that way. If he heard for certain that seven or more of the line were in chase of the enemy, he was to return. If the intelligence was not positive, he was to carry on to Barbadoes, join Cochrane, and seek out the enemy's fleet. If he found the French had left the Leeward Islands and gone north, Cochrane was to shift his flag to a frigate and remain in charge of the station, while Collingwood was to take the whole battle squadron to Jamaica, and in concert with Dacres to defend the island and seek to bring the enemy to action. Finally he was given as usual a general discretion to act as he found best on the spot, in order to prevent an attempt on any of the British West Indian Islands.[14]

The meaning of the Madeira destination was that steps had already been taken to watch that area. More than a month previously, when the precaution of organising the Flying Squadron was on foot, means had been adopted to supply it with intelligence of any escaping squadron it might have to chase. To this end two frigates had been withdrawn from Keith and Saumarez, with orders to proceed to Madeira with all possible despatch and cruise from forty leagues southeast of it to a hundred leagues north-west. They were to hold the station a month after arriving, and if an enemy's squadron was sighted one was to come home to report and the other to shadow the enemy till his course was determined.[15]

On the same day that Collingwood's orders were issued, corresponding instructions went forward for Nelson. He was informed that if he had made no detachment Collingwood would follow Knight's two ships to Barbadoes. As the effect of this would be to bring the squadron in the West Indies up to eighteen of the line with two or three three-deckers, nothing further would be required from Nelson. He was therefore to leave four of his squadron with Orde and bring home the rest, after making due provision for opposing any force the enemy had left in the Mediterranean. At the same time Gardner was told to send down a cruiser to get intelligence of Villeneuve's movements from Orde and carry it on to Madeira to meet Collingwood.[16]

It will be seen that up to this time the Admiralty had little doubt that Villeneuve was bound on the original mission which Napoleon had given him and of which they had had intelligence. As yet there is no hint that any apprehension of his sudden return to the Channel was felt at headquarters, or that Sir James Craig's expedition was in serious danger. The prevailing impression was that the objective of the Toulon fleet was Jamaica. It appeared that Nelson's resolute retention of his primary position had forced Napoleon to play into Pitt's hands. Denied all chance of operating within the Straits, Villeneuve had been driven to secondary colonial ventures and had left the Mediterranean free for the intended action in concert with Russia. No sooner, however, had the orders for the West Indies been issued, on this appreciation of the position, than it was all upset. By April 30th Gardner had sent in the letters he had received from Orde. Picture for a moment what they meant at headquarters. Nelson was no one knew where. The best information they had was Strachan's opinion that he had been thrown off the scent, and was almost certainly on his way to Egypt. Orde, moreover, without having ascertained anything more of Villeneuve's movements than that he had appeared at Cadiz, was quitting his station. Neither Admiral, therefore, would receive his orders for Craig's security, and both covering squadrons at the critical period were out of position. Whither Villeneuve was bound Orde could not tell. He might go north, he might go south, but, as we have seen, his carefully argued appreciation inclined him to think that the destination was westward with a view to doubling back to the Channel.

So far as is known, no one up to this time had seriously suggested such a probability, but from this moment at least it was never lost sight of. Still, knowing what Pitt did, it was quite as likely that Villeneuve's orders were to hold the approaches to the Straits and destroy Craig and Knight. They and their fifty transports, to say nothing of the convoys, were obviously in the direst danger of annihilation, and what such a shock would mean to the great Coalition in the crisis of parturition was too distressing to contemplate. The Government could scarcely flatter themselves that Napoleon had no suspicion of what was in the wind, for Craig's expedition did not stand alone. At Cork there was another similar one assembling under Sir Eyre Coote, which appears to have been intended for the security of India. The two together could scarcely escape French attention, and as a matter of fact, although Napoleon had not yet divined Craig's instructions, he had already an uneasy eye on the British military movements. Talleyrand's smooth pen had been presenting them to him as of no importance, except as evidence of the desperate political position of Pitt's Government. News had reached the French Foreign Office that at Lisbon they were in alarm lest the Tagus was the objective of the mysterious expeditions — a fear which Talleyrand regarded as somewhat extravagant. "Still," he said, "there is no project, however absurd, which we can safely reject as impossible in the existing state of opinion in England and the embarrassment of the Cabinet. If they must have an expedition its objective matters little to the real motive for undertaking it; and if, as is possible, all that is wanted is a display of enterprise, it is still more indifferent whether it is destined for Portugal or the North, or for the Levant or the Indies."[17]

Napoleon himself took the matter more seriously. Affecting to believe a vague rumour that Missiessy had taken Dominica and St. Lucia, he was persuading himself and his servants after his manner that his original mistake in getting the Rochefort squadron entangled in the West Indies was a stroke of genius. By throwing British strategy into confusion and diverting attention to distant colonies it was paving the way for invasion. The British expeditions served well to support his attitude, but reading between the lines of his correspondence we may well doubt if this was his real view of the enemy's new activity. Three days after receiving Talleyrand's news he wrote a memorandum upon it for Cambacérès, Arch-Chancellor of the Empire, whom he had left in Paris at his brother Joseph's side as the real head of affairs during his absence in Italy. This despatch breathes a different note. "It seems," he wrote, "that two expeditions of from 5,000 to 6,000 men each have left or are preparing to leave, one for the Great Indies and the other for the West Indies. They are neither militia nor volunteers they are sending: they are their best troops." The fact that the threat of invasion no longer availed to contain the flower of the British army in England clearly was unexpected and annoying. "If then," he continued, "our flotilla receives the signal and is favoured by six hours of fair wind, of fog, and of night, the English will be surprised and find themselves stripped of their best troops."[18]

This certainly was not what he really thought. Nothing is clearer amidst Napoleon's shifting plans than that at this time he had absolutely abandoned as a hopeless military operation the project of a surprise invasion by the flotilla alone. He may have believed it possible once, and popular opinion in England had believed it too. Now both knew better. The naval view had been accepted, and Napoleon's words can mean nothing but annoyance to find that his threat would work no longer. His self-esteem was sick, and after his manner he was treating it with a gentle course of self-deception. He persuaded himself he had fixed England's anxiety on her East and West Indian colonies, as he explained this same day to General Pino, his Minister of War in Italy. Pino had apparently been expressing anxiety about British action in the Mediterranean, but Napoleon assured him there was now no fear of England's assisting Austria except with money. His threat on India, he said, was forcing the British Government to send Lord Cornwallis thither with several regiments, and they had also found it necessary to despatch eight or ten thousand men to secure Jamaica.[19]

Such at least was the rosy picture he chose to paint, as he was about to cross the Alps in quest of his new crown. How much he really believed it is impossible to tell. All we can say with any certainty is that he was beginning to feel the irritation of Pitt's pin-prick. Probably he still believed the initiative was his, and had no suspicion as yet that an insidious process of wresting it from him had begun. It was of course too much for Pitt to flatter himself he had so well deceived the master of deception, and for him Villeneuve's appearance in the Straits' mouth must mean, first of all, that Napoleon was awake and after his manner was springing to meet the blow before it could fall. If it did not mean this, there was still Orde's suggestion, that he was bent after all on attempting the invasion, and attempting it under cover of a great naval concentration.

In a moment, then, the whole atmosphere at home was changed. It throbbed with high tension. We can feel the tremors still as we handle the papers which the crisis produced. Even Pitt was disturbed. He had spent the whole day on which the news arrived — that is, April 29th — in the House of Commons. There had been an exhausting and more than usually acrimonious wrangle over the Eleventh Report of the Navy Commission. In the course of it Pitt had announced Middleton's appointment, and had been brutally accused by Fox of trying to burke the inquiry into his friend's conduct. In the heat that was engendered a motion was made for the institution of criminal proceedings against Melville, and nearly all the leaders of the Opposition, regardless of the danger of the nation, ruthlessly tormented the Prime Minister by supporting it. It was a fierce struggle, but in spite of their acrimony, Pitt secured its rejection. Overwrought with the defence of his friend, he reached home at two o'clock in the morning to find Orde's news from the coast of Spain awaiting him. There was also a report from his Paris agent saying that the Toulon fleet was about to sail, that its destination was a mystery, but it was generally believed to be Ireland. The spy himself had reasons, he said, to believe it was intended for Jamaica, but in a second report, dated April 17th, he had assured Pitt the whole system of Napoleon was now directed to diverting the British Navy from his real attack.[20] The intelligence could only confirm Orde's view that a sudden concentration on the Channel was in the wind. Pitt could not go to bed, and at half-past two he sat down to give the alarm to his new First Lord.

"On returning from the House," he wrote, "I have just found these papers; they are of the most pressing importance. I will not go to bed for a few hours, but will be ready to see you as soon as you please, as I think we must not lose a moment in taking measures to set afloat every ship that by any means of extraordinary exertion we can find means to man. At such an emergency, I am inclined to think many measures may be taken to obtain a supply of men for the time, which would not be applicable to any case less immediately urgent."[21]

Barham had spent his first day of office in preparing to set on foot a reorganisation of the Admiralty in order to fit the distribution of work to the condition of the First Lord's being a sailor and responsible for the actual direction of the maritime war.[22] Perhaps he too was sitting up all night. At all events in the course of the next day, April 30th, a whole series of characteristically lucid orders were issued, which tell of acute tension and prolonged hours of labour. Those issued to the Admirals afloat are devoted primarily to saving Craig's expedition, in the second place to maintaining the blockade of Ferrol, and ultimately to the traditional closing in on the mouth of the Channel in case Orde's appreciation should prove correct.

To Calder went orders to retain Knight and his two ships, instead of sending them to the West Indies, if the imperilled expedition had come in touch with him. Craig and his transports he was to send back to Plymouth or Cork under cruiser escort. Knight on his part was informed that the need of the moment was to reinforce the Ferrol squadron in view of the possibility of Villeneuve's intending to break the blockade. If, therefore, he received the fresh orders before he had passed St. Vincent with the convoy, he was to bring it back to Ferrol, and follow Calder's orders as above. If Calder was not there, he was to carry on and close on Gardner off Ushant. If, on the other hand, he had passed

St. Vincent, and ascertained that Villeneuve had left Cadiz, he was to shift his flag to a frigate, send his two ships of the line to close on Calder or Gardner as before, and carry on with the convoy up the Straits under cruiser escort.

As for Orde, his instructions were to leave his cruisers to watch Cadiz, and join Calder immediately with his battle squadron. He would then be in command of both squadrons, but was to consider himself under Gardner's orders. This meant, of course, that the blockade of Cadiz was abandoned, and the new "Coast of Spain" Squadron reabsorbed into the old Western Squadron. It was explained to Orde that the object of the new disposition was, if possible, to maintain the blockade of Ferrol. Otherwise everything was to concentrate at the mouth of the Channel. If, therefore, it was found that Calder had already fallen back, Orde too was to close on Ushant. Assuming, however, that he and Calder were able to join hands on the Ferrol station the blockade was to be continued, but subject to this proviso. If they had reason to believe that a combined French and Spanish fleet was coming to Ferrol "under circumstances in which you may not think you can advantageously engage them," then they were to fall back together on Gardner at Ushant. Finally Gardner was directed to order Calder to close on him if the combined fleet were reported to be coming north.[23] If now we compare these orders with what Orde was doing, it will be seen that he was anticipating the intentions of the Admiralty exactly. Both he and they were following the well-known tradition, whereby it was secured that all disturbances of our strategical distribution only produced, as it were automatically, an overwhelming concentration at the vital time and place. Boldly as the fleet was spread, it retained in the alert instinct of its squadronal commanders a reflex power of shrinking back to the centre when any rough touch gave warning that dispersal was no longer wise. Orde acted on that instinct, and his action was approved by Barham. It were well to remember this before endorsing Nelson's hasty castigations well also to remember that Nelson never repeated them when he knew the facts.

In harmony with these instructions to the outlying squadrons, increased efforts were made to reinforce the central division of the Western Squadron. The *Prince George*, a three-decker, was ordered to join it immediately. Admiral Rowley was sent down to Chatham to press forward two new seventy-fours that were just completing, and orders went out to hire six or eight fast vessels as despatch boats.[24]

The underlying ideas of the whole group of orders is not far to seek. We have been attempting, they say, to pass a military force over uncommanded seas — seas, that is, in which no decision has taken place; our chain of covering squadrons has been broken through: therefore the expedition must be withdrawn, unless it has already passed the danger point. If, however, the enemy's movement is found not to be aimed at the expedition, we must assume it is aimed at the point of greatest danger, and we must make sure of the mouth of the Channel, the old focal point of British strategy.

It was this sure hold of British naval opinion on the unbroken tradition that was to render Napoleon's invasion as impossible as all the attempts of his predecessors. "Unhappily," says Colonel Desbrière, in speaking of the discredited French belief in a surprise of the Channel, "the English had long got wind of this danger, and convinced of its gravity had given a standing order, thanks to which the entrance of the Channel was fated to be held in crushing force. All the Napoleonic plans could only dash themselves to pieces against this primordial device so imperturbably followed."[25]

So it was that Barham began his memorable nine months' administration; but amidst all the strain and stress he found time to give to the Admiralty, out of the depth of his long experience, the organisation for war by which every call was to be met so brilliantly up to the day of final triumph. We cannot do better than attempt to grasp his system before proceeding further.

For himself he reserved no special function. "The First Lord," says his Memorandum, "will take upon himself the general superintendence and arrangement of the whole."

"The senior or first professional lord," it continued — and this was Gambier — "will do the same when the First Lord is absent. His duty will be also to attend to the correspondence of the day, but more particularly that of the ports, and all secret services" — that is, he had control of orders to naval bases and intelligence. "He will minute all such orders and letters as may come within his department and he may see necessary, and deliver the same to the Secretary to be acted upon."

His special sphere of action is then detailed. "He will, with the approbation of the First Lord, dispose of the movements of all ships on Home and Foreign stations, and give orders to the Admirals, Captains, and Commanding Officers of ships on service. He will distribute the seamen and marines. . . . He will attend particularly to the equipment of all ships and vessels of every description." His duties in relation to supply were thus confined to the fitting out of vessels already commissioned for active service which were thereby brought into his department. He was also charged with seeing that his orders had been obeyed by comparing them with ships' journals. Lastly he was "to take account of all promotions," but the First Lord was to sign the commissions.

Supply generally was in the hands of the "Second Professional Lord," who, so the Memorandum directs, "will receive from the Secretary (after they are read)" — that is, read to the Board at its daily sitting — "all letters and papers belonging to the Navy Board, the Transport Board, the Board of Sick and Hurt and Greenwich Hospital."

The duty of the Third Professional Lord was to superintend the appointment of all commissioned and warrant officers "under the inspection of the First Lord "and to keep all vessels complete with them. Vacancies for Captains and Lieutenants were to be "stated to the First Lord."

"The Civil Lords," so the paper concludes, "in order to keep the Professional Lords uninterrupted in the various important duties committed to their charge, will sign all orders, protections, warrants, and promiscuous papers daily issuing from the office. They will also assist the Board with their advice."[26]

In working this system Barham seems to have treated his colleagues as a staff under him — the First Sea Lord discharging approximately the duties of his Chief of the Staff, directing war movements but also seeing the material fit for service so far as regarded equipping and manning ships; the Second Sea Lord controlling the supply of material; and the Third, the higher personnel. Barham himself, so Barrow tells us, never sat on the Board. He seems to have concerned himself only with the larger movements of the campaign. "Lord Barham," he says, "at the advanced period of his life was satisfied to let things go on in their usual course, to remain quiet in his room, to make few enquiries and to let the Board consider and settle the current affairs of the Navy amongst themselves. In fact he never attended the Board; but when any doubtful question arose one of the Lords or the Secretaries took his decision on it in his own room."[27]

The impression which the passage gives is that Barham lived in Barrow's memory as little more than a figure-head. But it must have been also in his own room that he pondered over the shifting strategical exigencies of the campaign, anticipating each one as it arose, and having always ready in his mind the necessary orders for squadrons at sea. They are all preserved in the series of "Secret Orders," and all of them that deal with the main movements of the war-plan bear his signature. With "the current affairs of the Navy," as Barrow says, he did not concern himself. The higher direction of the war was one man's uninterrupted work.

To this he devoted himself with a singleness of purpose which set all etiquette at defiance. In the Barham Papers there is a long "Communication to the King "on the naval situation in September 1805, which begins with an apology for his not going to court. Owing to having, as he says, two Boards to superintend, meaning presumably the Board of Admiralty and the Navy Board, he cannot wait upon the King in person. In November there is another addressed to Pitt for submission to the Cabinet, which concludes with a hope that he will not be summoned to attend except for business connected with the fleet. There is nothing extant which can throw doubt on Barrow's assertion that he never sat upon the Board. His practice seems to have been, where war direction was concerned, to draft the strategical orders with his own hand, and to send the draft down to two or more of his naval colleagues for their formal approval and signature. In the truest sense he was the real director of the naval war, but in his eyes his functions as such did not exclude the control of the larger questions of material. For all his concentration of effort, he maintained, according to the old British tradition, a close watch on the Supply department — that is, he continued to control the Navy Board while exercising the functions of a Chief of the Naval Staff to Pitt, as the War Minister.

CHAPTER VI

Nelson's Dilemma

During all this time of tension not a word came of Nelson. So far as headquarters was concerned he had disappeared as completely and as mysteriously as Villeneuve, and there was nothing to throw doubt on Sir Richard Strachan's conjecture that he had gone again to Egypt. It was not so. For him, as we have seen, there was only one solution, and that only a partial solution, of the uncertainties of the problem. It was, not to go to the eastward of Sicily nor to the westward of Sardinia, until he knew something positive. Fixed in this determination he had taken up his position at Ustica off Palermo, and there he had to wait two days before he had anything on which he could act.

By April 10th a rumour had already reached him that a British military expedition was on its way to the Mediterranean. That so great a complication was to be added to his embarrassment without a word of warning was past bearing and almost beyond belief, and at his wits' end he was seeking relief, after his wont, in a letter to his friend Ball. "I can hardly suppose," he wrote early in the morning, "that any expedition would be sent to this country without my having some intimation, and I have not the most distant idea of such a thing. If they are sent, they will be taken; for the French know everything which passes in England. However I can do no more than I have done; for I am sorely vexed at the ignorance in which I have been kept." At this point he was interrupted by one of his captains coming on board, and when he sat down again to finish his letter the blow had fallen. "Hallowell," he continued, "is just arrived from Palermo. He brings accounts that the great expedition is sailed, and that seven Russian sail of the line are expected in the Mediterranean: therefore I may suppose the French fleet are bound to the westward. I must do my best. God bless you. I am very very miserable."

And well he might be. The stroke he had prayed and longed for through the weary months of his vigil was about to be played, and played apparently so badly that disaster seemed inevitable. He could not doubt, any more than the rest, that Villeneuve's objective was the doomed expedition. Why had he not been warned? He could not tell that the warning had been sent the moment the convention with Russia had been signed, and that it was still far from reaching him.[1] All he could know was that his whole plan of action was upset by a new factor. The position he had taken up would no longer meet the case. When he began his letter to Ball he had made up his mind "to stand towards Madelena and Cape Corse," apparently with the intention of ascertaining whether Villeneuve had doubled back, since from all his widely scattered cruisers came not a word of the lost fleet. But now the point of greatest danger had shifted to the mouth of the Straits, and without a moment's hesitation he resolved to move westward with all speed.

His idea was not to proceed direct to Gibraltar; for he now issued a "secret route," in which the first rendezvous was the south end of Sardinia (No. 71) and the second Formentera, the southernmost of the Balearic Islands.[2] The route would suggest that, in spite of his anxiety for Craig's force, his object was still to make sure that Villeneuve had not doubled back upon Naples, and his subsequent actions confirm the supposition that something of the kind was in his mind.

Bitter as was the cup of his dilemma it was not yet full. In spite of every effort and the splendid seamanship of his hardened squadron, he could scarcely make any progress to the westward at all. Persistent heavy weather from the west and north-west held him fast inside Sardinia. On the 11th he was no farther towards Formentera than the Island of Marittimo off the end of Sicily. Next day, full of his old doubt, he sent two more cruisers to look into Toulon, one to go inside Sardinia and the other round Toro. By the 15th, after four days' struggle, he was still beating round the south end of Sardinia, and here he was joined by two cruisers from Naples. One was a frigate of his own, the *Amazon*, which he had sent in for news, and the other the *Decade*, a smart frigate which had just made the voyage from England in seventeen days. She had brought out Colonel Smith, one of Lord Mulgrave's private secretaries, who had been sent specially to Elliot with news of the expedition and his secret instructions for its employment. Elliot had hurried her on to Nelson at the earliest moment, but her information was already nearly a week old.[3] "Lord Mulgrave," Elliot wrote, "informs me in great secrecy that a considerable body of troops was on the point of sailing for Malta, for the purposes with which you have been so long acquainted, Lieutenant-Colonel Smith, Lord Mulgrave's private secretary, who has brought me secret instructions upon this head, conceives that the regiments will have left England a few days after the departure of the *Decade*. Under this impression I think it highly material that you should not be ignorant of a circumstance, which, if known to the French, may have some weight with them respecting the destination of the Toulon fleet."[4]

To imagine Nelson's feelings on reading such a letter is not difficult. If Colonel Smith's surmise was correct, if the troops had really sailed before the end of March, it made matters ten times worse and the silence of the Admiralty ten times more exasperating. "Your Excellency's notice," Nelson wrote in indignant reply, "about troops being sent to the Mediterranean is the first word I have ever heard of it, nor have I an idea that any such thing could be in agitation without the Admiralty telling me, in order that I might meet and protect them." Had he been aware of the agitation at the Admiralty over Melville's downfall, he would have understood better, but of that he knew nothing to temper his anger. "Does your Excellency mean," he went on, "that *you* or that *I* have been long acquainted with it? If it is *you*, I dare say it is right; but if *I* am meant as being in the secret of the destination of those troops, I most solemnly declare my entire ignorance as to the force or destination, or even that *one* soldier is intended for the Mediterranean. I know certainly where many thousands are wanted; but, as I said before, I never will believe that any number of troops will be risked inside Gibraltar without an assurance of my protection: and that I should be directed to meet them upon some fixed station to the westward of Toulon, if not to the westward of Cartagena."

He was not to know the expedition was still wind bound at Spithead as he wrote, or that instructions such as he sketched were just starting from the Admiralty. For all he could tell the troops were already a fortnight out; and before he closed his letter —at midday —came news from a neutral just spoken that, nine days before, the Toulon squadron had been seen off Cape Gata bearing for the Straits before an easterly wind. "If this account is true," Nelson ended in despair, "much mischief may be apprehended. It kills me, the very thought."[5]

The acuteness of the danger seems almost to have thrown him off his balance. Yet even so he still held unshaken to the line he had followed all along. He was resolved that even the apparent certainty of the new danger should not beguile him to the westward till he had made absolutely sure the ground was good behind him. Accordingly he sent off yet another cruiser to look into Toulon, with orders to meet him at Formentera, the rendezvous to which he still held. She also bore a letter to the cruiser he had kept off Cape San Sebastian in the northeast of Spain, whom she was to relieve. "I am going," was his message, "to ascertain if the French fleet is not in Toulon and then to proceed to the westward, and this is all I can tell at present."[6]

It was not till two days later that his way was made plain before him and he knew he had been completely out-manoeuvred. He had just left Toro when away to windward Captain William Parker of the *Amazon* telegraphed that he had spoken a Ragusan who said she had seen the Toulon squadron, passing the Straits on April 8th, ten days since. And to add to the vexation he reported that the homeward-bound Levant convoy, which had already been caught once and which Strachan had been sent to protect, had left Gibraltar only a day ahead.[7]

Stunned and humbled by the news, Nelson changed the rendezvous to Rosia Bay (Gibraltar) and sat down to rearrange his plans. "I am going out of the Mediterranean after the French fleet," he wrote to Elliot in a tone of resignation in sharp contrast with his last indignant letter. "It may be thought that I have protected too well Sardinia, Naples, Sicily, the Morea, and Egypt from the French, but I feel I have done right, and am therefore easy about any fate that may await me for having missed the French fleet." So his pen wrote the words, but they are the words of a man who was neither sure nor easy. Next he began an apology to the Admiralty for his failure. "Under the severe affliction," he said, "which I feel at the escape of the French fleet out of the Mediterranean, I hope that their Lordships will not impute it to any want of due attention on my part, but on the contrary that by my vigilance the enemy found it was impossible to undertake any expedition in the Mediterranean." That had been his chief function, as he saw his duty, but would the Admiralty and the country understand? As yet he could not see clearly what the ultimate destination of his fleet should be. He merely informed them he was going to the westward and must be guided by what he heard when he reached Gibraltar, and that meanwhile he was taking precautions to preserve the command of the Italian seas during his absence.

For this purpose he formed the greater part of his cruisers into a squadron under the command of Captain Hon. T. Bladen Capel, of the *Phœbe* 36, with instructions to take station off Toro and between that island and Marittimo off the west end of Sicily, "for the purpose of intercepting any expedition which the enemy may attempt against Sardinia, Sicily, and Egypt." "I only mention it," Nelson wrote, "as the most likely place to fall in with any expedition which the enemy may attempt against those places from Toulon, but must leave this important trust to your judgment and to act, as from certain circumstances of information you shall judge best, to prevent their effecting a landing." The squadron, when it was concentrated as intended at Toro, would consist of five frigates and a bomb, and this force, with the Neapolitan squadron and the *Excellent* at Naples, he considered sufficient for the moment without counting on the arrival of the Russians.[8]

So to the last he clung to the base idea of his strategical principle. His dominant function was to keep command of the Mediterranean. For him that was always the end; the destruction of the Toulon fleet was only a means. To that end, therefore, he sacrificed more than half his cruisers —keeping only three frigates and a couple of sloops with his flag; and not even in the moment of his passionate desire to deal with the enemy's battle fleet, when cruisers meant almost everything, did he suffer it to turn him a hairbreadth from the higher purpose. No great captain ever grasped more fully the strategical importance of dealing with the enemy's main force, yet no one ever less suffered it to become an obsession; no one saw more clearly when it ceased to be the key of a situation, and fell to a position of secondary moment.

For a real insight into Nelson's character as a strategist there is nothing in his career so valuable as the period of trial that was now before him. At no other time are we permitted to see so deep down into the well-laid foundations on which his brilliant combinations were securely based. The dramatic attraction of his immortal chase has led to the growth of a legend that it was a stroke of inspired daring. But in truth it was a sober calculation patiently built up step by step with all behind made solid and secure and all in front reduced by slow degrees to such certainty as war ever permits. As a precedent for conduct in such a case there is nothing within our knowledge that can compare with the forging of the final decision —nothing that so fully reveals the working of a master mind in war. It must be followed day by day, even hour by hour where possible.

The day after he received Parker's report he was still only ten leagues west of Toro, but he had recovered himself and his purpose was settled. "Dead foul —dead foul," he wrote again to Ball, "but my mind is fully made up what to do when I leave the Straits, supposing there is no certain information of the enemy's destination. . . . I believe this ill-luck will go near to kill me, but as these are times for exertions, I must not be cast down whatever I feel." And again to Lord Melville, whom he believed still to be his chief, "I am not made to despair —what man can do shall be done. I have marked out for myself a decided line of conduct and I shall follow it up well."

It has often been assumed that this line was to make straight for the West Indies on an intuition that Villeneuve was gone there; but the rest of the correspondence shows it was quite the reverse. At a loss to locate his enemy and sure now that he had left the Mediterranean, he had resolved if he got no further information to play the old safe game which Orde had played, and which to the experienced Admirals of those days was a second nature —a golden rule when in doubt. So far was he from any determination to proceed to the West Indies that he had resolved to close on the Western Squadron at the mouth of the Channel.

In the course of the day Parker found the brig which Lord Mark Kerr had hired, and she brought an important new light. Not only was she able to bring Kerr's message that Villeneuve had passed the Straits ten days before, but she also carried later news that he had been to Cadiz and left again with some Spanish ships in company.[9] Nelson at once deduced that Villeneuve had not gone to the West Indies, and sat down to draw up the following appreciation for the Admiralty:—

"The enemy's fleet having so very long ago passed the Straits and formed a junction with some Spanish ships from Cadiz. . . . I have detached the *Amazon* to Lisbon for information, and I am proceeding off Cape St. Vincent as expeditiously as possible; and I hope the *Amazon* will join me there or that I shall obtain some positive information of the destination of the enemy. The circumstance of their having taken the Spanish ships, which were for sea, from Cadiz, satisfies my mind that they are not bound for the West Indies: but intend forming a junction with the squadron at Ferrol and pushing direct for Ireland or Brest, as I believe the French have troops on board. Therefore, if I receive no intelligence to do away with my present belief, I shall proceed from Cape St. Vincent, and take my position fifty leagues west from Scilly, approaching that island slowly, that I may not miss any vessels sent in search of the squadron with orders. My reason for this position is, that it is equally easy either to get to the fleet off Brest or to go to Ireland should the fleet be wanted at either station. I trust this plan will meet their lordships' approbation; and I have the pleasure to say that I shall bring with me eleven as fine ships of war, as ably commanded, and in as perfect order and in health as ever went to sea. . . . (*P.S.*) I shall send to both Ireland and the Channel Fleet an extract of this letter, acquainting the Commander-in-chief where to find me."

Once more, then, he was as clear-headed as ever, and eliminating minor matters was able to detach with precision the essential move. His spirit too was healed, and his letter to Lord Gardner rings with the old cheery note. He began to see, as indeed it proved, that his driving Villeneuve through the Straits was a strategical success, and he had little fear for what he would do outside. "My dear lord," he wrote, "if the Toulon fleet with that of Cadiz is gone your road, the ships under my command will be no unacceptable sight. If you do not want help, tell us to go back again. I feel vexed at their slipping out of the Mediterranean as I had marked them for my game. However I hope, my dear lord, that now you will annihilate them." From this time, moreover, there is no further sign of anxiety for the safety of Craig's expedition. The news of Villeneuve's having been to Cadiz to form a junction with the Spaniards must have assured him that the enemy had some other and higher aim.

A week of weary beating to the westward followed, but it brought no change in his view. At the end of it, in a letter to the Commissioner at Gibraltar, he expressed himself as unshaken in his conviction that the junction of the two squadrons indicated the relief of Ferrol, to be followed by a direct attack on the British islands, and not an adventure in the West Indies.[10] He was then nearing the Straits, and with his letter he sent the *Decade* forward to Gibraltar with directions to bring him the last word known there. Four days later, on May 1st, with Ceuta just in sight, he received a direct communication from the Admiralty which not only explained their silence on the subject of the expedition, but gave him hope it was safe. "I have this moment received your letter of the 1st of April," he immediately replied," acquainting me . . . that Rear-Admiral Knight with the *Queen* and *Dragon* were to sail in a day or two . . . having under convoy transports with 5,000 troops on board." It was the long-expected despatch directing him to take up a covering position. His relief was great, for now he knew the troops had not started so soon as

Elliot believed. There was good ground to hope, as he said, that as the *Fisgard* had left for England two hours after the French had passed, she would have arrived in time to stop the expedition sailing.[11]

On the 4th, as the wind still held ahead, he resolved to anchor in Tetuan Bay and employ the time in filling up with water, beef, and fuel. While thus engaged he received the first suggestion of what was really happening. It was a reply from Captain Otway, the Navy Commissioner at Gibraltar, telling him of the entire disappearance of the Combined Squadron and of the general belief that it had gone to the West Indies. The news certainly shook his former conviction, but though it filled him with new anxiety it was not enough to change his purpose. Of the sure intelligence he had hoped to get from Orde's cruisers there was none, and no matter how pressing was the danger in the west, he would not act on mere rumours. "I cannot very properly run to the West Indies," he replied to Otway, "without something beyond mere surmise, and if I defer my departure Jamaica may be lost."

His attitude to the dilemma was well expressed by his first biographers in a noteworthy passage. One of them, McArthur, knew him well and had come near to being his secretary. The legend of a heaven-sent inspiration was already arising when they wrote, and in their view it should be nipped in the bud as fraught with danger. "It was entirely inconsistent," they declare, "with Lord Nelson's great professional character and regard for the discipline of the service to take so bold a step until he had every reason to believe they could not have sailed in any other direction. . . . It is the more necessary to make this remark lest other officers, led on by the impulse of zeal unsubdued by the reflection he employed and the splendour of resolute pursuit, may erroneously indulge in a contrary idea to their own destruction."[12]

His whole conduct at this juncture amply bears out his biographers' remarks. The West Indies became a probable destination, that was all. Till there could be no room for doubt he kept an open mind, still resolved to close on the strategic centre, if no sufficient information were forthcoming. But meanwhile he prepared everything for the possible eventuality. On May the 5th he formally constituted his second-in-command. Sir Richard Bickerton, Commander-in-chief in the Mediterranean during his possible absence, with orders to carry out in every particular "the Admiralty instructions for the protection and safety of their Sicilian and their Sardinian Majesties' dominions, as well as preventing the enemy from effecting any expedition against Egypt." The squadron he would have for the work must at first be weak enough. Bickerton's flag was flying in the *Royal Sovereign*, but she was a first-rate and too valuable to be spared. Nelson meant to take her with him and intended Bickerton to shift his flag to any other ship he chose in the squadron that was to be left under his command. It was to consist of nearly the whole of Nelson's cruisers and any additional force that might arrive from home. There were over a score all told, and Nelson himself kept only four, so careful was he to make good behind him the ground committed to his charge.

As these orders were being prepared the wind at last came fair, and he moved for the Straits to pass on and meet the *Amazon* from Lisbon whence alone he could hope to get the light which would clear the fog. Lisbon for the moment was the centre of information, and there, while Nelson moves west on the fitful Levanter, we must look before the position can be grasped in all its bearings.

CHAPTER VII

How Nelson Made Sure

On the Tagus was being played one of the many under-plots of Napoleon's vast contest with Pitt. All through the long imperial struggle between England and France, Lisbon, the womb of the Oceanic expansion of Europe, had been recognised as a point beyond price. Napoleon, like all his predecessors, was resolved not only that Portugal must not be a British ally, but that even neutrality must be denied her. Following the precedents of the old Family Compact, it was a term of his convention with Spain that Portugal must be forced at least to close her ports to British vessels; and towards the end of February he had sent off General Junot, his aide-de-camp and Colonel-General of his Hussars, as ambassador to Lisbon to see that it was done. Junot was long on the road, for he had first to visit Madrid to stir the Spanish Government to greater naval activity, and not till the second week in April did he finally set out for Lisbon.

It was an evil moment. Our minister there, Lord Robert FitzGerald, was bracing himself for the coming diplomatic struggle, when on April 13th he received Orde's letters to say he had been driven off his station by Villeneuve. On the morrow Junot arrived, and FitzGerald could not doubt that in a day or two he would see the Toulon squadron in the Tagus and that Portugal would be forced into the Napoleonic system while he stood by helpless. "The junction of the French and Spanish fleets at Cadiz," he wrote home, "will now enable the ambassadors of both nations to hold what language they please here." There was no means of resistance. The Portuguese, it is true, were making an effort to restore their navy and had already secured the services of a British officer, Rear-Admiral Donald Campbell; but he had recently been sent to sea with a ship of the line and three cruisers to operate, ostensibly at least, about the Straits against certain Algerine pirates who had become troublesome.[1]

The language which Junot and the Spanish ambassador held soon made itself felt. Sutton, the officer whom Orde had left in command of his cruisers, found he was refused victuals at Lagos. FitzGerald protested and was told quietly the prohibition would not be enforced. Quarantine, moreover, was declared against the British vessels, and Sutton found it impossible to carry out Orde's directions that he was to hire boats to look into Cadiz. He could thus get no intelligence whatever. Of his sloops the *Wasp* alone was in touch with him: the *Beagle* had entirely disappeared. On April 24th, however, FitzGerald was able to report home, on direct information from Cadiz, that the allied squadrons had been seen sailing westward on the 10th. He sent the news off immediately by the English packet; and for Lisbon he could feel easier. But not for long. On May 2nd he was startled by an express from Sutton to tell him that on April 27th an officer of the *Wasp* had succeeded in looking into Cadiz in a Portuguese boat and had found the whole Combined Squadron there. If this were true, it meant that Villeneuve had come back, and the danger was as great as ever. FitzGerald could not believe it. He had just ascertained from a neutral skipper exact details of the allied squadrons as they had sailed together to the westward, and the reports from Cadiz were that every one knew they were bound for Jamaica. Still certainty in the matter was beyond his reach, and in his dilemma he fell back on a principle that is worth recording. The diplomatic and the naval intelligence were in conflict on a matter of moment, but the diplomatic situation turned on the situation at sea. It was primarily a naval matter, and therefore in consultation with Gambier, the Consul, a man on whose sagacity and knowledge every one relied, he concluded there was no choice but to act on the assumption that the naval intelligence was true. Accordingly they decided together to send it home at once and take such action as was in their power.[2]

Immediate action of some kind and on their own responsibility was absolutely necessary. They knew Knight and Craig were at hand. Only a few days before the *Orpheus*, a frigate that was cruising on the station, had gone out to try to meet them with a warning that Orde was gone. If she should fail to find them and Sutton's news was really true, they would be sailing straight into the lion's mouth. At all hazards they must be warned. Another English packet had just come in, and one of FitzGerald's staff was hurried away in her with orders to find them out. Twenty-four hours after he had gone the expedition appeared off the Tagus. Gambier sped out to them with the alarming news. He found the *Orpheus* had met them the day before, but they had missed the packet.

What was to be done? In view of what was going on in Lisbon it was an extremely delicate situation. But Gambier was at hand to advise and Knight and Craig did not hesitate. While the *Orpheus* was sent southward in search of trustworthy information as to the actual situation at Cadiz, to the Consul was committed a politely firm letter from the two commanders informing the Portuguese Government that they intended to take refuge in the Tagus, and that if any attempt were made to obstruct their entrance it would be taken as an act of hostility. The Portuguese were thus made as comfortable as possible with a plea of compulsion, and it had the desired effect. No opposition was offered, and next day the expedition quietly anchored inside the harbour defences.

The diplomatic air was immediately in a tempest. In the eyes of Junot and the Spanish ambassador, knowing as they did that Villeneuve was far across the Atlantic, the British movement could have but one meaning. It was obviously a device to forestall their game —a repetition of the successful British stroke of 1762. They had been expecting for some time that this was the real object of Craig's expedition and had warned Talleyrand of the danger. Their fear was now turned into stern reality. Junot stormed, the Spaniard threatened. It was a preconcerted trick, they protested, between the Portuguese and Pitt to secure the forts with British troops, and they vowed they must have at once either an ample and satisfactory explanation or their passports.

As we know, Pitt's military force was far too deeply engaged to permit him any such design, but the suspicions of the two enraged ambassadors were so far justified that Craig was actually making arrangements to seize the sea defences at the first sign of a French fleet in the offing. "It would have been excellent fun," wrote one of his officers in recording the curious incident.

Aranjo, the Portuguese minister, was at his wits' end. If he could not pacify Junot and his colleague it meant a Franco-Spanish invasion. If he broke with the British, retribution might come more swiftly still, for Nelson at any moment might appear. He could not afford to offend either party. He appealed to FitzGerald, hoping Craig did not mean to stop long, and FitzGerald could only assure him that the expedition would stay no longer than the day he got further intelligence of the enemy's movements which he was expecting hourly by the *Orpheus*.[3]

So the matter had to rest. Threaten as the two ambassadors would, they were helpless. Neither cared to take the extreme step of demanding their passports, and while they still hesitated the tension was relieved. On the third day the *Orpheus* came back with confirmation of FitzGerald's belief that Villeneuve had not returned, and with what was still better, the long-expected tidings that Nelson had passed the Straits. Thereupon Knight made the signal to weigh, and prepared to go out to meet him.[4]

Some fifty miles beyond Cape St. Vincent, the *Orpheus* had fallen in with Parker in the *Amazon*, whom it will be remembered Nelson had sent forward to the Tagus to seek the information on which his final decision was to rest. Together they proceeded off St. Vincent —the rendezvous Nelson had given —and there Parker handed over his mails and despatches to the *Orpheus* to be taken on to Lisbon, while he waited to meet Nelson with the news which the *Orpheus* had given him. By this means a couple of days might be saved. It was the Nelsonian way, and Nelson himself had been doing the like. The fair breeze had come before he had completed his stores at Tetuan, but he would not waste the wind. Off Gibraltar it failed, and he anchored again to try to complete. But in five hours it came fair, and he was away once more for St. Vincent, burning for the information which must decide his course.

He was still, as he said, as much in the dark as ever; but since he left Tetuan the probabilities had changed. In his letters to the Admiralty he no longer says that if he hears nothing he shall close on the Channel, but that probably he will go to the West Indies. The cause of this change is scarcely doubtful. At Gibraltar he had got into contact with Admiral Campbell and the Portuguese squadron, and Captain Hargood of the *Belleisle* tells us he received from him "important information as to the destination of the French squadron." Not a word of this appears in Nelson's correspondence, and naturally enough, since Campbell's part in it was unneutral service, which if known would get him into serious trouble. What it was we can surmise with tolerable certainty. In any case it was regarded as so important by Junot and his colleague that, on Campbell's return to Lisbon, they insisted on his dismissal and he had to go home to die in poverty and neglect.[5]

Yet it was not Campbell's information that brought Nelson to a final decision. There must be greater certainty still before he could take the crucial step, and this he hoped to get off St. Vincent either from the *Amazon* or one of Orde's cruisers, which he now knew had been left to watch. It was on the evening of May 6th, the same day he saw Campbell, that Nelson had left Gibraltar. Meeting with light airs, it was not till the morning of the 9th he had made St. Vincent. His destination was still uncertain, and his stores for a voyage across the Atlantic still incomplete. "We have heard nothing of the French fleet since they left Cadiz on the 10th," wrote Hardy, his flag captain, as they sighted the cape. "It is therefore strongly believed by Lord Nelson that they are gone for the West Indies, and of course we shall follow them if we hear nothing of their destination from Lisbon, from whence we expect the *Amazon* will join tomorrow." Up to this time, therefore, the question was still open, but after his manner Nelson made the best use of the delay till certainty could be attained. The storeships which Orde had sent into Lagos were still there, and with evident enjoyment he decided to move thither and help himself to all he wanted. "Here we are, my dear Campbell," he wrote to his friend next day from Lagos, "clearing Sir John Orde's transports . . . completing ourselves to five months, and tomorrow I start for the West Indies. . . . Admiral Knight . . . is at present off Lisbon with the convoy of troops. I wish he would come here; but he has been deceived by false information that the Combined Squadrons were still in Cadiz —I wish they were."[6] In the evening he moved back to St. Vincent, and at ten o'clock the same night Hardy added a postscript to his letter. "We are now off St. Vincent, and his lordship has made up his mind to bear up for the West Indies in the course of tomorrow."[7] Thus to a few hours we can tell when it was Nelson took his momentous decision, and we can tell, moreover, exactly on what information it was taken.

The first light on the actual situation that he obtained was from his old friend Sutton in the *Amphion*, who was still at the post where Orde had left him. It was also the fullest, though Nelson in his Journal would not admit it. All he says is that at half-past seven in the evening of the 9th she joined company, "and I ordered Captain Sutton under my command, who informed me he had gained no intelligence of the enemy since their leaving Cadiz." But this was not the whole story, for Sutton was able to give him negative evidence which could leave no doubt that the enemy had left European waters. Two days earlier he had spoken the *Lively*, a frigate that was little more than a week out from the Channel, and this is what she had to tell. She had left Spithead as late as April 27th and only seven days before her captain had been on board Gardner's flagship, where he heard that Orde was falling back on Ushant, and that nothing had been heard of Villeneuve. On the morrow, as he sped south, he had seen the junction between Gardner and Orde actually made, and a little later he passed a convoy northward-bound which had not been molested. Nelson therefore could be certain that for more than three weeks after the Combined Squadron had left Cadiz it had not been heard of anywhere to the northward.

Now according to Captain Parker of the *Amazon*, it was this intelligence, at least as much as his own, which caused Nelson to make up his mind. Writing to his father to explain why the fleet went to the West Indies, he says, "Lord Nelson was satisfied from the very recent accounts from Lisbon, as well as from England, brought in seven days only by the *Lively*, that the enemy were not gone to the north, and instantly made up his mind to go to the West Indies."[8] Parker then believed that it was the negative intelligence that had most to do with removing Nelson's hesitation —that is, he could be certain he was not wanted off Ushant.

The *Amazon* herself rejoined about an hour later, bringing all the Lisbon news. Amongst the papers handed over to her by the *Orpheus* was the deposition of an American skipper to whom the *Orpheus* had spoken. He had left Cadiz on May 2nd and was able to report the exact composition of the Combined Squadron, the number of troops it carried, and the names of the commanders. "The reports of their destination," he said, "were various. By some it was supposed they were destined for Ireland: and by others, with great probability, for the West Indies, particularly Jamaica." So perfect a confirmation of the intelligence which Nelson had from Campbell, from home, and from Lisbon, must have cleared away the last shade of doubt, and then and there he sat down to inform the Admiralty he meant to go.[9]

The only trouble was that the enemy had now a whole month's start of him. Yet he did not despair of being in time to save Jamaica and the other British islands. So great was his confidence in the superior seamanship of his fleet, he was sure with luck and judgment he could gain many days upon the chase. But every hour was precious and yet he could not give the word to go. He now knew Craig's expedition had put into Lisbon on the false information that had been received as to Villeneuve's having returned to Cadiz, and his last orders from home were to see it safe on its way. From the American skipper's report, moreover, he had learnt what the actual state of affairs at Cadiz was. A number of ships of the line were fitting there for sea in hot haste, and in spite of his eagerness to be gone he determined he must await the arrival of the expedition and see it safely into the Gut.

Next morning, to his great relief, Knight met him off Cape St. Vincent with the Admiralty orders relating to the expedition. These he at once sent forward to Bickerton that he might do what was necessary to co-operate with Craig, while he himself made such arrangements for the safe passage of the convoy as would justify his leaving the station without an hour's delay. To this end he directed Knight to take the transports down wide of Cadiz and Tarifa and then run straight along the Moorish coast into Gibraltar.[10] Beyond that point there was still the Cartagena squadron to consider. At all costs it must be rendered powerless; and after a short deliberation, Nelson resolved, in spite of his relative inferiority to the Combined Squadron, to hand over the *Royal Sovereign* to Knight.

No decision of Nelson's is more eloquent of his grasp of the true end and meaning of naval warfare. He was about to pursue and try to bring to action a numerically superior force, and Captain Parker used to say that one of the conditions on which he relied for success was that Villeneuve had no three-deckers, and that "he reckoned on the great superiority in close action of three batteries of guns over two."[11] Yet so firm was his grasp of the war-plan and the place his fleet had to fill in it, that at the last moment he gave up a 100-gun ship to secure directly the true and paramount end of his operations. In naval warfare there is nothing more difficult than a correct adjustment of action between the ever-competing claims of the ulterior and the primary object —between striking directly to secure the object of the campaign, and using the indirect but more drastic method of a concentrated stroke at the enemy's fleet. Here we have a decision on the point from Nelson in the zenith of his powers, and it is surely difficult to overestimate its value.

At home the decision was well received. "He seems to have acted most handsomely," wrote Lord Hardwicke on opening Nelson's despatch to Ireland, "as indeed he always does for the public service, in weakening his own force for the security of the convoy under the *Queen* and the *Dragon*."[12]

The same evening, some twenty miles to the southward of St. Vincent, the two squadrons parted company. Knight to see his convoy safely into Gibraltar, while Nelson bore up on his long chase, taking with him his remaining ten of the line and the frigates *Decade*, *Amphion*, and *Amazon*. The last the Admiralty heard of him was by a letter written on May 14th, as he approached Madeira, to assure them that even if Villeneuve had not gone to the West Indies, little harm could come of his chase. "If they are not there," he said, "the squadron will be back again by the end of June —in short, before the enemy can know where I am." This element in the reasoning which brought him to his decision must not be forgotten —the moral effect of an unlocated fleet. How rightly he calculated the factor we shall see presently in Napoleon's inability to make up his mind where Nelson had gone or in what quarter the "fougueux amiral" would reappear, no less than in the paralysis which the uncertainty produced on Villeneuve's will.

CHAPTER VIII

Collingwood's Flying Squadron

Of all parts of the art of war there is none perhaps of higher value than the interpretation of intelligence. At the end of our long series of maritime wars with France, the faculty of interpretation had reached in the sea service its fullest powers. So wide was the theatre, so slow the means of communication and so precious every rare item of news, that sharp necessity had developed an acuteness of sense that gives at times an impression of second sight. The whole service was as it were irradiated with an alert sympathy, a mutual understanding between the War Staff and the fighting lines, by which admirals afloat seemed always to see into the mind of the Admiralty and the Admiralty to rest assured of what the admirals would do. It was a factor in the struggle which Napoleon failed to take into account, or even to appreciate. In his overweening self-confidence he would not believe that the British sea service possessed a strategic intuition as great as his own on land. Yet it was even greater or at least more formidable than his —for in the one case it depended on a single master-mind, in the other it was an instructed instinct that was alive and active in every centre of direction. At every turn of the campaign we feel its quickening impulse, and nowhere more strongly than in the process by which the Admiralty came to the same conclusion as Nelson, and in the action they took in consequence.

It will be remembered that on first receiving Lord Mark Kerr's intelligence that Villeneuve had passed the Straits, they regarded Jamaica as his probable objective, and ordered Collingwood with part of the Flying Squadron to Madeira. His instructions were to reinforce the West Indian station, should he ascertain that that was the enemy's destination and that Nelson had not himself anticipated the movement. Then came Orde's news, with the suggestion that Nelson had been diverted to Egypt and that Villeneuve's operations indicated an attack on Craig's expedition, to be followed by a concentration at some western rendezvous for seizing the command of the Channel. We saw also how steps were promptly taken with the object of saving Craig and securing a counter concentration on Gardner off Ushant.

But even as the necessary orders were being signed, tidings reached Plymouth which gave a new and clearer light upon the situation. Again it came from one of Orde's cruisers, and this perhaps will explain why the Admiralty took a view of his conduct so different from the reprehension which modem critics have made his undiluted portion. His reception at home was perfectly normal. He had requested to be relieved, and on his arrival he was directed to bring his squadron to Plymouth for a refit and to strike his flag, but his conduct as a whole was approved.

The cruiser in question was the long-lost *Beagle*, the sloop which Orde had left with Sutton to watch the Straits and which it will be remembered had disappeared into space.

The mystery was now explained. On April 9th, being then under Cape Spartel, sheltering from the Levanter with the Portuguese squadron in company, she had sighted some strange vessels passing the Straits on the heels of the homeward-bound Mediterranean convoy. So suspicious was the situation that after comparing notes with one of the Portuguese cruisers, Captain Burn, her commander, had decided to beat into Tangier for intelligence. There next day he heard from the Consul that it was the Toulon squadron to the number of thirteen of the line and five frigates which he had seen passing the Straits, and that both Orde and the convoy were in serious danger. Thereupon he immediately made sail again to look for the Admiral off Cadiz. Next morning outside the Straits he saw the strangers again, steering to the westward, and the Portuguese squadron still on the watch off Cape Spartel. They too must have seen the movement westward or at least part of it, and hence the importance of Campbell's information to Nelson. On reaching the Cadiz rendezvous Burn found Orde already gone, and no trace of the Toulon squadron inside. But to seaward he could see the four belated Spanish vessels beating out also to the westward. It was obvious they had just left Cadiz, and till the evening of the 12th he kept them in sight. Having thus fixed their course he hurried away to try to find the Admiral at St. Vincent. On his way he spoke an American bound for Toulon, who said he had seen a squadron of five of the line to the westward. Accordingly Burn stood out in that direction, but Orde, as we know, had turned south, and though the *Beagle* beat north and west till the 18th she failed to get touch with him. Once, it is true, she came within thirty miles of the squadron, but still finding no trace of it, Burn decided, as soon as he had made sufficient westing for a fair wind, to hold away for Ferrol.[1]

In this Burn showed admirable judgment. For Orde was then to the westward of him making for the same point. The *Beagle*, however, being more weatherly than the squadron, had got a day ahead, and all she found off Ortegal was one of Calder's cruisers, the *Indefatigable*, of which Moore, the captor of the galleons, was still in command. He took her to the Admiral, who as usual, in the wild westerly weather that had brought the *Beagle*, up, had taken the squadron under Cape Prior for shelter. Of Orde there was no news, though he was then actually passing north, only a hundred miles to the westward. Accordingly, after communicating all she had seen, the *Beagle* made her way direct for home, probably by Calder's orders. Her information was indeed priceless, for it was actually later and more certain than anything Nelson had obtained before he decided to chase; and with it she anchored in Plymouth Sound on April 30th.

Her invaluable report was in Barham's hands on May 2nd. It was not entirely satisfactory. Captain Burn had said nothing explicitly of Villeneuve's squadron, but as he had looked into Cadiz it was to be assumed from his silence it was not there. Nor had he seen the four Spaniards actually leave Cadiz. Still the inference was pretty clear. Unfortunately, however, he had omitted in his report an item that was indispensable for a trustworthy interpretation of his news. In those days there was no thought of training officers in a scientific method of reporting intelligence, and Captain Burn had omitted to say how the wind was when he parted company. Till this was known there must be doubt as to whether the course observed was a true one or not, and before making any fresh distribution Barham sent down for the *Beagle's* log.[2] Still something could be done. The threat to Jamaica was clearly intensified. A packet was on the point of sailing for the West

Indies, and that night went off warning to the Admirals, with instructions that General Myers, Commander-in-chief in the Leeward Islands, had been given authority to detach two or three thousand of his troops to Jamaica in case of need, and that Cochrane was to do all he could to expedite their transport.[3]

Two days later Barham had made up his mind. He had indeed a practical certainty — which Nelson did not arrive at till five days later —that Villeneuve's destination was the West Indies, and he determined to act at once. His first step was to tell Gardner to send away Collingwood and his five of the line. Collingwood's orders were, as before, to go to Madeira, ascertain whether Villeneuve or Nelson had passed, and act accordingly, leaving word what he had done for the Consul to send back to Gibraltar and Cadiz. If there was no certain intelligence he was to go straight on to Barbadoes and co-operate with General Myers for the security of Jamaica.[4] As, however, the whole matter was still uncertain, Gardner was given discretion to detain the detachment if he thought it desirable, in view of any fresh information that might have reached him. Collingwood's orders were to be handed to him in a sealed packet at the moment of sailing and not to be opened till he was clear of the Channel.

Before the despatches went out there arrived Orde's message that he was falling back on Gardner.[5] Thereupon Knight's orders had to be cancelled. He had been told, it will be remembered, he was to reinforce Calder at Ferrol. He was now again ordered to send his two ships direct to the West Indies as a reinforcement for Collingwood, if Nelson had not gone there.[6]

In all these arrangements Barham's grip on the central point was never relaxed. In spite of all the distant calls he clung to it with a tenacity that was beyond Napoleon's calculations and made hopeless all his sanguine attempts to dissipate our home concentration. After the receipt of Orde's appreciation pointing to a hostile concentration in the west, Gardner was strictly enjoined that all orders for detachments such as Collingwood's were to be read as conditional on his having enough force to keep eighteen of the line with his flag. Subject to this minimum he was also, if possible, to keep Calder's squadron up to eight.[7] At the same time corresponding directions were framed for Nelson in order to provide for filling the gap in the home fleet which Collingwood's detachment would make. He was authorised, if he had not followed Villeneuve, to leave in the Mediterranean as many ships of the line and cruisers as were needed to watch such force as the enemy had in Toulon and Cartagena. With the rest he was to proceed off Cadiz, and leaving there five cruisers to report movements to Calder and home, he was to close on Gardner; or if he preferred he might remain in the Mediterranean himself and send his superfluous ships home under Bickerton.[8]

The instructions for detaching Collingwood reached Gardner on May 9th. He immediately proceeded to complete the necessary ships with stores, and just as Nelson was making up his mind to go to the West Indies, he sat down to inform the Admiralty that as he had no further intelligence he intended to detach Collingwood at once.[9] On the morrow, however, it began to blow hard from the west with a big sea, and the work of completing the ships for foreign service was stopped. Gardner, therefore, ran to the Lizard for smooth water; but as the heavy weather continued he ordered Collingwood into Causand Bay, and after handing him the sealed orders he himself returned to his station off Ushant.[10] Meanwhile the Admiralty had decided to increase Collingwood's squadron, and on May 10th had sent to Ushant an order that Gardner was to give him nine of the line.[11] On hearing what had happened and that the two Admirals were no longer together, fresh orders were sent direct to Collingwood at Plymouth. He was to add to his squadron three of the line that were on the point of sailing with sealed orders (probably to Gardner or Calder), and as before to go to Madeira, and if he found Nelson was in pursuit of Villeneuve to return to Plymouth.[12]

Everything was now in order for making sure that the enemy would not have a free hand in the West Indies long enough to do serious harm. Hardly, however, were the orders on the road, when a despatch reached the Foreign Office from FitzGerald at Lisbon containing the unlucky false news that Villeneuve had put back to Cadiz and announcing that Craig's expedition had taken refuge in the Tagus. Without a moment's delay word went off to both Ushant and Plymouth to stop Collingwood until further orders. Next day, in fear he might be already gone, an urgent demand went forward for a frigate to go down to Cadiz instantly, find out the truth, meet Collingwood with her report at the Finisterre rendezvous, and then bring home his despatches which would explain what he had decided to do.[13]

That they should know this as soon as possible was vital, in view of the fresh instructions which had to be thought out for him. The situation was one of extreme difficulty. Little credit was given to the report of Villeneuve's return, but the possibility had to be faced. If it were true, it would mean that his first movement to the westward was a feint to draw attention to Jamaica, and Pitt, it must be remembered, had just been warned by one of his most active agents abroad that Napoleon was intent on making false movements in order to conceal his actual line of operations. The supposed return to Cadiz indicated that the real objective was either in the Mediterranean or, as Orde had argued so forcibly, the Channel. Of the two the Channel was the less likely, for Napoleon was in Italy. Moreover it so happened that the political situation called acutely at the moment for the security of the Mediterranean. The convention with Russia was trembling in the balance. A despatch from Leveson-Gower had arrived on May 9th —the day the last orders were issued to Gardner —to say the treaty had been signed with the objectionable article relating to the evacuation of Malta. It was actually, therefore, in the midst of the naval crisis that Woronzow had his stormy interview with Pitt in which he had to inform the hard-pressed minister that the Czar demanded the absolute and unconditional assent to the Malta article as a *sine qua non* of his ratification of the treaty.[14] Pitt, so the ambassador tells us, received his communication like a thunder-clap. To increase the difficulty of his position he had heard from St. Petersburg that the Czar was again complaining bitterly of the British delays in fulfilling the promises of military action in the Mediterranean; and here was Craig hard and fast in Lisbon, unable to move.[15]

The point on which the Czar insisted was the one above all others on which it was impossible for Pitt to yield. Already, on first hearing from Gower of the proposed new condition, Mulgrave had been instructed to address a strong note of protest to Woronzow. It was absolutely essential, he wrote, to Great Britain, and particularly in view of French designs on Egypt and India, to have "a secure port in the Mediterranean not liable to capture on a sudden attack at the commencement of war." If his Britannic Majesty were disposed to sacrifice Malta he knew he could get a separate peace that would absolutely secure his own position, but what he wished to obtain was the permanent independence of the Powers of Europe. It was in this note that he had claimed that England was the legitimate successor to the Naval Knights of St. John of Jerusalem. Charles the Fifth had established them at Malta as guardians against the then existing enemy of Christendom, and it was only as a British naval port that the old stronghold could serve that purpose now.[16]

Accordingly Pitt, in reply to Woronzow, told him with equal firmness that the Czar's demand meant the breakdown of the alliance. Neither the King nor he could grant it if they would. Any government that consented to give up Malta would be flung from power in a universal howl of indignation. Woronzow privately shared Pitt's view, but he continued loyally to urge the Russian case, till Pitt was forced to cut him short with the ultimatum already recorded. His last words should be recalled. "So," he said, "however great our grief, we are compelled to abandon hope of seeing an agreement consummated, since its express condition is our renunciation of Malta. We will continue the war alone. It will be a maritime war."[17]

Thus at the unlucky moment when the false intelligence from Lisbon came to hand the whole situation turned on the command of the Mediterranean, and to leave the enemy concentrated at its entrance and free to act was impossible. It was there Collingwood must go, and go in strength. To send him in inferior force was to court disaster. The probability, on Strachan's report, was that Nelson had gone to Egypt and his co-operation could not be counted on. Collingwood might have to fight alone, and if he fought the political situation demanded that it must be with the assurance of a real victory. Sweden and Prussia were both hanging back, and even the shock of Napoleon's coronation as King of Italy had failed to stiffen the irresolution of Austria. Nothing but a victory, decisive and indisputable, could serve Pitt's turn. Anything less would certainly destroy the faint hope that still existed of forming his great coalition.

But could he venture to give Collingwood the necessary strength without loosening the hold on the Ushant position? The last word, it will be remembered, had been to direct Gardner on no account to reduce his force below eighteen of the line. To give Collingwood what was wanted would bring the Ushant station below the minimum. It was a dilemma that called for the highest courage and resolution, and the nicest balancing of risks. Not even the decision which Nelson had just taken demanded a greater measure of warlike virtue, but like him Pitt and Barham did not flinch. In two days they had made up their minds to run the risk and strike for the command of the Mediterranean. On May 17th, accordingly, Collingwood's final orders went forward. At Plymouth he had already eleven of the line with his flag, but that was not enough. He was therefore to rejoin Gardner and obtain from him a flag-officer with another three-decker and two more seventy-fours. With this powerful squadron he was to proceed to Lisbon, where he would find Knight and add his two ships to his command. He would then have a force of three three-deckers and thirteen others, and be in a position to proceed off Cadiz and clear up the situation. If the Combined Squadron was there he was to blockade it. If he found it had gone to the West Indies and Nelson after it, he was to reinforce him in proportion to the enemy's strength. The rest of his force he was to send back to Plymouth. If Nelson had not gone he was to go himself with twelve sail, so as to bring the force on the West Indian station up to eighteen; and if he ascertained the enemy had a larger force than this, he was to take as many more as were necessary. If, on the other hand, he found the enemy had gone into the Mediterranean he was to follow them, and in case of meeting Nelson he was to show him the new instructions and follow his orders.

Corresponding orders were issued to Nelson, on the assumption that the report of Villeneuve's return to Cadiz was true. In that case, if he met Collingwood he was to blockade the Combined Squadron with twenty of the line, but to be at liberty to form such detachments as he thought necessary to watch Cartagena and Toulon.

Thus was the main situation dealt with, but there remained further complexity. To add to the difficulty there was another military force to protect. In view of the danger which seemed to threaten the West Indies it had been decided to divert thither the force which was gathering at Cork under Sir Eyre Coote to reinforce India. He had accordingly been appointed Governor and Commander-in-chief of Jamaica, and was under orders to sail as soon as possible. This resolution had been taken early in April, apparently on news of the complete pacification that had followed Sir Arthur Wellesley's successes and on the reports of the Foreign Office spies as to Napoleon's real objective. Orders had already gone to Commodore Hood to throw out his cruisers to receive the expedition, but it was also necessary to cover its passage out of the danger zone. There was a suspicion that Villeneuve's real object might be to cruise about Madeira for the East Indiamen; if so, Coote would certainly be caught. If possible he must be stopped. But his sailing orders had already gone forward and the countermand might come too late. Collingwood was therefore informed that in going or sending to the West Indies he must provide for covering the passage of the expedition till it was past Madeira.[18]

Though the effect of the new disposition was to reduce Gardner's force to fifteen of the line against Ganteaume's twenty-one, the risk was probably not so great as it appears or beyond what a sound defensive basis demanded. Of his fifteen ships three were only sixty-fours, which at that time hardly counted as ships of the line; but, on the other hand, no less than nine were three-deckers,[19] and in Plymouth and Portsmouth were Orde's squadron and several reserve ships. All of them were actively refitting, and with a few exceptions they were capable of taking the sea at twenty-four hours' notice. Moreover Barham had in mind a device which would certainly secure him a respite of a week at least. It was simple enough. Gardner was instructed, as soon as Collingwood joined him, to look into Brest with the whole force before he detached the squadron destined for Cadiz. Such a display of strength could be relied on to keep Ganteaume quiet till he was able to ascertain what Gardner's real force was, and by that time fresh ships would be ready.

Such then was the solution of the difficult strategical problem with which Pitt and Barham so suddenly had to deal. Interesting as it is, it has long been forgotten, for it was destined never to be carried out. The great mass of our old strategical lore, which served us so well and cost so much to obtain, has passed into oblivion for similar reasons. Only by patient excavation can it be recovered, and only by the recovery of the unexecuted schemes can we hope to be safe from the danger of crude generalisation based on the comparatively few cases that survived above the surface.

Two events at the last moment occurred to stop this particular movement and to commit it to oblivion. As Collingwood sailed from Plymouth to join Gardner, Gardner received the despatches which Nelson had sent him from Toro to announce his intention of coming off Scilly, if he heard nothing of the Combined Squadron from Lisbon.[20] Gardner immediately sent a cruiser to the rendezvous and forwarded Nelson's despatches to the Admiralty with a request for instructions. The Admiralty, however, decided that no directions could be given until further intelligence of Nelson's squadron should be received.

Close on the heels of this surprise came another, and this time it was one that called for prompter action. On May 22nd, as Gardner and Collingwood were before Brest making the joint demonstration which Barham had directed as a preliminary to Collingwood's parting company, word came in from Calder that one of his cruiser captains, Maitland of the *Loire*, had located an enemy's squadron, ten days before, some five hundred miles to the westward of Ferrol. Shadowing it till nightfall he was chased off, but not before he ascertained it was the Rochefort squadron (details of which he had obtained from an American) and that it was making for Cape Ortegal.[21] With this information he made off to Calder, and on the 14th found him in his usual position off Cape Prior. Calder promptly assumed that Missiessy intended to make a landfall at Cape Ortegal on his way back to Rochefort, and at daybreak next morning he was off that point. Not finding the enemy there, as he hoped, he concluded he must have kept more to the north, and he determined to make a push north-north-east to cut him off if, as he expected, he was running down the latitude of Rochefort. This was a move on which he could venture without prejudice to his blockade, for the wind was blowing hard from the south-west, foul for the Ferrol squadron to get out. In the evening, however, it unfortunately came into the north, with every sign of shifting still further. With a chance of an easterly wind he dared not leave Ferrol open, and he felt compelled to desist. There was nothing for it but to send the *Loire* on to Gardner and to take his squadron back to its station.[22]

Here then was news which materially altered the situation from what it was when Gardner and Collingwood received their last orders. In the first place Missiessy's inexplicable reappearance, coming as it did when the report of Villeneuve's return to Cadiz was still uncontradicted, shook to their foundations the deductions on which Barham was proceeding. It was Missiessy's supposed presence in the West Indies that gave colour to the indications of a campaign or a concentration in that quarter. What then could his sudden return mean? And why was he coming back just as Villeneuve was going out? Or was it possible that Villeneuve was never intended to go? In the second place —and this is what concerned Gardner and Collingwood most nearly—it meant a serious increase of force in their immediate neighbourhood. What ought they to do in view of the discretion allowed them? The two Admirals conferred together and agreed there was no doubt that the three-decker and four of the line, which Maitland had seen, were safe back in Rochefort or possibly L'Orient. For Gardner to give Collingwood the reinforcement that had been ordered would now reduce the Ushant squadron to a dangerous weakness, and taking advantage of the latitude which had been originally given him in case of fresh information, he decided to retain with his flag the five ships of Graves's division which formed the last addition to the Flying Squadron and to send Collingwood down with the remaining nine.

The reason he gave to the Admiralty was this: "As five of the enemy's ships are returned from the West Indies and the Vice-Admiral (Collingwood) is directed to detach such proportion of ships to the West Indies as . . . the enemy may have sent there, fourteen ships would be more than he would now require to take down." As for the blockade of Cadiz, he felt that it would not be prejudiced by his action. "I hope," he concluded, "the steps I have taken will meet with their lordships' approbation, as, should it be ascertained that the Toulon fleet is returned to Cadiz, the five ships I have detained can very soon be sent after the Vice-Admiral, and probably reach the point of his present intended destination nearly as soon as himself."[23] The Admiralty did approve his conduct, but while waiting for directions he did not think himself entitled to use the detained ships either to blockade Rochefort or reinforce Calder who badly needed relief. All he did was to detach Collingwood on the 23rd with his nine of the line, and wait for further orders.

CHAPTER IX

Modifications Of Napoleon's Plans

As things actually stood, Gardner's action exactly fitted the situation. May 20th was the day on which Napoleon had to recognise that his scheme for a concentration in the West Indies had broken down. After urging Ganteaume by every means in his power to get to sea without fighting, he had informed him, if he could not escape by midnight on the 20th, he was to stay where he was for a different combination. It was on the 20th, too, that Missiessy put into Rochefort, sick and dispirited, and with his squadron entirely unfit for action.

So far as the campaign was concerned his mission had been a failure. When he had sailed at the beginning of the New Year, it had been for the purpose of colonial attack to which Napoleon, having laid aside his invasion, intended to devote his navy. Missiessy's special function was to throw supplies into the French islands, capture Dominica and St. Lucia in concert with the local forces, and then to raid and levy contributions on the smaller British islands. In pursuance of these instructions he reached Martinique on February 20th, and next day, after consultation with the local officers, proceeded against Roseau, the capital of Dominica.

The surprise was complete. Appearing off the place under British colours he was welcomed as a friend. General Prevost, the governor, actually sent off one of his staff to do the honours, and the officer did not discover the trick till he was on board Missiessy's flagship. General Lagrange, who was in command of the French troops, was consequently able to land with scarcely any resistance, and to seize positions so good that Prevost found Roseau untenable. He therefore decided to allow the local force to capitulate; but before Lagrange realised the craft of his move he had withdrawn the whole of the regular garrison, and was in full retreat to a fortress in the extremity of the island known as Fort Cabril. The moment Lagrange detected the movement he saw its danger, and begged Missiessy to detach a division to cut off the British retreat. A flat calm prevailed, and Missiessy protested not a ship could stir. Lagrange begged for the squadron's boats. Again the Admiral refused. To risk paralysing his squadron by exposing its crews in a military operation was a responsibility he did not feel called upon to take, and the result was that Prevost secured himself in a position that turned the tables upon the French. Fort Cabril could only be reduced by a siege, and for a siege the expedition was wholly unprepared. Accordingly while news sped to Europe of the capture of the island, Missiessy found himself compelled to withdraw and to rest content with a contribution of 100,000 francs from Roseau, and about a score of small prizes captured at their moorings.

For the present at any rate no attempt was made upon St. Lucia. Missiessy preferred to continue his way northward for less hazardous operations, and after landing at Guadaloupe the troops which he had brought to reinforce the garrison, he proceeded to raid the small British islands that lay beyond. From Nevis, St. Christopher's, and Montserrat he exacted ransoms, but there his activity ended. In his view it was now time to return to Martinique in order to meet Villeneuve and combine with him in the larger operations which Napoleon's instructions enjoined. The damage he had done was considerable. The ransoms and thirty-three prizes actually produced £40,000, but this of course did not nearly cover the cost of the expedition, and the British position in the Leeward Islands remained unshaken.

To the French authorities the most galling point in that position was the Diamond Rock, a desert islet that rose in a rugged cone barely a mile from the south-west point of Martinique. Its strategical importance was out of all proportion to its size. Not only did it lie upon the direct route from Europe to Fort de France and St. Pierre, the political and commercial capitals of the colony, but it also broke the coastwise line of communication between those places and the rich southern and western districts from which they were supplied. When in 1803 Commodore Samuel Hood, with his broad pennant in the *Centaur*, was blockading Martinique, the rock had proved a serious hindrance, since the coastwise traffic was constantly escaping his cruisers by stealing inshore of it. The French regarded its splintered, surf-beaten shore and precipitous escarpments as inaccessible, but Hood did not, at least not for his "Centaurs." He resolved to possess it, and use it as a "block ship" and as a base for his inshore boat operations. He tried, and by miraculous skill in a few hours the thing was done. "Were you to see," wrote an eye-witness during the subsequent proceedings, "how along a dire and, I had almost said, a perpendicular acclivity, the sailors are hanging in clusters hauling up a four-and-twenty pounder by hawsers, you would wonder! They appear like mice hauling a little sausage. . . . Believe me, I shall never take off my hat for anything less than a British seaman." High aloft they created and armed an inaccessible fastness, and below made a little battery at the landing-place. Lieutenant Maurice of the *Centaur* was placed in charge with the rank of commander, and the islet was officially rated in the Navy List as "His Majesty's Sloop, Diamond Rock." Here for two years the little garrison of a hundred men had lived in pure enjoyment a Robinson Crusoe life amongst the caves, incessantly raiding and cutting out, and proving an unendurable thorn in the side of Martinique.[1]

The harrassed French governor, unable to touch it, had been counting on its reduction when Missiessy and Villeneuve should meet at Fort de France. But by the time Missiessy got back from his expedition to the northward, a frigate had arrived with news that Villeneuve's first attempt to get out had failed, that the combination was cancelled, and that the Rochefort squadron was to return to France. In Missiessy's eyes this meant he was to return immediately. In vain the governor entreated him to devote a fragment of his force to the Diamond Rock before he left. In spite of his vehement protests Missiessy refused, and forthwith sailed away in accordance with his programme to throw the last of his troops and supplies into St. Domingo, as he passed on homeward-bound.

With Missiessy's premature departure the great combination on which Napoleon was staking his success received its first serious blow. From the outset Napoleon had been uneasy that something of the kind might happen, and when, on receiving Austria's submission, he found himself compelled to resume the invasion he had sent a revocation of Missiessy's order to return. Villeneuve was to try again, and Missiessy was to remain and meet him. The order did not reach Missiessy in time to stop him. Indeed, as soon as Napoleon heard Villeneuve had left Toulon, he realised that this would probably happen, and he set about constructing the first of those interminable modifications of his plans which ended not only in reducing his Admirals to a state of helpless bewilderment as to what he really expected them to do, but also in leaving his own mind in serious confusion as to what orders he had actually given, and what they had actually received.

It was on April 11th — the day after the junction at Cadiz was effected — that he drafted the new plan. As yet he had heard nothing of Villeneuve beyond the fact that he had left Toulon, but he did know that Ganteaume had failed to get out and that Missiessy would probably be on his way home. Having therefore to face the probability that his first combination would break down, he fell back on the discredited plan of getting a surprise command of the Channel by Villeneuve's fleet alone, and began to paint another of his rose-coloured pictures. He assumed that Gravina would join at Cadiz with eight of the line, and there were two more just ready for sea at Rochefort under Admiral Magon. These he would send out direct to Martinique, if Ganteaume failed to get out by May 10th. Villeneuve's fleet would thus be brought up to twenty-two of the line, a force sufficient to enable him to return round the north of Scotland into the North Sea, set free Marmont's corps and the Dutch squadron in the Texel, and come on to Boulogne.

His reasons for believing this plan feasible are a striking example of how entirely he failed to fathom either the subtlety or the strength of British strategy. Villeneuve, he assured himself, would meet no force sufficiently strong to oppose him, because Ganteaume would always detain a squadron of twenty of the line before Brest, and Missiessy's return would absorb another squadron to blockade him in Rochefort.[2] How hopeless it was to force the British government to keep such a force before Brest we have already seen, and events were to show that no squadron in Rochefort could tempt Barham to weaken unduly the central point.

Sanguine as was the scheme, it was too sober and narrow to sit easily on Napoleon's contempt of his enemy's ability. He did not remain constant to it for two days. By April 13th he had an entirely new plan in his head. The rumour that Dominica and St. Lucia had fallen had reached him and he was more sanguine than ever. It was at this time, too, that intelligence of the feverish activity in the British naval ports, as well as of the two expeditions and of the formation of Collingwood's Flying Squadron, inflamed him with the belief that his devices had upset his enemy's equilibrium, filled their counsels with confusion, and that, in their dismay, they were scattering formidable squadrons and the best of their troops to the ends of the earth.[3]

It was, moreover, in an hour of supreme exultation that the new idea came to him. He was on his way to Italy, not too sure of how the French provinces regarded his assumption of the Imperial crown. He had reached Lyons, where, passing in state through the streets, he received an ovation. With the shouts of the adoring populace in his ears, he felt the world was his oyster and with his fleet he could open it. The possibility of securing the command of the Channel by an overpowering and unexpected concentration again took possession of him, and that night the last plan was cancelled. Instead of waiting till May 10th, Magon was to sail immediately, and carry orders to Villeneuve that if in thirty-five days from the receipt of them Ganteaume had not appeared at Martinique, he was to assume he had been unable to break out, and Villeneuve with twenty of the line, the least number which Napoleon believed he would have, was to return to Ferrol. There he would raise the blockade, call out the fifteen of the Gourdon-Grandallana squadron, and with the whole proceed to join hands with Ganteaume off Brest. Then together they would force the Channel with an overwhelming fleet of fifty-six of the line and appear before Boulogne. There they would find the Emperor in person, who would himself give them their final orders, and "on their successful arrival," he said, "hung the destinies of the world."[4]

The new arrangement, of course, was not to come into force if Ganteaume appeared. Villeneuve was still to wait for him the specified period, but not in inactivity. The delay was to be made good by reducing St. Lucia, if it had not fallen, and such other of the British islands as were within the means and time at his disposal.[5]

That a man of Napoleon's ability should have given such orders is only to be explained by the intoxication which the success of his policy was producing. As he journeyed in triumph towards Italy, he found France worshipping at his feet, and beyond glittered within his reach the Iron Crown. Austria and Prussia were ignominiously looking on in silence at this last and most flagrant breach of his engagements, and England, his only active enemy, seemed at her wits' end. The sole merit of the new scheme above the rest is that he seems now to have faced for the first time the real conditions of the problem. It appears to contemplate winning a road across the Channel by battle. Yet he does not realise — and here lay its most vital defect — that the battle off Brest must be fought by Villeneuve alone, and that to escape defeat he must come in overwhelming force. He still believes, for all that Ganteaume and Decrès can say, that Ganteaume will be able to co-operate, as though it were a case of two armies which he could move as he would. Moreover, in spite of the tremendous difficulty of the task, in spite of the paramount necessity of concentration of effort, he bids Villeneuve squander his force prematurely in attempting colonial conquest; and to complete the perversity of it all he assumes throughout that his enemy will do all the foolish things he wishes him to do. Surely never was a project more contrary to the principles we are accustomed to call Napoleonic.[6]

It must further be remembered that these ambitious orders were signed before Napoleon had a word of news as to how Villeneuve had fared after leaving Toulon, or of what Nelson was doing. They left Paris for Rochefort on April 17th. It was not till the 20th that Napoleon, who had just reached Italy, heard from Genoa that Nelson, as late as April 10th, was still south of Sardinia and not in pursuit.[7] Two days later came news from Spain that on the same day on which the new idea had come to him, Villeneuve had safely effected a junction with Gravina at Cadiz and had gone on his way. It was a disappointment that only five Spanish ships had joined instead of the eight he had expected, but he immediately set about providing the remaining ships of his ally with a fresh part to play. Still with sanguine infatuation building on the presumed folly of his enemy, he was convinced that, as Nelson was not in pursuit of Villeneuve, he had been again enticed to Egypt. More elated than ever with the prospects of his new plan, he determined to secure his advantage by measures which would hold Nelson in the Mediterranean. For this purpose he would form a new Toulon squadron. We have seen how his first idea for using Missiessy, if he should miss his last orders and return, had been to keep him in Rochefort to occupy a blockading squadron. Now he was minded to bring him to Toulon and to persuade the Spanish Government to let their Cartagena squadron join him there. Godoy, Prince of the Peace, was then all powerful at Madrid, and Talleyrand was instructed to approach him on the subject of the new combined squadron. "My intention," Napoleon wrote, "would not be to order the squadron out, but to make it a menace, and as I shall have there [at Toulon] a camp of four or five thousand men, I shall cause the English great uneasiness. If the Prince of the Peace will not adopt this course, then I think the Cartagena squadron ought to go to Cadiz."[8] For his purpose of drawing the attention of the British to the Mediterranean the alternative of a squadron at Cadiz, controlling the entrance to the Straits, had almost as high a diversionary value as a new Toulon squadron. To increase the effect of what he hoped for, while waiting for an answer, he industriously scattered through the European press reports that Villeneuve had evaded the British watch and had landed ten thousand men in Egypt.

By such transparent devices he could think to beguile Nelson and give Villeneuve and Gravina a free hand. Decrès was therefore directed to send them ampler and more explicit orders for attempting the conquest of the British Leeward Islands. They were to expel the English, not only from Dominica and St. Lucia, but from St. Vincent, Antigua, and Barbadoes as well, and possibly even to recapture Tobago and Trinidad.[9] Never did even the elder Pitt in his most sanguine moments devise a programme so entirely unrelated to the time and force available.

If the fault which Napoleon most severely reprehended in his Marshals was that of making for themselves pictures favourable to the enemy, his own besetting naval sin was making pictures favourable to himself. The one over which he was now gloating represented England trembling for India, Cochrane half-way there, and Nelson, with his eye on the French corps at Taranto, devoting himself to the defence of Egypt. The West Indies he saw defenceless till such time as a British force superior to Villeneuve's squadron could be detached from the Home Fleet. The picture was false in every line, but Napoleon would not see it, and hard on the heels of Magon, who sailed with the earlier orders on May 1st, the *Didon* frigate carried the new ones, bidding Villeneuve and Gravina oust the English from the West Indies as a *hors d'œuvre* to the full meal that was spread for them in the Channel.

Having thus taken the first steps which his unreal picture suggested, he produced in the following week an equally sanguine plan for Villeneuve's final move on England. It was elaborated in every detail, and every detail was rose-coloured. He did not know Magon had already sailed. The Iron Crown of Italy which he was about to set on his head had filled the measure of his intoxication; time and space were ceasing to exist; the wilderness of ocean over which he was scattering his squadrons was but a chessboard on which he could move them as he would, to the utter confusion of a purblind and nerveless adversary.

For the final movement, as he now formulated it, temporary command of the Channel by surprise still had a place, beside the idea of real command, won in a great and decisive action. Villeneuve, after he had returned to raise the Ferrol blockade and had formed his junction with Gourdon and Grandallana, would be left free to choose the method that seemed best at the last moment. Napoleon still believed that all that was wanted was three, or on second thoughts four, days' command before Boulogne. Villeneuve might gain it either by joining Ganteaume or by leaving him to occupy the main British squadron and going north-about to take the enemy's position in reverse down the North Sea. It was not unlikely that the British Admiralty would direct its chief attention to preventing a junction between the Brest and Toulon squadrons and would endeavour to deal with Villeneuve in detail. To this end they would probably move Cornwallis out a considerable distance to meet him. If they did, it would only facilitate his operating by surprise. Instead of approaching Brest he could run round Cornwallis, make the Lizard, and from there rush the Channel, or if the wind were not favourable he could go north-about to the Texel. If, however, he decided on joining Ganteaume and a battle, he could either previously bring out the Rochefort squadron on his way to Ushant or leave it where it was to occupy its own blockading squadron. If possible he was not to fight till the junction with Ganteaume was complete, but if a preliminary action could not be avoided, he was to fight as near to Brest as possible, so as to permit of Ganteaume's co-operation. Lastly, in case events prevented any of these plans succeeding, he could fetch out the Rochefort squadron and concentrate with the Cartagena squadron at Cadiz for further orders.[10]

It was an ingenious method of breaking the strength of the interior position held as of old by our Western Squadron. But as before it was the design of a soldier, framed on the lines of land warfare and the movement of armies. Its fatal defect was, as we shall see Decrès presently pointing out, that it made no deductions either for the superior mobility of fleets and the peculiar limitations of that mobility imposed by conditions of wind and tide. In short, so far as it rested on a junction between Villeneuve and Ganteaume, it was a plan based on the false analogy of an army relieving a beleaguered garrison. If we are investing a fortress it is always possible for the two sections of the enemy's force to co-operate to a greater or less extent, but there is no recorded case in sailing days of a blockaded squadron having been able to take effective part in an action between a relieving force and the blockaders.[11] The difficulty was partly due to the fact that a wind that was favourable for the relieving force to attack was usually foul for the blockaded force to come out; and partly to the fact that if the blockading force moved away to meet the attack and left the port open, still the difficulty which the blockaded force always had in locating the blockaders, if out of sight of its signal stations, prevented its moving out except at great hazard until it actually heard the engagement in progress. Napoleon, in short, omitted from his calculations two primary conditions of naval warfare; one — that at sea there was a lee and a weather gage which did not enter into analogous problems on land, and the other, that it is impossible to tell under a day or two whether a naval blockade has been raised or not.

So things stood when on May 20th midnight sounded the knell of the West Indian concentration, and the new orders for a concentration in home waters came into operation. This was the day Napoleon had finally fixed as the latest on which Ganteaume was to attempt to break out, and henceforth the door was shut on him till Villeneuve should appear to open it. With that Napoleon had to rest content so far as Brest was concerned; but for Missiessy's squadron to remain idle was another matter, and since the Spanish refusal to accept his idea of a new Toulon squadron his restless mind was at work again on schemes for putting it to the best advantage. He had just heard from Spain, that the Government had decided the Cartagena squadron must come to Cadiz. The reason is curious. If the British Government were at a loss to fathom the meaning of Missiessy's unexpected return, the Spanish Government had a knot still more difficult to untie, and much more disturbing. For them the dominating fact was that Nelson had appeared at the Straits at the moment when Craig had reached Lisbon. Craig they knew was now waiting at Gibraltar, but where was Nelson? On what was he bent? As Godoy remarked to the French ambassador, the answer to this question was nothing to the Emperor but everything to Spain. Nelson had last been heard of off St. Vincent. He was thus a month behind Villeneuve and pursuit could scarcely lead to anything. Clearly Spain must be prepared for a blow at one of her arsenals — probably Caraccas in Cadiz Bay. Salcedo and his squadron must come round from Cartagena for its defence, and this would be done so soon as they knew where Nelson was and that the passage through the Straits was clear.[12]

Napoleon was equally perplexed as to the meaning of Craig s expedition, but less disturbed. As usual he decided it was going to do what would most nicely suit his plans. "The famous secret expedition," he wrote to Decrès, "put into Lisbon on May 7th, and sailed again on the 10th. It is composed of two ships of the line, a corvette and fifty transports carrying 5,000 to 6,000 men. It seems to have taken refuge in Lisbon for fear of Villeneuve. Where is it going? It is a problem. My opinion is that it has nothing in reason to do except to take the Cape or to carry assistance to Jamaica or the Windward Islands.[13] If it is destined for Malta, so much the better. Nothing will prove more strongly the ineptitude of the English Cabinet; for these plans of continental operations based on detachments of a few thousand men are the plans of pygmies. If then you hear that this expedition has gone to Malta, rejoice; for the English have deprived themselves of 6,000 men and of a certain number of ships. All the reports I get from England agree in saying that the English are embarking troops on all sides."[14]

This criticism of Pitt's strategy has been taken as Napoleon's real opinion, and even as a condemnation of that amphibious form of war which had become characteristic of British methods. But such an interpretation is by no means certain. To begin with, no one familiar with his correspondence can have failed to notice a habit he had of branding movements which he had not foreseen as *inepties* or *sottises*, and the more disconcerting such movements were, the more contemptuous was his language. His success and self-confidence seem to have brought him to a state of mind, in which he could not or would not believe his own appreciations could have missed any reasonable eventuality; and if an opposing commander acted in a way which he himself had failed to anticipate, the only explanation he permitted was that the man was a fool and a blunderer. Such a process of thought was but a piece of the perverse self-deception which was probably his greatest defect as a commander. In this case it is unusually striking; for in a month or two, as we shall see, he was speaking of the expedition in a tone of serious alarm. Moreover the letters should not be read alone. Those he wrote on the same and the following day, suggest that his real feeling was one far removed from contempt.

They were the two busy days which preceded the ceremony of his coronation at Milan, and over the pageantry of the preparations there is clear to see the shadow of Pitt's coming coalition, the first doubt as to whether the initiative of the campaign is to be his own.

On the eve of his great stroke for incorporating Italy in his empire, which had already caused him so much misgiving, he sat pouring out despatch after despatch, filled with new anxiety. To Marshal Berthier, his Chief of the Staff, there are two for reinforcing and rearming Corsica and his chief Italian ports. To Cambacérès, his right hand in Paris, he writes: "You can contradict loudly the news that is being spread of a treaty of alliance between England and Russia. Make it known indirectly on 'Change and elsewhere that Russia, on the contrary, has refused to listen to any hostile proposals." Fouché, who controlled the press bureau, is told to insert in the papers that at St. Petersburg the French are growing more popular, that the English are disliked, that the project of a coalition has fallen through, and that in any case Russia will not intervene and is too remote to engage on her own account directly and effectively. "Be careful," he tells Barbè-Marbois, "to read the English papers, and to get them by the quickest way. Do not stop at a thousand louis more or less and send me such information as may interest me, above all the movements of ships and announcements of all preparations of all expeditions." "Monsieur mon Beaufrere et Cousin," he writes testily to Prince Murat, "what you write me about the conclusion of a treaty of alliance between England and Russia is nonsense: it is entirely false. These reports, which the English spread to get themselves out of the mess for the moment, are fabrications." In the evening, after the fireworks and illuminations were over, he was even haunted with the possibility of his enemy playing their old game of supporting insurrections in France itself: and he wrote again to Fouché: "In the state of disorganisation and embarrassment in which England finds herself, it is possible she may seek to renew trouble in the interior of France. But I can't think she will make much of it. That string is worn out like so many others."

It is possible that his orders for strengthening the Italian ports had their origin in a desire to provide secure points of refuge for a small frigate squadron he was about to send out for a cruise under his wayward brother Jerome, who had just returned from his escapade in America and in whom he hoped to find the Admiral he was seeking. But all the rest of the letters suggest strongly that the meeting of Craig's expedition and Nelson gave an ugly turn to the growing rumours of an Anglo-Russian alliance, and that for the first time Napoleon was forced to doubt whether his invasion threat would so effectively paralyse British initiative as he had expected.

On the morrow his preoccupation with Craig at Gibraltar and the possibility of English and Russian co-operation in the Mediterranean continues. "It is urgent," he writes, "to get the Cartagena fleet to Cadiz and to blockade Gibraltar, if the English do not keep a superior squadron in those seas;" and yet again to Fouché: "I have already told you that the treaty of England with Russia is false. It is a trick of the English Cabinet. Their intrigues have broken down completely. Even when you see this treaty printed in the English gazette and Pitt announcing it to Parliament, you can say it is not true." The same day he hears that the British fleet before Brest has been firing a salvo, and it gets on his nerves. He discusses it with Decrès, is afraid it may mean a regrettable incident for Magon, and he ends by assuring the Minister that "England is entirely abandoned by the continent, her situation is worse than ever."[15]

To add to his troubles he could get no news of Missiessy. He had not yet heard of his return. As the Spanish fear of Craig had ended all hope of a new Toulon squadron, he had decided to send him back to Villeneuve. But as the days went by the probability of his being too late or even shut in by blockade grew more and more disturbing, and Napoleon began deluging Decrès with projects for using him in some other way. In spite of "the state of disorganisation and embarrassment" in England, everywhere he looked he saw a British squadron in the way. The problem was how to employ Missiessy so as to occupy or entice away an equal British force and yet have him at hand at the decisive moment. "If I send Missiessy to Cadiz or to Toulon," he wrote to Decrès on May 29th, "and the English evacuate the Mediterranean, it is evident the English will have on the day of the battle of Ushant, six more vessels against me, which I ought to make Missiessy contain." There was, to be sure, the possibility of sending him to Cadiz to fetch the Cartagena and Cadiz squadrons to Ferrol, but to this course there were two objections. He believed Calder had ten of the line before Ferrol, and Missiessy, if he succeeded in rallying both the Cadiz and the Cartagena squadrons, would have fifteen. "But is it prudent," he says, "to attack ten English vessels with five French and ten Spanish?" Moreover a concentration at Ferrol, like all concentrations at the wrong time and place, would do more harm than good. It would attract at least twenty of the enemy, and then Villeneuve would be unable to get there without fighting and the difficulty of the Brest junction would be reproduced. For the same reason he could not send him to Brest, for even if he could slip in, that again would only lead to an increase of the British force at the mouth of the Channel — the force, that is, which it was his special object to reduce. There was no way, he finally decided, but for Missiessy to operate an independent diversion. If he was blockaded in Rochefort he would occupy at least six of the enemy, and could conform to their movements. If on Villeneuve's approach the blockade was raised he must go out and make a demonstration on the coast of Ireland. "This movement," he writes, "will give London a fit of nerves (*la, crispation*) and oblige them to detach six of the line." Meanwhile Missiessy would disappear into the ocean and turn up off Ferrol in time to meet Villeneuve.

As further reports began to reach Milan of the rapid succession of orders that had been issuing from the British Admiralty since Villeneuve's escape, the picture which Napoleon was painting for himself gained in colour. "The disorder of the English is extreme," he wrote to Decrès. But if Napoleon deceived himself Decrès had his eyes open, and on June 1st he sat down to warn his sanguine master of the serious mistakes he was making. "What seems certain," he wrote with grave sarcasm, "is that, if the English Government has not divined your Majesty's thoughts, it is none the less true that they have been penetrated by the London journalists."[16] He felt sure Cochrane had not gone to India, but was in the West Indies, and he warns Napoleon that if Nelson goes there too they will have together eighteen of the line, "of which several are three-deckers," and that a premature action there is highly probable. "The low speed of some of Admiral Villeneuve's vessels," he argues, "leaves little hope that he will be able to avoid an engagement. On this hypothesis the die is cast, and a fortnight hence the God of Battles will have given judgment." Even on the other hypothesis that Cochrane was not there and Villeneuve might get away without fighting, his predicament would be even worse. Nelson would immediately follow him back, "and if he despairs of reaching Ferrol in time, he will send thither a fast frigate, and himself make for Brest, which will give the enemy an immense force at that point."

To redress the balance Napoleon was of course relying on the junction between Villeneuve and Ganteaume being made before the "Battle of Ushant" was fought, and Decrès as delicately as he can tries to convince him the thing is impossible. "I will make no comparison," he says, "with two columns of an army, a case in which the smallest accident may often upset the most nicely calculated junction. . . . Whatever the winds on which Admiral Villeneuve makes for Brest it is possible these winds may be foul for Admiral Ganteaume's fleet. For this junction to operate with success, Admiral Villeneuve must appear before Brest at a moment favourable for the fleet to get under way." Even so it will be impossible for Villeneuve to avoid sustaining for a time single-handed the whole force of the enemy. "If Admiral Villeneuve's fleet has not force sufficient to constrain the enemy to refuse battle, he will have to measure strength with him for at least ten hours before he can be joined by the Brest fleet. The issue of such an action fought with such a proportion of vessels will leave the victor with an effective force sufficient to sustain a second attack." In other words, if all goes as well as possible, no victory can be expected to be decisive enough to give certain command of the Channel.

But he goes still further, pointing out technical reasons why it is impossible to hope that things will go so well. By no process of intelligence will it be possible to make certain that Villeneuve shall arrive when wind and tide are right for Ganteaume; in all probability, therefore, the Brest squadron would not be in a position to support Villeneuve till the day after he appears. Moreover there was a likelihood of Villeneuve's finding the enemy off Ushant in much greater strength than Napoleon has allowed for. It was quite possible they would have not merely the regular blockading squadron, but also the whole of its reserve, as well as the Ferrol squadron and eventually Nelson's too. He reminds his master that of the whole force on which he relies to deal with such a concentration of highly trained squadrons, nineteen vessels will be Spaniards just out of harbour, commanded by inexperienced officers and poorly equipped. Finally he begs that Villeneuve may be given orders not to risk an action unless he finds his own squadron in a superiority of at least six to that of the enemy.[17]

It is doubtful whether this luminous appreciation, with its first forecast of what actually happened, was ever completed. A curious feature of it is that though Decrès clearly did not put much trust in Nelson's being enticed away, yet he dared not say openly that he was not the simpleton Napoleon professed to think him. Still he felt bound to hint that it was just possible Nelson might do the right thing, and he adopted a method of conveying the suggestion, which was as ingenious as it was delicate. "His boasting," he says, "only equals his ineptitude (*ineptie*) — and I use here the proper word — but he has one striking quality, which is to have no pretensions with his captains except for bravery and luck; whence it follows that he is accessible to advice, and in difficult situations, though he is nominally in command, it is another who actually directs."[18]

Whether or not Decrès ever ventured to forward his crushing criticism, it certainly had no effect in shaking Napoleon's obstinacy. A week later he reproved his minister for not having "a mind exclusive enough for a great operation." "It is a fault," he said, "which you must correct, for it is the art of great successes and great undertakings." Decrès in despair begged him to come back to France. "I don't know," Napoleon replied, "why you say so much of my return to Paris. Nothing is better calculated than my journey to hide my projects and cheat the enemy." Always this besetting dream of his enemy's imbecility! Unconvinced he continued incessantly to elaborate his plan, in spite of news that kept coming in to show how airy was the castle he was building.

Salcedo had tried to get round to Cadiz in order to attack Craig at Gibraltar, but had been forced by the weather to put back and was now held in his port on rumours that both Orde and Nelson were in the neighbourhood. The falsity of the rumours was not penetrated by Napoleon. He embraced them to add colour to his picture. For him they meant a further chance of weakening his enemy on the Ushant position. Missiessy could now be sent to make a demonstration in the North Sea and off the Texel, and Marmont should emphasise it by such a display of activity ashore as would compel the British Government to take it into account. The basis of it all was pure illusion. It was quickly demonstrated that owing to the strength of the British interior position between Cadiz and Cartagena it was impossible for the two squadrons either to get together or between them to contain a force superior to their own. In a week Salcedo tried once more to get round to Cadiz, but only to hurry into port again in alarm, on tidings that Collingwood had arrived to re-establish the command of the Straits' mouth.[19]

Still nothing availed to dilute Napoleon's optimism, or his belief that he had completely confused his enemy and broken their concentration. He had heard that a Flying Squadron of twelve of the line had been detached from the Ushant fleet, and till the actual announcement that Collingwood was blockading Cadiz he believed he had gone to India. As to Nelson he was equally sanguine. Though he did not know where he was for certain, he had little doubt he was either in England or the Mediterranean, and was convinced that Missiessy's cruise would complete his effort to upset the equilibrium of his enemy. "The uncertainty and confusion," he repeated, "that the London Admiralty is in, declares itself on all sides. Orders and counter-orders and the greatest indecision — that is the actual state of things."[20]

Yet even as he wrote, these orders and counter-orders over which he was exulting had brought, not confusion, but the quiet re-establishment of the long line of blockade which Villeneuve's escape had thrown momentarily out of gear. So nicely adjusted was the interlocking of the parts, so well practised the hands at the levers, that every uncertainty had been met by a simple turn. Each part in answer to the adroit impulse slipped smartly into its appointed place. From the Texel to Cartagena the chain was drawn tight and every gate was locked upon the impotent squadrons of which Napoleon had yet to construct a fleet.

CHAPTER X

Restoring The Command — Ferrol And The Straits

To pass from the imaginative and almost feverish correspondence of Napoleon at this time, to the coolly calculated orders of Lord Barham and the confident motions of the British commanders gives an impression of quiet mastery that is the note of the campaign from now onwards.

Ignorant that Missiessy's reappearance was a mistake, the Admiralty's first deduction from their intelligence was that no serious attack or concentration was intended in the West Indies. It even indicated a possibility that Villeneuve was not bound thither at all, and word was immediately sent after Collingwood instructing him to go no further than Madeira without fresh orders. On the same reasoning Pitt decided not to divert Sir Eyre Coote's expedition to the West Indies, and an express was hurried off to Drury, who in Gardner's absence was commanding the Irish station, to stop him, or supposing he had started, to recall him if possible.[1] There was a possibility that Villeneuve had gone to India after all, as Napoleon was trying to make his enemy believe. But the Government was not to be enticed into making so wide a dissipation of its fleet except on the surest evidence, and they contented themselves with a warning to Sir Edward Pellew, who commanded on the station.[2]

The discretion which Gardner had exercised in withholding Graves's division from Collingwood received formal approval, and he was directed to devote it to the blockade of Rochefort, with instructions to intercept the French squadron if it put to sea and to follow it wherever it went. Gardner received the order on June 5th, when Collingwood had been gone a fortnight. Decrès had just heard of this weakening of the Ushant fleet, and seeing in it a chance for Ganteaume to strike, was appealing to the Emperor for the necessary orders. But Napoleon would not quit the plan which seemed to be working so well. He was the last man in the world, for all his faith in the principle of destroying the enemy's forces, to hazard an action except for some clearly seen end. "To what can a battle lead?" he replied. "To nothing. Simply put in the papers that the English have sent eight (*sic*) of the line before [Rochefort] and that they have weakened by so much their Brest blockade . . . and that it is inconceivable why the French fleet does not profit by the occasion. Next day, in another paper, say that it is most extraordinary that journalists permit themselves such reflexions; that before condemning or approving the conduct of an admiral in an affair of this nature, they should know what are his instructions, and that probably, as the Emperor has not communicated them to the journalists, all their talk on the subject is quite futile."[3]

The prompt closing of Rochefort reduced all his schemes for the employment of Missiessy to the *pis aller* of conforming to the movements of the blockading force. But in any case the squadron could not have sailed for some weeks — so exhausted were its crews, and so great the need of repairs — and a fortnight after Missiessy had put into the port, Graves had appeared. With his own 80-gun ship, two three-deckers, and three others, he was in a marked superiority over what the enemy was reputed to have. Thus by the time Napoleon knew Missiessy was back he was already firmly held to his moorings. Graves indeed, on his arrival, found the squadron so entirely unfit for sea that he forthwith submitted to Gardner whether it was necessary to keep anything but a frigate off the port. Gardner replied — and the point is interesting in relation to the old practice of war direction — that he did not feel authorised to recall him or any part of his detachment without special orders from the Admiralty. The orders he got were to withdraw two ships of the line and to add them to his own squadron or to that of Calder before Ferrol.

The position of this squadron had been causing Gardner some anxiety. Calder had been complaining that his force was inadequate to watch the port. Besides his own three-decker the *Prince of Wales*, he had only an 80-gun ship, four seventy-fours, and a forty-four, while Gourdon and Grandallana had between them eleven of the line actually ready for sea, and three more in a forward state. To add to the inequality, one of Calder's ships had been severely damaged aloft, and four others would soon need relief. So strongly did Gardner feel Calder's weakness that it had been his intention, to send him the whole of Graves's division. This addition to the Ferrol squadron, after the units requiring refit had been sent home, would have given it a strength of ten of the line, of which three would be three-deckers, besides an 80-gun ship — a force which by the ordinary rule of calculation would have made it superior to the Combined Squadron inside. The Admiralty order to attach Graves to Collingwood and subsequently to send him before Rochefort had stopped the movement, and made it impossible for Gardner to detach anything to Calder without bringing his own squadron below the established minimum of eighteen.

His anxiety, however, was needless. Barham was quite alive to the situation and had already provided for it. The nature of these orders and the manner in which they were interpreted by the Admirals concerned, are highly interesting. They afford a typical example of what long war experience had established as to the discretion which the man on the spot might permit himself in reading his orders, and the certainty and fearlessness with which officers in those days could weigh the spirit against the letter.

It will be remembered that Barham's first idea after hearing of Villeneuve's escape was that Knight's two vessels, the *Queen* and *Dragon*, which formed Craig's escort, should proceed with Collingwood's Flying Squadron in chase, if Nelson had not gone himself. If Nelson had pursued, Knight was to send both vessels to Orde, who was then believed to be still on his station. This was on April 27th. Three days later came Orde's despatch which told of his falling back on Ushant, and contained his appreciation, which pointed to the probability of a concentration of the enemy's squadrons somewhere to the westward. To hold the Ferrol position in strength was therefore of the last importance, and it became absolutely necessary to reinforce Calder. Consequently, it will be remembered, Knight was instructed that if he had not passed St. Vincent with his convoy, he was to come back to Ferrol. If he had, he was to shift his flag to a frigate at Gibraltar and send his ships of the line to Calder, or if Calder had raised the blockade they were to carry on to Gardner.

The first of these orders Knight received when he reached Gibraltar. By that time Nelson had already detached Sir Richard Bickerton in the *Royal Sovereign*, and had placed Knight under his orders. Bickerton of course decided, as Nelson was pursuing, to keep Knight's ships with his flag. His intention was, in accordance with Nelson's instructions, to use the squadron for covering Craig's passage to Malta and meeting a Levant convoy then due. He informed the Admiralty that in taking upon himself to do this instead of sending the ships to Orde as they had directed, he was influenced by the dominant consideration, that when the Admiralty issued the orders they did not know that the squadron in Cartagena had become active, and had already once been to sea. The whole tenor of the order indicated that had they known this they would certainly have wished Craig's escort to remain for his protection. Before, however, he could act, the second orders arrived, as to reinforcing Calder; whereupon Bickerton considered he was no longer justified in using his discretion in the light of the local situation. "I must give up," he replied, "the objects I had and obey, though it will expose the convoy and transports to the [Algeçiras] gunboats and the Cartagena squadron. As I certainly am not strong enough to meet and attack this force advantageously, backed as it is by the Cadiz squadron, which must amount to five of the line . . . I do not feel myself at liberty to deviate from their lordships' orders when there is no reasonable hope of my being able by an action with such a superior enemy to confine the Cartagena squadron within the Straits, or to prevent the junction of at least the larger part of them with that of Cadiz; and when it is considered that their lordships' future arrangements will be made under a full conviction that the ships of the line under my orders have joined the squadron under Sir Robert Calder or Lord Gardner's fleet." His principle may be thus enunciated — that in dealing with explicit orders no exercise of discretion that may confuse the war-plan is permissible to an officer on the spot, unless he sees in the local conditions, unknown to headquarters, the certainty of delivering a decisive blow at the enemy's naval force or possibly of paralysing a part of it greater than his own.[4]

The decision was one which called for the highest qualities of a commander. In obeying his orders in spite of his knowledge of the local situation, he was exposing an important military force to present risk of being destroyed by a combined attack from Cadiz, Cartagena, and Algeçiras. Fortunately, in the General he had to deal with a man of as high and sound a military spirit as his own. Directly he received the orders he showed them to Craig, and Craig in spite of the dangers staring him in the face agreed there was but one thing for Bickerton to do. To make the position perfectly clear, he sent home a despatch to the War Office to assure them Bickerton's conduct to him throughout had been "most confidential and cordial." Of his departure with the squadron he had not a word of complaint. "His doing so," he says, "is with my perfect concurrence and acquiescence." Though he well knew the Admiralty despatch had been written without information of how large and active was the enemy's force about the Straits, yet he did not feel justified in pressing Bickerton on that account to vary his orders. The view he took was that all the instructions which the Admirals had communicated to him had a certain "general tendency," and this, he said, was "invariably that of assembling a great naval force to the westward, an object which under the present circumstances might be of a magnitude to supersede every other."

No utterance could more clearly reveal how intimate at that time was the sympathy between the best men in the two services and how complete was their mutual understanding of the principles of combined warfare. Faced as Craig was with the prospect of his force being left almost without defence in seas swarming with the enemy, he did not forget that for England there was one condition of affairs to which everything else must be subservient. In the Admiralty orders he perceived indications that the moment was at hand for a supreme decision in a great fleet action, at the vital strategical point. If so it was a moment for which everything, even his own force, must be risked; and he did not flinch. Not even by a word would he tempt his colleague from the supreme duty.[5] On the morrow, May 17th, Bickerton sailed with his three ships for Ferrol, leaving Knight in command at Gibraltar to make such dispositions as he could with the few cruisers and gunboats available for the safety of the convoy and the observation of Cartagena.

Ten days later, as Bickerton neared Finisterre, he met Collingwood coming down with his nine ships of the line and a frigate, and was able to place him in possession of the actual state of affairs. Collingwood, as we know, had been given a wide discretion as to the disposal of his own force. The two Admirals held a long consultation and had little difficulty in coming to a conclusion as to how far Collingwood's orders might be modified to meet the local conditions. From Bickerton Collingwood learnt that Nelson with only ten of the line was in chase of Villeneuve with eighteen. He also learnt the important new fact that both in Cadiz and Cartagena there were active squadrons. Seeing the comparative strength of Nelson and Villeneuve, and that Cochrane had no more than six of the line, he ought by his orders to have despatched two of the line after Nelson to bring the whole naval force in the Leeward Islands up to eighteen also. But in view of the fact that since his orders were received Missiessy had returned and that the enemy's force in the West Indies was thereby reduced by five ships, he decided not to do so till further orders. Bickerton's urgent representation convinced him that the situation demanded taking his whole force down to the Straits to secure the local command. "In view," Collingwood wrote home, "of the active preparations in Cartagena and Cadiz and that a convoy is expected from Malta I shall proceed off Cadiz with the utmost despatch . . . and take station there." He hoped their lordships would approve this departure from his orders, since the activity at Cartagena was unknown when they were drawn up. "I consider," he concluded, "the spirit of my orders demanded that I should not leave so large a force at liberty to sail in execution of their plans." Here then was a clear case of modifying explicit orders. They were not merely "instructions"; and Collingwood's despatch bears the Admiralty endorsement, "Approved under the circumstances."[6]

In consideration of Collingwood's consent to take this course, Bickerton sacrificed his only cruiser to inform the Admiralty. The despatches of the two Admirals were received on June 8th and instantly orders were returned to them fully accepting their view of the situation. Bickerton, who in obedience to his orders had gone on to Ferrol, was to shift his flag to the *Queen* and, leaving the *Royal Sovereign* and his two-decker with Calder, was to go back to the Straits and place himself under Collingwood's orders.

Collingwood thus became Commander-in-chief of the regular Mediterranean station from Cape St. Vincent to the Levant with a force of ten of the line besides the *Excellent* which was still on guard at Naples, and the strong force of cruisers which were exercising the control within the Straits. His orders were to establish a close blockade of Cadiz and of St. Lucar, the adjacent port of Seville. Hitherto, with a view apparently of conciliating neutrals, and especially Americans, a commercial blockade had not been strictly enforced. But on the urgent representations of the officers on the station of the activity in the Spanish dockyards, and the abundance of supplies that were pouring in, the two ports were now definitely closed.

While Collingwood occupied the Cadiz station, Bickerton, as Nelson had arranged, was to command inside the Straits; but he was to report frequently to Collingwood and obey all his orders for the disposition of ships. To begin with, however, for the special purpose of getting Craig forward to his destination, Collingwood was to give him four of the line, thus dividing the battle squadron between them.[7]

This arrangement Collingwood was unable to carry out in full. On June 8th, the day his orders were being issued by the Admiralty for the blockade, he had taken up his station before Cadiz, but after parting with Bickerton he had reconsidered his decision to postpone the execution of his orders to reinforce Nelson. On thinking it over it occurred to him that possibly Cochrane might do what Nelson afterwards did — he might think it his duty to follow his fleet, and was perhaps already in European waters on Missiessy's heels. His departure would seriously weaken the naval force in the West Indies, and to restore the position he now sent away to Barbadoes his two fastest seventy-fours. When therefore, on June 22nd, Bickerton rejoined him from Ferrol he had only seven of the line instead of nine. As there were in Cadiz two first-rates and two two-deckers, he felt he could not reduce his own force below four. Acting however in the spirit of the order, he divided his battle squadron with Bickerton, giving him three. It was a force, he explained to the Admiralty, inferior to that in Cartagena, but he trusted it was strong enough to prevent Salcedo's sailing till Bickerton could be joined by the *Excellent* from Naples. With this force Bickerton parted company, and two days later he appeared again off Gibraltar.[8]

It was high time. In his absence both Craig and Knight had been having many anxious hours. It was only the timely arrival of Collingwood, as we have seen, that saved the expedition from an attack in force by Salcedo, but even when he was scared back their troubles were by no means at an end. Across the bay they could see the Algeçiras gunboats continually increasing in numbers. Knight did his best with the small force at his command. Anchoring the convoy in close order, he covered it with the only two cruisers he had, a frigate and the *Beagle*, who had returned to her station, kept one or two gun-brigs and gunboats patrolling, and had guard-boats out at night. Campbell, the Portuguese Admiral, moreover, had come into the bay and had anchored his squadron in such a position that the Spaniards accused him of wilfully covering the transports from attack. He certainly kept Knight supplied with information to the best of his ability. By the time, however, the expedition had been thus exposed for a month things looked so threatening that it became imperative to make other dispositions. General Fox, the governor, had obtained information that an attack was intended in a few days, and that the gunboats at Algeçiras now numbered forty, besides many more at Cartagena. Together Fox and Craig laid the facts formally before Knight and a joint council was held. The Admiral suggested taking the whole convoy to sea, and offered to hoist his flag in the frigate for its protection, if the Generals would give him a detachment of troops to complete the companies of both his cruisers, and assist in arming some of the transports. They readily agreed, and the whole convoy was taken out of the bay to the eastward of the Rock, where it continued standing off and on across the Gut "in delicious weather."[9]

The device entirely succeeded. The transports were well out of reach of Algeçiras, and the appearance of Collingwood off Cadiz effectually deterred any movement on the part of the Cartagena squadron. So far from thinking of offence, Salcedo was busy with harbour defences, and the flotilla of gunboats of which Fox had heard was being hastily equipped for the protection of the port. Indeed the whole attention of the Andalusian authorities was fixed on making preparations against the attack which, since Craig had put to sea, he seemed about to deliver at some undetermined point.[10]

In this situation the convoy was found by Bickerton on his return, and on June 25th, without anchoring, he led it on with a fair wind up the Straits. Hugging the African coast, he detached the *Beagle* to report what Salcedo was doing. Off Cape Tenes, well to the eastward of Cartagena, the *Beagle* rejoined, reporting Salcedo at anchor. Thereupon Knight determined to send Craig on his way under an escort of three frigates, while he himself parted company to constitute a covering squadron for the army's passage by taking station before Cartagena.[11]

So in the face of all Napoleon's active and undefeated squadrons the passage of the expedition had been secured. The first step towards Pitt's enveloping attack had been taken, and as Craig passed quietly on his way to the westward all was in labour with Napoleon's counter-stroke. The concentration for the great invasion had begun.

CHAPTER XI

Operations In The West Indies

At home the last that had been heard of Nelson was as he approached Madeira, three days after he had parted company with Craig. The Admiralty had received a short note assuring them that if he had made a mistake and the Combined Squadron was not in the West Indies, he could be back again off Cadiz by the end of June before the enemy could know where he had gone, and that then he would proceed to England, leaving such a force behind him as the service required.[1] His faith in the safety of his move and the influence of an unlocated fleet was fully justified. We have seen how Napoleon believed he had not left European waters, and before the French headquarters were sufficiently assured of his departure to base any action on it, he appeared again at Gibraltar.

To Lord Camden, the Minister for War, who had asked him to give Craig his co-operation and advice, he had written a longer letter explaining the difficulties of the political situation. In his opinion — matured as it was by the practical experience of the last war — it would be a mistake for Craig to land in Sicily at once. Any such move would be the signal for a French advance on Naples. The King would certainly not consent to it. But the moment the French made a movement independently, our troops would be received with gratitude. In this advice Nelson was endorsing the Government's own view, nor had he anything to add except once more to urge the importance of securing Sardinia.[2]

Thus the last thought they had had from him, was for the safety of the station he was leaving behind. All that man could do, indeed all that was necessary, he had done. To speak of him as having abandoned the Mediterranean is to misconceive his careful attitude. Strategically his conscience was clear, and henceforth he could absorb himself freely in what was before him to the westward.

He was already at work. During the previous days, in view of a meeting with Villeneuve's superior fleet, he had been drawing up a tactical memorandum, which he ordered Captain Parker of the *Amazon* frigate to distribute to the fleet on May 15th.[3] The nature of this memorandum is quite uncertain. Clarke and McArthur believed it to be one they saw amongst Lord St. Vincent's papers, and Sir Harris Nicolas in his collection of Nelson's letters followed them. But the document was undated and there are insuperable difficulties in assigning it to this occasion. Internal evidence shows that when Nelson drafted the document he was contemplating an action against a fleet of eleven or twelve sail with a force about equal to it: but now he had before him the prospect of engaging a much larger squadron with inferior numbers. "I am going," he had written to Acton a few days before, "to the West Indies where the enemy have twenty-four sail of the line: my force is very very inferior. I only take ten with me and I only expect to be joined by six."[4] He meant, of course, Cochrane's squadron, and it was certainly the general expectation in the fleet

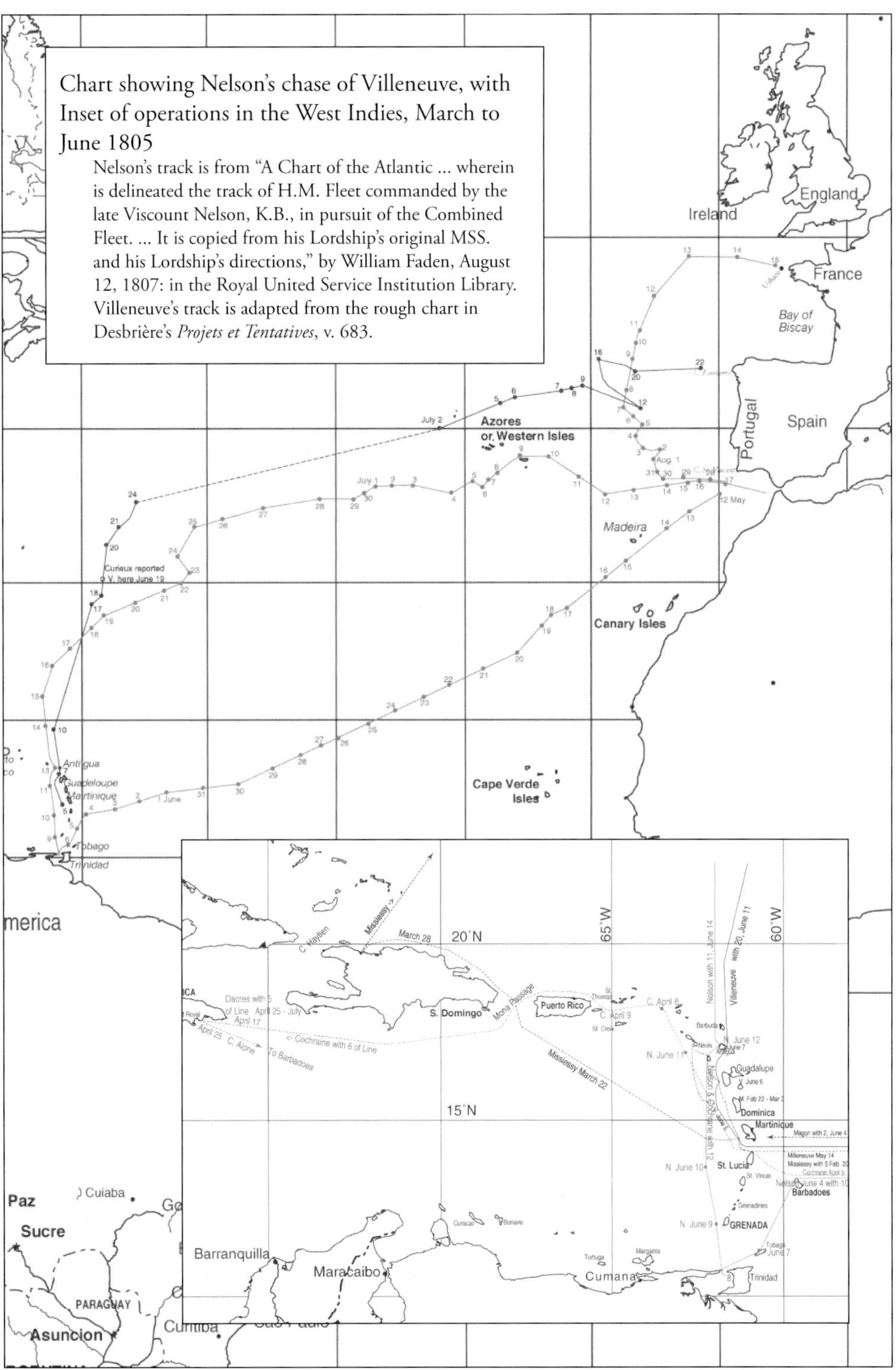

Chart showing Nelson's chase of Villeneuve, with Inset of operations in the West Indies, March to June 1805

Nelson's track is from "A Chart of the Atlantic ... wherein is delineated the track of H.M. Fleet commanded by the late Viscount Nelson, K.B., in pursuit of the Combined Fleet. ... It is copied from his Lordship's original MSS. and his Lordship's directions," by William Faden, August 12, 1807: in the Royal United Service Institution Library. Villeneuve's track is adapted from the rough chart in Desbrière's *Projets et Tentatives*, v. 683.

that these six vessels would be united to Nelson's flag when he reached the West Indies.[5] The loss of the memorandum of May 15th is greatly to be deplored; for few documents in Naval History could be of higher interest than one which contained Nelson's ideas of this time, on dealing with a superior enemy.

In order to ensure the co-operation of Cochrane's squadron, he had sent forward a frigate from Cape St. Vincent, but he was destined to be disappointed, owing to the difficult situation of affairs in the West Indies. Cochrane, in his pursuit of Missiessy, had reached Barbadoes on April 5th, little more than a month before Nelson had left the Straits. There he heard his enemy had just been reported in the neighbourhood of St. Domingo. In these circumstances his own inclination and the tenor of his instructions bade him continue his chase, if only for the safety of Jamaica. He scarcely waited to take over the formal command of the station from Commodore Hood: he did not even anchor, but leaving Hood in local command with one of his own ships, the *Spartiate*, to assist him in holding the station and supporting the local cruiser squadron, he held away with the rest — six in number — in hot pursuit and high hope of an encounter.

On April 9th he reached St. Thomas in the Virgins, where he ascertained Missiessy had already been to St. Domingo and landed his troops. He also received information that the French were expecting a second expedition, and that the combined force was to attack Jamaica. It was information too probable to ignore, and, little dreaming Missiessy was already well on his way back to Rochefort, he made up his mind he would be on the point of returning to Martinique to join the new comers from France for the grand attack. Here, then, was a fine chance of nipping the combination in the bud by intercepting Missiessy on his way. Doubling back, therefore, he passed along the south side of Puerto Rico and turned up into the Mona passage, between that island and St. Domingo. There he took station expecting every hour to see his adversary fall into his mouth. When, however, he did not appear, and all the information Cochrane could get pointed with increasing cogency to Jamaica as the point of danger, he felt there was nothing to do but to act on the instructions he had received from the Admiralty. They directed that if on his arrival he heard the Rochefort squadron had gone to St. Domingo, he was to reinforce the Jamaica station with six of the line. To Jamaica, therefore, he decided to sail with the whole squadron.[6] It was a resolution that demanded no little loyalty and self-sacrifice. For it meant depriving himself of almost the whole of his squadron. He had no intention of remaining there himself. His place was on the Leeward Islands station. Indeed he only stayed the few days necessary to hand over to Dacres five of his six vessels, for Dacres had nothing else of the line, and then on April 25th, keeping only his own flagship the *Northumberland* 80, he began the laborious task of working his way back to Barbadoes.

Such was the situation when on May 14th the Combined Squadron appeared at Martinique. Villeneuve was immediately assailed by the military authorities to attempt something against the British islands. But there were difficulties in the way. The orders with which he had sailed strictly enjoined he should go to Fort Royal and hold himself in readiness to join Ganteaume the very hour he should appear. How then could he entangle his fleet in combined operations? And apart from this difficulty he had still to face the menace of an unlocated enemy. A powerful squadron had been reported about St. Domingo and Puerto Rico. It was of course Cochrane's, but at Martinique they knew not what, nor where, nor how strong it was. Was it a squadron from England in chase of him, under the impression his objective was Jamaica? That was Villeneuve's first thought — it was impossible for him to tell. Meanwhile what could he attack with safety? Dominica and St. Lucia were the only islands within his reach, but he knew both were on their guard, and the recent example of Dominica showed they could not be reduced by a *coup de main*. Still, not being able to bring himself to spend the whole of his forty days waiting in inaction, he decided to send three frigates to cruise against the enemy's commerce, and endeavour to glean intelligence both from local craft and vessels arriving from Europe.

This done, he turned his attention to removing the disgrace of the Diamond Rock where Captain Maurice and his crew were still defiantly installed and active. Their last exploit — a favourite diversion — had been to entice one of Villeneuve's belated Spanish consorts close in to the rock by hoisting French colours and to salute her with a dose of their twenty-four pounders. It was beyond all endurance, and the day after the frigates left, Villeneuve sent against the rocky "sloop" a detachment of two of the line, three cruisers, and a dozen gunboats with a force of troops, under Captain Cosmao of the *Pluton* 74. It was not till the 31st that they were able to reach the landing-place. Seeing the overwhelming force opposed to him, Maurice abandoned the shore battery, and retired all his "crew" to his fastness aloft. The French at once effected a landing, but soon found themselves in a scrape. Maurice's position was absolutely inaccessible without scaling-ladders; the troops, who had been sea-sick for two days, were starving; and so heavy was the shower of stones and musketry that the defenders poured down that neither food nor water could be fetched from the squadron. Even the boat-guards could not remain at their post. Many were killed and wounded, and all had to take shelter in caves below the fastness. They were themselves, as it were, besieged, and had to watch three gunboats get adrift and break up on the rocks. Day after day the ships bombarded the garrison, but till scaling-ladders arrived nothing could be done. A party of five-and-twenty men tried with ropes, but they were all taken prisoners.

Maurice's gallant resistance was not without result. The day the attack opened there arrived at Martinique the *Didon*, which it will be remembered had sailed two days after Magon, charged with Napoleon's new orders of April 29th and a copy of the previous orders which Magon was bringing. Her news was that Ganteaume, though hourly expected to sail, was still in Brest, but that, as Nelson had gone to Egypt, Villeneuve himself was not likely to be molested. Villeneuve also learnt that Magon had sailed from Rochefort with two of the line and 800 more troops to swell his force, and enable him "to continue his attacks on the British colonies." This was the order which directed him to employ his energies in this way for thirty-five days after Magon arrived, and if at the expiration of that period Ganteaume had not appeared, he was to return to Ferrol, and not to the Canaries as was provided by his original orders. With twenty of the line and 12,000 men, which with the local forces and his own he would have at his disposal, Napoleon, as we have seen, thought it possible he might be able to expel the British entirely from the Leeward Islands and even from Trinidad. The orders, however, concluded with a proviso that these enterprises were to be kept "subordinate to the grand object of the essential operation which was to crown his Majesty's arms."

Villeneuve was aghast. The new orders assumed he had been engaged already in attacking the British islands. Apparently Napoleon had forgotten what orders he had given him. So far from having been told to operate against the British colonies, he had been strictly enjoined to do nothing but hold himself in readiness to sail with Ganteaume the moment he appeared. If only, he said in his reply, he had been told before he might have done something. But now it was too late. The English had been warned of his coming by the frigate which he knew Orde had sent out, and they were now on their guard everywhere. He had even been three days trying to take a paltry rock. Fifteen of his original forty days were already expired, and as for waiting thirty-five days after Magon's arrival, it was out of the question. His stores would not permit it. "Still," he wrote to his exasperating master, "as I see you condemn in advance the inaction to which my orders alone chained me . . . I will only say it has been to me insupportable. Be that as it may, as soon as the Diamond Rock is finished, we will start to attack Antigua or Barbuda."[7]

All this time the siege of the "sloop" had been proceeding, and it was not till June 3rd that any impression had been made. On that day the French, having procured the necessary scaling material, had succeeded in getting up the back of the Rock. Maurice saw himself faced with an assault, and by this time he had not a cartridge nor a drop of water left. He decided accordingly that further resistance was useless, and putting out a flag of truce, was allowed to march out of his fastness with the honours of war. The number of his effective men the French returns put at 107, and he had only lost two killed and one wounded. The French put their landing force at 260, but Maurice believed they had 1500 ashore from first to last, and that they lost thirty killed and forty wounded. They themselves acknowledge a loss of at least fifty. In any case it was a gallant and useful defence, and when Maurice was court-martialled for the loss of "His Majesty's late sloop Diamond Rock" he was honourably acquitted with a high expression of admiration.[8]

The day after the surrender the French detachment rejoined the flag, and as they did so Magon appeared. Villeneuve, resolved not to lose another hour, made immediate preparations to proceed northward against Antigua and Barbuda. And well it was he did so, for even as Magon joined him the batteries of Barbadoes were saluting the Mediterranean squadron.

Nelson had gained ten days on his chase, and believed he had gained more. He was on fire to be gone. The six of the line he had expected were not there, but Cochrane was. He had arrived only two days before, after his weary beat back from Jamaica, and the same evening he was joined by Laforey in the *Spartiate*, who since the receipt of Orde's warning and the Admiralty orders to cover Eyre Coote's arrival, had been cruising to windward on the look-out for the transports and convoys from home. Nelson therefore had now twelve of the line, and the enemy, so he believed, had only eighteen, a supposition which the local information confirmed. Disappointing as it was, a superiority of a third in no way restrained his ardour. His only doubt was where to find them.

Now it so happened that the day before word had come in from General Brereton, the Commander-in-chief at St. Lucia, that the enemy had been reported to him as having been seen passing Gros Islet bay at the north-west of the island on the night of the 28th, and his belief was that the movement indicated an attack on Barbadoes or Trinidad. A possible explanation of this unfortunate piece of intelligence is that at the Gros Islet signal station they had seen the cruiser squadron which Villeneuve detached that day, and in the dark the anxious watchers had taken it for a fleet. General Myers, commanding at Carlisle Bay, had, however, no suspicion of its inaccuracy, and immediately sent it off to Nelson by his military secretary. As the enemy had not appeared at Barbadoes it could only be assumed they had gone to Trinidad, and by this time they would have landed their army. Myers, therefore, suggested that he should be permitted to accompany the fleet with 2,000 men that he had available. It would mean a day's delay, but Nelson felt he could not say no. "I cannot refuse so handsome an offer," he wrote, "and with the blessing of God on a just cause I see no cause to doubt the annihilation of both the enemy's fleet and army."

He himself had expected to find the Combined Squadron to the northward, but the intelligence was precise, and he felt himself bound by it.[9] Brereton he had known well in the old Mediterranean days as an energetic and capable staff-officer in the Corsica operations, and felt he was a man to be trusted. On the morrow, therefore, with Myers and his troops hastily embarked, he sailed for Trinidad in high hopes of a decision.

In the interval of waiting he had issued a new order of battle — to include Cochrane's two ships — which is of considerable interest, for in it we can detect a foreshadowing of the order he used at Trafalgar, at least in two important points. In the first place, like the order of the famous memorandum, it was an "Order of Battle and of Sailing" in two divisions, modified from the one he had issued at the Gulf of Palmas in March. In the second place, it shows his heaviest ships not distributed in the usual manner, but massed at the head of his own division after the fashion which Rodney first introduced into the Signal Book from Bigot de Morogues, and which Nelson was the first to employ on the day of reckoning. No accompanying tactical memorandum is known to exist, nor is there any express intimation that he intended to fight in two separate lines, though the actual disposition of the ships was similar to the one used at Trafalgar and would have lent itself to that form of engaging.[10]

In this order, early on the 6th, he made for Tobago, which lay in the direct course to Trinidad. Captain Bettesworth in the *Curieux* brig, one of the station cruisers, had been sent ahead for intelligence. On the morrow off the island he met Nelson with an important report. The previous day an American had informed the Tobago authorities that he had been boarded off St. Vincent by one of the ships of the French fleet, and that it had proceeded south. This information was of course false, and probably intended to mislead, but unfortunately it was confirmed shortly afterwards by the sight of a private schooner making the agreed signal for the enemy's fleet at Trinidad. Surely never had Admiral worse luck than Nelson on this occasion. It was not intended as a signal to the fleet. It was the private arrangement of an enterprising Tobago merchant, who, anxious to know what the fleet was, had sent out his clerk to reconnoitre, and the signal he had arranged for reporting a British fleet happened to be the same Cochrane had established for the enemy at Trinidad — a serious lesson as to the dangers of amateur signalling in time of war. Its effect was of course to remove all Nelson's doubts. Signalling to prepare for action, he immediately hurried on. As he came in sight of Trinidad he was mistaken by the British military posts along the shore for the enemy, and according to rule they retired to concentrate on their main position, firing the blockhouses behind them. The flames in the dim morning light gave the final touch of certainty. The enemy had obviously landed, and Nelson pushed on through the Dragon's Mouth right into the Gulf of Paria, assured he had before him at Port of Spain another battle of the Nile.

As they opened the harbour and not a sign of an enemy was to be seen, they could scarcely believe their eyes, so certain and doubly corroborated had been the intelligence. What Nelson felt not a single letter reveals. His self-restraint is admirable; the best of him came out; he simply cast all intelligence to the winds and immediately turned back, resolved to act on his own judgment.

Early next morning, the 8th, as he was re-passing the Dragon's Mouth, he was met with a despatch from Captain Maurice telling him that Diamond Rock had fallen and that the Combined Squadron had not yet left Martinique. There was hope still. Maurice also informed him that he had been assured by his captors that the Ferrol squadron had recently joined. This Nelson was sure could not be true, for had it come Maurice himself must have seen it. "I have my doubts," he wrote to the Governor of Barbadoes, "respecting the certainty of the arrival of the Ferrol squadron . . . but, my lord, powerful as their force may be they shall not with impunity make any great attacks. Mine is compact; theirs must be unwieldy; and although a very pretty fiddle, I don't believe that either Gravina or Villeneuve know how to play upon it."[11]

No one knew better than he the deterrent power of a fleet actively in being; and away he held northward, intent to prove the truth of his theory. Next day he was off Grenada. Maurice's news that the enemy had not yet moved was confirmed, but shortly afterwards he was met by a cruiser from Dominica bringing word that on the evening of the 6th, three days before, the whole Combined Fleet had been sighted off the south end of Guadaloupe steering north. "Whether the enemy's object is to attack Antigua or St. Kitts," he wrote to the Admiralty, "or to return to Europe time will show," and under a press of sail he carried on, giving successive rendezvous at Montserrat and Antigua.

This time the information was true. It was early on the morning of June 5th, as Nelson was steering to the southward for Trinidad, that Villeneuve had moved north, "with the intention," as he wrote in his official report, "of making an attack on the Island of Barbuda."[12] Passing along the lea side of Dominica the French saw a British convoy and its escort under the guns of a protected anchorage, but they left it alone. Villeneuve was bent on reaching Guadaloupe to pick up another battalion, and this done he held on his way. The same night — that is, the 6th — when Nelson was nearing Tobago — he was steering to pass between Antigua and Montserrat.[13] "At ten o'clock in the morning," he proceeds, "after having doubled Antigua, we had word in the north-north-west of a convoy of fourteen sail under escort of a single schooner. I ordered a general chase, and by nightfall the whole convoy was taken except the escort ship."[14]

With the exception of the reduction of Diamond Rock, this capture was the only positive result of the operations from which Napoleon hoped so much. It was a convoy homeward-bound, which had assembled in the usual way at St. John's Road, Antigua, to await the coming of the other divisions from the southward with the regular escort. But the merchants, on hearing that the Rochefort ships had joined Villeneuve and that the Combined Fleet with 10,000 men was about to attack the island, had fallen into so unfortunate an alarm that they had memorialised the governor to demand immediate convoy from the local cruisers. On the governor's representations Captain Nourse, the senior officer at St. John's, had ordered Lieutenant-Commander William Carr of the *Netley* schooner to take them home.[15] The reward of their panic was to fling their ships into Villeneuve's lap. Carr, of course, could do nothing. The moment he sighted the advanced frigates of the enemy he signalled his merchantmen to make away and save themselves, while he kept the *Netley* lying-by to watch the enemy till they were within gunshot. Then as he ran, chased by two frigates, he had to watch the French fleet spread to pick up his dispersing convoy. By sunset, when he succeeded in dropping his pursuers, he had seen the whole of it captured.

He was now in as difficult a position as a young officer could well have to face. He had nothing left to escort home, but he had despatches for the Admiralty from Captain Nourse, his senior officer. On the other hand, he had located the enemy and knew their approximate force. What ought he to do? Should he carry on home with his despatches or return and report to the Admiral the vital information upon which he had stumbled. In his dilemma he took the extreme step of opening the despatches. He found in them nothing but Nourse's explanation of why he had ordered the *Netley* home. All doubt was then removed as to the direction in which his duty lay, and he promptly decided to return to find Nelson.[16]

At the same time Villeneuve had obtained equally important information. From his prisoners he learned that the British Mediterranean fleet had arrived at Barbadoes twelve or fourteen strong. It was what he had dreaded all along, and he had no more spirit in him. "This force," he wrote, "joined to that of Admiral Cochrane, which is about in these seas, would be enough to balance the combined forces, even if it were not superior, seeing the strength of the ships, of which several are three-deckers." In his eyes it made every enterprise against the enemy's possessions impossible. The utmost he could do would be to go back to Martinique and await the time fixed for his return to Europe, "in painful inaction," as he said, "disastrous to the health of his crews." Even that would take ten days and might expose him to a battle, and where could he refit afterwards? Even a victory, which he clearly did not expect, would render his return to Europe impossible. The truth was he found himself brought up against one of the vital defects of Napoleon's ill-considered plan. There it was inevitably staring Villeneuve in the face, and in his distress he consulted Gravina. The condition of the Spanish crews permitted of but one answer. Ganteaume or no Ganteaume, they must lose not a moment in returning to Europe. Hastily the prizes were committed to a frigate, the local troops crowded into four other cruisers to be returned to their garrisons, and on June 10th they held away with all speed for the Azores.

Was ever the weakness of surprise command more strongly exhibited? Was ever clearer proof of how the apprehension of counter-surprise by an active and unlocated force always neutralises its apparent possibilities? "We have been masters of the sea for three weeks," wrote one of Villeneuve's most observant officers, "with a landing force of 7,000 to 8,000 men and have not been able to attack a single island."[17] Yet Napoleon could still dream of conquering the world, by a few hours' command of the Channel.

The decision to which the vice of the Emperor's scheme drove the two entangled Admirals was none too prompt. On the 10th, as they were transhipping the troops,

Nelson was signalling Montserrat for his rendezvous. Next day he sent in there for intelligence, but they could give him none of any use — nothing indeed but a report from an American skipper that the Combined Fleet had left Guadaloupe with the intention, as it was supposed, of attacking Antigua. To Antigua therefore he pushed, but only to find, as he approached the island, no sign of the enemy. He was now faced with the necessity of making a decision at least as great and really more difficult than that he had come to off Cape St. Vincent a month before. On the morning of the 12th, as he waited for his cruiser to bring news from the shore, he was again in the same uncertainty as that which had tormented him at Gibraltar. From "under Antigua" he wrote to the Admiralty: "If I hear nothing of the enemy at Antigua I shall stand for Prince Rupert's Bay [that is, back to Dominica] and form my judgment; but, I feel, having saved these colonies and two hundred and upwards of sugar-loaded ships, that I must be satisfied they have bent their course for Europe before I push after them." Here was the same inspiration divining his enemy's intention and the same restrained determination not to act on inspiration alone. The ink was not dry before the information he awaited was obtained. Word came in that the French troops which had been taken from Guadaloupe had come back and disembarked. Then he was practically sure. "Therefore," he wrote, "I am pushing for the anchorage of St. John's [Antigua] to land the troops and hope to sail in the morning after them for the Straits' mouth."

Thus before he had Carr's intelligence he had practically made up his mind, and Bettesworth, in the *Curieux*, was sent off with his despatches to inform the Admiralty that Villeneuve was on his way back and that he was after him. In the evening he anchored at St. John's and proceeded to disembark his troops. By morn on the morrow they were all ashore, and the fleet got under way. Scarcely had it done so when the *Netley* came in to remove all doubt from his mind and report the enemy far stronger than he had thought. Before dark she had counted no less than thirty-two sail.[18] Carr's report of the enemy's force in no way altered Nelson's intention to get at them if he could. It rather raised his hopes. Instead of thirty days, he was now only four or five behind Villeneuve, and there was every prospect of a meeting. True, he thought it probable the Spaniards would be detached to Havana, but the possibility of their remaining with Villeneuve was faced and did nothing to check the chase. He would not even retain Cochrane, who was ordered to return to his station. Nelson was content to keep the *Spartiate*, and so had eleven of the line with his flag.

With this slender force he was ready to fight, but in certain conditions only. As before, when he believed his strategy had forced Villeneuve from the Mediterranean, his object was partly gained already. He had forced the enemy from the West Indies, and he could now weigh risks more calmly. "Do not imagine," he is reported to have said to his assembled captains, "that I am one of those hotbrained people who fight at immense disadvantage without an adequate object. My object is partly gained. If we meet them we shall find them not less than eighteen, I rather think, twenty sail of the line, and therefore do not be surprised if I should not fall upon them immediately. We won't part without a battle. I think they will be glad to let me alone, if I will let them alone, which I will do till we approach the shores of Europe or they give me an advantage too tempting to be resisted."[19]

With these ideas in his mind he disappeared once more into the Atlantic, leaving Cochrane in no easy frame of mind. So skilfully had the French directed attention to Jamaica that he could not share Nelson's view. It will have been noticed that throughout all these operations the reinforced squadron at Jamaica had made no move. They had been waiting on the defensive at Port Royal ready to do their best against the expected attack till reinforcements arrived. So far, it may be said, they had been enticed away, but in fact they were not off the board. As we have seen, it was their presence in the West Indian seas that convinced Villeneuve he could do nothing. But for Cochrane the menace still existed. Ten days after Nelson had left, he was back at Barbadoes writing anxiously to the Admiralty that he was sure Jamaica was the objective. He did not know, curiously enough, where Nelson had gone, but from what he had said in conversation, Cochrane was afraid he thought Villeneuve had gone back to the Mediterranean.[20] He was naturally anxious. He was alone on the station, for Hood had gone home with a convoy. It was not till three weeks later that the *Ramilies* and *Illustrious*, which Collingwood had sent to reinforce Nelson, appeared in Carlisle Bay, to relieve his mind. Yet no sooner had they arrived than he received a report of the Combined Fleet having been seen steering a course which pointed to its intended junction with the Brest and Ferrol squadrons. If Nelson, as he believed, had gone to the Straits, the crisis would be acute. In a moment all thought of his own comfort was cast aside. With the usual insight into the mind of the Admiralty he decided to send both the ships back at once with two convoys that were due to sail. "Every line of battle ship that can be spared," he wrote to the Admiralty, "from hence may be wanted in the Channel," and almost as he penned the words an identical order was being drawn up at the Admiralty.[21]

It was a belief of the old Spaniards that Drake had a magic mirror in which he could see all the movements of his enemies and count their numbers. In a sense it was true, and in that sense he had handed it on to his successors. That mirror was the tradition he had founded, and they had polished it by rich experience till it became a living instinct for naval war to which every man could turn for guidance. Cochrane, one of the least of Drake's heirs, could see in it plainly the stress and strain that was prevailing in home waters, and it told him the crisis of the campaign had come, as indeed it had.

CHAPTER XII

How Lord Barham Met The Crisis

Towards the end of May Cornwallis had reported himself fit for duty, but owing to the dislocation caused by Villeneuve's escape and Missiessy's return the Admiralty decided it was better to postpone making any change in the main command. By the end of June, however, when the situation had been restored, he received orders to relieve Lord Gardner, who was to return to his old post at Cork and resume the management of the cruisers on the Irish station.

The centre of disturbance had passed away westward. No one as yet could tell it was moving back again, and in the home area there was calm. As the hour approached for which Napoleon had worked so long and elaborately, he was more than ever bent on lulling his enemy into security, or at least diverting British attention from his focal point, He was still in Italy employing the last days of his sojourn in developing the military and naval resources of his new kingdom, and in particular at Genoa, whose ancient status he intended to revive with a naval yard and arsenal.

His continued absence so far from Boulogne would serve well, he believed, to deepen the impression he wished to create, and seeing what was in his mind he could not approve of Ganteaume's desire to make continual sorties. Such demonstrations could only serve to keep the enemy on the alert. He even doubted the wisdom of keeping the whole fleet out in the Bertheaume anchorage and wished to have some of the ships sent back into port. "My intention," he wrote to Decrès, "would be to lull the English to sleep as much as possible about the Brest squadron, in a natural manner, however (*sans affectation*), and direct all their attention on the Texel. Write in this sense to Marmont. . . . . I myself will cause a picket of my guard to march on Utrecht, and on my arrival in Paris, I shall announce my departure for that place. That will make them afraid that Villeneuve is going there and will induce them to weaken before Brest, which is the great point." He assured Decrès the trick would serve. "There's nothing," he said, "so short-sighted as the English Government. It is a government absorbed in party politics (*chicanes intérieures*), which turns its attention wherever there is a noise."[1]

It was an error not confined to Napoleon or to his age — to assume that the energy and spirit with which British politicians play the Parliamentary game denote incapacity for war and real statesmanship, or at least neglect and blindness in large imperial issues. Still it is difficult to believe that so great a soldier, who was not wont to underrate his enemies, could really have expected by means so trivial to gull the old hands against whom he was playing into breaking their hold on the long-tried position. Yet he himself sent Marmont elaborate orders on the subject. "The English," he wrote, "have at Yarmouth no more than three vessels of a higher rate than sixty-fours. I want to draw more to that point to further my operations." Marmont himself is to keep away from the Texel, but in the second week of July he is to embark a division, move the squadron as far out in the roads as safety will permit, and arrange a *mise en scène* which will suggest a distant expedition. Then on July 20th he is suddenly to put all his army in motion, get it afloat in the course of the week and embark in person with pilots for the voyage to Ireland north-about. The Dutch Admiral and his officers are not to be told the real meaning of the movement. "It will look," he says, "as if you were only waiting for a gale to drive off the English blockading squadron and let you out, which will necessarily compel the English to keep there a squadron of at least ten of the line and give them all kinds of uneasiness." Finally, in view probably of one of the many strokes he was contemplating for the Rochefort squadron, Marmont was warned not to think his embarkation was a mere parade. It was quite possible it might become a real operation.[2]

The disturbing power of an army by the sea with transports and escort alongside — a specially English device — is often questioned. Here at least is evidence of Napoleon's faith in it — a faith, it must be said, that was not a little justified by the confusing effect which his garrisons in the Neapolitan ports had had upon Nelson's judgment; and in this case, as we shall see, it did have a certain effect.

Though the idea of combining the Rochefort squadron with Marmont's corps attracted Napoleon's imagination for a while, he never regarded it very seriously. What he really hoped to get out of the isolated squadron for the effect he wanted was a raid as far possibly as the mouth of the Baltic, which would threaten British commerce and a descent in Ireland. The main trouble was to find a commander fit to conduct so daring and hazardous an enterprise. With Missiessy Napoleon was disgusted, and particularly for the lack of energy and initiative he had displayed in the West Indies. "I choked with indignation," he told Decrès, "when I read he had not taken the Diamond;" and again, "That Rock will be an eternal monument of shame to this expedition." He had counted on the squadron being out again within a week of its arrival, but in place of the news he expected he received lamentations from the old Admiral that he was ill, that he doubted if he was fit for sea again, and that he wanted to go to Paris to see his wife. Unable to think of any one to replace him, Napoleon after his manner fell to coaxing and trying to appeal to his ambition. Decrès was to tell him he was the link on which the great combination depended and that he could not go to Paris. "However," he wrote, "I think Madame Missiessy is a reasonable woman with a little ambition. Get her to go to Rochefort. It is only right that Admiral Missiessy should see his wife. Let her make him understand he must finish the campaign."[3] But all was useless, and Missiessy finally gave up the command on the ground of ill-health.

Napoleon's first idea was to replace him by Rosily, an old officer whose reputation rested on his cruiser work in years gone by under Suffren. But he was tired of old Admirals and resolved to inaugurate a change. "There is no good blinking the fact," he wrote to Decrès before Missiessy s final resignation, "henceforth I must choose my Admirals from young officers of thirty-two years of age, and I have enough cruiser captains with ten years' active service to select six to whom I may entrust commands. . . . Meanwhile make the Rochefort squadron sail with Missiessy or some one else."[4]

The man Decrès chose was Allemand, Captain of the *Magnanime*, one of Missiessy's ships of the line. He was reported to have shown high ability and spirit during the expedition and, as events were to prove, no selection could have been better. His influence was felt immediately. By the end of the month there was so much activity in the port that Graves was regretting the two of the line that had been removed from him on his first optimistic reports. The squadron was accordingly brought up again to five of the line and Graves himself was relieved by Admiral Stirling, in the *Glory* 98 — an intrepid officer, who had been serving as Navy Commissioner at Jamaica and had just come home on promotion to fly his flag for the first time.

At Ferrol it was equally difficult to conceal the imminence of the crisis. Calder's intelligence system was perfect. An Englishman, who had been both British and American consul before the war, had remained on in the latter capacity and was furnishing the Admiral with regular information. Napoleon had just sent down orders that Gourdon and his Spanish colleague, Admiral de Grandallana, should move the thirteen of the line, which they now had complete for service, out to Coruña, so as to be ready to put to sea the moment Villeneuve and Gravina appeared. Before Gourdon could acknowledge the order and point out its impossibility owing to the lack of anchorage room at Coruña, it was in Calder's hands. The consul had sent it out to him by an English-American skipper who sailed on July 3rd. Calder had just been reinforced with the two seventy-fours which Graves had reported he could spare from before Rochefort, but he had had to send home his largest three-decker, the *Royal Sovereign*, to refit. This left him with but nine sail of the line, only two of which were three-deckers. He did not think such a squadron sufficient for the blockade, but assured his chief "that everything in his power should be done for his majesty's service with such a force as their lordships should deem adequate to the critical service he was employed upon."[5]

Further south Collingwood was also on the alert, keeping a close watch on Cadiz with three of his battle squadron, and holding the Straits with the fourth off Cape Spartel and a frigate at Gibraltar. Inside the Mediterranean Bickerton with his battle squadron was in a position off Cartagena to cover the passage of Craig's expedition while his cruisers formed its escort and secured it against an attack from the Toulon frigates. These vessels as well as others in Genoa were also being watched by the cruiser squadron which Nelson had committed to Captain Capel, and he had been blockading one of them in Villefrance, the port of Nice. The disposition Capel had adopted was principally directed to preventing any expedition passing to Sardinia. The *Excellent* was still at Naples — a comfortable pledge of British policy and a symbol of the power that was at Elliot's back, and Bickerton, realising her political importance, had refrained from calling her to his flag. At Malta, Sir Alexander Ball had a fifty-gun ship and four or five cruisers for the protection of the Levant trade. There was also a frigate at Constantinople, which had gone thither with our Minister, and at Trieste was a brig for commerce protection. The military command of the Adriatic was further secured by a Russian squadron at Corfu, which by the end of July amounted to four of the line and ten cruisers.[6]

Such, then, was the actual naval situation at the end of June. It remains to consider how Napoleon appreciated it, and we have it all in an elaborate memorandum he prepared for Decrès. He saw eighteen of the line before Brest, six before Rochefort, eight before

Ferrol, and not more than four in the Mediterranean. Of Nelson and Collingwood he knew nothing. The only information he had was a false report that they had met off Cape St. Vincent on May 15th, and had then disappeared. Possibly they had gone together to the West Indies, but he did not think this likely. He persuaded himself that while Nelson proceeded there alone to join Cochrane, Collingwood had been sent to the East Indies. If this were true. Nelson would lose several days at Barbadoes making his junction with Cochrane and filling up his ships, and in the interval Villeneuve, having heard of his arrival, would have time to get clear away. The only result, then, of Nelson's chase would be that Villeneuve would not wait his allotted time and the crisis would come a little sooner than was intended. He would meet the situation by making an earlier return to Boulogne. "I shall hasten my coming," he says, "by some days, because I think Nelson's arrival in America may push Villeneuve to leave for Ferrol."

Still he could not conceal from himself that Villeneuve might be caught and blockaded in Fort de France, and in his heart he doubted whether the great combination could ever come off. His memorandum concluded with yet another change of plan, in which ultimate reliance is placed on the Brest squadron alone. Two lines of operation on which it might act were submitted for Decrès' opinion. If Ganteaume saw a chance of getting out, should he shape his course as though he were going to attack Ireland, but instead of doing so, plunge into the Channel and come before Boulogne with his own squadron alone; or should he first go down and pick up the Ferrol squadron and enter the Channel with thirty-three of the line? "It is an involved game (*jeu mêlé*) no doubt," he wrote, as indeed it was, "but one that will always be something to fall back upon, if Villeneuve gets blockaded. . . . Write of it all the same to Ganteaume as a general theme to find out what he thinks."[7] What Ganteaume did think, as we shall see presently in his crushing reply, was that it ignored the fundamental consideration on which the British system of defence was securely based.

Two days after Napoleon had penned this final appreciation, the outlook of the British Admiralty was cleared at last by certain information that Villeneuve had been to the West Indies. He had reached Martinique, it was said, on May 13th with sixteen of the line. The news was brought to Liverpool by a "running ship" — one of those adventurous merchantmen who preferred the enjoyment of a hungry market to the unprofitable security of a convoy. Sent up to Pitt by the Mayor, it was in his hands by July 1st. The same day he forwarded it to the Admiralty with an intimation that he had decided to reissue Sir Eyre Coote's orders for the West Indies. All this time the expedition had been waiting at Cork for instructions. Coote was now directed to embark his troops immediately and the Board was required to provide him with convoy.[8]

This resolution of the Cabinet by no means indicates that Napoleon had succeeded in diverting Barham's attention to the West Indies. It was merely a precaution; for the same day the news was received the Admiralty sent off to Collingwood and Calder a warning to be on their guard against Villeneuve's sudden return.[9] Barham, in the ripeness of his rich experience, evidently had as little doubt as Napoleon as to what would be the effect of Nelson's breaking in upon the Caribbean Sea. Indeed every British Admiral in European waters was expecting Villeneuve's reappearance somewhere. At this very time Collingwood was writing: "I think it not impossible I shall have all these fellows coming from the West Indies again before the hurricane months, unless they sail from there directly for Ireland, which I have always had an idea was their plan; for this Bonaparte has as many tricks as a monkey. I believe their object in the West Indies to be less conquest than to draw our forces from home. The Rochefort squadron seems to have had nothing else in view."[10] And these were the men that Napoleon thought he had deceived.

The only uncertain point was the home port for which Villeneuve would make. Should it be Cadiz or any point in the Mediterranean there was cause for considerable anxiety. How weak was the position at the mouth of the Straits, Barham did not know till July 7th. On that day a despatch from Collingwood reached the Admiralty informing them that on second thoughts he had obeyed their order to send two of the line to Nelson.[11] As he had been told to divide his squadron with Bickerton, Barham correctly inferred from this that he would have only four of the line with his flag, and the old First Lord sat down in the solitude of his room to grapple with the situation. The result was one of those priceless strategical minutes in which the old British lore lies embalmed and almost forgotten.[12]

It begins with an exact statement of the actual disposition of the force available. "Now off Brest, 22; off Rochefort, 5; off Ferrol, including 2 from Rochefort, 12;" and two others immediately available, besides 5 in reserve to replace ships coming in to refit. This, he says, meant from 38 to 40 of the line "manned and stored," disposable for Brest, Rochefort, and Ferrol, that is, for the "Western Squadron." What he proposed was to detach immediately from Cornwallis ten of the line to reinforce Collingwood off Cadiz. "Because," he explains, "I take it for granted that only four remain there. That makes a strong force at the very spot where they may be expected."

He was at one, therefore, with Nelson as to Villeneuve's most probable destination. To this extent Napoleon had led them both astray, but not for a moment did Barham neglect the alternative possibility that the Combined Squadron might return to a French port in the Bay. Indeed his minute is mainly devoted to providing for this eventuality. His plan for dealing with it is based on striking Villeneuve before he can get within distance of his destination whatever it might be, or in touch with any of the three blockaded squadrons in Brest, Rochefort, or Ferrol. It was obvious that one or more of the blockading squadrons must be used for the counter-stroke. The problem, therefore, was how to deliver the blow at a sufficient distance to seaward and at the same time prevent any of the blockaded squadrons from moving. The solution was worthy of his genius.

He would use the Ferrol and Brest squadrons for his striking force, each on its own line, but in such a way as not to raise either blockade. "Let the Ferrol squadron," he wrote, "get three additional frigates and be ordered to stretch north-northwest of Ferrol by means of frigates and show themselves off Ferrol itself occasionally and at such undetermined periods as to disguise the real object of their cruise." As for Rochefort, it is to be kept strictly blockaded; but he adds, "Let the fleet off Brest, reduced for the moment to 12 sail, but reinforced by the *Defence*, *Goliath*, and *Zealous* to 15, be ordered to stretch out to the south-south-west in a direct line for Cape Finisterre, and by means of frigates keep up communication with the Ferrol squadron."

The plan was certainly daring, and particularly in his handling of the Brest squadron. At first sight it seems to entail a serious loosening of the defensive basis of the campaign. It appeared to involve, moreover, not only the possibility of opening the Channel, but also of the Ferrol squadron escaping to break the Rochefort blockade.

Barham was not blind to this aspect of his disposition, but he calculated, and as it was to prove afterwards, calculated rightly, the risk had no real existence. "Before these plans," he argues, "were developed to the enemy the cause for their existence would have ceased; that is, the Combined Fleet would have returned for Europe, or the uncertainty with regard to their motions would be at an end." At any rate the moral effect of success would be so great as to justify whatever risk was entailed. "The interception of the fleet in question," he concludes, "on its return to Europe would be a greater object than any I know. It would damp all future expeditions and would show to Europe that it might be advisable to relax in the blockading system occasionally for the express purpose of putting them in our hands at a convenient opportunity." In other words, the moral effect would be to relieve materially the almost unendurable strain of the great blockade; for whenever any part of it was temporarily relaxed the enemy would suspect a trap was being laid for him.

Such was the masterly plan with which Barham intended to meet the difficult and uncertain situation. Forty-eight hours proved the soundness of his calculations. Before the enemy could know what the new disposition meant, he rightly judged the fog would be cleared and it would not be wanted. Before his draft could even be reduced to the form of orders the light came. For at eleven o'clock at night on July 8th Captain Bettesworth of the *Curieux*, direct from Nelson, rattled up to the door of the Admiralty.

On the 7th, as Barham was quietly working out his plans, the *Curieux* was anchoring at Plymouth. She had made the passage from Antigua in twenty-four days. In hot haste Bettesworth had posted to London, but only to find, so the story goes, that Lord Barham had gone to bed and that no one dared to rouse him. At an early hour the old man awoke and fell into a fury when he knew what had been awaiting him. For it was not only Nelson's despatches Bettesworth had to deliver, but having taken a more northerly course than the Admiral, who was making for the Straits, he had sighted Villeneuve and determined his course. It was on June 19th, as high as latitude 33° 12′ and in longitude 58° — that is, some 900 miles north-northeast of Antigua — that he had seen him, and the Combined Fleet was still standing to the northward. Till there could be no doubt Bettesworth had shadowed them, and then made all sail home with his all-important news. That Villeneuve had stood so far to the northward could only mean he was making for the Bay, and not, as both Barham and Nelson expected, for the Straits. What was to be done? In half-an-hour Barham had decided.

The historian James, who was provided with official information on the incident by the First Lord's secretary, tells us that without waiting to dress and growling that seven or eight hours had been lost, he wrote out the necessary orders and sent them off. The story has been doubted, but it has certainly some foundation. Amongst his papers there still exists a rapid minute which he dashed off to meet the situation. It is written at speed with several interlineations on a small scrap of paper in eloquent contrast to the long memorandum, which he had just completed.

Cadiz was no longer the centre of anxiety, and with extraordinary decision and directness for a man of eighty years he recasts in half-a-dozen lines his previous scheme. Calder was clearly in the most immediate danger and also in the best position for striking Villeneuve before he could get a landfall. But to reinforce him from Cornwallis, as he had intended, was not without danger. To Cornwallis might almost equally well fall the chance of first contact, and if he were weakened it was now doubtful whether ships detached from him to Ferrol could be replaced from his reserve in time.

The problem was thorny, and it is clear that for a while Barham was in two minds about it. As he first drafted the minute it ran: "My idea is to send the intelligence immediately to Admiral Cornwallis, who may be directed to strengthen Sir Robert Calder's squadron with as many ships as will make them up to 15." This was in accordance with the memorandum of the previous day, which provided that "Rochefort is to be kept strictly blockaded." But on second thoughts it must have occurred to him that the risk of weakening the Ushant position was too great — that in fact he was trying for something beyond the resources that were immediately available. The only sound solution was to concentrate on the two most vital points. For this the Rochefort blockade must be sacrificed, and Stirling be ordered to join Calder.

Accordingly before completing the minute he amended it in this sense, and in its final form it ran as follows — the italicised passages being those which he inserted: "My idea is to send the intelligence immediately to Admiral Cornwallis who may be directed to strengthen Sir Robert Calder's squadron with *the Rochefort squadron and* as many ships *of his own* as will make them up to 15, *to cruise off Cape Finisterre from,* 10 *to* 50 *leagues to the west.* To stand to the southward and westward with his own ships, at the same distance for 10 days. Cadiz to be left to Lord Nelson. 9th July."[13]

On the minute as thus amended the famous orders of July 9th were framed. No strategical decision has received more unanimous applause, yet now that we know Barham hesitated, it is open to any one to speculate as to which was the better alternative. As things turned out the first disposition would have met the case amply. It would have saved a deal of trouble from the Rochefort squadron and that trouble might well have been much worse than it was, for in the weeks before Trafalgar it seriously endangered Nelson's communications, and not only was it an abiding menace to our trade, but it came near to losing us the Cape of Good Hope. Yet such judgments *ex post facto* must be made with caution. It must be remembered that to devote a squadron to blockading Rochefort was to play Napoleon's game. It was what he expected and desired, and if Barham in his tried wisdom refused to permit any consideration to loosen his grip on the Ushant position few will be found to assert he was not right. "When in doubt make sure of the mouth of the Channel," was a maxim too long sanctified by its fruits to be lightly transgressed.

At all events it was approved at the time by his colleagues. It went forward as amended, and upon it were framed the following orders: "Admiral Cornwallis — Intelligence being received by H.M. Brig *Curieux* that the combined French and Spanish squadrons, which passed Antigua on the 8th ultimo, had been seen by that vessel in latitude 33° 12′N., long. 58° W., steering at first N. by E. but afterwards altering their course to N.N.W.; and there being grounds to suppose that it is their intention to make some port in France or Spain; you are hereby required and directed to strengthen the squadron off Ferrol under the orders of Vice-Admiral Sir Robert Calder with the ships off Rochefort under Rear-Admiral Stirling, and to instruct the Vice-Admiral to proceed without loss of time off Cape Finisterre, from whence he is to cruise for the enemy to the distance of 30 to 40 leagues to the westward for the space of six or eight days. You are further required and directed to stretch with the fleet under your immediate command about the same distance to the south-westward and for the same space of time; at the expiration of which the several squadrons are to return to their respective stations. — (Signed) Barham, J. Gambier, Garlies."[14]

It was all done in about three hours. By nine o'clock in the morning the Admiralty messenger was away, and as he thundered down the Portsmouth road Napoleon was in the act of leaving Turin for Boulogne "to change the destinies of the world."

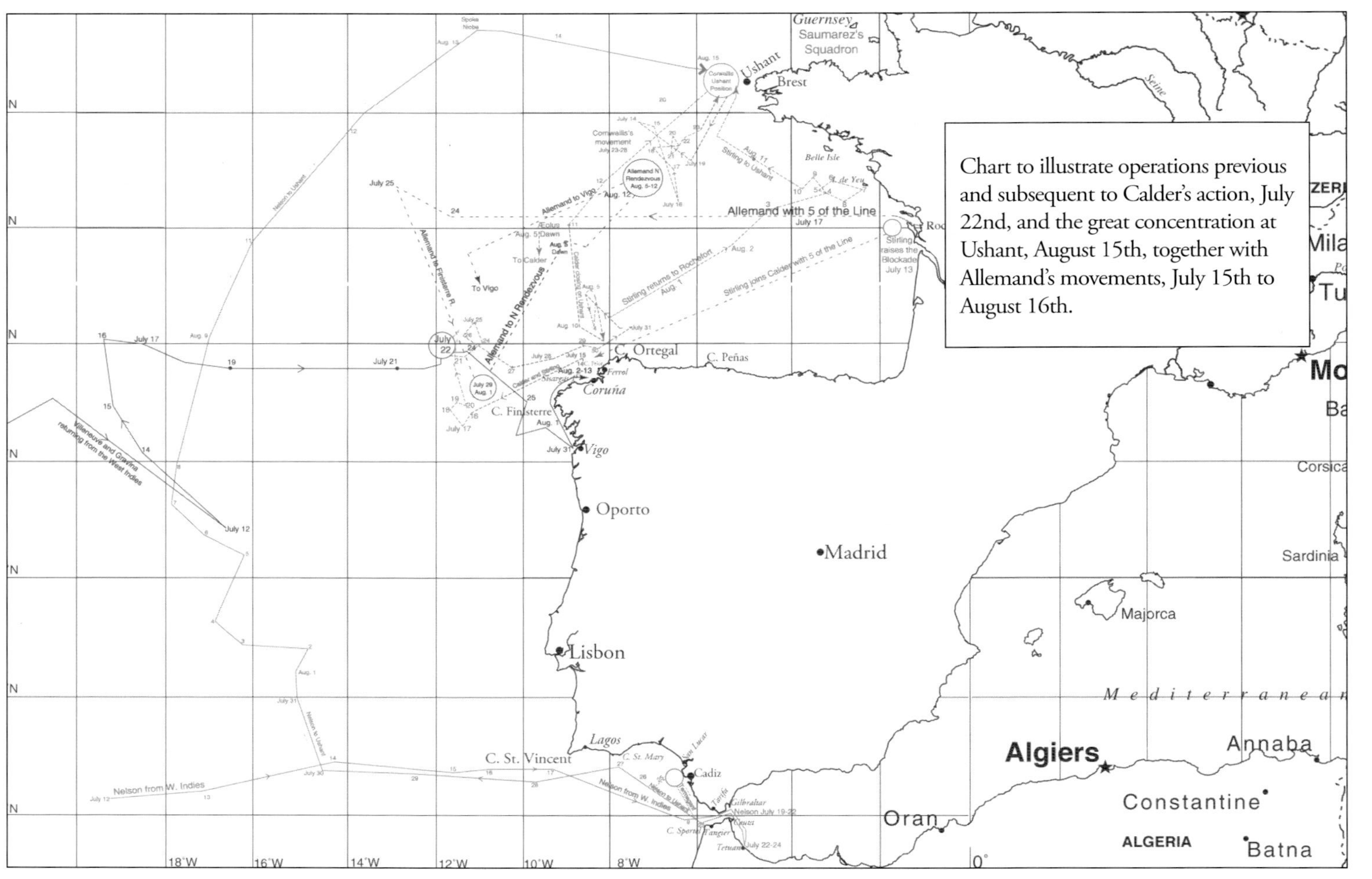

Chart to illustrate operations previous and subsequent to Calder's action, July 22nd, and the great concentration at Ushant, August 15th, together with Allemand's movements, July 15th to August 16th.

CHAPTER XIII

Cornwallis Opens Brest

Cornwallis joined the fleet off Brest in the *Ville de Paris* 110[1] on July 7th, the same day that the *Curieux* reached Plymouth, and after Gardner took his leave he found nineteen of the line with his flag. On the 9th the *Terrible* 74, on her way home from Ferrol to refit, gave him the information, which Calder had obtained from the American Consul, that the enemy were under orders to move to Coruña to be ready for Villeneuve. Scarcely had he received this intimation, which told him that the hour of action was at hand, when a despatch vessel arrived from the Port Admiral at Plymouth with Bettesworth's news that Villeneuve was making for the Bay. Cornwallis immediately sent it on to Stirling and Calder, with a warning to be on their guard against being surprised or caught embayed. At the same time he was joined by Sir Richard Strachan in the *Caesar* 80, whom he placed in command of an inshore squadron of five of the line. But no sooner was this disposition made than Barham's orders arrived to upset it. By the evening of the 12th the necessary directions were on their way to Stirling and Calder, and Cornwallis, having left a cruiser squadron of six sail to watch Brest, was moving out and away to the south-westward in pursuance of Barham's plan of operations.

With his flag he had now a splendid battle squadron of twenty sail, which, including as it did no less than seven three-deckers and three 80-gun ships, was greatly superior to that of Villeneuve and Gravina. His instructions, it will be remembered, as finally drafted were "to stand to the south-westward 30 to 40 leagues for 10 days," and he interpreted them with the freedom that was obviously intended. At first he stretched about south-south-west, "in the direct line for Finisterre," as Barham's original orders had provided. This course he held for about 100 miles and then turned up to the north-westward, crossing the natural approaches to Brest until he reached a rendezvous he had given from 70 to 80 miles south-west of Ushant, and there he remained till the evening of the 15th. So far not a sign of the enemy had been found, and Cornwallis seems to have conceived a strong impression that they were not making for Brest at all. No letter exists to enable us to see into his mind. All we know is that, leaving a cruiser on the rendezvous, he now stretched away south down to the latitude of Rochefort.

Of all the moves in the campaign none will seem quite so daring as this. It will be observed that it went somewhat beyond the orders which Barham had given him; to stretch 30 to 40 leagues south-west of Ushant. Cornwallis clearly had his own view of the most likely ground to secure his chief's objects, and he saw it approximately at a point where the latitude of Rochefort intersected the direct line between Ferrol and Ushant. In this position he might hope to intercept Villeneuve on two of his three possible courses. It was equally good whether the enemy made Ferrol and then came on to Brest, or was making for Rochefort direct and running down its latitude in the usual way. But to all appearance it left the direct line to Brest dangerously open at the critical moment. Still, that Villeneuve would take the direct line and not seek to avoid an action by a more devious course was improbable, and in any case the approaches to that port were well covered by the squadron cruisers. What, however, seems the most serious risk of all was that the move left Ganteaume free to come out and reach the Channel. The danger looks all the more grave since, as we know, the last word which Ganteaume had had from Napoleon was a suggestion that he should attempt this very stroke the moment he saw a chance. Imagine, then, the excitement which Cornwallis's withdrawal caused at Paris when it was reported, quickly followed as it was by news of the disappearance of the squadron before Rochefort.

On July 10th, the very day that Cornwallis received the new disposition, Napoleon reached Fontainebleau. He had come in three days and a half from Turin; but for his eagerness it had not been nearly fast enough, and he was scolding at the state of the roads and grumbling that the Empress had insisted on stopping everywhere for her meals. Once at work again, plans poured out from him more feverishly than ever. The first was one for elaborating his feint from Holland by a sham expedition, which Marmont was to prepare at Helvoetsluys.[2] Next were produced a long set of instructions destined to meet Villeneuve off Ferrol. Once more it was impressed upon him that his object was to be master of the Straits of Dover, if it were only for four or five days. Wide discretion was given him in the means he might adopt. He might join both the Brest and Rochefort squadrons, or either of them, as he saw fit; and, if only the latter, he might go north-about and join the Texel squadron. If as the result of having to fight an action he found the object was beyond his power to attain, he was to content himself with releasing the Ferrol squadron and taking it down to Cadiz, but on no account was he to enter Ferrol. Clearly Napoleon was contemplating failure with an eye behind him on action in the Mediterranean, and Decrès' draft of the instructions emphasises the apprehension. "His Majesty," he wrote to Villeneuve, "desires that the fleet under your command shall carry through the great project of the invasion of England, conceived so long since by his genius, but so much time has gone by since the issue of your original orders, so many things may have happened, that in his wisdom the Emperor considers he should not give you an absolute order to that effect in spite of his persistence in this great design, but rather rely on your sagacity and boldness."[3]

Finally Allemand's orders were completely changed. In all probability the appearance of Villeneuve off the coast of Spain would cause the raising of the Rochefort blockade. Instead, however, of going out according to his previous instructions in order to make diversions on the coast of Ireland and in the Narrow Seas, he was to wait for the word from Gourdon and then go straight to Ferrol. But it was all too late. The day the order was penned Stirling moved away, and on the morrow Allemand, seeing the coast clear, put to sea — under his old instructions. In pursuance of them he pushed out due west straight for the point which Cornwallis had reached.

Meanwhile Napoleon had received another blow, which may well have been the cause of the doubtful tone in his order to Villeneuve. Ganteaume had sent him his answer to the theme he had propounded. If the Brest squadron got to sea should it rush the

Channel, or should it go first to pick up the Ferrol squadron? Ganteaume knew too much of his profession to have the slightest doubt and too much character not to state it. "If," he wrote, "the fleet, in leaving Brest, was fortunate enough to elude the vigilance of the blockading squadron, there exists no doubt that it ought to make for Ferrol in preference to Rochefort. . . . But if, in accordance with the first part of the question in your despatch, we venture into the Channel with no more than twenty-two vessels which compose our fleet, it would not be long before we were observed, or before the vessels we had eluded would get contact. To these they would not have failed to join the whole of the force at their disposal on the coasts and in the ports of England, and then it seems to me the chances would be against us. The Channel is too narrow a sea to allow of being there without detection or of manoeuvring with success in the face of superior force." Cornwallis, he calculated, had twenty-one sail, of which twelve were three-deckers, besides five of a supposed Irish squadron, and fifteen in reserve.[4] "To attempt," he continues, "an expedition so important as that of Boulogne in a sea so stormy as the Channel, and one which is not always practicable for the boats employed in that expedition, I think we must be able to count on having the passage free for at least a fortnight. With only twenty-one vessels we should be in constant fear of seeing thirty suddenly appear, whose force would be nearly double that of our fleet."[5] Here, then, from Ganteaume's own pen is reason enough why the movement opening Brest entailed little risk. Did Barham see into his mind when he gave the order, or Cornwallis when he more than obeyed it? It is not unlikely. At all events they knew that since 1744 no enemy, however numerous, had dared to penetrate the Channel with an undefeated fleet behind it, and in that year it was only the weather that saved it from destruction as it saved the Armada. Both cases ended in a disastrous *sauve qui peut*. It was the kernel of our traditional defensive strategy, as it stood firmly based on the Western Squadron. No fleet could hope to reach Dover without being brought to action, and the further it got the greater were the advantages of the home fleet and the more crushing the results of failure.

To such considerations Napoleon had always shut his eyes, and Ganteaume's reply filled him with resentment. "I cannot in the least understand Ganteaume's immobility," he wrote to Decrès on the 18th. "How is it possible that, he who is in possession of all my projects, lets the enemy disappear without making any movement? I anticipated in my instructions that the enemy must disappear from Brest. Now for four days, it seems, they have not been seen, and this, added to the disappearance of the Rochefort squadron, can hardly leave any doubt about Villeneuve's arrival." He was in a fever of impatience, for he believed the crisis had come some days earlier than he had expected. Decrès was therefore to send Ganteaume a peremptory order to drive off the British cruisers and see what was behind them. If he found the battle squadron had moved far out to meet Villeneuve he himself was to go straight to Boulogne.[6]

Two days later the Emperor heard from his spies of the arrival of the *Curieux* and the news she brought. It did nothing to shake his belief that Villeneuve was close at hand. It must be some other news that had led to the alteration of the British disposition, for he was convinced the Admiralty could not have made up their minds so quickly and got the orders off in time. It must be that their home cruisers had located Villeneuve, and he issued orders for immediate action. Berthier was told to get the Grand Army embarked at once. "Every moment presses," Napoleon urged; "let the four Marshals know. There is no longer an instant to lose." The orders to Ganteaume were repeated with increasing emphasis. Napoleon himself wrote him a letter telling him he was to go out and fight any force before Brest, if he found it less than sixteen of the line. If the enemy were gone to Ferrol or far to sea to meet Villeneuve, he was to go straight to Boulogne. "There," he said in his sanguine way and in spite of what Ganteaume had written, "there all is prepared; and there, master of the sea for three days, you will enable us to end the destiny of England. . . . When you receive this letter we shall be in person at Boulogne-sur-Mer, and all will be on board and moored outside."

Surely never did a great commander talk more wildly. Had he lost his head, or was it just a theatrical display? The picture he painted had no relation whatever to the actual possibilities of the situation. The flotilla returns of July 22nd and August 3rd show that he had filled the ports of embarkation with over two thousand vessels of all kinds, scheduled to carry some 150,000 men and nearly 10,000 horses.[7] So vast a throng of shipping fairly choked the ports, and yet more were under orders to concentrate from the Flemish depôts. Elaborate organisations existed on paper, plan had succeeded plan, all beautifully symmetrical but none of them corresponding in the least to the conditions which actually existed. Instead of 150,000 men ready to embark, there were only 90,000; instead of 10,000 horses, there were less than 3,000. Boulogne itself was blocked with transport for 73,000 men, and there were only 45,000 to use it. Worse still, no one had any idea how long it would take to get the flotilla to sea. The movement had never been tried as a whole; no plan of operation had yet been settled, and it passed the wit of man to devise one.[8]

" If, then" — so runs the judgment of those best able to decide — "in an organisation essential for the success of his enterprise, where order and rapidity of embarkation were factors of the first importance, his genius indulged itself in systems simply symmetrical, bearing no relation either to the actual state of the troops and their service, or to the means of embarkation accumulated in the ports, we must surely ask ourselves if he ever seriously intended to make a sudden departure."[9]

What indeed could he have meant? In spite of his assurance to Ganteaume, he made no attempt to leave Paris, and yet the orders were not withdrawn. It mattered little, for before the Admiral could act on them, Cornwallis had completed his eight days' cast for Villeneuve and was back again before the port.

After reaching the latitude of Rochefort on July 16th he did not remain there, but began working back at once towards the north-east, with his fleet disposed in battle order and exercising battle tactics. On the 18th he returned to his assigned position from thirty to forty leagues south-west of Ushant, and in this region he remained cruising to and fro in open order. On the 20th, as his advanced ships could find nothing, he sent frigates to look into Rochefort and L'Orient, while he continued to hold his cruising ground two days more. Then as his allotted time was expiring, he began to make back to his Ushant position, and on the morning of the 24th he showed himself again to the Brest signal stations.[10]

So Barham's plan was justified in the result. So great is the advantage of secrecy with a blockading fleet that he might well be sure that Ganteaume would not be able to detect the movement in time to act before it was over. And if he had done so? If he had acted on

Napoleon's orders and stolen up Channel? It could only have meant his destruction, as he himself well knew. Cornwallis's frigates would quickly have warned him, and with his seasoned crews and knowledge of the Channel he must surely have overtaken Ganteaume and crushed him with his superior force and training. And if Ganteaume had reached Boulogne uncaught, and the flotilla with no settled method or organisation had tried to cross? Why, then, there must have been, with the aid of Keith's squadron in the Downs, a tragedy almost without parallel in the history of war. There is nothing to show that Barham deliberately set the trap, but trap it was; and so far as the evidence goes, Napoleon was only kept from leaping blindly into it by the crafty French seamen whom he treated with so much contempt.

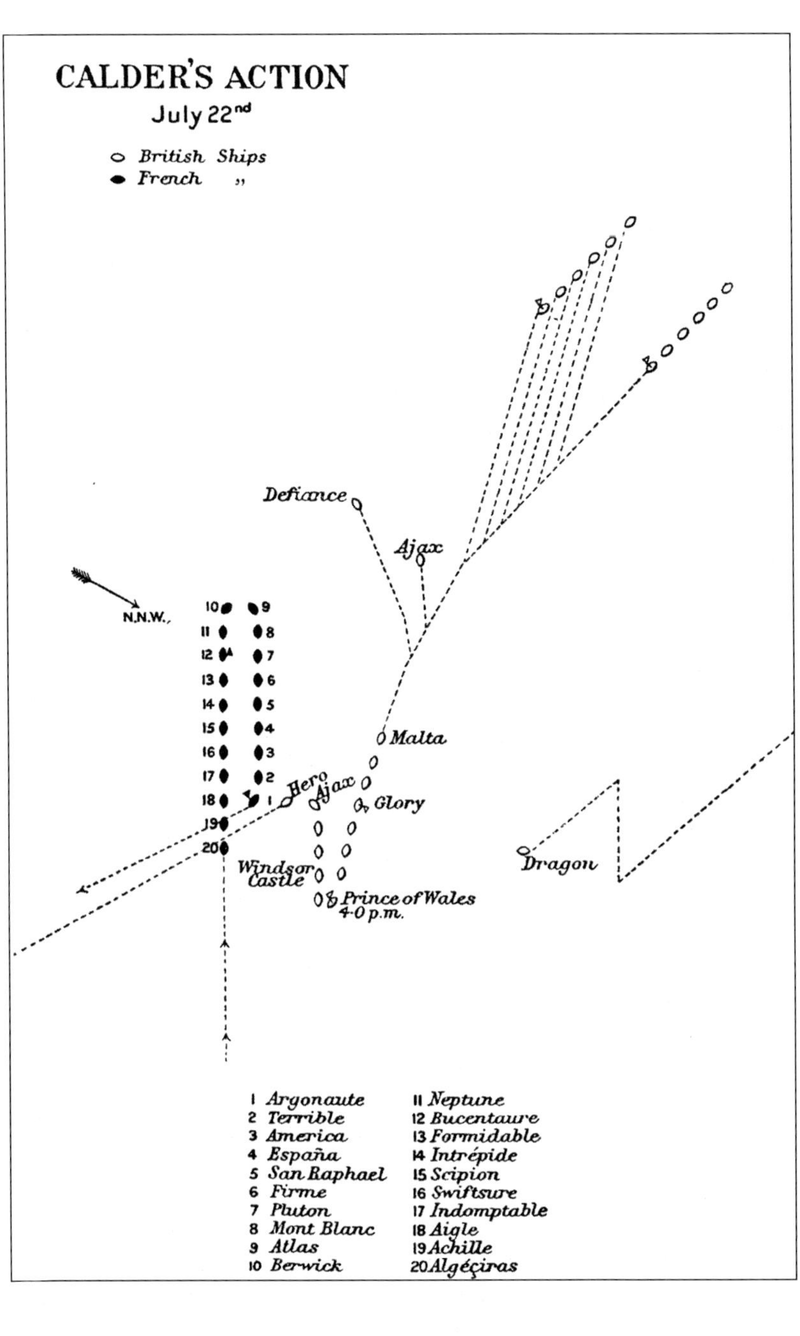

CALDER'S ACTION
July 22nd
British Ships
French ,,
Defiance
Ajax
N.N.W.
Malta
Hero
Ajax
Glory
Windsor Castle
Prince of Wales
4·0 p.m.
Dragon
1 Argonaute
2 Terrible
3 America
4 España
5 San Raphael
6 Firme
7 Pluton
8 Mont Blanc
9 Atlas
10 Berwick
11 Neptune
12 Bucentaure
13 Formidable
14 Intrépide
15 Scipion
16 Swiftsure
17 Indomptable
18 Aigle
19 Achille
20 Algéçiras

CHAPTER XIV

Calder's Action

With Ganteaume still held fast in Brest it was to Villeneuve and the Ferrol concentration that Napoleon had to look. But there Barham's design had proved equally successful. On July 22nd, as Cornwallis was closing in again to resume his close blockade, the blow had fallen which was to prove decisive of the campaign, so far at least as concerned Napoleon's offensive action against England.

Calder's action off Finisterre is one that has been little regarded. Dimly seen in the penumbra of Trafalgar, and through the cloud of a court-martial, which had nothing to do with it, its tactical significance has escaped serious investigation. Yet its place in the history of tactics was surely worth appraising, if only for the sake of the school to which Calder belonged. The three schools under which the final development of sailing tactics had taken place were those of Rodney, Howe, and Jervis. Rodney's, after a long and successful rivalry, had been supplanted by that of Howe. The finish and precision which Kempenfelt's genius had given its system had carried it beyond anything that had yet been seen, and it still dominated the service. Of this school Nelson was an adherent, if indeed his eclectic mind can be said to have belonged to anything less than all schools. He certainly had a strong leaning to the freehanded school of Jervis, which differed widely from the other two, and it was in this school that Calder had been trained. It is, therefore, no matter of surprise if a study of the facts should suggest that the experience of this neglected action was at the bottom of the most brilliant conception of the Trafalgar memorandum. In any case the indications of its influence on the tactics which Nelson employed are striking enough to call for the closest attention to every attainable detail.

It was in the evening of July 12th that the cruiser which Cornwallis sent to Stirling brought him his orders to raise the blockade of Rochefort and join Calder.[1] In the night he slipped away, and on the 15th, as Cornwallis was making his bold stretch to the southward, Barham's second concentration was complete. Waiting only an hour or two for darkness to conceal his movement, Calder stole away in his turn for his appointed station to the westward, leaving a brig to keep a close watch on the Ferrol squadron.

His own force now numbered, besides four cruisers, fifteen of the line, of which four were of 98 guns, and one, the *Malta*, a splendid 80-gun ship of greater burden than any of the three-deckers.[2] The remaining ten, with the exception of the *Dragon*, a powerful seventy-four, were all small and old two-deckers, two being of sixty guns only. Still as the combined force he was to meet was supposed to number only sixteen with no three-deckers, he could go on his way with a light heart, so far at least as Villeneuve's fleet was concerned.

With what he was leaving behind him it was different. Stirling had to report that at Rochefort he had left nine of the line and several frigates ready to sail, and there was now nothing to prevent their joining the Combined Squadron in Ferrol. He knew, moreover, that a chain of signal stations had been established from Ferrol westward along the coast in order to give warning of Villeneuve's approach, and enable Gourdon to come out to meet him the moment he appeared. His only chance of success then was to strike and crush Villeneuve before he could make the land and get in touch with Ferrol. It was to this end that Barham had directed that he should proceed off Cape Finisterre, and cruise thence thirty or forty leagues to the westward for six or eight days.[3]

By July 19th he was already about a hundred miles west by north of Finisterre. Here he got fresh news of Nelson just a month old. On June 17th, when Nelson was about six hundred miles north from Antigua in chase of Villeneuve, he had spoken an American cutter which had seen the Combined Squadron on its way home three days before. Any doubt which Nelson may have had of his adversary's destination was thus removed. He believed indeed he was hard on Villeneuve's heels, and must catch him before he could make his port. Full of this hope, on June 19th, he had sent away the *Martin* sloop to warn Gibraltar and the Mediterranean, and the *Decade* frigate to carry the news to Lisbon for Ferrol and Ushant.

This news now reached Calder by the Lisbon packet, and he began to work north-westward to cross Villeneuve's probable track, believing he must be somewhere close at hand. Nor was he mistaken. On the 12th, the day Stirling left Rochefort, Villeneuve had actually been within three hundred miles of the coast about due west of Oporto, but there the prevailing northerly winds forced him to go about, and for four days he had to stretch back to the westward before he could make his latitude.[4] It was not till the 17th that he was again able to head to the eastward for Ferrol.

On the morning of the 22nd Calder was some three hundred miles west by north of that port. Here having reached the limit of his cruising ground he wore S.W. by W., and expecting contact at any moment signalled for the fleet to prepare for action and to close.[5] He had two advanced ships, the *Defiance* and *Ajax*, and his two frigates spread as usual six or seven miles ahead, while the *Dragon*, his best seventy-four, had been chasing a strange sail about the same distance to leeward. The wind was light, about north-west, and the weather misty enough to reduce the range of vision very low. But shortly before noon the *Defiance* was able to make the signal for a strange fleet of twenty-four sail and then twenty-seven to the south-south-west. Calder at once bore away towards them to the south-west, and as he did so he formed close order of sailing in two columns and cleared for action.[6]

The noon positions of the opposed flagships show that the bodies of the two fleets were then about sixteen miles apart, and so thick was the weather that for two hours neither could make anything of the other. Villeneuve had his squadron in sailing order in three columns, the Spaniards to starboard and to leeward, and a light division of two of the line and two frigates thrown forward.[7] His course was about east direct for Ferrol, but when his light division reported the advanced ships of the enemy he altered it like Calder more towards them to find out what they were. About one o'clock his light division was able to report a British fleet of twenty-one sail approaching him, whereupon he signalled to form the close-hauled line of battle on the Spaniards and to clear for action. At this time it became brighter, and the *Defiance* and *Ajax* were able to make out the strangers definitely as an enemy with ships of the line. On taking in their signal Calder merely reduced his intervals by half a cable and held on as he was.[8] No attempt was made to weather his opponent, his intention being apparently to interpose his squadron between Villeneuve and Ferrol and to engage him to leeward.

As yet neither could make sure of the other's battle force. The weather had thickened again so much that the two fleets could only just see each other dimly through the mist. As the Combined Squadron formed the close-hauled line of battle with the wind now at west-north-west, it was of course heading to the northward. Gravina himself was leading, and the two fleets thus held on towards each other for an hour in the fog. It was not till past two o'clock that it began to lift again, and then Calder's advanced frigates, which had run down the enemy's line, were able to signal his exact force. Villeneuve had ordered his light division to fall into station in the rear, and the frigates had counted from twenty to twenty-two of the line.[9]

To the British Admiral so large a force must have been a severe surprise, and since his reputation for hard fighting afterwards fell so low, it is agreeable to draw close attention to the spirit with which he dealt with the unexpected situation. In effect that situation was that he found a numerically superior fleet coming up close-hauled to windward of him, and an action imminent. The last word of Lord Howe and Kempenfelt on the subject had been that the proper thing to do in these circumstances was to attack the van and the rear to prevent being doubled on, and to leave the centre alone; or if the organisation was in three divisions, the centre was to engage so much of the enemy's centre as it could.[10] In other words they adopted Lord Torrington's famous principle. But this Calder did not choose to do. He was not of the Howe-Kempenfelt school. His battle experience had been gained as Jervis's first captain at St. Vincent on the famous Valentine's Day, and it was but natural that he should share Jervis's mistrust of formal tactics. Instead, therefore, of accepting the recognised form of attack — and in spite of the enemy's force no thought but attack was in his mind — he chose to do what Nelson did at Trafalgar and concentrate on the enemy's rear and centre. The effect would be to engage the part of the enemy's line which was not yet formed and to leave the Spaniards alone. How far these considerations were in his mind we cannot tell, but we may at least credit him with the bold and original resolution he took.

Towards half-past three the two fleets were about eight miles apart and bore from each other about N.E. and S.W. Calder still made no attempt to get to windward, but after calling in his advanced ships he signalled to prepare to engage, and then to form the order of battle to the south-south-west, a course which led him frankly to leeward.[11] A few minutes later he signalled for another point to starboard, and then the fog closed down again and once more the two fleets lost sight of each other. When it lifted a quarter of an hour later they found themselves running nearly parallel on opposite tacks just out of gunshot.

For Villeneuve the line Calder was taking could have but one meaning. Dominated as French naval opinion was, and as opinion must always tend to be everywhere, by the last great action, he was convinced that the tactics of the Nile were in the British Admiral's mind and that Calder meant to double on his rear.[12] It was not yet in order, and with a view of supporting it Villeneuve passed orders up the line to Gravina for the fleet to wear in succession the moment he heard firing in the rear. It happened, however, that Gravina just then caught sight of a French frigate through the mist repeating the preparative signal that had been made, and luckily for Villeneuve he began the movement immediately.[13] At the same moment the *Hero*, which was leading the British line — an old and weak seventy-four under Captain Alan Gardner — had reached the enemy's centre, and Calder, seeing the moment had come for his manoeuvre, signalled to tack in succession. His object was to bring his fleet close under the lee of the part he meant to engage and on the same tack as the enemy, and directly the signal was hauled down, he hoisted "Engage the enemy's centre," and a quarter of an hour later "Close order."[14]

Thus not till the last moment did he let his captains know the plan of attack, and it so happened that the van ships did not take in the determinative signal to engage the centre. In the log of Captain Gardner it does not appear at all; in that of the *Ajax*, who had taken her station astern of him, it stands simply as "engage the enemy." The fact was that before the signal could reach Gardner at the head of the line he had been driven to act on his own initiative. As he led to the northward along the enemy's line he suddenly became aware of a large Spanish ship coming down upon him free upon the opposite tack. It was Gravina's own flagship as she led the movement to save the French rear. Here, then, was Calder's intended attack completely parried. It was too thick for the Admiral to see what was happening, nor could Gardner see Calder's flagship. What was he to do? If he held on the fleets would pass again on opposite tacks, a form of engaging which had long been condemned as incapable of producing a decisive result. He determined, therefore, on his own responsibility to go about and lead the fleet on the same tack as the enemy. Before he could get round Gravina was upon him, and gave him a broadside while he was still in stays. Fortunately the Spanish flagship had got a list to port from bad stowage, and her fire was not well enough directed to do much harm. Gardner was, therefore, able to continue the movement, and in this way about five o'clock the action began, but in an entirely different form from that which Calder had intended.

Immediately after opening fire Gravina found he had reached the rearmost ship of his own fleet, and in accordance with verbal orders he had received from Villeneuve in passing, he hauled to the wind and stood west-south-west across the French wake to cover their rear. It was not for three-quarters of an hour that Calder knew what had happened. At that time he was hailed by the *Ajax*, the *Hero's* second astern, who had tacked after Gardner. She, however, had hove-to, and getting engaged with two of the enemy she had been driven out of the line to leeward, and had thought best to bear up to warn the Admiral, who had just reached the point for tacking.[15] There was nothing for it now but to confirm the movement. By this time six ships had followed Gardner's lead. The flagship was the seventh, and Calder, hoisting the "General" to tack in succession, went about himself.

Thus his well-meant attack was spoiled by circumstances over which he had no control, and by the accident of Gravina's tacking before Villeneuve intended. Calder was now committed to a concentration on the van and centre, an evil method of engaging which led inevitably to a counter concentration on his own rear as the enemy's rear came up. He had, moreover, only twelve ships in action. The *Hero* as well as the *Ajax* had been driven out of the line before he himself tacked, and the *Barfleur* 98, the fourth ship, was now at grips with Gravina. And not only were the two weak leading ships gone, but the powerful *Dragon* was still beating up from to leeward, and indeed did not succeed in rejoining till the action was over.

The *Malta* in the extreme rear brought up against the twelfth ship of the enemy's line, which happened to be the headmost of their rear, also an 80-gun ship, carrying the flag of Rear-Admiral Dumanoir, but most of the French rear never got into action. Thus after all Calder had succeeded in attacking an equal part of the enemy's line, but what happened afterwards no one could tell even approximately. The fog settled down again thicker than ever as the fleets stood away to the west-south-west closely engaged. For the most part they could not even see what they were firing at, and let fly at the flashes of each other's guns. Villeneuve himself as he came about did not know whether the enemy were to port or starboard. Friend could hardly be told from foe. The *Malta* as she rounded into action fired on a British frigate. So the blind fight went on till the night closed down upon it, and it was not till nine o'clock that all was still.

By that time the British found themselves in possession of the two rearmost ships of the Spanish squadron, which after an heroic resistance had fallen to leeward disabled into the midst of the British fleet. It was the *Windsor Castle* 98, it would seem, that had contributed most to the success and suffered most severely, losing her foretopmast and forty-four men killed and wounded. "She did splendidly," said an officer who was present, and to judge by the casualties, it was she and another three-decker — the *Prince of Wales* — that did most of the damage. Nowhere else was much harm done, except in the British rear. Here the *Malta*, in the place of honour, with the *Thunderer* 74 next ahead, suffered the inevitable concentration, but not without inflicting serious loss upon their adversaries. Both ships, however, were severely cut up, and the *Malta* lost as many men as the *Windsor Castle.*[16]

"A very decisive action," Calder wrote in his despatch next morning, "which lasted upwards of four hours, when I found it necessary to bring-to the squadron to cover the captured ships." Villeneuve saw it differently. "The enemy then made off," he wrote in his report. "He had had several vessels crippled aloft, and the field of battle remained ours. Cries of joy and victory were heard from all our ships."[17]

The claim of neither Admiral was ever endorsed by competent opinion. Events, it is true, went far, at least strategically, to justify Calder's boast that the action was decisive, but Villeneuve's vaunt of retaining possession of the field had no justification. The actual result of the battle was that Calder had maintained his position, barring Villeneuve's approach to Ferrol and the Galician signal stations; he had captured two of the line from a superior force, and had inflicted on his enemy three times the loss he himself had sustained. So far Calder had certainly won a victory. His conduct in the action received the commendation of the Admiralty, and was never called in question. He certainly believed he had done well, and in the early hours of the night sent word down the fleet that he meant to renew the battle in the morning.

When day broke, however, he found his fleet widely scattered. The van were far away to windward towards the distant enemy; the frigates and prizes, together with the *Windsor Castle* and *Thunderer*, were out of sight somewhere to leeward. To add to his anxiety for their safety the returns of damages to rigging which he received were so serious as to forbid an attempt to work to windward, and he decided that his only course was to call down the van and then bear up to get in touch with the cripples to leeward.

As had happened so fatally in Byng's case Calder's first spirited determination to renew the action had been weakened by secondary considerations when the stir of excitement was over. The despatch which he now resolved to send to Cornwallis exactly explains his altered view of the situation. "The enemy," he wrote, "are now in sight to windward and when I have secured the captured ships and put the squadron to rights, I shall endeavour to avail myself of every opportunity that may offer to give you some further account of these combined squadrons. At the same time it will behove me to be on my guard against the combined squadrons at Ferrol, as I am led to believe they have sent off one or two of their crippled ships last night for that port. Therefore possibly I may find it necessary to make a junction with you immediately off Ushant with the whole squadron. *P.S.* I am under the necessity of sending the *Windsor Castle* to you in consequence of the damage she sustained in the action."[18]

On the morrow no such opportunity as he indicated occurred. It is true that Villeneuve did make some show of renewing the action, but he always asserted that Calder refused to let him close. Calder, on the other hand, maintained that Villeneuve, with all the advantage of the weather position, refused to come within reach of him. On the 24th the wind shifted in Calder's favour, but still he made no attempt to engage. The enemy was barely in sight and in his opinion it was out of his power to force an action without risking his prizes and crippled ships or permitting Villeneuve to get touch with the Spanish signal stations. His view was that so long as he maintained a position which forbade Villeneuve to gain his object without fighting, he secured the fruits of his victory. He always contended that in this resolution he followed the example of Howe and Jervis. Neither the one after the First of June, nor the other after St. Vincent, had behaved differently, and yet neither Howe nor Jervis had a second equal and unshaken fleet threatening him from behind. "Circumstanced as I was," he said, "it appeared to me to be impracticable to force the enemy to action with such advantage as would justify me, even if I had nothing to apprehend but the opposing squadron. But when I reflected that sixteen sail were at Ferrol, who might have come out to the assistance of the combined fleet, or . . . . be pushing to England, the invasion of which was an event daily expected, I felt by renewing the action I should run too great a hazard and put my fleet in a state of danger which I could not have been justified for doing. I therefore thought it best to keep my squadron together and not to force the enemy to a second engagement till a more favourable opportunity. At the same time conceiving that their object was to join the ships at Ferrol, I determined to prevent them."

This he certainly did. On the morning of the 25th the two fleets were no longer in sight of one another; wind and sea were rising; and Villeneuve, fearing for his shattered ships, resolved to abandon the attempt to hold up for Ferrol and bear away for Cadiz instead. Even this, as the weather grew wilder every hour, soon seemed too great a hazard. Gravina was consulted as to the possibility of getting into Vigo, and the result of the conference was that they turned back and ran for that port for refuge.

Of this movement Calder could have no knowledge. His two frigates were too deeply engaged with the crippled ships to keep touch with the enemy, and all he knew was that the Combined Squadron had disappeared to the southward. In the circumstances he could not but think that he had done all that was required. In a successful action he had maintained the vital Finisterre position; he had foiled the Ferrol concentration, and he felt that he could take his own line. His first care was to see the *Windsor Castle* and his two prizes as far to the northward on their way home as would render them reasonably safe from attack either from Rochefort or Ferrol. This done he held away back for the original rendezvous Cornwallis had given him in hope of getting in touch with Nelson, who might be expected to appear any day. If Nelson was not to be found it was his intention to return off Ferrol.

What judgment must be passed on Calder's conduct? It is probably one of the most difficult cases in history — a case of delicate choice between the primary object of destroying the enemy's fleet and the ulterior object of defending England against invasion. Most modern writers condemn him out of hand as a man of little heart, who did what was obviously the wrong thing from sheer pusillanimity. His brother officers, after hearing the evidence for three days and being in touch with the sentiment of that golden time, were not so sure. For six hours they sat in secret and anxious debate before a decision was reached, and then they condemned him to be reprimanded. But for what? "For not having done his utmost to renew the said engagement and to take and destroy every ship of the enemy." With that he was charged, and of that he was assuredly guilty. But in Calder's view, to put the charge in that way was to beg the whole question. In his view it was his duty in the circumstances not to renew the action and not to try to destroy every ship of the enemy. His duty was to keep his fleet in being and prevent the enemy getting to Ferrol. The modern conception of warfare is such that probably any tribunal of naval officers would condemn him again today, but in those days the creed of the primary object was not so ripe. To condemn Calder for a mistake is one thing; to brand him as a fainthearted blunderer is another.

He himself believed that, like Byng, he was the victim of popular outcry. In publishing his despatch the Admiralty had suppressed the last passage which hinted at the possibility of his not being able to renew the action. The country consequently in a condition of elated expectation was looking every day to hear of the completion of the victory, and what they got was news of a retreat. The revulsion of the disappointment, he always maintained, was what hounded him to his fate. But the truth is the Admiralty and Government were at one with public opinion; and now that we know the soul of Barham's plan we can see why it was so. He had taken great risks to secure a great moral result. His object was to establish an abiding dread that though hostile squadrons might slip out of their blockaded ports, the penalty of their success would be never to return. At the cost of a sacrifice admirably judged he had placed Calder in a position to secure that end, and Calder had not secured it. At the psychological moment he had looked behind him in confused anxiety for matters which did not concern him, and for which Barham had provided amply. It was a lapse of warlike spirit for which it was impossible to forgive him, and a court-martial was inevitable.

His real defence was never raised. It was, that the situation, the real inner intent of Barham's orders, was never explained to him, and he did not know that his one and only duty, whatever the result to his own fleet, was if he once got hold never to let go so long as he had a tooth left.

This principle — to fight to a finish when in doubt — has become an axiom in modern naval opinion, but it was scarcely so when Calder fought. The hardest part of his case is that he fought the action under one standard, and was tried for it under another. Between the action and the court-martial Nelson fought and won Trafalgar. Trafalgar set up an ideal of hot-pressed action and a sentiment of confident superiority which did not exist when Calder fought, anywhere but in Nelson and his band of brothers. Nelson, of course, had no doubt in the matter, and deeply as he sympathised with Calder he put his finger at once upon the black spot. "He appears," so he wrote to the Second Sea Lord, "to have had the ships at Ferrol more in his head than the squadron in sight. . . . He lays stress upon other considerations than fighting the enemy's squadron, if he could have done it, *which he denies to be possible.* I have ventured to recommend Calder to keep to that; *prove it* and his character is retrieved."[19] In Nelson's eyes, then, the one and only excuse for not concentrating effort on the squadron in sight was the impossibility of bringing it to action. He himself would certainly have gone at Villeneuve again, and so would Monck in older days; but can we say with any confidence there were two flag-officers in the service at the time who would not have erred with Calder, knowing only what Calder knew. The better way, then, is not to indulge in facile condemnation, but to try to realise with humility the tremendous power upon overwrought nerves of the "considerations other than fighting" which led him astray. So may a man best strengthen himself against doing likewise in like case.

CHAPTER XV

Movements After Calder's Action

Defensible or indefensible, Calder's misapprehension of what was required of him had brought to the ground Barham s bold conception for a counter-stroke. Napoleon's plan to all appearance had so far succeeded that we were thrust back upon the defensive, and nothing in the campaign is more interesting than the automatic manner in which the wide-flung fleet shrank back to the strategical centre, to meet the threatening concentration.

Nelson was the first to move. Convinced like Barham that Villeneuve's destination was Cadiz, he had set his course from Antigua straight for Cape St. Vincent, sure that the best way to bring his chase to action was to make that landfall before him. "The enemy," wrote Canton Bayntun of the *Leviathan* on June 21st to Nelson after he had got wind of Villeneuve from the American skipper, "the enemy cannot be far ahead, and by our taking a more easterly direction it is possible (if he be bound that way) we may arrive off St. Vincent before him. Your lordship each night forms a part of his dreams."[1] The *Decade* which he had sent on to Lisbon, was to meet him at the cape. He made it on July 17th, but of the enemy there was no news whatever, except that Missiessy had got back to Rochefort two months since. Nothing had been heard of Villeneuve and after sending to communicate with Collingwood, Nelson moved down to Gibraltar to renew his stores On the 20th he went ashore — being the first time for all but two years that he had set foot out of the *Victory*. He had still a remnant of hope that he had forestalled Villeneuve, and would be able to fight him as he approached the Straits; but he now received a letter of welcome from Collingwood containing an appreciation of the situation which differed entirely from his own.

Throughout the war Collingwood's service had been in the Channel, and his ideas inevitably took the colour of his station. This station bias appears to be as constant as anything in war — a condition of the human factor that has to be taken into account. Every commander is predisposed to see in his own theatre of operations the objective of those of the enemy; and as Nelson, against the balance of probability as it seems to us now, clung to his apprehension for the Mediterranean, so Collingwood had not got rid of his preoccupation with the Channel. It would be unsafe, therefore, to argue that because in the main he was right in this case and Nelson wrong, that his strategical penetration was greater than Nelson's. The view he now laid before his chief was that Villeneuve's object was to bring out the Ferrol and Rochefort squadrons, and so appear off Ushant with thirty-four of the line, and there be joined by twenty more from Brest. Cornwallis by concentrating the three divisions of the Western Squadron would not have more than thirty. "This," he says, "appears to be a probable plan. For unless it is to bring these great fleets and armies to some point of service — some rash attempt at conquest — they have been only subjecting them to chance of loss, which I do not believe the Corsican would do, without the hope of adequate reward."[2]

Nelson, however, still clung to his waning hope. His intention was, as he informed the Admiralty, to proceed to Tetuan for fresh victuals and water. In the meantime, he said, he was sending to Collingwood and Bickerton for the orders they had received in his absence, and if he found them to contain nothing to the contrary, he would then, after providing for the blockade of Cartagena, take station outside the Mediterranean and wait for further instructions. If, however, he heard Villeneuve had made for the Bay, he would forthwith join the Ferrol or the Ushant squadron, as circumstances seemed to require.[3]

The interval he employed in restoring the situation in the Mediterranean. He could not understand the existing disposition, with Collingwood's fleet divided between Cadiz and Cartagena, and nothing at all with Knight at Gibraltar to control the Straits. But above all he was concerned for Craig at Malta. He found orders recalling the sloops from that station to join Collingwood. So active were the enemy's privateers, and so incapable the island of feeding itself unless the adjacent waters were free, that he knew this would mean the starvation of the garrison. His first letter to Barham, on hearing of his appointment as First Lord, was to protest against the arrangement. He even took upon himself to cancel it and order the cruisers back again. Nor did he stop here. He reorganised the whole command into three sections, and sent home a requisition for the force required for each. Collingwood was to command from St. Vincent as far as Cape Spartel on the Moorish coast for the blockade of Cadiz and Seville. Knight was to have the Straits or Gibraltar section extending from Spartel to Malaga with a substantial cruiser squadron under his flag. Bickerton, whom he sent for in person, was to have the rest, with explicit directions as to how he was to dispose his force for the blockade of Cartagena, the defence of Sardinia, Sicily, Naples, and Malta, and the protection of the Levant trade. These arrangements were completed on July 22nd, and then Nelson moved out for Tetuan, little dreaming that to the northward off Finisterre another was enjoying the feast he had prepared so laboriously for himself.

On the 24th, still hungering for news — for not yet had he received one material word —he weighed for the rendezvous he had given off Cape Spartel, where all his cruisers were to meet him. He had got no further than Tarifa, just outside the Gut, when at about, half-past three in the morning of the 25th, the *Termagant*, a sloop recently out from England, came into the fleet. She had been into the Tagus on her way down, and had brought on a Lisbon newspaper containing an account of the arrival of the *Curieux*, and the news she carried. Nelson's mind was made up in a moment. Clearly Villeneuve had been making for the Bay, and thither he would go. A strong Levanter was blowing, making it difficult to speak with his old friend Collingwood. Important as an interview was, he would not waste a breath of the fair wind. Word was left for cruisers to join him at St. Vincent, or if he were not there, at Ferrol — unless there was reason to believe he had taken a different course. In that case they were to look for him at Ushant or Ireland, or in the last resort Spithead. So it was that just as Calder was moving to the distant rendezvous off Finisterre in hopes of meeting him, Nelson was making in all haste to join hands with him.[4] On the second day he was off St. Vincent, but here he encountered the prevailing northerly winds. To proceed up the coast to Ferrol would mean interminable delays, and would involve the risk of leaving the Ushant squadron unsupported at the critical moment. In his hands, and his hands alone, lay the possibility of redressing the balance which Collingwood had calculated so anxiously. There was nothing for it but to reach wide to the westward, and he sent word to Cornwallis that he was coming to him, or to Ireland, as intelligence might dictate.

It was an unhappy decision, for which nobody can be blamed. Had Calder but sent word to the southward immediately after the action it might have been avoided, but he had no cruiser to spare. Had he but sunk his two worthless old prizes it might have been done. As it was, in default of information, Nelson had to assume his enemy had gone to the north, and was forced to make for the point of greatest danger. Had he but joined Calder what a world of acute anxiety would have been spared! what successes would have lain in his path! Trafalgar might never have been fought, and Barham's great idea might have been fully realised.

Ahead of him was a strategical tangle into which he must have torn with resounding advantage. From the Finisterre rendezvous Calder had sent the *Dragon*, his untouched seventy-four, to look into Ferrol. She returned with the surprising information that everything there was just as they had left it. Gourdon and Grandallana were still at their moorings, and neither Villeneuve nor the Rochefort squadron had appeared. Calder could only conclude that Villeneuve had made for Cadiz, and was destined to fall into the hands of Nelson and Collingwood. With a quiet mind he accordingly decided to resume his blockade. His original intention had been to leave the *Dragon* behind him in case Nelson might still be coming north, but as there was now little likelihood of this, he took her with him and left the rendezvous bare. By July 29th he had reconstituted the blockade with fourteen of the line, but two days later he decided to send home his 80-gun ship, the *Malta*, to repair her damages.

Meanwhile Villeneuve found himself at Vigo in what he called "a most distressing situation." He had neither orders nor intelligence; the port was without defence or any means of repairing his ships; scurvy and dysentery were playing havoc with his crews, and besides the two ships he had lost, three others, as the result of the action, were unfit for service. In this plight he had summoned Gourdon to come to him, but Gourdon could only reply it was impossible. He had not yet been able to get out to Coruña. There was nothing for it then but for Villeneuve to try to get to him at the risk of another action. "May a new meeting," he said, "be more fortunate than the first." By hook or by crook he scraped together a month's water and victuals for the fifteen vessels which now constituted his squadron, and on the last day of July, leaving his sick and wounded behind with the three disabled vessels, he put to sea intent on reaching Ferrol without an action. Outside on the morrow, August 1st, he was fortunate enough to find a strong south-westerly breeze, and with all speed he stole away northward, close along the shore.

And where was Allemand? Why had he not made Ferrol? Three days after Stirling had disappeared from Rochefort he had put to sea, with his broad pennant in the *Majestueux* 120. His squadron besides comprised four two-deckers and five cruisers — an ideal force for the work he had in hand. It must be recalled that the last orders which had reached him were to make a demonstration off the West Coast of Ireland, and be back at a certain rendezvous 40 leagues west of Ferrol in time to meet the combined squadron on its return from the West Indies. His main object, in fact, as laid down by Napoleon, was to bring about the long-sought junction with Villeneuve. It was characteristic of Napoleon's inexplicable elimination of the enemy from his naval dispositions, that the rendezvous he fixed for the meeting was well within the area which Calder had been directed to cover.[5] Indeed, it was just 40 miles south-east of the point where the battle of July 22nd was actually fought, and the Emperor's naive surprise when he realised it we shall see presently. The time fixed was the end of the month. Allemand was to be on the spot from July 29th to August 3rd, but here was another miscalculation. The order assumed that Villeneuve would not start home till thirty-five days after Magon arrived. A possible interference by Nelson had been ignored, and now Nelson's hot pursuit outwards had had the effect of driving Villeneuve home, not only too soon to meet Allemand, but too soon to receive the despatch which explained the new arrangement for his junction with the Rochefort squadron.

To make matters still more confused, the effect of Stirling's blockade had been seriously to delay Allemand's sailing under his original instructions, and the consequence was that when he did get away and opened his sealed orders, he found the time limited for his Irish demonstration had already expired. It was for this reason that Napoleon had sent down an order to stop him. It arrived too late, and Allemand put to sea with the old instructions. They directed him to proceed west 400 leagues, so as to avoid the British squadrons off Ushant and Ferrol, and appear off Ireland from the westward between July 4th and 9th. There he was to cruise for a week, and then run down to the Finisterre rendezvous to meet Villeneuve. If, therefore, he followed his orders strictly he should have begun to make for the rendezvous the day he left Rochefort. But it was characteristic of the man's high spirit not to look too closely at the letter of his orders, but to try to do his best to carry out their intention. He determined, therefore, not to give up the Irish diversion without an effort. "Although the term had expired," he wrote to Decrès, "I thought, my lord, that without missing my first rendezvous, 40 leagues from Ferrol, I could, with favourable winds and by cutting short my route, still show myself off Ireland."[6]

With this idea he held away due west, as directed, all unconscious that, instead of avoiding the Ushant squadron, his course was taking him straight to the southernmost point which Cornwallis had made in his sweep for Villeneuve. But while he was preparing to weigh, Cornwallis, as we know, had turned back, and when Allemand on July 19th reached the fatal point, he found nothing there but the *Ranger* sloop which Cornwallis had left behind him to try to get wind of the Combined Squadron from neutral merchantmen. She was promptly captured and sunk. An examination of her officers disclosed her mission, and put Allemand on his guard, and next day he issued a ruthless order that every neutral that had been in sight of the squadron while on its true course was to be captured and sunk.[7]

On the following day, the 21st, he found himself nearly 150 leagues west of Rochefort. The wind was drawing into the west-north-west; it was foul for him to go on; and as yet he had not traversed half the distance to the westward which had been laid down in his instructions. But it was fair for Ireland. At the risk of falling foul of Cornwallis he could shorten his route, as he said, and make up for the time lost at Rochefort. This he resolved to do, and hauled up to the northward. But it was all to little purpose. The wind kept veering continually further to the north, and though for three days he struggled on he could make little progress. True, he captured a fine vessel from Guernsey, from which he got a set of large scale charts of the Irish coast, but by the 23rd he saw his attempt was hopeless. While still over 300 miles from his goal, he had to heave-to in a stormy northerly wind; all chance of reaching Ireland in the time available was gone, and next day he bore up for his Finisterre rendezvous.[8]

In all naval story there is probably no adventure so full of fantastic fortune as this incredible cruise of Allemand's Pursuing a plan that was crossed at every point by Barham's finished disposition, he sped from danger to danger as his master's wilful blindness had doomed him. Wandering in the midst of well-disposed squadrons hungering for his destruction, again and again he escaped by a hairbreadth — appearing and disappearing like a phantom fleet — his every move forestalled, yet always sheltered by some bewildering turn of fortune or happy stroke of judgment. When we consider that the whole episode was born of that little interlineation in Barham's order, whereby he altered his mind at the last moment and sent Stirling to Calder its mythical colour is complete. It is as though some unseen power were resolved to remind the veteran First Lord how helpless was his art against the Fortune of War

As Allemand had begun, so he continued to the end. His cruise had opened by his making straight for the spot where Cornwallis had been waiting for him, and having escaped by mere chance, he was running blindly into Calder's arms. But his star was still bright. He reached the point of danger on July 28th, a day before he was due, and it was also the very day Calder had moved away to resume the blockade of Ferrol and had left the rendezvous bare.

Here then he remained unseen his allotted time, sending out cruising ships to look for Villeneuve. On August 3rd one of them rejoined. Of Villeneuve there was no trace, but she had ascertained from an American, homeward bound from Bordeaux, that on the last day of July Ferrol was blockaded by a squadron of fourteen of the line. Thereupon, in accordance with his instructions, Allemand moved to a second rendezvous which had been given him, about 160 miles south-west of Ushant and just outside the Ushant-Finisterre line — in fact just about the limit of Cornwallis's advanced cruisers.[9] At the hour of starting he found he was being watched by a frigate—she was the *Æolus*, of which more presently — but after his manner he sailed a false course east-south-east till he saw her disappear towards Ferrol, and then he was able to proceed northward undetected.[10] As he reached his point on August 6th, another of his cruisers came in to report that, from information obtained from a Swede, she had definitely located a squadron of eleven of the line with three threedeckers cruising about 60 miles north of Cape Ortegal. As we shall see this was also Calder, but Allemand could not tell what to make of it. He could only conclude it was another squadron in search of him, and that he must have passed close to it in the night. He naturally became anxious. His orders were to remain where he was for a week. The idea apparently was that at this point he would be able to fall in with Villeneuve after he had released the Ferrol squadron, and would be coming north for Ushant. But Napoleon, in his extraordinary infatuation, had omitted to consider that this would be exactly the area which his enemy would be watching most closely, and so it was. Allemand immediately found himself observed by a little cloud of cruisers, peeping at him over the horizon or pushing their attentions home. In vain he tried to get hold of them; every one slipped nimbly through his fingers.[11] All he could come by were one or two merchantmen and a British privateer cutter just from home. But this last capture only added to his trouble, for he learnt from her that as she was sailing from Plymouth two Spanish prizes had been brought into the Sound. Evidently an action had been fought, but was it with Villeneuve or with the Ferrol squadron? Two days later further information was obtained from a Portuguese prize. She had been boarded a few days before by the *Dragon*, and her skipper could confirm the action. It was Calder who had fought it, against whom he knew not, but he was sure the squadron of eleven of the line that had been seen to the north of Cape Ortegal was the same which had fought the action. What then was it that was blockading Ferrol? To make the position still more difficult, the Portuguese skipper had also to tell that he had been boarded by the *Phœnix* (a frigate of which we shall hear more). She appeared to be looking for Calder, and had told him that Villeneuve had been sighted by the *Curieux* flying homewards with Nelson at his heels.[12]

It was more than the harassed Commodore could endure. There were still thirty hours to run of the time he was to remain on the northern rendezvous, but he decided it was madness to remain to the end. "My position in the Bay," he wrote in his report, "has become disturbing, my lord. The squadron blockading Brest must know my position by the frigate which escaped the *Armide* [*i.e.* the *Naiad*], The squadron blockading Ferrol and the one which is cruising in latitude 45° and longitude 11° [that is, to the north of Cape Ortegal] are also informed of it by the frigates which have watched me. My station is too plainly disclosed for it to be prudent for me to remain till the 13th. It is almost impossible, my lord, for a vessel from Villeneuve to reach me. It will be captured by the quantity of enemy's ships which are cruising in every part of the Bay." He accordingly concluded by saying he intended to avail himself of the discretion which his instructions allowed him, and run for safety to Vigo. And this he did there and then, stretching far to the westward to get out of harm's way.

Except in one important point the actual situation differed little from his appreciation. On August 1st, the day after Calder had returned to the blockade of Ferrol, and Villeneuve had left Vigo for the same port, the strong south-westerly wind which was carrying the Combined Squadron so happily to its destination, forced the British Admiral well to leeward of the blockaded port. The result was that Villeneuve found nothing in his way, and was able to run into Coruña without firing a shot. On the following day, in accordance with Barham's instructions that at the end of the specified period all squadrons were to return to their regular stations, Calder ordered Stirling to return to Rochefort. If he found the port empty he was to join Cornwallis. Calder himself with his remaining nine ships took the position from 40 to 60 miles to the northward of the port in which the mysterious squadron had been reported to Allemand. Here he continued day after day laboriously holding up against strong south-westerly winds. His reason is nowhere stated; it was not his usual practice. In such weather his rule was to run for shelter behind Cape Ortegal.[13] It is to be presumed, therefore, that he was looking out for Allemand. Not that he had any definite information, for the *Æolus*, who had just located the Rochefort squadron, had not yet reached him. But seeing how anxious he had been about it after the battle, it is natural he was expecting it would make an attempt to reach Ferrol. He was therefore lying in Allemand's path, and according to the sound British method was keeping wide of the port of destination in order to deal with him before his friends inside could come to his aid.

Had he been at the Emperor's elbow he could not have judged more correctly. A direct movement on Ferrol, if Stirling raised the blockade of Rochefort, was actually what Napoleon had enjoined on Allemand in the orders which did not reach him. But Calder was doomed to disappointment. His move, as we have seen, had come to Allemand's ears and had effectually headed him off, and after cruising in vain for a week — that is, till the 9th — Calder sent the *Dragon* to look into Ferrol to see if by chance the Rochefort squadron had slipped in. The same evening she returned in company with the *Æolus*, bearing news that Allemand was at sea to the westward, and that not he but the whole Combined Fleet was in Ferrol. To remain with his slender squadron facing a force of thirty of the line obviously about to sail, to say nothing of Allemand's five, was in Calder's eyes useless; and, as Orde had done earlier in the campaign, he decided it was his duty to close on Ushant. On the 10th, therefore, he stood north, leaving the *Dragon* behind to watch the port and move towards the Finisterre rendezvous to look out for Nelson. Thus for a third time Allemand had the narrowest possible escape, and his prudence in leaving the rendezvous before his allotted time was justified. By his orders he should have held it till the 13th, and on that day Calder on his way north passed by it only twenty-four hours after Allemand had left, and nothing but his sagacious disobedience saved him from destruction.

So far as Napoleon's plan was concerned the Rochefort squadron was, of course, still in the air. Otherwise to all appearance, by the junction of the other French squadrons at Coruña, the combination had been so far successful. Still the Admirals knew it was only an appearance. On August 2nd as the Combined Squadron were making the junction at Coruña, the Emperor was at last on his way from Paris to Boulogne. On the 3rd, he began issuing his final orders from the camp of the Grand Army, and on that day Gravina and Villeneuve were writing to Decrès under honeyed phrases a solemn warning that the Emperor's plan was impracticable. "I will say to your Excellency," wrote Gravina, "that the plan of operations could not seem better conceived — it was divine. . . . But today it is sixty days since we left Martinique, and the English have had plenty of time to send warning in advance to Europe and to reinforce their Ferrol squadron. . . . All this, in my opinion, has much disconcerted the plan, brilliant and well laid as it was. Now the enemy knows our force. . . . It is only natural that on our leaving here they will not hesitate to give us battle, and by sending forward their scouts to warn their Brest squadron they will be able to shadow us and choose their time for a second battle before we can make our Brest landfall. In this way they can defeat the plan of campaign, which certainly was very fine and interesting." From first to last the French frankly recognised Gravina's loyalty and courage, and coming from his devoted pen such criticism, for all its courteous phrasing, was in the last degree scathing.[14]

Villeneuve, ill and depressed, was entirely of the same opinion, and besides endorsing Gravina's strategical views, he gave Decrès frankly his real estimate of his late "victory." It had, in fact, shattered the last remnants of his confidence in the plan and his squadron. "The enemy," he said, "were warned; they had been reinforced; they did not hesitate to come and attack us with a force numerically very inferior. . . . In the fog our captains, without experience of an action or of fleet tactics, had no better idea than to follow their second ahead, and here we are the laughing stock of Europe."[15] To complete his despair, he had received, as he was entering Coruña bay, one of Napoleon's impatient orders, forbidding him peremptorily to put into Ferrol. He was to anchor at Coruña, and wait there for Gourdon and Grandallana to come down and join him. The result was that Gravina, who was leading, found himself too far in to obey the signal, and was forced to go on, while Villeneuve had hurriedly to anchor at Coruña with half his ships running aboard each other in the confined anchorage. At Coruña there were no stores or water to be had, everything was eight miles away up at Ferrol in the depth of the bay; and there, to complete the trouble, Gourdon, the Commander-in-chief, lay to all appearance dying, and Grandallana was intriguing to get Gravina's command. Moreover, as the squadrons lay scattered between the two ports, it was impossible to get them out in one body, and Calder the day before had been reported in the offing. Villeneuve professed himself ready to go out the moment his fleet was revictualled, but it was without hope of avoiding or winning an action. "Eight of the line," he wrote, "keep in sight of the coast at eight leagues. They will profit by the lesson given to Admiral Orde; they will shadow us. I shall not be able to close with them, and they will fall back on the squadron before Brest, or that before Cadiz, according as I make for the one port or the other."

The news that Allemand was out and under orders to join him did nothing to relieve, what he called, "the bitterness of his soul." He had been told of the commodore's two rendezvous, but knowing, as every seaman must know, how ill chosen they were, he despaired of finding him at either, and Decrès, lost in the confusion of the Emperor's orders, had forgotten to tell him that Allemand's point of retreat was Vigo. As the period for Allemand's holding the Finisterre rendezvous had just expired, the only chance of getting into touch with him was to send to the northern one, on the fringe of Cornwallis's station. One frigate was all Villeneuve would risk on the enterprise, and on August 6th, just as Allemand reached the rendezvous, Captain Milius, of the *Didon* 40, went out with orders that the squadron was to come to Ferrol, and if Villeneuve were gone it was to follow the further instructions that would be found awaiting it.[16]

A famous cruiser episode of the highest interest was the result. On July 20th, in response to Calder's urgent entreaty for more cruisers, and Barham's instructions to keep up communications, Cornwallis had sent down the *Niobe* 38. On the 29th, immediately after he received news of the action, he despatched another, the *Æolus* 32, Captain Lord William Fitzroy, and, later still, the *Phœnix* 26. They were to look for him on his Finisterre rendezvous. The *Æolus* was also charged with a despatch, which probably contained Cornwallis's rendezvous, as he was expecting Calder would shortly come north, and Fitzroy had further orders to look out for enemy's squadrons in the Bay as he crossed it. If he located one, he was immediately to push on before it to report to the admiral for whose station it appeared to be making.[17] This was the vessel which, as we have seen, had sighted Allemand on August 4th just as he was about to leave his first rendezvous; and on the 5th, having seen him steer his false course east-south-east, had gone off to warn Calder. On his way down to the rendezvous Fitzroy ascertained from the communicative American, by whom Allemand had obtained the same information, that Calder had resumed his blockade, and he accordingly altered his course for Ferrol. The result was that, on the afternoon of August 7th, about 60 miles north-west of Finisterre, he sighted the *Didon*, who, after ascertaining that he was not one of Allemand's cruisers, turned and ran from him off her course south-west. Fitzroy gave chase till dark, and seeing it was impossible to close without a long pursuit, decided that in view of the importance of the intelligence he bore, and the clear tenor of his orders, it was his duty to haul off and continue his mission to find Calder. And this, as we have seen, he did.[18]

Meanwhile the Didon, having run far to the south-west, and finding herself no longer observed, determined to make another effort to get north to Allemand's rendezvous. Hauling her wind again to the north-west, she headed almost straight for Calder's Finisterre rendezvous, and sure enough at daybreak on the 10th she sighted a strange cruiser in the distance that at once gave chase. Now it so happened that Milius, like every one else, had just boarded the American from Bordeaux, who by this time must have been entering into the humour of his position with thorough enjoyment. He informed Milius that the stranger was certainly the British cruiser *Phœnix*, on board of whom he had been summoned the previous day. She had only twenty guns, he said, but her captain and officers had so high a conceit of her and themselves that they would certainly fight. But in fact the Yankee was lying. There was sport in hand, and he would not spoil it. It was true he had been on board the *Phœnix*, as he said, but having asked to be shown round the ship, he found her commander, Captain Baker, had disguised her to look like a sloop. In fact, she was a frigate of thirty-six guns. But Baker had bought some cases of claret from him, probably at his own price, and having been otherwise handsomely treated he went back to his ship in high good humour, determined to play the English captain's game.

The result was all that Baker could wish. The *Didon* had now only three days to reach Allemand's rendezvous before he would be gone, and Milius, believing he had nothing but a weak enemy in his path, determined to fight his way through. His decision will probably be applauded as correct and seamanlike. His case differed essentially from that of the *Æolus*. He had definite material intelligence to convey to a definite spot, and, unlike the *Æolus*, he could not get it through in time without clearing an inferior enemy's cruiser out of his way. To run was to fail in his mission, to fight was to secure a chance of success. He chose to fight, and a very famous cruiser action was the result.

Both the commanders and both the frigates had the reputation of being amongst the smartest in the service. The *Didon* in size, force, crew, and speed was decidedly superior.[19] Baker, however, was confident, and being determined not to let her escape him, manœuvred to get to leeward before he would fire a shot. In the process, so brilliantly was the *Didon* handled, he was raked three or four times without being able to effect his purpose. So severely mauled was his rigging that further manoeuvring was impossible, and in desperation he ran straight at his opponent. Then at last the two vessels were fairly engaged side by side at pistol shot. Carronades, grape, musketry — everything got home at its best. A fresh attempt to rake which the *Didon* made, and which Baker cleverly parried, brought them yard-arm to yard-arm, the stem of the *Didon* almost foul of the starboard quarter of the *Phœnix*. Both men promptly tried to board, but so superior was the French strength that it was all Baker could do to keep his own decks free. For a while it was a rough affair of pikes and muskets, till Baker got a gun to bear out of his cabin window with terrible effect. Still the action raged almost muzzle to muzzle till both vessels were no longer under control, and they fell away from each other breathless to repair damages.

It had become calm with a big swell, and each commander was eager to be the first ready to catch a return of the breeze. Here the *Phœnix* had the advantage. Though her rigging and sails were in rags, her spars had suffered the least. The *Didon*, it is true, had lost nothing but her maintopmast, but so badly was her foremast wounded that before it could be secured she rolled it overboard. The *Phœnix*, on the other hand, was already nearly under control again. All essential knotting and splicing were complete as the breeze came back. In a few minutes her tattered sails began to draw, and she was bearing down again to renew the action. The *Didon* had already lost over seventy killed and wounded; she was absolutely helpless; and Milius ended a gallant and well-managed action by hauling down his flag.[20]

Baker had won, but his position was by no means easy. Nearly all his officers were wounded; he had less than 200 men to manage some 350 unwounded prisoners, and a dismasted prize, 200 tons bigger than himself, to get into safety. Taking her in tow, he made away to join Calder off Ferrol, but ere he reached his destination he fell in with the *Dragon* making for the Finisterre rendezvous to try to fall in with Nelson, with intelligence that the blockade was raised and Allemand at sea. Her news was such as made it madness to try to get north, and under her escort Baker turned back to get out of harm's way.

For the supreme hour had come: everything was in movement for the final cast, and it was Baker who, by his fine action, had ensured that at the crisis of the campaign, in spite of Napoleon's exhaustive ingenuity, the Rochefort squadron should remain as it had begun, lost and in the air — in touch with no one, and unable in any way to affect the issue.

CHAPTER XVI

General Situation At The Crisis

The turning-point of the campaign was at hand, but the hour was big with far more than the crisis of a campaign. A hundred years of rivalry for the lordship of the sea was drawing to culmination, and the protagonists, as in some old drama of destiny, were fairly face to face upon the imposing stage. On the cliffs of Boulogne, at the zenith of his powers, was the greatest master of war the long struggle had produced, alert and straining for the catastrophe amidst the sound and pomp of the Grand Army. Over against him, unknown to fame and bent with his eighty years, a sailor sat alone in the silence of his room at Whitehall. Unseen and almost unnoticed he was gathering in his fingers the threads of the tradition which the recurring wars had spun, and handling them with a deft mastery to which the distant fleets gave sensitive response. The splendour of quick success and an unrivalled genius for war was arrayed against hard-won experience and the instinct it had bred, and it was arrayed in vain.

Ever since Napoleon had realised with reluctant conviction that to pass his army across the Channel by stealth or its own force was impossible, he bad been exhausting his strategical ingenuity to secure the temporary command. He had run the gamut of every device his predecessors had ever tried. No trick or compelling movement had been neglected to dissipate the force that barred his way, to entice the persistent guard from its impregnable position, or by surprise to fling upon it an overwhelming mass of his own strength. For seven crowded months he had schemed and striven with the utmost power of his genius and with nearly the whole seaboard of Europe at his call; and yet when the hour came his squadrons were still impotently divided; and far from clearing the way for their union, his efforts were only drawing together at the old strategical centre practically the whole available battle strength of his enemy.

For Barham and Cornwallis it had been a time of acute anxiety. The *mise en scène* which Napoleon had directed Marmont to arrange in the Texel — his latest device to loosen the British grip of the Channel — had had its effect. Since the second week in July intelligence reports had been coming in from Holland of a sudden activity in the Helder. All transports had been moved out to the Texel Roads, three ships of the line ordered thence to Flushing had been told to stand fast, seven of the line and four frigates were ready for sea, and ammunition was pouring in along the roads from Amsterdam. Our agent was not deceived. Every one believed it meant a genuine movement, "but I," he said, "am enabled to tell you the truth. The plan is now for certain to risk a stroke on Ireland, and all that is done on our [that is, the Dutch] coast has no other object than to mislead the enemy." A few days later, however, came more emphatic information of Marmont's activity, and the Government felt they could no longer leave things as they were.[1] Then, as always, the threat of troops and ships in action together could not be ignored. They suggested naturally that Napoleon was contemplating getting a squadron into the Texel north-about, and as according to the First Lord's calculation, the Ushant squadron had then twenty-five of the line, it was decided to reinforce Lord Keith in the Downs, and Cornwallis was ordered to send him three seventy-fours.[2] Keith's own attitude was one of resolute incredulity, but he told the Government, if they attached any importance to the news, he advised that Admiral Russell, who under his orders was watching the Dutch coast from Yarmouth, ought to be directed never to leave the Texel. He would reinforce him as soon as possible and keep a frigate at hand, so that he himself could take command if anything happened. Meanwhile he had ordered Admiral Vashon, who from Leith was controlling the northern section of his command, to warn his cruisers on the Norwegian coast to be specially vigilant.[3]

The anxiety of the Government, however, increased. Four days later information came in from Lord Strangford, our *chargé-d'affaires* at Lisbon, that Villeneuve's instructions were certainly to return north-about and release Marmont's force in the Texel.[4] It was intelligence which, as we know, was not entirely without foundation. The idea was actually one of the alternatives with which Napoleon's brain was teeming. Strangford had received the information direct from Paris; the *Curieux's* report of Villeneuve's course endorsed it, and the danger became more serious. That very day the Admiralty issued an order to Cornwallis that be must send three more of the line to Lord Keith "with all possible despatch," and at the same time Rear-Admiral Drury, who was still in command of the Irish station, was directed to keep a vigilant watch for "any part of the enemy's squadron," and if anything appeared to send word by fast sailing vessels to Ushant, to the Admiralty, and to Nelson at Lagos.[5]

Lord Keith was still sceptical. On receipt of Strangford's information he replied that he attached little credit to it, but in deference to the Government's view he had repeated his orders to Vashon, and had instructed Russell that in case of need he was to fall back to the Downs.[6]

Barham's attitude to the flotilla theatre of operations is well shown by an interesting episode which occurred just at this time, and which marks the sharp distinction he drew between the defensive and the offensive parts of the plan of campaign. The young captains of the advanced cruisers were seizing every opportunity of striking at the belated sections of the French flotilla as they passed to the ports of concentration, and even at the Boulogne units when divisions came out for practice. On July 17th and 18th a more than usually serious affair of this kind had occurred, as Admiral Ver Huell was passing a strong section from Dunkirk to Boulogne. The attack had been pushed home with so much energy and daring that considerable damage was inflicted on Ver Huell's vessels; but the movement was not stopped, and the British cruisers engaged had suffered somewhat severely from the shore batteries. Keith reported the incident, with commendation of the brilliant behaviour of the officers concerned. But it was all quite contrary to Barham's ideas, and while fully recognising the courage and devotion of the attempt, he informed Keith that this kind of operation was not in accordance with sound strategy. He was to understand that it must not occur again. On no account were attacks to be made on the flotilla under the shore batteries by the cruisers of his command. "It may be," he said, "the means of losing them when they may be required for more material service." In other words, in the defensive area of the British plan, the forces were to remain on the defensive, and on no account to attack except when a clearly favourable opportunity for a counter-stroke presented itself.[7]

The main function of Cornwallis was, of course, to cover the defensive position of Lord Keith, and to prevent a hostile battle fleet from disturbing it. So impregnable indeed was Keith's position, so long as it was undisturbed from the ocean, that that of Cornwallis was the real key of the situation. For this reason he had been told, it will be remembered, that all orders for detachments were to be regarded by him as conditional on his keeping eighteen of the line with his flag. The second order to send three vessels to Keith was consequently difficult to deal with. He received it on August 4th, just after he had heard from Calder that Villeneuve had disappeared after the action, and that he had resumed the blockade of Ferrol and sent Stirling back to Rochefort. So far all was well, but he had now only just eighteen of the line with his flag; the detachment would reduce the squadron below the prescribed minimum. Nevertheless, Cornwallis obeyed and sent away his three weakest ships, which were also those best suited to the service on the Dutch coast.[8] Apparently the dangerous weakness to which the central position had thus been reduced was quickly realised, for on July 30th the three seventy-fours were ordered to return to Cornwallis's flag.[9] It was just at this time the Admiralty received news of Calder's indecisive action, and his own opinion that Villeneuve would probably get into Ferrol, and that he himself would have to close on Cornwallis. Barham was already of opinion that a rapid concentration of every available ship off Ushant was the simple and only solution of the disturbed situation. The closing in of the Western Squadron was already provided for, and on August 3rd an order was sent down to Nelson to come up and join it, after detaching whatever he regarded ay necessary to enable Collingwood to maintain the blockade of Cadiz.[10]

The broad strategical principles underlying these dispositions, and Barham's fundamental views as to the functions of the Western Squadron in the war-plan, are clearly indicated in a memorandum which he sent at this time to Cornwallis. It will be seen that his duties were far from being merely defensive. Subject to the primary exigencies of defence in home waters, his fleet was the active centre from which minor counter attacks were to be flung off as opportunity or need arose. "I had wrote you," the memorandum runs, "a private instruction, when we first heard of the Rochefort squadron being at sea, to send four ships of the line to intercept them, but the alarm from the eastward obliged us to send those ships to Lord Keith, which would otherwise have come to you." . . .

"It is truly mortifying not to be able to seize such opportunities when they offer, and it will be my study to keep your fleet as strong in numbers as possible, so as to allow you to detach squadrons for annoying the enemy, as often as you hear of them being in your neighbourhood without waiting for orders from home."

"As the Western Squadron is the mainspring from which all offensive operations must proceed, it shall be my care to keep it as strong and effective as possible."

"The enemy to the eastward are active in appearance, but as many things must concur to bring such an armament to sea, they cannot attack us unobserved."

"I hope you have an opportunity of communicating frequently with Sir John Saumarez, so that information of an attack to the eastward may be as early as possible, in case your assistance should become necessary."[11]

Lord Barham therefore, it is clear, while holding resolutely to the main defensive position, was alert to strike in any direction the moment the tortoise should show its head. As for Pitt, just as little as the old First Lord had he suffered the preoccupation with home defence to loosen his grip on the main offensive intention of his policy. And this is a point of the highest importance, if we are to judge rightly the masterstroke by which the situation was eventually solved. Whatever Napoleon might think, he had failed to wrest the initiative from Pitt's hands. The Treaty of Coalition, it is true, had not yet been ratified by the Czar, but during the last week of July news reached the Government from St. Petersburg which pointed to a speedy conclusion of the whole matter. The Czar's idea of the Coalition, it will be remembered, was to use it as an armed mediation for forcing Napoleon to abandon his intolerable policy of aggrandisement, and to assent to a general settlement of Europe on terms acceptable to England and the other Powers. We have seen how the terms demanded by England in regard to her position in the Mediterranean were not approved by the Czar. The last despatches from Gower, received on July 3rd, had announced that Austria was equally irreconcilable on the point, and that although she was mobilising her army she was not to be trusted. Russia, however, might possibly act alone, and the Ambassador had been given to understand she was going to bring her force in Corfu up to 25,000 men. General Lacy had actually reached Naples, and he seemed ready to co-operate with Craig in South Italy. Moreover, although the Czar would not ratify the treaty, he was already acting on it. He had arranged with Pitt that a Russian envoy charged with the mediation should represent both countries. The man chosen for the mission was Novosilzow, one of the Czar's most confidential servants, and he was on the point of starting for Paris. On his way he was to stay at Berlin and endeavour to press the halting Prussian Government into line.[12] The news which now came to hand was that Napoleon's defiant annexation of Northern Italy had exhausted the Czar's patience. "Such an act," wrote Gower, "at the very moment when a Russian plenipotentiary was expected in France charged with propositions of which the professed object had been the general arrangement of the affairs of Europe, is considered so gross an insult to both Sovereigns whose sentiments that plenipotentiary was empowered to declare, that his Imperial Majesty had judged he could not . . . permit Monsieur Novosilzow to proceed." An express consequently had been sent to recall him.

So far all was well, but Gower had to report that feeling at the Russian Court was almost equally sore at Pitt's insistence on the retention of Malta, and his categorical refusal even to consider a modification of the Maritime Code. To Gower's explanations and arguments they had responded by reproaching him with the fact that no answer had been received from London to the proposition the Czar had made for an extended plan of operations and an increase of the British subsidy in return for an increase of the Russian troops. Fortunately at the moment a despatch arrived from London frankly accepting the new proposals, and the sky began to clear. Gower said he had not been able actually to secure the ratification, but that he had no doubt he would be able to announce it in his next despatch.[13]

At the same time Worontzow, at the Russian embassy in London, received information from Novosilzow at Berlin that Austria was coming round. She was beginning to realise, he said, that force was the only remedy, and though apparently acquiescing in Napoleon's seizure of the Iron Crown, was only waiting for the right moment to declare her adhesion to the Coalition. Prussia, too, was inclining to repent her subservience. "They see more clearly," wrote the Russian envoy when he reached Berlin, "Buonaparte is no more a guardian angel, but an out-and-out devil, and they are persuaded that this devil will gobble Germany if they let him alone and persist any longer in their inaction."[14]

Of the effect this intelligence had upon Pitt's mind there is no direct evidence. But the action he took suggests that his quick eye for a situation saw in it the moment of all others for high action. Though England was in the crisis of her defence against the long-threatened invasion, he did not hesitate to give new impetus to his measure for attack. Certainly it was the hour at which England at all risks should show she had the power and the will to strike, for all Napoleon's effort to bind her hands. What at least is certain, is that in the height of the disturbance which the news from the Texel was causing, and regardless of the resulting strain on the Navy, Pitt laid fresh burdens upon it. The Russian demand had to be honoured, and on July 27th he decided that the Commander-in-chief in the Mediterranean was to concert measures with Craig to carry out the joint action in Italy, which the "extended" Russian plan demanded. This meant providing transport and escort for 25,000 troops from the Black Sea, as well as for the 6,000 of Craig's force at Malta.[15]

But this was not all. For in a separate despatch from Gower there was news of a fresh danger against which England must be prepared to strike alone, whether the Powers took action or not. "The state of affairs in Constantinople," wrote the Ambassador, "is at this moment extremely critical." The Russian Ambassador at the Porte had sent his Government word that General Joubert had arrived there with a personal letter from Napoleon to the Sultan and a large sum of money, to secure adherents to the French interests. A new Grand Vizier devoted to France had come to power; a typically indiscreet Russian governor had committed an untimely violation of Turkish territory; our own Ambassador had not yet appeared, and the negotiations which had been in progress for a Russo-Turkish Alliance had been broken off.[16] Here then was a recrudescence of the old danger which Nelson had scotched at the Nile, and for all his preoccupations Pitt would not leave it alone. At Cork there was still Eyre Coote's force waiting in inaction. When it was known that Villeneuve had left the West Indies, it had been ordered to stand fast a second time. Coote's appointment as Governor of Jamaica, however, was not cancelled, and General David Baird had succeeded him in command. This force then was now disposable, and Barham was informed that the Government intended to use it for a secret expedition to capture the Cape of Good Hope. It would consist of between six and seven thousand men, and the Admiralty was to provide a battle squadron and cruisers for the escort under Sir Home Popham.[17]

For all the serious state of affairs in Turkey, the idea is open to an obvious criticism. If Pitt was really focusing his plan of campaign on a combined offensive movement against Napoleon in Italy in concert with Russia, elementary strategy demanded that he should concentrate all disposable force upon that movement. It can only be said it was no mere question of elementary strategy. The situation was confused by the mutual suspicions of the parties to the still incomplete Coalition. Though its prospects were certainly brightening, the British ministers could not suddenly dismiss their suspicion that the continental Powers concerned were perhaps playing for their own hands, and might at any moment come to terms with Napoleon and leave England in the lurch. If so, Pitt's great scheme to cover India by forcing Napoleon back from his advanced position in the Mediterranean would fall to the ground. In so precarious and unstable a diplomatic situation, was it or was it not good strategy to prepare a second line of defence for our Eastern trade and possessions? No one but a beginner in the study of war would presume to answer the question with confidence. The answer would seem to turn on the reality of the Turkish danger, and on the exact degree of reliance that at the time could be placed upon the prospect of the Coalition. Of that there was certainly no better judge than Pitt. In any case the enterprise cannot be dismissed as a mere eccentric or sporadic attack having no organic connection with the main issue. It way in fact an essential part in the comprehensive scheme of Imperial defence.

Its higher strategical purpose was clearly set forth in Pitt's instructions to Lord Cornwallis, the Governor-General of India. Castlereagh's despatch, which conveyed them, informed him that since it was possible that India might require reinforcements before they could be sent out from home, he was authorised in case of need to call on Baird and direct Admiral Popham to cover the passage of the force against interference from the French base at Mauritius. But it was only to be done in case of urgent danger to India. "The whole of this instruction," Castlereagh explained, "proceeds upon the principle that the true value of the Cape to Great Britain is its being considered and treated at all times as an outpost subservient to the protection and security of our Indian possessions. When in our hands it must afford considerable accommodation and facilities to our intercourse with those possessions, but its occupation is perhaps even more material as depriving the enemy of the best intermediate position between Europe and India for assembling a large European armament for service in the East Indies," as well as for the intercepting and protection of trade. Lord Cornwallis therefore, before making a call on the expeditionary force, was to consider fully on these lines the relative advantage of summoning Baird to India or holding the Cape.[18]

The reasoning is plain. In the previous winter, when Napoleon began to regard the invasion of England as impracticable, he had formulated a plan for such an attack on India as Castlereagh's despatch indicated. Seeing how confident the Government was in the impregnability of their home defence, there was every possibility that Napoleon would shortly be forced back once more on Colonial attack as a means of containing the British forces; and Joubert's appearance at Constantinople gave strong colour to the apprehension that India would be the possession chosen. If so, no success in the Mediterranean could prevent his making such an attack, particularly if he secured the co-operation of the Porte. Moreover, howsoever strong our position in the Mediterranean and the Near East, it would still be open to him to turn it by way of the Cape. So long as it was in the hands of his Dutch vassals it was a real danger. It gave him a line of operation at least as formidable as that by way of Egypt and the Red Sea, or of Turkey and the Persian Gulf. To mass all our available force on the one line was to leave the other open. It lay over an open sea, and it was consequently impossible to secure it by naval force alone, as in the case of the narrow seas at home. It is therefore unsafe to dismiss the idea with contempt by applying crudely the simple test of concentration. It was in effect a concentration of effort upon one object, but from geographical exigencies and the existing political conditions it was more than doubtful whether the correlative concentration of force could surely be effective on one line of operations only. In any case the whole question will serve as a warning that the broad combined problems of Imperial defence are not to be solved off-hand by the facile application of maxims which are the outcome of narrower and less complex continental conditions.

Such then were the involved considerations through which Pitt and Barham had to steer their course, as they faced the crisis in the Narrow Seas. They are considerations which at first sight may appear to have little to do with it, but in fact it will be seen that they determined the crucial movement which we have now to consider: and no right judgment of it is possible unless they be kept firmly in mind.

CHAPTER XVII

The Masterstroke

It was on August 10th that Villeneuve intended to begin his final movement from Coruña. "I am sailing," he wrote to Decrès on that day, "and I shall make for Brest or Cadiz according to circumstances. The enemy observe us here too closely to leave any hope of concealing our movement."[1]

Light westerly airs prevailed, and owing to part of the fleet being up the Ferrol arm of the bay it was not till the 13th that he had all his force together outside. So severe had been the punishment which Calder had inflicted upon the original Combined Squadron, that even as reinforced by the divisions of Gourdon and Grandallana, it only numbered twenty-nine of the line. Of these fourteen were the raw Ferrol ships that had had no sea or fleet training whatever, and of the whole number only one, the *Principe de Asturias* 120, was a three-decker. Six were 80-gun ships and the rest seventy-fours. The cruisers numbered six frigates and four corvettes. There was still, however, a fond hope that the *Didon* might get touch with Allemand, and that the addition of his squadron would bring the whole Combined Fleet up to thirty-four of the line with another first-rate.

It was precisely during these days that the British counter-concentration was taking place off Ushant. Stirling having found Rochefort empty came in on the 13th just as Villeneuve was getting his squadrons together outside Coruña, and the same evening Cornwallis's cruisers signalled the approach of Calder. Next morning, before Villeneuve had been able to move, he joined, and the following day, the 15th, Nelson appeared.

Ever since the 9th, when he had made enough westing to drop the northerly winds, he had been steering a course for his original rendezvous fifty leagues west of Scilly. By noon on the 13th he was about 150 miles short of it, and in the course of the afternoon he fell in with the *Niobe*. She was three days from Cornwallis, and could report that when she parted company nothing had been heard of the Combined Squadron in the Bay. She had, however, spoken a Portuguese, who said he had sighted it a short time previously steering north. Assured by the information that Ireland was not in danger, Nelson immediately bore away to the eastward, signalling the Ushant rendezvous, and by six o'clock on the evening of the 15th he was saluting Cornwallis's flag.[2]

Without even calling on Nelson to report himself, Cornwallis, on Barham's instructions, ordered him and the *Victory* home for their long-earned rest. Stirling in the *Glory* was also sent in with several other vessels that required a refit. In the end he had some thirty-six of the line with his flag, or on their way to join it, besides the *Dragon* and *Goliath*, which were to the southward in search respectively of Nelson and Calder. Considering its preponderance in three-deckers, and its high efficiency, it was a force that completely commanded the situation. Had the allied Admirals come north, even with Allemand in company, they certainly must have been defeated long before Ganteaume could have come to their assistance.[3]

Such then was the actual situation. What did Napoleon make of it? Did he doubt from the first — even before the concentration was complete — that all hope of the invasion was at an end?

On August 3rd, as we have seen, he had reached Boulogne, displaying an inspiring confidence that the command of the Channel was about to pass into his hands. But that is by no means conclusive that he saw his way clear for attempting his hazardous enterprise. The indications of a coalition in his rear were too ominous to be ignored. Austria was massing troops in Venetia and the Tyrol, constant communications were passing between Naples, Corfu, and Malta, and a levy *en masse* of the Neapolitan militia was reported by St. Cyr to be going on in secret. Before quitting Paris Napoleon directed Talleyrand to prepare an ultimatum for both the Austrian and Neapolitan courts, and then, without saying a word to his ministers, he had suddenly left for Boulogne. The day after he reached the coast, he approved the text of the Austrian note, and directed that Naples was to be threatened with instant invasion if the report of the general enrolment proved correct. He had no doubt, as he afterwards confessed, that these threats would prove effective, and that he would be left free to proceed with his invasion.

Such was his state of mind when, before the ink of his last order was well dry, urgent Spanish despatches came in from Talleyrand. They announced nothing less disturbing than that Nelson had almost certainly reappeared at Gibraltar, and was believed to have entered the Mediterranean.

Talleyrand made no secret of what it meant. Villeneuve was no one knew where, and all the far-sighted minister could see was that, if he attempted to approach the Channel under the delusion that the British concentration was broken, he was doomed to destruction. The position was alarming in the extreme. Napoleon's sudden and quite unexpected departure from Paris filled Talleyrand with dread lest his master's gambling spirit had got the better of him, and that at last he really meant to stake everything on the desperate throw from which he had so long held back. "This unexpected news," he wrote to Napoleon, "has made an impression upon me which I try in vain to calm. This kind of agitation is only to be endured by those of your servants who are supported by your presence." Then he proceeded to tell his master plainly that he was beaten. He was sure that Nelson would come north, and he calculated that his arrival would give the English a line of at least fifty-four vessels. "This unforeseen concentration," he urged, "leaves no doubt that the project of invasion is impracticable for the moment; but as the reality of this project cannot but gain the strongest confirmation by the presence of your Majesty at Boulogne, it is probable it will decide the English to mass at some Channel rendezvous, and this disposition will give the Combined Fleet time and means to get into a Spanish port."[4]

Napoleon after his manner did not deign to traverse his minister's conclusions; he simply refused to admit the facts. "All this news about Nelson," he wrote to Decrès, "seems doubtful. What the devil could he be after in the Mediterranean? Do they want twenty of the line there?" At this time, it is to be remembered, he had not heard of Craig's arrival at Malta, and not a word of Villeneuve. He knew nothing of his arrival in Europe or of the battle. He still believed not only that he had frightened his enemy into an abject defensive, but that they had no suspicion of his great plan. "They little know," he added, "what they have got hanging in their ear. Everything here is going well, and certes if we are masters of the passage for twelve hours, England has lived. I can't make out why we have no news from Ferrol. I can't believe Magon never reached him [Villeneuve]. I am telling Ganteaume by telegraph to keep out in the Bertheaume Road."[5]

Three more days went by and then came news, not of Villeneuve, but again of Nelson. After watering and revictualing at Gibraltar and Tetuan he had come back out the Straits, and as long since as July 25th he had been seen from the Cadiz signal stations making for Cape St. Vincent.[6] This same day, whether before or after receiving the news, we cannot tell, Napoleon told Talleyrand not to send off the note to Vienna before he had seen it again, and directed his Guard to leave Paris for Boulogne. Then on the morrow came news at last of Villeneuve. It told of his indecisive action with Calder and how he had put into Vigo to refit, but it expressed his intention of proceeding at once according to the plan to join hands with the Ferrol divisions and come on to Brest. Napoleon chose, or at least pretended, to see in all this the realisation of his hopes. He immediately had a victory proclaimed, and announced that Villeneuve had fulfilled his mission, but at the same time he ordered his Guard to stand fast in Paris.[7]

He was clearly at his wits' end. As the vigilant financial world saw him apparently resolving to hazard the desperate throw his credit was falling dangerously, and he was strenuously trying to restore it by elaborating the success of Villeneuve's action. To Villeneuve himself, who had written in the lowest spirits, he sent word to point out encouragingly that the British success was really insignificant, and that he still hoped he would proceed with his mission. He persuaded himself, on information from his spies in England, that the Admiralty believed the Combined Squadron had gone to Cadiz or was coming to the Texel, and once more he urged Marmont "to do the impossible" to draw the English in his direction. He must occupy at least twelve of the line. It was indeed the impossible; for ten days were still to pass before Marmont saw half that number barring his exit. They were all weak ships that were fit for nothing else, and that was the utmost force ever devoted to him. The only effect of the feint, as we have seen, was for a moment to interfere with Barham's arrangements for reinforcing Cornwallis in order to permit of his detaching a force to strike at Allemand.[8]

By stubbornly ignoring the news of Nelson and by crediting the British Admiralty with childish simplicity, Napoleon seems at this moment, if ever, really to have believed that his hour had come, and for three days was all amiability and encouragement. But on the 13th the note was changed. Word came in from Villeneuve that, instead of forming his junction outside Ferrol and immediately coming on, he had entered the port before the Emperor's stringent prohibition had come to his hands. Napoleon was beside himself. It is of this day that Daru, the head of his War Office staff, tells the well-known story. The Emperor sent for him, and he found him raving up and down the room railing coarse abuse upon his unhappy Admiral. Then, suddenly stopping, he cried, "Sit down there and write," and with that he dictated without a check the whole of the orders for his immortal campaign of Austerlitz.[9]

Whatever truth there may be in the story, it must not be taken to mean that Napoleon had wholly abandoned his idea of invasion. It may have been intended merely to give emphasis to his threat to Vienna. The same day he ordered Talleyrand to see the Austrian Ambassador and urge instant demobilisation in the strongest terms. "Already," so the minister was to tell him, "he (Napoleon) has suspended the execution of his projects of hostility, and has recognised that he cannot cross into England with 150,000 men when his southern frontiers are menaced."[10]

Whether or not he meant what he said there is no sign yet that he had admitted himself beaten. That same fevered day, with increasing passion, he poured forth letter after letter to Decrès with the instructions he was to send to Villeneuve. By fair means or foul the despairing Admiral must be heartened, cajoled, or bullied into getting to sea again. If this was not the real object of these extraordinary documents — if Napoleon really believed in the possibility of what he wrote — he had entirely lost grip of the situation. In his frenzy — for it was hardly less — he pictured the British squadrons deceived by his fancied diversions and scattered upon the seas — off Ireland, in the North Sea, in the Mediterranean, everywhere but where they were — in the act of gathering at the fatal point. Calculation after calculation of the British force and disposition he showered upon Decrès and Villeneuve, each more groundless, more sanguine than the last, and all full of glaring contradictions and false estimates. But his labour was thrown away; for at that moment Villeneuve was already sailing from Coruña with his path barred before him. It was no longer a question of what he did or left undone. The game was played, and Napoleon was outmanœuvred.

For all his fierce refusal to admit the truth which Talleyrand had told him, he was even then preparing to face it. On those same critical days — the 13th and 14th — he was actually directing Talleyrand to issue his revised ultimatum to Austria. "The answer," he wrote, "is easy to forecast. It will contain denials, protestations — in a word, dilatory phrases. That will not do for me. My decision is made. I will attack Austria and be at Vienna before the month of November, to face the Russians if they show themselves."[11] Possibly then he had already half realised his failure. On the 15th, not knowing that Villeneuve had sailed, he wrote again in despair at what seemed to him the invincible ineptitude of his Admiral. On his head he visited the results of his own confused orders, and could not see they had brought their own reward. His failure to grasp the foundations of the game, which every British Admiral knew by heart, is almost incredible in so great a genius for war. In this very letter he naïvely exposes what can only be called the simplicity with which his fantastic plan had been framed. "What I find so extraordinary in all this," he says, "is that the place of Allemand's rendezvous . . . is just the position where the battle was fought." Surely the barest knowledge of the theory and practice of naval warfare would have taught him that that was just the most natural thing to expect. His confident egotism would not recognise that he was playing against past-masters of a game at which he was only an amateur. What he took for astute strategical inspirations were to his opponents the commonplaces of their craft, and while he stood fuming between bewilderment and wounded self-confidence, making confusion worse confounded, the men of the old tradition were playing in sure mastery high over his head.

It was now they delivered their masterstroke. In all the campaign there is no movement — not even Nelson's chase of Villeneuve — that breathes more deeply the true spirit of war, and yet nothing in it has been more severely criticised. Let us see then exactly how things stood. The middle of August was the actual crisis of Napoleon's long prepared threat. He himself was at Boulogne, alert to give the word at any moment, and the Grand Army and its transport were ready or as nearly ready as Napoleon's genius could get them. But at the vital moment the great concentration of the British battle fleet at the mouth of the Channel was also complete, and it made the movement of the Grand Army impossible. So long as that concentration held England was impregnable, even to the most formidable attack that had ever threatened her. On the other hand, the main fleet of the enemy was at Ferrol free to come north, but also free to go south for Cadiz and the Mediterranean. For all Barham or Cornwallis could tell this was the game Napoleon was playing — the game that Talleyrand was actually urging his master to play. In the eyes of the British Admirals the whole project of the invasion was so desperate that they could not believe it was real, and, with experienced penetration, they detected in it a device to force upon them a concentration off Brest, which would leave Villeneuve free to strike to the southward. To prevent such a movement of the Combined Fleet was, as the British war-plan stood, no less important than to overwhelm it if it came north. What then should Cornwallis do? Should he rest content with the control of the invasion theatre: or should he strike to control the whole theatre of the campaign? Should he be satisfied with impregnable defence, or should he risk it to deprive the enemy of all initiative? "The Western Squadron is the mainspring from which all offensive operations must proceed." Lord Barham was even then writing the words to him, but the letter had not yet arrived.[12] There was not a day to lose; at any time Villeneuve might be moving, and if Cornwallis waited for orders from the Admiralty it might be too late to act. Surely higher responsibility never rested on an Admiral at sea. Yet there is not a sign of hesitation in the stout old officer. To wait for orders was to abandon the game. In his room at the Admiralty Barham was telling him to strike when he saw the chance, "without waiting for orders from home," and he did not wait, even for the permission.

Not for more than twenty-four hours did he hold the concentration. On the 16th, the day after Nelson joined, Cornwallis signed orders to Calder to take eighteen of the line, which, with the *Dragon* and *Goliath* already to the southward, would give him twenty, and proceed off Ferrol, there to use his utmost exertion to prevent the enemy sailing again, or to intercept them if they attempted it. The squadron detailed included five three-deckers and seven of Nelson's squadron, with his second-in-command, Rear-Admiral Louis, at their head in the *Canopus* 80 — and seeing the high condition of the force contrasted with that of Villeneuve's sickly, heterogeneous, and demoralised fleet, it may be taken as fairly its equal. Such at least was Villeneuve's own opinion.[13]

Though at the time Cornwallis believed on Calder's report that Allemand had probably joined Villeneuve, and would have raised his force to well over thirty of the line, he could spare no more, but even this danger would not deter him from the bold stroke the situation demanded.[14] He had in fact divided his fleet, keeping the minimum of eighteen of the line with his flag, of which about ten were three-deckers.[15]

This was the move which Napoleon characterised as an *insigne bétise* when he heard of it. "What a chance Villeneuve has missed!" he wrote. "By coming down upon Brest from the open he might have played prisoners' base with Calder's squadron and fallen upon Cornwallis; or with his thirty of the line have beaten the English twenty, and obtained a decisive superiority."[16] It is in this opinion that so many modern critics have followed him. Forgetting, as we shall see, under what a smart of irritation he uttered the snarl, they have solemnly endorsed his testy criticism. We are told that the great movement is "condemned by the simplest and most generally admitted principles of warfare," that it was "a strategical blunder," "a blunder which might have proved fatal," and more to the same effect.[17]

It is a point that goes to the root of naval strategy, and only by a careful study of the case in detail can we understand why at that hour in which the war experience of centuries culminated the judgment of the veterans concerned was unanimous, without hesitation, and clean contrary to that of their recent critics.

As to the risk involved — the possibility of Napoleon's game of "prisoners' base" — let us first take the official British view. Certainly it was not that the result of an action between Villeneuve and Calder would be as Napoleon professed to believe, and there is nothing in the whole war to support the Emperor's sanguine opinion. On all the evidence an action fought out between the two squadrons would have put both of them off the board, and this was Nelson's view. When the division of the fleet was known he was consulted by the anxious ministers. "This I ventured without any fear," he wrote, "that if Calder got fairly close alongside them with twenty-seven or twenty-eight sail, by the time the enemy had beat our fleet soundly they would do us no harm this year."[18]

Nor did Cornwallis fear for his own position the possibility of "prisoners' base." Besides the *Dragon* and *Goliath* he had three cruisers watching Ferrol, as well as two or three others in the neighbourhood.[19] "Should their lordships," he wrote, in reporting the detachment of Calder, "be pleased to order the ships in any other direction it may easily be effected." Clearly he considered them as strategically still under his hand. In his view they were still concentrated in the real sense of the term, within supporting distance of each other. "I have thought," he concluded, "the step I have now taken might meet with their lordships' approbation, as a means of keeping the enemy's squadrons in check, if that from Rochefort is still at sea."[20]

Now the critics omit to observe that their lordships did approve. It was only natural they should, for the moment they heard of Nelson's return they sent Cornwallis an order to do just what he had done, with only one small difference. They were dissatisfied with Calder's conduct after the action, and he was not to command. Barham and Cornwallis then were independently at one upon the movement — a fact which should make critics pause. The order was signed on August 19th, and it bade Cornwallis retain eighteen of the line off Ushant and detach Sir Charles Cotton, his own second-in-command, with two flag-officers under him, off Ferrol. He was to give him twenty of the line and as many more as he might have at his disposal up to thirty-two.[21]

It was not that they did not realise the gravity of the situation at home. Only ten days before they had given Cornwallis formal warning "that the enemy have it in contemplation to attempt immediately the invasion of this country from the ports of Holland and Boulogne." It was the period of spring tides, when the Dutch squadron would be able to put to sea, and in a private letter to the Admiral Barham had called special attention to the danger. "I just write one line," he said, "to apprise you, ministers look to an invasion soon, and have given directions to all the military corps. I have done the same privately to the Admirals at all the ports. I take it for granted you will take a near station during the spring tides in order to reinforce the Eastern force if necessary."[22] The imminence of the danger then, such as it was, was fairly faced, but none the less both Pitt and Barham were determined not to be forced back upon the defensive — determined not to devote to it more force than they felt gave them a sufficiently firm grip upon the threatened invasion, and determined not to be intimidated out of their offensive plan of campaign. To have kept the fleet massed where it was would have been to surrender the initiative to Napoleon, to have acted tamely upon the defensive. And it is curious that the critics who most severely condemn the movement are just those who are the most fanatical prophets of the offensive.

"This division of the fleet," writes the most weighty of them, "which is condemned by the simplest and most generally admitted principles of warfare, transferred to Villeneuve all the advantage of central position and superior force, and was stigmatised by Napoleon as a 'glaring blunder.' . . . This censure was just."[23] But how did it transfer the central position to Villeneuve? If against all probability he had dared to face the concentration which he knew was to the north of him; if by a miracle he had succeeded in eluding Cornwallis's cruiser screen and had got between him and Calder, he would in a sense have obtained it, but only in regard to our defensive area. Looking at the whole theatre of the campaign, he had the central position already. At Ferrol he was interposed between our main force and Collingwood with the Mediterranean fleet. On our keeping control of the Mediterranean rested our engagement with the Powers of the Coalition. Pitt at the moment was absorbed in fulfilling that engagement. It could only be done by preserving the initiative which we had gained at Malta and Corfu, and for that it was essential that we should forthwith wrest the central position from Villeneuve. Having gained that position, Napoleon had the choice of striking at the Channel or within the Straits, and as the political situation had developed in the past weeks, it was vital to deny him the choice. The seeds which Pitt had sown so patiently were ripe for the counter-attack. As Cornwallis had said, the enemy's fleets must be "held in check" and the control of military action in the Mediterranean placed beyond doubt. Had the movement not taken place, as Codrington wrote of Villeneuve's fleet on the eve of Trafalgar, "this immense force would probably by this time have been already in Toulon to co-operate with the French army in Italy."[24] The central position of the whole theatre, in fact, stretched from Ferrol to Brest, and it was this position that Barham and Cornwallis decided at once and simultaneously to re-occupy.

It is obvious, then, that if the movement be considered in the light of the whole situation, it was one which has ample justification in the universal principles of strategy. But beyond those principles lay a further vindication in the special exigencies of maritime war. The case indeed affords a typical example of the frequent error which, arises from attempting to measure naval strategy by the elementary maxims derived from warfare on land. The question once more was not purely military. It was distorted by the intrusion of commerce protection. It was the season for the home-coming of the great convoys. The concentration at Ferrol directly threatened them, and the necessity for securing their approach was a dominant consideration in Lord Barham's mind. "Ferrol," he wrote to Cornwallis, "is the great object till our East India and West India fleets are arrived, and which may be in the course of a fortnight. The heavy frigates, as far as you can spare them, cannot be employed better than meeting them towards the coast of Ireland." That is, he was in the usual way to provide a covering squadron against the enemy's battle squadron and strengthen the convoy's escort as they reached the danger area of the home terminal. And then Barham added, "We have at this moment received yours, and you have entered completely into my views."[25]

It may be urged by purists trained in the continental school that such deflections are essentially heretical. But in truth each case must be decided on its merits as a balance of advantage against risk. It is for a naval power to command the sea for all purposes if it has the power. In this case we shall see, as we proceed, the safety of these particular convoys was an object of so much importance as to justify any reasonable risk, while to suffer a concentration to be forced upon us which would leave the enemy free to strike them with impunity would have been to admit an inability in the fleet which nothing in the situation could excuse.

And was there any real danger? Bold as was the division of the fleet, a closer examination of the conditions will show that it was well within fair risk of war. From the prisoners taken in Calder's action the condition of the Combined Fleet was well known. We also knew how inadequate were the resources of Ferrol to supply so large a force as Villeneuve's for the time necessary for a campaign in the Channel. His respect for Nelson's unlocated fleet was fully manifest, and to war-ripened judgments like those of Barham and Cornwallis it must have seemed morally certain that Villeneuve would never venture to come north on his own responsibility. It was true Napoleon might force on him the desperate movement, but in that case there was a consideration well known both to Barham and Cornwallis that practically ensured its failure. They knew the Combined Fleet was so much exhausted and that the resources of Ferrol were so inadequate to supply it, that one of two things must happen. Villeneuve might either wait in the port long enough to complete his stores for a Channel campaign, in which case Calder would be in plenty of time to blockade him, or he might hurry out with his supplies incomplete, in which case it would be impossible for him to keep the sea long enough to carry out Napoleon's intentions. If, therefore, he moved before Calder arrived, it would mean almost certainly that he was bound for Cadiz or to attack the convoys.

Finally, if these calculations proved false —if Villeneuve in desperation did stake everything on the chance of "playing prisoners' base" with Calder and striking a swift blow at Cornwallis alone, what would be the results? It is usual to assume that the Ushant fleet was inferior to that of Villeneuve. But it is to be remembered that Cornwallis had ten three-deckers and the rest all seasoned ships of eighty and seventy-four guns, as against Villeneuve's motley twenty-nine partly French and partly Spanish. Of these ten at least were mere floating barracks, and amongst those ten his only three-decker.[26] Now with such a force Cornwallis had two possibilities before him. If he chose or was forced to fight, the effect must be that Villeneuve's fleet would be fit for little afterwards. If he avoided and played the old game of Howe and Kempenfelt, moving to the westward till Calder rejoined, experience showed that Ganteaume and Villeneuve together would not dare enter the Channel without having first brought him to action.[27]

Every precaution to meet such a situation was taken. Orders of the most urgent description had been sent to the Port Admirals to get everything to sea that would float, and Barham calculated that he had ready or nearly ready for emergent service in the Channel 15 three-deckers, 4 eighty gun ships, and about 35 other two-deckers belonging to the Western Squadron alone; and besides these there were 9 two-deckers at sea with Lord Keith and 5 more fitting in the Thames.[28] Had the worst happened that Barham's strategy risked, had Villeneuve attempted to do what every Admiral in Napoleon's service knew to be madness, then there must have come upon the enemy in the narrow unfamiliar waters of the Channel — so dreadful with memories both for French and Spaniards — a catastrophe more terrible than the Armada — more decisive than Trafalgar itself.

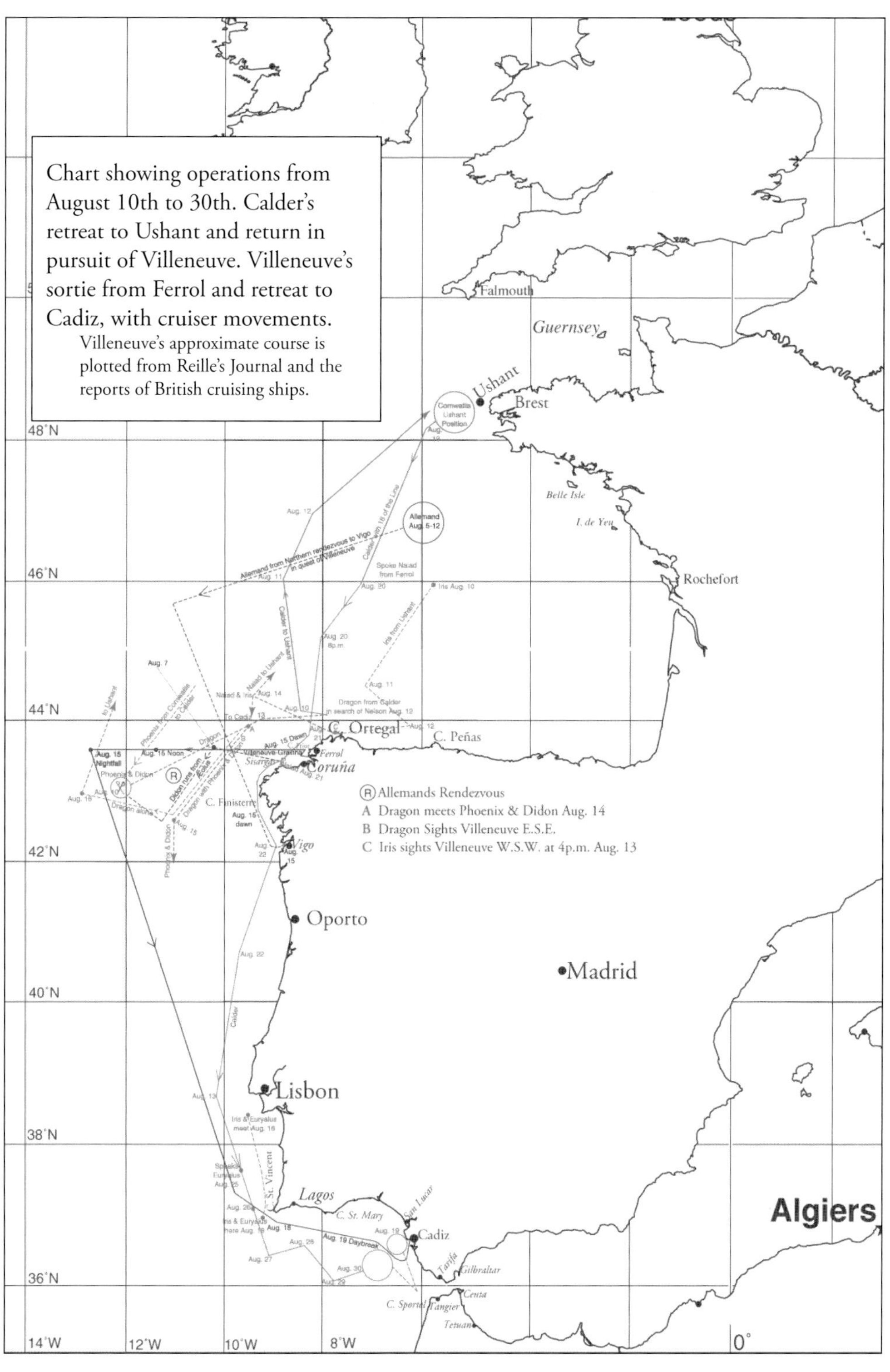

Chart showing operations from August 10th to 30th. Calder's retreat to Ushant and return in pursuit of Villeneuve. Villeneuve's sortie from Ferrol and retreat to Cadiz, with cruiser movements.

Villeneuve's approximate course is plotted from Reille's Journal and the reports of British cruising ships.

CHAPTER XVIII

The Solution Of The Crisis

From the above considerations it will be seen that in the opinion of the responsible men the danger attending the division of the fleet was not for a moment to be weighed against the decisive advantage such a division alone could secure. The moral strength of the British position had been accurately calculated, but at the same time it must not be supposed the utmost care was not taken by material means to guard against the remote probability of a surprise from the south. Ferrol had not been left unwatched for a single day. On the contrary, Cornwallis had taken elaborate measures to keep touch with it. It was on August 9th that Villeneuve had begun to move his fleet outside, and that Calder had sent the *Dragon* to look into the bay. On the 10th she had returned with the *Æolus* fresh from locating Allemand. Their report was that all the Combined Fleet had come down to Coruña—a with the exception of eight vessels still windbound up at Ferrol. It was on this report that Calder had gone north to close on Ushant, and no sooner was he away than the *Nimble* appeared. She was a sloop Cornwallis had sent off to communicate with Stirling and Calder. Directly she was sighted by Villeneuve's cruisers she was chased off, but not before she too had seen Villeneuve at Coruña. Five sail were under way as though they had just joined — a fact which could only confirm Calder's impression that Allemand had arrived. Forthwith she sped back to warn the Admiral at Ushant. She reached him early on the 14th, just after he had had the news from Calder. It was now he determined to divide his fleet; and the *Nimble* was immediately sent down again with other cruisers to keep observation till Calder should arrive.[1]

What it was Villeneuve really meant to do has always been a matter of doubt. Did he or did he not intend to make any attempt to join hands with Ganteaume? In the despatch he sent to Allemand by the *Didon* he had said if he found any difficulty in getting to Brest his definitive destination would be Cadiz.[2] On the 10th he wrote to Dècres the letter already quoted: "I am sailing, and I shall make for Brest or Cadiz, according to circumstances. The enemy are watching us here too closely to leave any hope of concealing my course."[3] He had no idea but what Calder was still off the port, but this was not the worst. The moral effect of Nelson's implacable chase had been extraordinary, and every one in his heart believed he was somewhere below the horizon with Calder, waiting till he had them well away from their port to strike his blow. The last news of him was that he had been seen speeding from the Straits towards Cape St. Vincent, and the inference that was drawn we have in a despatch written by General Beurnonville, the French ambassador at Madrid, to Talleyrand before it was known that Villeneuve had sailed. "We cannot reasonably suppose," he argued, "that the English squadrons are not concentrated, and to that I attribute the clinging of our admirals to Ferrol. Nelson and Calder have not less than twenty-seven of the line, several of which are three-deckers."[4] In the opinion of Lauriston, the General in command of the troops in the fleet, the probability of such a concentration had entirely upset Villeneuve's equilibrium. "Indeed, Sire," he afterwards wrote to the Emperor, "the fear of Nelson has got the upper hand of him." The General himself was not free from the oppression. "It will not be long," he wrote in the same letter, "before we have Nelson down upon us; for we have learnt that with those eleven vessels he has sworn to follow us, even if it be to the Antipodes."[5]

For three days more the westerly winds held the Ferrol division fast and delayed the final concentration. As they dallied in inaction, every hour was adding to the chances of Nelson and Calder getting together to intercept them the obsession increased daily: and by the 13th. when the windbound ships eventually were able to reach Villeneuve, the last drop of his spirit seems to have ebbed away. Lauriston at least believed that by the time the fleet was under way and the final despatches had been sent off to Paris, Villeneuve had abandoned all intention of attempting to effect the junction with Ganteaume. "We are going definitely to Cadiz," the Admiral had said to him; "I have told the minister so."[6]

What Villeneuve had really written to Dècres in his last despatch was this: "I am about to sail, but I don't know what I shall do. Eight of the line keep in sight of the coast at eight leagues. They will follow us; I shall not be able to get contact with them, and they will close on the squadron before Brest or Cadiz, according as I make my course to the one port or the other. . . . I do not hesitate to say — to you — that I should be sorry to meet twenty of them. Our naval tactics are antiquated. We know nothing but how to place ourselves in line, and that is just what the enemy wants."[7]

In face of this letter we might well dismiss Lauriston's story as an intentional perversion. His attitude was frankly hostile to Villeneuve, and his report was written with the avowed object of persuading Napoleon to supersede an Admiral who had lost his nerve, had entirely forfeited the confidence of the fleet, and was unfit to command it. But the General is, to a great extent, confirmed by the most careful and impartial authority we have — the *Journal* of Captain Escaño, Gravina's chief-of-the-staff. Under August 13th he enters simply, "We sailed for Cadiz," and this appears to have been the general belief.[8]

Whatever may have been Villeneuve's inmost intention, it is certain that he recognised the movement he had been ordered to make as one it was impossible to carry out with success, and probably without disaster. "Seeing that I had no confidence," he afterwards explained, "in the condition of my ships, in their sailing, and in their power of manœuvring together, the concentration of the enemy and the knowledge they possess of all my movements since I reached the coast of Spain, leave me no hope of being able to fulfil the grand object for which the fleet was destined."[9]

Every hour confirmed his depression. No sooner was he well started to the north-westward, than a sail was reported to the north-east. He at once went about, signalled to clear for action, and ran back under Cape Prior, keeping the port still under his lee. The precautions which Cornwallis had taken were beginning to work. The strange sail was the *Iris* 32, one of the cruisers he had just sent down to communicate with Calder. Immediately after leaving Cornwallis she had seen the *Naiad* escaping from Allemand's cruisers, and after speaking her had proceeded to Ferrol to inform Calder. Not knowing that he had raised the blockade, she at first mistook the Combined Fleet for our own Ferrol squadron, but she quickly discovered the truth, and was chased off to the northward by a frigate. Concluding, from the confusion that reigned in the enemy's fleet, they must be just out of port and on the point of sailing, she stood in again in the morning. During the night Villeneuve had resolved to resume his course and had tacked under cover of darkness, hoping probably to conceal his movement, but there again was the *Iris* watching him as closely as ever. This time the whole light division chased her off, but not before she had counted the combined force exactly; and when about two o'clock she dropped the fleet, she had fixed its course a little north of west.[10]

By this time she was not alone. To the south-eastward had appeared Captain Dundas in the *Naiad*. She was another of the cruisers which Cornwallis, on deciding to divide his fleet, had sent down to watch Villeneuve till Calder arrived. She herself had sighted some of the Combined Fleet in the morning, and the two captains seem to have had little doubt its movements indicated Cadiz as its destination. They decided, therefore, that while the *Naiad* carried the news to Cornwallis, the *Iris* should proceed to warn Collingwood of his danger.[11]

Dundas reached Ushant early on the 19th, and Cornwallis immediately sent him back with another cruiser, the *Hazard*, to carry to Calder fresh orders and one of his lucid appreciations. "The enemy," he wrote, "are most likely bound for Cadiz or up the Mediterranean. It is hardly to be supposed that they have provisions enough to enable them to go to any distant part. The first object is to overtake them before they can get into port. It is not likely they have any troops on board, and, in that case, very improbable that they should steer for Ireland, nor do I think they would venture to cruise for any time in hopes of meeting a homeward-bound convoy." Calder, therefore, was to "go in pursuit of the enemy instead of going off Ferrol."[12]

No sooner were these orders well away than Cornwallis received from the Admiralty secret information of the approach of one of the convoys already referred to. It was that from the East Indies under Admiral Rainier. He was informed of the secret route it was to take, and was directed to have special regard to its safety if the movements of the enemy suggested it was their objective.[13] To Cornwallis the instructions made no difference. He had discounted the danger already, and so far as was necessary or compatible with the higher strategy, he had provided for it. In any case, at this moment he had other fish to fry.

On the following morning, the 21st, his advanced frigate signalled that the enemy were coming out of the harbour. The fact was that for the past two days Napoleon in his last sanguine moments had been telegraphing to Ganteaume the most peremptory orders to get out of Brest and anchor outside in the fortified anchorage of Bertheaume, so as to be ready to put to sea the moment Villeneuve was signalled.[14] It was an order that had to be obeyed, and Ganteaume was now carrying it out. Without a moment's hesitation Cornwallis stood in with his whole squadron, and finding the French lying in disorder across the mouth of the port, he boldly anchored for the night close in off the Black Rocks, determined to attack in the morning in spite of the batteries. Surely it was not the resolution of a man who would run away from a force even twice his strength. At daybreak both fleets weighed and formed battle order. As they stood for one another it looked as if Ganteaume meant to accept battle, but just before he came within gunshot he tacked and held back again. Cornwallis made a desperate attempt to close and cut off his rearmost ships, but the tremendous fire of the batteries rendered it impossible, and he was forced to retire. He had led the attempt in person, and was wounded by a spent fragment of shell, a fact which the tough old admiral did not think worth mentioning in his despatch. The loss incurred was trifling — the gain was the moral effect in checking any attempt of Ganteaume's to exercise his fleet, and to render still more hopeless the prospect of his being able to make any move to join hands with Villeneuve should he appear.

Meanwhile Villeneuve held on his course apparently something north of west, as the *Iris* had reported.[15] As he dropped Ferrol, everything was confirming his conviction that an enemy's fleet was watching him. The various British cruisers, together with the *Dragon*, which, delayed on her way to the Finisterre rendezvous by the recent westerly winds, was then passing some thirty miles to the north of him, had been magnified by his scouts into two of the line and two frigates, and were assumed to be the inshore squadron of a blockading fleet; and to confirm this view fourteen sail had been reported to Villeneuve, apparently by a mistaken signal in the north-east.[16] Then eight more were signalled in the north-west, but on examination they proved to be neutrals.[17] Then at last he spread his wings to the increasing north-east wind and left Ferrol fairly to leeward; but even so, he was not to shake off the spectre that haunted him.

On the 13th, it will be remembered, Captain Griffith in the *Dragon*, proceeding from Calder on his mission to get into touch with Nelson, had met the *Phœnix* towing the *Didon*, and had turned her back. In company they were steering for the Finisterre rendezvous, when next day about two in the afternoon the *Dragon* boarded a Dane bound for Hamburg. With a view probably of covering the *Phœnix* and her prize, Captain Griffith informed the skipper that he was part of a fleet of twenty-five of the line; and to increase the impression, when he let the Dane go, he played the old trick of making imaginary signals to a distant admiral. Scarcely had he completed his performance when he was aware of a strange fleet in the east-south-east. For an hour or so he watched them, while an advanced frigate came up to observe him. About six o'clock, to his great satisfaction, he saw her board the Dane he had hoaxed and then hurry off to join her fleet. The sun was just setting, but before it was too dark he was able to count twenty-six sail standing, as it seemed, about north-westward.[18] Whereupon he and his consorts turned to the southward away from the danger with all reefs out. Next morning nothing was in sight. So dismissing the *Phœnix* and her prize to make the best of their way to Gibraltar, Griffith hauled his wind, presumably with the intention of getting touch again with the fleet he had sighted.[19]

Meanwhile, in the early hours of the 15th, Villeneuve had received the report of the cruiser that had sighted the British ships and boarded the Dane. Villeneuve himself says nothing in his despatch of the false news that had been obtained. All we know is that, although the prize which the frigate had seen in the possession of the *Dragon* and *Phœnix*, was believed to be the *Didon*, the Admiral would make no attempt to rescue her. He simply held on as he was, straight for Allemand's first rendezvous, on the chance apparently that he might have returned there. At noon he was close upon it, but of Allemand there was no sign.[20] Yet in fact they had been within an ace of running into one another. At daybreak Allemand on his way to Vigo found himself between that port and Finisterre.[21] By yet another of the fantastic chances of his cruise he must therefore have crossed Villeneuve's track close astern of him in the night, both being possibly without lights, and neither had seen the other. Allemand, however, now got tidings from a neutral that Villeneuve had been to Vigo, and thither he hurried in hope of getting definite instructions.

As for Villeneuve, he continued to push west further and further from his lost colleague. Whatever his original intention on leaving Ferrol, there can be little doubt he had now made up his mind what to do. Neutrals visited had confirmed his worst fears. "It appears," says Lauriston, "by all the reports which various ships made to us since leaving Coruña, that Nelson has gone north, having heard of our putting into Vigo, and without doubt after making his junction with Calder."[22] After all his sanguine master's efforts to disperse the British fleet — the fundamental condition of success — it was clear to him it was more closely concentrated than ever, while his own concentration had failed. The consensus of all the intelligence confirmed the hopelessness of his getting touch with Allemand. If he went north in accordance with Napoleon's plan he must go with what he already had, and what he had was a fleet only in name. The movement from Ferrol had proved it to be a mere mass of ill-assorted units incapable of acting as a squadron at all. To proceed was madness. The whole plan of campaign had obviously broken down. In his orders of July 16th, which had reached him at Ferrol and under which he was now operating, there was the following proviso: "The Emperor has kept in mind the case in which by eventualities impossible to calculate the situation of the fleet would not permit you to undertake the execution of his plans which would have so great an influence on the fate of the world, and in this case only the Emperor desires to concentrate at Cadiz a mass of imposing force."[23] In Villeneuve's eyes the case had arisen. The enemy, as he explained in justifying his move, had obviously penetrated the Emperor's plan, and it had failed. "Their concentration of force," he said, "was at the moment more serious than in any previous disposition, and such that they were in a position to meet in superiority the combined forces of Brest and Ferrol." Added to this a stormy wind had been blowing for two days from the north-east; it was likely to continue, and he dared not hold his ill-found ships against it. Till nightfall, therefore, he held on as he was, and when darkness came to shroud his movement he turned back to Cadiz.

What Gravina thought of it we cannot tell. Escaño, his chief-of-the-staff, loyally draws a veil over it all without a word of comment. That day and the three that followed he enters all together in his journal. "In these days," he says, "there occurred nothing more noteworthy than the capture of a merchant vessel, which was burnt. We chased all craft that were sighted, and pursued our course down the coasts of Galicia and Portugal."[24] Nothing more noteworthy than a merchantman burnt! The pathetic loyalty of that entry! For every man knew that what had happened was no less than that the whole initiative was being surrendered to the enemy, and no one could see there was any help for it. "The captains," wrote Lauriston to the Emperor, "have no heart left to do well. Attention is no longer paid to signals, which are kept flying on the masts two or three hours. Discipline is completely gone."[25]

His movement to the southward was not observed by any British cruiser, but ahead of him was the *Iris* speeding down to Collingwood to carry warning of what was likely to happen, and spreading the news far and wide as she went. Early on the 15th, just before she reached Finisterre, she had fallen in with Sir William Parker in the *Amazon*, whom Nelson had sent on ahead of him off Ferrol for intelligence. His orders were, if he judged Nelson had not gone there, to proceed off Ushant or Ireland. Hearing the *Iris*'s intelligence, and that the *Naiad* was taking it to Ushant, Parker decided to proceed direct to Cork, where he arrived on the 24th, just in time to enable Admiral Drury to stop the East India convoy and Baird's expedition then on the point of sailing.[26]

Meanwhile, on the 16th, the *Iris* as she held on for Collingwood fell in with Henry Blackwood, king of cruiser captains, in the famous *Euryalus*. His presence there was a curious piece of the Fortune of War. He really belonged to the Irish cruiser squadron. At the end of July, when the attention of the Admiralty had been directed to the Texel and to the possibility of Villeneuve's coming into the North Sea, he had been sent to Drury at Cork to enable him to watch the north coast of Ireland. On his way from Spithead, however, he had got news of Calder's action with the report that it had forced the Combined Squadron to go south to Cadiz. On reaching Cork on August 2nd, he reported this to Drury, who the day before had received an order to inform Nelson immediately at Lagos if any of his ships should succeed in locating Villeneuve. Thinking it was now useless to watch the north coast, Drury took upon himself to send Blackwood straight off the station to find Nelson.[27] It was of course far too late to find him, and on arriving off the Tagus Blackwood heard from Lord Strangford that Nelson had left Lagos, and that he had been seen on August 5th a hundred leagues west of Lisbon standing to the North.[28] Strangford had also received information of Villeneuve's intentions. A spy of his in the household of the Spanish Ambassador had seen a letter of Gravina's written just after the action, in which he said, with much sarcasm upon his French colleagues, that they meant to go into Cadiz, revictual, and get into the Mediterranean before the British could come up with them.[29]

Whether this information also was given to Blackwood is uncertain, but he at once turned back in hopes of finding Nelson off Finisterre. So it was he fell in with Captain Brace in the *Iris*, and heard his news, that Villeneuve was out and making to the westward.

It of course altered the whole situation, and Blackwood with characteristic grasp and fearlessness of responsibility at once took it firmly in hand. It was on the *Iris*'s intelligence, he says, that he judged Villeneuve's destination after leaving Ferrol must be to the southward, and that he was then somewhere close to him. Alone neither he nor Brace could do anything effective. In such circumstances he felt that cruisers must be coupled, and on this sound principle, as he explained to the Admiralty, he ordered Brace to stay by him. Cruising in company they would try to locate the Combined Fleet, and then if they got touch, the ship which proved to be the faster should shadow it while the slower one carried the information to the Admiral. He further argued that he was no longer under any obligation to find Nelson, for Parker in the *Amazon* had learnt from the *Iris* all he knew himself, and she had gone to Nelson's rendezvous. He therefore decided, after sending his news into Lisbon, to proceed with the *Iris* to Cape St. Vincent, as the only sure point to get touch with the enemy, and wait there forty-eight hours. On the 18th he was off the Cape, and there he heard from a Dane that there was a large fleet to the westward working in towards him. It could only be the Combined Squadron. His way was now clear. He decided at once to stay where he was and shadow Villeneuve, while at the same time he sent off the *Iris* to carry the news to Ireland, and if possible to Cornwallis.[30]

It was on the 19th she parted company, three days after Calder had received his orders from Cornwallis to take his half of the fleet to the southward. For two days he had been held close to Ushant with baffling breezes, but now he had caught the north-easter, and was surging across the bay direct for Ferrol with his eighteen of the line. Before him, believing as he did that Allemand must have found Villeneuve, was the prospect of having to encounter nearly twice his own number. But there was no sign of the flinching of which he was to be accused for his recent conduct: no sign of anything but eagerness to be off the port. Early on the morning of the 20th, being then in the middle of the Bay, nearly half-way to his station, he spoke the *Naiad* on her way north to inform Cornwallis that Villeneuve was out, and the prospect grew more serious still. He signalled for all flag-officers, but after a short conference proceeded under a press of sail. His course was now more to the westward, as though to cross his enemy's track if he meant to come north. Later on, however, he altered it again direct for Ferrol, sending forward the *Attack* gunboat to look into the port, and by noon on the 21st he was on his old station just north-west of Ortegal.[31] Here the *Pickle* met him with information that Allemand had put into Vigo. It was welcome news. It meant there was still a chance of overwhelming him before he could join Villeneuve. He might well be in the act of making the attempt, and Calder promptly stood southwestward flying the signal to prepare for battle, and clearing for action. His purpose is nowhere expressed, but it can be deduced clearly from his actual movements. In the evening he had taken a position off the Sisargas Islands, about five-and-twenty miles west of Coruña. As this was the usual landfall for ships bound from Vigo, and as Calder still apparently believed the Combined Fleet was at Ferrol, it is obvious he was in hope of intercepting Allemand at this point before he could complete the concentration.

His judgment was as sure as his action was prompt; for it so happened that this was actually the point for which Allemand was making at the time. Off Vigo, on the 16th, he had received Villeneuve's orders to look for him at Ferrol, and if he found him gone, then off the Penmarcks on the South Breton coast. Next day Allemand had hurried away, and ever since had been trying to double Finisterre against persistent easterly and north-easterly winds, on which Calder had come down.[32]

While he was thus occupied somewhere off Finisterre there came into Calder's fleet the *Nimble*, who, it will be remembered, after bringing to Cornwallis the first news of Villeneuve's sailing, had been immediately sent back with fresh instructions for Calder. Reaching Ferrol the previous day, she found Calder's scout, the *Attack*, and learning where the Admiral was, had made all sail to him with news she had just obtained from a Portuguese skipper. It was of the last importance. For it told how just a week before Villeneuve had sailed with twenty-nine of the line and ten cruisers, his exact force, and that his course had been west either for Cadiz or San Domingo.[33] Thereupon Calder signalled to bear up, and held on to the westward. Apparently he suspected Villeneuve had gone to Vigo to pick up Allemand. By nine next morning he had doubled Finisterre, and thence he threw forward a chain of cruisers to Vigo. By yet another miracle he saw nothing of Allemand, who must have been close by to seaward of him. At all events four days later the phantom squadron made the Sisargas Islands, and next day, finding Villeneuve had left Ferrol, Allemand held away north to meet him off the Penmarcks.

In the evening Calder's cruisers reported that the Rochefort squadron had left Vigo four days previously, sailing north, and at the same time another cruiser, the *Poulette*, came in, who reported she had been down to Cadiz in search of Nelson, and had been sent back by Collingwood a fortnight since. In all that time she had seen nothing of Villeneuve, but thought it quite possible that she had passed him in the night, and that he might be to the southward. Here then for Calder was a problem of peculiar anxiety, little less exacting, indeed, than that which Cornwallis had just had to decide. Had Villeneuve gone north or south? Allemand's reported course — the only certain news — must have suggested the north, but then nothing had been seen of him. Probably it was this persuaded Calder that his own intuition must be correct, and he boldly decided to go south. His explanation to Cornwallis was this. Having no certain news of the enemy, he had resolved to bear along the coast for St. Vincent and Cadiz. There he expected to find Collingwood if the enemy had not passed that way. If they had, and Collingwood had been driven off, he would have left a rendezvous, where he would endeavour to join him. "If they have not gone south," he said, "I assume Admiral Collingwood [who was his senior] will approve my joining you off Ushant."

All next day he held on, having sent a cruiser ahead to Lisbon for intelligence, and early on the 24th his anxiety was at an end. A cutter came in from the ever active Consul Gambier, with information that left no doubt that Villeneuve was in Cadiz. Once more the flag-officers were called to council, and then away they sped to lock the door.[34]

The news was true enough. By sunset, twenty leagues short of Cape St. Vincent, Calder had the whole story from the *Euryalis*. As Blackwood had expected, he had got touch with the Combined Fleet within a few hours of sending the *Iris* away. He had been severely chased, but refused to be shaken off. Though he escaped capture, he found it impossible to get through the scattered throng of ships to inform Collingwood. He was, however, able to warn the *Phœnix*, for whom there was still no rest, and she turned north again for England with her prize.

Collingwood therefore came near to being taken by surprise at anchor before Cadiz. "I must tell you," he wrote to his wife on the 21st, "what a squeeze we had like to have got yesterday. While we were cruising off the town, down came the Combined Fleet of 36 sail of men-of-war. We were only three poor things with a frigate and a bomb, and drew off towards the Straits."[35] Still he had had two days' warning of what to expect, probably from Gambier. He was dreaming of his family and his domain — "the oaks, the woodlands, and the verdant meads" — but he was ready. His idea was to keep the Straits open so as to be able to fall back on Bickerton at Cartagena and his own fourth ship at Tangier, and force anything that pursued him to pass the Straits. But in truth he was in little danger, so low had the spirit of his enemy sunk. The spectre of Nelson's unlocated fleet was still haunting the Admiral, and his cruisers, mistaking signals, kept sending in confused reports of squadrons in the vicinity. At the last moment they told how a Swede had recently seen eight vessels within the Straits and twelve more at Gibraltar, besides the three before Cadiz. "It is Nelson," cried Villeneuve, "who is there with twenty-three of the line." Fearing an immediate attack on his cumbrous fleet, his only idea was to get it into safety as soon as possible. Gravina with the light squadron made a push to cut off Collingwood, but he was soon recalled, and on the 20th the whole fleet ignominiously re-entered Cadiz.

Next day, to complete the exasperation of the French and Spanish captains, Collingwood quietly resumed his station before the port. It was a fine resolution, especially when contrasted with that of Orde. But it would be unjust to regard the two cases as identical. Orde had to deal with a fresh squadron at the outset of a great adventure; before Collingwood was an exhausted force that had failed in its mission, and was in retreat. Somewhere to the north must be a fleet which had headed it back, and that fleet must soon be on its way to support him. Still, without disparaging Orde, high praise must be given to Collingwood. He at least could only guess how demoralised his enemy was, and he expected them to sail again at once. "They are gone into Cadiz," he wrote to Gambier on the 20th, "for the purpose of replenishing their ships, and are expected to sail again soon, reinforced by eight from that port." And again next day to his wife: "We have been looking into Cadiz, where their fleet is now as thick as a wood. I hope I shall have somebody come to me soon, and in the meantime I must take the best care of myself I can." He had not long to wait. The moment Bickerton heard what had happened, though he himself was sick ashore, he abandoned his watch on Cartagena and sent his ships to join his chief. By the 28th the two squadrons were together off Cadiz, and two days later Calder appeared.

So ended the *insigne bêtise*. Instead of waiting tamely on the defensive, Barham and his colleagues by sheer boldness and sagacious penetration had secured both Channel and Mediterranean. They had refused to play into Napoleon's hands. Whatever his game might be they had it in hand, so far as it was possible for the fleet to hold it. What he had to do must now be done with his army alone. His whole fleet — with the exception of Allemand's little lost squadron — was in fetters, and the great crisis was at an end.

CHAPTER XIX

The Return To The Offensive

The campaign was now transformed. As between France and England, England had regained the initiative. In technical phrase, "an offensive return" was open to her. It was hers to attack, while France, so far as England was concerned, was forced back upon the defensive. It was the situation for which Pitt had been working with so much quiet perseverance ever since he came to power — the situation which Napoleon had never yet taken into account. As all the world knows, the way he eventually dealt with it was magnificent — the crowning exploit of his military career, but his recognition of the situation was slow and stubborn. The shock to his pride and his prestige was so severe as to upset his equilibrium — to blind him with savage exasperation — and in passionate rebellion at the treachery of his Star, he refused to admit that Pitt had beaten him. For three fevered weeks — just the three weeks in which Nelson was taking his uneasy rest ashore — he struggled against the humiliating truth. When at last he faced it, he saw Europe a live magazine beneath his feet; and Pitt, instead of cowering before him as he thought, was secretly stretching out a linstock to explode it. Then in his heroic recklessness of means he arose, and in a desperate effort to quench the insidious flame he flung away his fleet. That in a word is the dramatic conclusion we have yet to trace.

It was not till August 22nd that Napoleon knew that the Combined Fleet had come out from Coruña, and that his fierce denunciations of his Admiral for unreasonable delay were unjustified. Once more he was sanguine, or at least desperate. Clinging stubbornly to the belief that it was still possible that Villeneuve might be coming on to Brest, he telegraphed to Ganteaume that he was not to permit him to enter the port to re-victual. He himself was to put to sea immediately his colleague was signalled, and taking the whole force under his command was to proceed up Channel without a moment's delay. At the same time Dècres was directed to inform Villeneuve that if after all he did go to Cadiz he was forthwith to get on board two months' supplies and come north without a moment's delay.

They were surely counsels of despair, but he had caught the first glimpse of Pitt's linstock. Till that moment he seems to have had no doubt that his truculent menaces would avail to keep Austria and Russia quiet. But now he learned that Craig had reached Malta with 6,000 troops and was already in close communication with the two Russian Generals, Lacy at Naples and Anrep at Corfu. Trivial as was the force, it had for Napoleon a significance that was not to be measured by its numbers. There were reasons why it gave a fresh colour of seriousness to the Austrian mobilisation which he had fully expected to see dissolve at his demand as it had done earlier in the year. It was clear some further emphasis must be sought to give weight to his threat. As a counterpoise to the pressure which Russia was exerting on Berlin, he had already taken the cynical step of offering Hanover to Prussia as the price of her support; and he now suddenly demanded an immediate answer.[1] Accordingly on the very day when the arrival of Villeneuve's despatches from Ferrol had left the whole situation in uncertainty he gave peremptory instructions that the King must be told to make his choice at once. If he accepted "the present" Napoleon offered, so the ambassador was instructed to say, and it had the effect of overawing Russia and Austria and setting his hands free for the maritime war, he would be content. But the offer could only stand for a fortnight. Once he struck his Ocean camp he could not stop, and it would be too late. The maritime war-plan would have failed, and the Prussian diversion not be worth the price.[2]

Whatever the connection of this cold-blooded stroke of diplomacy with British military movements, it is certain that they were causing Napoleon some uneasiness. The old law which gives to such expeditions as Craig's a disturbing power out of all proportion to their intrinsic force, was beginning to work — the old law which Frederick the Great and the Elder Pitt had understood so well. It was in the power of Craig to secure a foothold at Napoleon's weakest point, and it was impossible to tell what was behind the little advanced guard. Baird was on the point of sailing to the southward, but whither, the Emperor knew not. Nor was this all. Since the end of July, Pitt had been preparing on his father's principle to have in readiness a much larger force, "either to menace or attack the enemy or their maritime frontiers." Castlereagh thought it might be made up perhaps to 35,000 infantry and 10,000 cavalry, and that meanwhile without any prejudice to internal defence a corps of 10,000 men might be concentrated in the neighbourhood of Portsmouth and Cork, with a sufficiency of transports standing by in constant readiness and fully equipped and victualled for foreign service.[3]

It was an old device. Napoleon himself was even then endeavouring to use it with Marmont's corps and the Dutch transports in the Texel, and yet so certain is its power of disturbance that even he found it could not be ignored. "Monsieur Talleyrand," he wrote the day after he sent his peremptory demand to Berlin, "the more I reflect on the situation of Europe the more I see it is urgent to take a decisive line. I have, in reality, nothing to expect from Austria's explanation. She will only reply with fair phrases, and gain time to prevent my doing anything this winter. . . and in April I shall find 100,000 Russians in Poland, supplied by England with equipment, horses, artillery, &c., and 15,000 to 20,000 English at Malta, and 15,000 Russians at Corfu. I shall then find myself in a critical situation. My decision is made."[4]

Even so, he still clung or pretended to cling to the hope of Villeneuve's appearing at the eleventh hour. "If he follows his instructions," the letter went on, "joins the Brest squadron, and enters the Channel, there is still time; I am master of England. If, on the contrary, my Admirals hesitate . . . I have no other resource than to wait for winter to cross with the flotilla. . . . In this state of affairs . . . I run to the most pressing. I strike my camps and replace my war battalions by my third battalions, which will still give me a sufficiently formidable army at Boulogne." Finally Talleyrand was told to prepare a manifesto as a declaration of war against Austria, but it was not to be issued. By keeping it secret till the last moment, Napoleon meant to gain a fortnight on his enemy.

The truth is he had received from Dècres a protest which put the arrival of the Combined Fleet beyond the pale of possibility. The harassed Minister did not doubt that Villeneuve had gone to Cadiz, and he could not bring himself to forward him the order to come back with the Spanish squadrons in Cadiz and Cartagena. At last his master's extravagancies had stung him to something like rebellion for the sake of his own maltreated service. "At your Majesty's feet," he wrote, "I implore you not to associate Spanish vessels with your squadrons. . . . I know no situation more painful than my own. I beg your Majesty will consider that I have no interest but that of your flag and the honour of your arms. If your fleet is at Cadiz, I implore you to regard this event as a decree of destiny, which is reserving you for other operations. I implore you not to make it come back from Cadiz into the Channel. . . . I implore you, above all, not to order it to attempt this voyage with two months' victuals, because Monsieur d'Estaing took, I think, seventy or eighty days coming from Cadiz to Brest, and perhaps more.[5] It is above all at this moment — when I may stop the issue of orders fatal, as I think, to your Majesty's service — that I ought to insist strongly. Would that I might be more successful in this case than I have been before! But it is misery for me to know the trade of the sea, for this knowledge wins no confidence nor produces any effect on your Majesty's plans. Indeed, Sire, my position is becoming too painful. I reproach myself for being unable to persuade your Majesty. I doubt if any one man could. May it please you, for naval operations, to form about you a council, a naval staff — such as may seem fit to your Majesty. . . . A Minister of Marine, dominated by your Majesty in all that concerns the sea, must serve you ill and become as nothing for the glory of your arms, if even he does not become harmful."

A letter so loyal, so wise, so broken-hearted, even Napoleon could not ignore. It was probably this which turned the scale, heavily weighted as it already was. On the morrow the routes for Vienna were issued to Marshal Berthier, and on the 25th Napoleon informed Talleyrand that all was over with the invasion. As yet the failure was not laid at Villeneuve's door, but frankly on his own misjudgment of the military and political situation. "I could not have believed the Austrians so stiff," he said; "but I have been so often mistaken in my life that I no longer blush for it."[6]

Though Napoleon's front was now definitely facing to the eastward, he himself stood fast at Boulogne. The movement had to be masked. A fortnight had to be gained before Austria's suspicions should be aroused, and, further, there was his rear to secure. He had at last to face the fact that England was no longer on the defensive; her army was free to attack, and so soon as all was in order for his change of front he began to give it serious attention.

Berthier received the marching orders on August 26th, and next day Talleyrand was told to extend his Naval Intelligence Department to the British land forces. The head of the department was "to keep a box with divisions for all the movements of the English army, including the artillery, and reserving places for the movements of the generals and staff officers;"and as soon as it was ready he was to send him a travelling duplicate for his own use.[7] During the next few days he was much concerned with the subject, making arrangements to prevent a descent at Boulogne for the destruction of the flotilla, and bidding Marmont before marching eastward to assure the Dutch that this same army could be moved rapidly to their defence if they were attacked from the sea in his absence. Duroc, the Envoy who had just been sent to Berlin to force the King of Prussia to a decision, was told that Napoleon did not care much whether he got rid of Hanover or not. If Prussia refused it, he would merely garrison Hameln with 3,000 men, and he was in hopes that he would bring 30,000 or 40,000 English to besiege it. "Frederick," he said, significantly, "did not take long to get from Prague to Rosbach."[8] Forty thousand men, almost exactly Castlereagh's figure, was the force which he calculated England might have at her disposal.[9] Napoleon must have put the British disposal force at a lower strength, for he fixed the Boulogne defence army at 25,000 men, with officers and cadres enough besides to form the flotilla crews into regiments. "The English," he told Berthier, "will then be unable to attempt anything with less than 40,000 men."[10]

It was in the midst of these preoccupations that he heard from London for the first time of the division of Cornwallis's fleet and gave vent to his angry criticism. Not only had he failed to scatter the British fleet when he did not want it to concentrate, but he had failed to force it to keep concentrated when he least of all wished to see it spread. He saw himself outwitted by the seamen he despised, and his only relief was to call them egregious blunderers, and to begin to pretend to himself that the fault was all Villeneuve's for missing so grand a chance. Yet we can now see that if Villeneuve had come north at once on reaching Ferrol, as Napoleon wished, he would have fallen into the arms of the complete British concentration. If, on the other hand, he had come north after the division and had got into the Channel by evasion, he would have found no army at Boulogne. It was not even till two days after the order for demobilising the flotilla that Napoleon knew Villeneuve was in Cadiz. The decision to attack Austria before she was ready had been taken a week earlier and quite independently of whether his fleet would come to Brest or not.

It was on September 1st the news reached him that Villeneuve had actually retired to Cadiz,[11] and that same evening the *Euryalus* was heaving-to off the Needles. Blackwood had brought up his tidings in ten days from St. Vincent, and that not a moment might be lost he left his ship outside the Solent and went ashore at Lymington. Thence he took a chaise and four and galloped through the night, rousing Nelson at Merton in the early morning with his stirring news, as he passed on his way to the Admiralty.[12]

To the Government he brought welcome relief from a period of strained anxiety. For what he had to tell was not only that Villeneuve was in Cadiz, but also — and this Napoleon did not yet know — that Calder had locked the door upon him. It will be recalled that the most pressing anxiety which the partial success of the French plan had caused the Government was not so much for the invasion, which they considered they had well in hand, as for the military expeditions and the home-coming convoys. The concentration at Ferrol placed them in immediate danger and the apprehension was seriously increased by Villeneuve's hasty sailing for Coruña before he could have re-victualled. The course he had steered to the westward threatened a dash at the East Indiamen. Or if this were not so, still they might be the objective of Allemand. They were a source of more than usual anxiety. Not only was the convoy extraordinarily rich, but in the *Trident* 64, its escort ship, were two men the country could ill afford to lose. One was Admiral Rainier, who was coming home in command after being relieved on the station by Sir Edward Pellew. The other was a passenger — no less a man than Sir Arthur Wellesley returning from his brilliant campaign against the Mahrattas, the campaign which had removed all fear of effective French interference in India. A secret route had been sent out to meet them at St. Helena, but none the less the danger was disturbing.[13]

The capture of this priceless convoy would mean not only the loss of a brilliant soldier but a disastrous blow to the national finance, and commercial and family influence alike demanded that it must be secured at any cost. So great indeed was the anxiety that on August 27th, when as yet there was no suspicion that Napoleon had abandoned the invasion, Cornwallis was told that so soon as he was strong enough he would have to detach a division of four or five of the line a hundred leagues west-south-west of Scilly in order to receive the threatened Trade. Calder had already been directed to cover its arrival, if he found Villeneuve and Allemand seemed to be making it their objective; and Cornwallis's new instructions provided that if the detachment found Calder operating to this end it was to consider itself under his orders.[14]

It was on this burning question — the real objective and the whereabouts of the Combined Fleet — that Nelson was most eagerly consulted by the Ministers when he reached London. He had struck his flag on the evening of August 19th in grave anxiety as to what his reception would be. In his own eyes he had failed and been outwitted. He was soon reassured. His heroic dash to save the West Indies had reawakened all the old enthusiasm for the hero of the Nile and Copenhagen. At Portsmouth he had met an ovation, and by the time he reached London it was unrestrained adulation. So extravagant did it grow that the more sober spirits felt called upon to protest. "Should the mad project of invasion," wrote the editor of the *Naval Chronicle*, "ever be attempted, the public would feel additional security from having the hero of the Nile on our coast. But we greatly lament that ill-judged and overweening popularity, which tends to make another 'demi-god' of Lord Nelson at the expense of all other officers in the service, many of whom possess equal merit, and equal abilities, and equal gallantry with the noble Admiral."[15]

But nothing could stem the tide. People, city, and Ministers were all at one, and Nelson to his no small discomfort found himself regarded as a magician, as though he were in possession of Drake's fabled mirror in which he could see "all the movements of the enemy's ships, all that passed in them, and count their crews." On August 23rd, his first day in London, he saw both Castlereagh and Pitt, and found them "full of the enemy's fleet," and expecting him to say where it was. "I am now set up for a conjurer," he wrote next day to Keats of the *Superb*, his most trusted counsellor, who had come ashore with him; "and God knows they will very soon find I am far from being one. I was asked my opinion against my inclination, for if I make one wrong guess the charm will be broken."

Barham alone held aloof. The two great seamen hardly knew one another, and to the First Lord's cold, hard-headed intellect there must have been something antagonistic in Nelson's full-coloured genius. It is probable that, in common with many others, he regarded him as a poseur, whose vanity was wont to make the most of his achievements, and whose impulsive nature — for so it seemed on the surface — was not to be relied on in a vital crisis. The crucial question was, of course, whom should he entrust with the Mediterranean command. There the naval interest now centred with acute emphasis. Nelson with his rich experience was, of course, the natural choice; but Barham clearly shared Nelson's own doubts as to whether his recent conduct had been as well considered as it might have been, and the national hero was met on landing with a cold request to send up his Journal. Nelson in reply submitted that he did not know such a thing was expected of a Commander-in-chief. But he had kept one for the two periods of his chase, and this he sent up — and with quick effect. "Lord Barham," we are told on the best authority, "on receiving . . . Lord Nelson's Journals, perused the whole narrative with an attention which enabled that Minister to form a more complete idea of the Admiral's character; and Lord Barham afterwards liberally declared he had not before sufficiently appreciated such extraordinary talents. This opinion of the noble Admiral's late proceedings was immediately communicated to the Cabinet with an assurance from Lord Barham that an unbounded confidence ought to be placed in Nelson, who was, above all others, the officer to be employed on the station he had so ably watched, and whose political relations he had so thoroughly understood."[16]

From this moment he was treated frankly as the man of the hour — the embodiment of the policy of a bold counter-attack in the Mediterranean into which Pitt's war direction had ripened. Barham consulted him freely on the naval requirements, and this occupied the greater part of his time, and was fruitful, as we shall see, in new developments. But to the Ministers his political knowledge was of equal value. Our relations on the Continent were still in the greatest uncertainty. A week before Nelson landed, a King's Messenger had arrived from St. Petersburg. In his last despatch Gower had led Pitt to expect an announcement that the Russian treaty had been ratified. But now he could only tell that the Czar was still hanging back. At St. Petersburg they had been pressing him further on the question of Malta and the Maritime Code, but he had firmly refused even to discuss the points. The Minister had then hinted at the prospect of mediation being resumed. Gower, however, was unmoved, and assured his Government that the treaty would probably be ratified in a few days without the mediation article. His hopes of Austria were still more sanguine. The Czar had been assured she had definitely decided to take action at once, so as not to leave the choice of time to Napoleon, and it was said she had already concerted a plan of campaign with Russia. Under this arrangement, as communicated to Gower, 55,000 Russians were to enter Galicia in the middle of August, and in two months they would be in line with an Austrian army on the frontier of Bavaria. It was calculated — and most unhappily calculated — that this would enable them to anticipate Napoleon by twenty days. The Archduke Charles was to command the allied army without interference from Vienna.[17]

All this was well so far as it went, but there was nothing yet on which Pitt could build securely. By the time, however, that Nelson reached London the position had become more stable. Gower, as he expected, had been able to announce the ratification of the treaty, and that concerted action was opening. The Russians were to commence their march through Austria on August 20th, and a force of 16,000, men for Stralsund was only awaiting transport. For its support they begged that the Hanoverian troops in England should be sent to join it, and that the British Government would hasten to come to terms with Sweden as to the amount of her subsidy.[18]

Clearly, then, the time for drastic action on the other flank of the French had come. But unfortunately the situation in Southern Italy was in the last degree precarious, and here Nelson's intimate knowledge was a godsend. The difficulty was that nothing was as yet known as to the arrangements Elliot had been able to make with the Russian Generals for co-operation with Craig. It was not even known whether Craig had reached Malta.[19] The last information from Elliot was that an envoy had arrived from Paris who, with ruthless brutality, was trying to browbeat the Neapolitan court into a recognition of Napoleon's new title. At any moment they might give way, and Lacy, the Russian General, wanted to have his troops brought over from Corfu immediately. He was urgently pressing for Craig's co-operation, but not a word had been heard from him.[20]

It was quite possible, therefore, that under Napoleon's violent pressure the feeble resistance of Naples might break down, and Craig, even if he arrived in time, might find the moment had come for a forcible and adverse occupation of Messina to save Sicily from the wreck of the Neapolitan kingdom. Seeing how long Nelson had been pressing for troops to meet this very situation, he naturally became anxious to know how Craig's force was to be used, but Castlereagh could not yet give him a definite answer. "As the man said of the Parson," Nelson wrote to Ball, "he preached about doing good, and so Ministers talked of our troops doing good to the Common Cause." In the turbid mist that shrouded the situation Nelson clung to his old idea of securing Sardinia as the key of the difficulty. So long as he had that island for a base, he was sure he could place Sicily beyond Napoleon's reach.[21]

He was listened to with respect, and indeed was eventually furnished with means to the amount of £40,000 for the organisation of the Sardinian forces in case of need. The point just then received new emphasis. On September 1st came another despatch from Gower, saying that Austria had authorised a plenipotentiary to sign her adhesion to the Coalition, but she was making all kinds of difficulties over details. With her appetite for Northern Italy unassuaged, she made special objection to the restoration of the King of Sardinia as a term of the ultimate settlement of Europe. She also wished, in spite of the recent Russian experience, to try mediation as a means to her end before committing herself to actual hostilities; but nevertheless she expected Pitt to commence paying her subsidy at once. Naturally Gower had refused, and he now warned Mulgrave that the character of the Austrian Court was so weak and vacillating that, unless she could be forced to commit herself during a momentary fit of vigour, she was not to be trusted. The military arrangements she proposed were equally unsatisfactory. She intended, of course, to use her main army in Northern Italy, and she was demanding that Craig's force should march with Lacy's Russians to join it. The proposal was out of the question. It would destroy the value which the expedition derived from its amphibious nature — the only real value it had — and would jeopardise Sicily. Gower again had refused.[22]

In the same bag with this despatch was a second giving details of the intended movements of the Russians for the coercion of Prussia and their requirements in Northern Europe. "I am to press," wrote Gower, "the advantage to the cause which would be derived by a demonstration on the English coast, and that a collection of transports in the Downs and the movement of troops upon the shore would not fail to add considerably to the embarrassments of Bonaparte." They further hoped that when operations began a British force would appear in the Elbe and land.[23]

These measures did not appeal to Pitt. The hour for scheme had not yet struck, and he was not to be drawn into ventures beyond the force at his disposal or beyond what the precarious situation warranted — and the situation was obviously precarious. Indeed, the whole plan of action had a half-hearted ring about it that was not to his mind. It was the work of a joint council of war upon which the Austrian representative was General

Mack. High as was his reputation as an administrative soldier, he was not a man to inspire confidence, and the suggested dispositions savoured strongly of his hand. Pitt, therefore, had no hesitation in supporting the attitude Gower had taken up. "The proposals and plan of operations," wrote Mulgrave in his reply, "present rather the laboured details of obstacles to any attempt at opening a campaign against the French than a system of active and vigorous operations." As to the special Russian demands, he was to say that England was ready to subsidise everybody, but that it was useless to send any force to the Elbe and Weser to co-operate with the Swedes and Russians until the main operations had developed. This, of course, was strictly in accordance with the principles on which alone such expeditions could materially affect a Continental campaign.[24]

To what extent Nelson was consulted on the main scheme of the great Coalition is uncertain. But one contribution he made to it is very noteworthy. He had known Mack when in 1798 that admired officer had been sent down to command the Neapolitan army, and he was convinced nothing good could come of operations committed to his charge. Though not consulted by the Government in the matter, he did his best to warn them through his old friend the Duke of Clarence, and that in no measured terms. "If your Royal Highness," he is recorded to have said, "has any communication with Government, let not General Mack be employed, for I know him to be a rascal, scoundrel, and a coward."[25] It is probable that his deep interest in foreign politics led him to make other suggestions. "No Minister," wrote his devoted chaplain, "ever better understood the tone of the times he lived in." True, he himself says he was so short a time in England, and not more than four times in London, that he could hardly talk of anything seriously but naval affairs.[26] Still, his contemporary biographers assert that "he visited various departments and showed Ministers the dangers to which they were particularly exposed in the Mediterranean, the errors that had too long been persisted in, and the events and changes that might be expected to take place in Europe from the prevailing aspect of its political horizon."[27] The statement is confirmed by Wellington's well-known account of their dramatic meeting in Castlereagh's ante-room, when the "Sepoy General" came to report himself on his safe return, and Nelson was waiting to take his leave. At first impressed adversely, like Barham, with his egotistic conversation, "so vain and so silly as to surprise and almost disgust me," he changed his opinion when Nelson found out who he was. "Then," said the Duke, "he talked of the state of the country and of the aspect and probabilities of affairs on the Continent with a good sense and a knowledge of subjects both at home and abroad, that surprised me equally. . . . In fact, he talked like an officer and a statesman."[28]

It would be worth much to know what were the ideas of Nelson's that so deeply impressed the great soldier — to know whether perchance they discussed the policy Pitt even then had in mind and which Wellington brought to so full a fruition. The idea of pressing Napoleon from the sea at his weakest point was at least an old and favourite one with the Admiral. Years before he had discussed it with another famous soldier of the Revolution. Dumouriez was then in exile at Acton, finding relief for the disappointment of his marred career in advising the British Government on the defence of England. He had just presented them with the last of his elaborate appreciations, and now seeing in Nelson the embodiment of his own and Pitt's policy of counter-attack in the Mediterranean, the neglected General found new hope of measuring swords at last with the man who had supplanted him. "My constant desires are to cooperate with you in Italy," he wrote. "All my hopes at the very point of the Continental war are in your counsels to your Ministry to provide me with a foreign army of Italians or Austrians to attack the upstart Corsican through the centre of Italy." He had already submitted a plan to Vienna. "And if," he continued, "I receive the command of the diversion, we will realise together the projects we formed at our first meeting in Hamburg, against the barbarian usurpator whom we equally abhor."[29]

It was with his mind filled with these preoccupations that Nelson had been trying to enjoy his rest down at Merton. From his first interview with Pitt he seems to have understood that he might be called on at any moment to resume his command.[30] But till Villeneuve's fleet was located and the situation cleared he could only wait, holding himself ready for the summons at any moment. Both he and his friends knew it must come. Lord Hood told him on August 26th he felt sure Villeneuve had gone to the Mediterranean or Cadiz, and that he would certainly have to go to sea again.[31] The naval tension of that last week in August was as high as the political. Alert for the great summons, Nelson would accept no invitations. In refusing one on the 29th he says, "Every ship, even the *Victory*, is ordered out, for there is an entire ignorance whether the Ferrol fleet is coming to the northward, gone to the Mediterranean, or cruising for our valuable homeward-bound fleet"; and again the same day, expressing the same doubts, he says, "My time and movements must depend upon Buonaparte. We are at present ignorant of his intentions."[32]

It was four days later that Blackwood in the grey dawn broke in upon him with the glorious news. Nelson immediately followed him to London, and found all excitement at the release of the strain. "Thank God! Thank God!" wrote the veteran Lord Radstock, "a thousand thousand times that these Jack o' Lanterns are once more safely housed without having done that mischief which was justly dreaded. The papers tell us you will shortly be after them."[33]

That his hour had come he took as a matter of course. It was the call for which he had been waiting. The first order that left the Admiralty after Blackwood's chaise had rattled down Whitehall was one to stop the *Victory* — probably it was Nelson's first request.[34] The next was to Cornwallis cancelling the directions he had received to send Cotton to replace Calder in command of the southern half of his fleet. Then a day passed in which there is nothing but one of the cruel orders that tell so harshly the strain of the crisis. Men were lacking for the ships that were to reinforce Nelson, and all station commanders received directions to press seamen from the homeward-bound convoys. The next day is silence, and well it might be; for it so happened that the day on which Blackwood reached the Admiralty with the longed-for news, was also the day on which came in the first reports that the Boulogne camp was breaking up. The revolution in the campaign had come about — an entirely new phase had begun, and all day Barham was at work upon a remarkable series of orders to meet it. On the morrow they were complete. [35] Their purport must be dealt with later. Suffice it now to say that when Nelson's were put into his hands he found them of a nature which fully confirms what we are told of Barham's conversion. "In confidence in his zeal and ability," the old Mediterranean station was to be restored as far west as St. Vincent, and it was to be placed in his hands with full liberty to distribute his squadron as he pleased. He was given in fact a free hand, subject only to two provisos. He was to prevent the enemy from putting to sea, and he was to protect the Mediterranean convoys.[36]

Of the military operations it was still impossible to say anything definitely. But the prospect was brighter. The Admiralty's news that Bickerton had seen Craig's expedition safely as far as Cape Bona had come opportunely to hand the day after Blackwood's arrival. On September 5th were received two despatches from Sir Arthur Paget, our ambassador at Vienna. The first was filled with despair at Austria's insisting on a preliminary attempt at mediation, but the second announced that the Austrian Foreign Minister, Cobenzl, had just informed him that he had couched his demands to Napoleon in such a way that war was inevitable.[37] In the same hour, too, there was a despatch from Elliot. The Queen, he said, was prostrate at the insolence with which the French envoy had delivered Napoleon's harsh ultimatum. The end seemed at hand, and the Russians, impatient for action, were growing suspicious at hearing nothing from Craig. Still there was hope. The attitude of Austria had prevented any reinforcement of St. Cyr, and Elliot himself had been doing his best to allay the impatience of the Russians by putting them in communication with Captain Sotheron of the *Excellent*, the senior British naval officer on the station.[38]

Immediate action was now taken. The crisis was clearly acute. There could be no doubt that Craig had reached Malta, and by this time would be in communication with Lacy; and on the morrow the Admiralty was requested to order all transports at Gibraltar to proceed to Malta forthwith.[39]

On the same day, moreover, full confirmation was received of the reported abandonment of the invasion. The cutter, *Courier*, had just cut out of Tréport a French schooner which had left Boulogne on the 2nd. Her skipper asserted that the flotilla there was being dismantled, and that the troops had marched off into the country six days before, "because of a new war with Russia." Napoleon, he said, was still at Boulogne when he sailed, but was expected to leave in a day or two. The Tréport division of the flotilla was also found to be landing its stores and ammunition.[40]

By this time, therefore, it was obvious that henceforth the head and front of British action was in the Mediterranean area, and that Nelson was the central figure. Flattering as was the position, he regarded it without enthusiasm. "I hope," he wrote to his friend Davidson on the 6th, "my absence will not be long, and that I shall soon meet the combined fleets with a force sufficient to do the job well; for half a victory would but half content me. But I do not believe the Admiralty can give me a force within fifteen or sixteen sail of the line of the enemy. . . . But I will do my best, and I hope God Almighty will go with me. I have much to lose but little to gain: and I go because it is right, and I will serve the country faithfully." He had had scarcely more than a week's real rest to restore the long strain upon his shattered constitution, and the situation before him was one of the utmost difficulty. It was not so much a question of how to defeat the enemy — of that he had little doubt — it was how to entice or force them to a decisive action. Unless this could be done, the only prospect before him was another long winter blockade.

This problem was now his main pre-occupation. In his last interview with Castlereagh, after his meeting with Wellesley, the advisability of using a military force for the purpose of forcing Villeneuve's hand had been discussed. Whether the suggestion came from Nelson, or the War Minister, or possibly from Wellesley, is not clear. Castlereagh implies that Nelson was in favour of it, and says distinctly that the Admiral only refrained from pressing for military assistance because he regarded the season as too far advanced for the operation to be undertaken that year.[41]

The fairest promise of bringing the enemy to action by naval means alone lay in the inferiority of the force which would be at his disposal at least for some time. But here lay also his chief trouble; for an action with inferior force could hardly prove decisive, and it was a decisive action that would be expected. To this alternative, however, he reconciled himself. His general plan was to conceal as far as possible the amount of his force in hopes of tempting Villeneuve to commit himself to an attack. All day on September 11th he was at the Admiralty issuing orders as Commander-in-chief. On the 12th he took leave of Pitt and Castlereagh, and on the morrow, after a day at Merton, he set out at night for Spithead. The enthusiasm of his reception at Portsmouth next morning did something to lift the weight of anxiety that oppressed him. Early in the morning he went off to the *Victory* and rehoisted his flag. Two of the Ministers, Canning and Rose, accompanied him to see him off.[42] They dined on board, and then Nelson made the signal to weigh, little dreaming that, as he began to face his almost hopeless task, Napoleon in the self-same hour was issuing, in untaught disregard of his enemy, the very order he prayed for — the order which would solve the insoluble and deliver Villeneuve into his hands.

Yet so it was — as though Fate had willed that no touch should be wanting to the dramatic intensity of the campaign as it pressed to its catastrophe. It was on August 30th, amidst the littered wastes where the Ocean camp had been, that the Emperor signed the decree demobilising the Flotilla. The following day, with his eye on the British army, he was busy arranging for its defence against a descent from the sea. It was at this time he must have received from Villeneuve the despatches which told of his return to Cadiz; for on September 1st Dècres, on Napoleon's instructions, was sending him fresh orders to meet the changed aspect of the campaign. "With those thirty-six of the line," the Minister wrote, "his Majesty's will is that his flag and that of his allies command the whole of the Andalusian coasts and the Straits, because he regards it as impossible that the enemy can confront you there with an equal force. It is said at this moment that England is preparing a convoy and some sort of expedition which is presumed to be destined for the Mediterranean. His Majesty's will is that you should take all fitting precautions to get warning of the approach of this expedition and to destroy it."[43]

It would seem that fresh news must just have come in about Baird's expedition at Cork and that it increased Napoleon's annoyance. Still he did not anticipate that it would lead to any serious naval developments, nor was a fleet action any longer in his mind. While Dècres was penning the new orders for Villeneuve, Napoleon himself was sketching out a fresh plan of operation for his naval force, by which it was to be broken up into a number of cruising squadrons and devoted to commerce destruction. Besides three cruiser squadrons it was his intention to establish no less than seven others from his battle force — three from the Brest fleet, and four from Cadiz, employing thirty of the line and eleven frigates.[44]

With this unsatisfactory project in his mind he set out next day for Paris, brooding over the blow his prestige had suffered from his ignominious failure to invade, and over the tremendous campaign he had to face in order to recover it — and as he brooded his anger burned hotter and hotter against Villeneuve. It was in these days that he finally persuaded himself that the whole fiasco was due to Villeneuve and to Villeneuve alone; and on the 13th, as Nelson was passing his last quiet hours at Merton, he sat down to concoct his famous Legend of the Invasion — a legend which to this day has lost little of its vitality.

"I meant," he wrote, "to concentrate forty or fifty ships of the line in the port of Martinique by combined operations from Toulon, Cadiz, Ferrol, and Brest [yet it had never been his idea that the Ferrol squadron should go there]; to bring them back suddenly on Boulogne; to make myself master of the sea for a fortnight [it had always varied before from a few hours to four days]; to have 150,000 men and 10,000 horses encamped on this coast [yet he had never had two-thirds, of that strength]; and immediately on the signal of my fleet's approach to land in England and seize London and the Thames. This project failed to succeed. If Admiral Villeneuve instead of entering Ferrol [which he never did] had merely called out the Spanish squadron [it was Franco-Spanish and could not have got out sooner for the wind] and had sailed for Brest to join with Admiral Ganteaume, my army would have landed and it would have been all over with England." And yet he knew full well, if Villeneuve's stores had permitted him to do so, he would have fallen into the midst of the overpowering concentration that awaited him off Brest. So he goes on to try to explain away his original mistake in believing the operation feasible with the armed flotilla alone. It was absolutely useless, he says, but if he had collected ordinary unarmed transports the English would at once have penetrated his design of bringing his massed fleets into the Channel. The costly creation and armament of the flotilla was solely intended to deceive them as to the direction from which the real danger was coming and it was successful. "The enemy were duped," he says with heroic effrontery. "They thought I meant to pass by main force with the pure military strength of the flotilla. The idea of my real project never dawned on them." The unblushing misrepresentation of what he knew to be the facts almost takes away the breath. But that a man of Napoleon's imagination should have penned such a document is less astounding than that it should ever have been taken seriously. It obviously reflects nothing but anxiety for his shattered prestige, and was simply a political manifesto designed to save his face, in which his freedom with the facts of the case was only bounded by his genius for gauging the limits of popular credulity.[45]

The anxiety under which he invented his great fable is clear to see in the next document which came from his pen. To add to his trouble it would seem that further information had just reached him from Italy of the danger that threatened the right flank of his vast movement. His scheme for a world-wide campaign against British commerce was suddenly laid aside, and the following day fresh orders went off to Villeneuve, which gave the Combined Fleet a new and pressing function. So immediate was the necessity for bold and prompt action that he would not even permit Dècres to tell the unhappy Admiral what he thought of him. With one more appeal to his courage and audacity, he told him not to wait for six months' stores, as he had been enjoined in the last orders, but to be content with two, and get to sea at once to save the situation. "Having resolved," he said, still holding back from admitting he was on his defence — "having resolved to make a powerful diversion by directing into the Mediterranean our naval forces concentrated at the port of Cadiz, combined with those of his Catholic Majesty, we would have you know that our intention is that, immediately on receipt of these presents, you will seize the first favourable opportunity of sailing with the Combined Fleet and proceeding into that sea. . . . You will first make for Cartagena to join the Spanish squadron which is in that port; you will then proceed to Naples and disembark on some point of the coast the troops you carry on board to join the army under the orders of General St. Cyr. If you find at Naples any English or Russian ships of war, you will seize them. The fleet under your command will remain off the Neapolitan shores so long as you may judge necessary to do the utmost harm to the enemy, and to intercept an expedition which they intend to send from Malta. Our intention is that wherever you meet the enemy in inferior force you will attack them without hesitation and obtain a decision against them. It will not escape you that the success of these operations depends essentially on the promptness of your leaving Cadiz."[46]

It is in this apprehension for St. Cyr and particularly in the threat from Malta, that we get the key of the rest of the campaign, and how it was that Pitt, by his little expedition, forced Napoleon to sacrifice his fleet to Nelson. On the following day the Emperor wrote again to Dècres explaining, without disguise, that the primary object of the new orders was to deal with Craig's expedition and prevent any further action of the same kind in the Mediterranean. So absolutely essential did he regard the movement that a day's reflection had convinced him that he could not risk leaving its execution to Villeneuve's nerveless hands. He must be superseded by a more vigorous officer. Admiral Rosily, who had been originally intended to replace Missiessy, was the man he chose, and Dècres was told he was to order him to set out for Cadiz forthwith and take over the command if the fleet had not put to sea.[47]

So the old device which Pitt had inherited from his father worked the miracle — by sheer force of strategical law and by no clearly expressed intention. Nelson at least never alludes to the possibility of its proving a solution of his difficulty, and as Rosily's orders were being written — and it was these that eventually did the work — he was clearing the Channel with Blackwood and two of the line that had joined from Plymouth, all unconscious that his arch-enemy was stretching out to him the crown of his career.

CHAPTER XX

Securing The Communications

All's well that ends well; but the strain which had prevailed at the British Admiralty until Villeneuve had been located and safely housed had driven home certain lessons. It was clear that the existing cruiser system was far too loose and unscientific to ensure such an effective command of European waters as Pitt's intended operations demanded. Barham at all events set himself, in concert with Nelson, to organise his cruiser control on sounder lines for the rest of the campaign. Drury, who at Cork had been directing the most important squadron both for intelligence and commerce protection, had shown little grasp of his functions, and was Constantly being found fault with by the Admiralty. And as for the captains, the leading idea with many of them was that when sent off on detached service they were to enjoy the luxury of "a cruise" with a chance of distinction and prize money. The freedom in which they sometimes indulged themselves was outrageous, and the whole system cried out for severe restraint and organisation.[1]

Circumstances were favourable for an improvement. The release of the strain on Keith's squadron caused by the abandonment of the invasion set a good many cruisers at liberty, while at the same time a new means of increasing the power of communication was available. With the latter there can be no doubt Nelson had a good deal to do. Barrow relates that in the morning of the Admiral's last day in London, he was at the Admiralty inquiring earnestly about a code of signals just then improved and enlarged. "I assured him," he writes, "they were all but ready: that he should not be disappointed, and that I would take care they were at Portsmouth the following morning." But even so, Nelson could not rest. He looked in again in the evening, the last thing before leaving for Merton. Barrow was staying late on purpose to see them off. "I pledged myself," he says, "not to leave the office till a messenger was despatched with the signals, should the post have departed, and that he might rely on their being at Portsmouth the following morning. On this he shook hands with me . . . and he departed apparently more than usually cheerful."

What Nelson was so anxious to have was the famous code which he was soon to immortalise, entitled *Telegraphic Signals or Marine Vocabulary*, the recent invention of Sir Home Popham. As yet it had not been fully adopted into the service, but at the outbreak of the war in 1803, it had been so far recognised as to be issued to ships of the line.[2] Apparently it had been issued to Keith's cruiser squadron, where the inventor had been using it with great success. Under Popham's direction indeed it proved so great a convenience, especially in bad weather when personal communication was impossible, that its value could no longer be doubted. Accordingly, during the time Nelson was being consulted by Barham, it was decided, apparently in some haste, that every ship should have a copy, and the decision seems closely related to the new system of cruising.

This system was based on the modern idea of cruiser lines. The most important one was to be established by the Irish Admiral, to extend from Cape Clear to Finisterre. The order was one of those forwarded in those famous days of hard work that followed Blackwood's arrival and brought Nelson in hot haste up to London. Lord Gardner, whose sick-leave had expired, and who was about to relieve Drury at Cork, was informed that his frigates were to cruise in a line between Cape Clear and Finisterre, in order to keep up as direct a communication as possible with the other stations, and for the protection of the trade and the annoyance of the enemy. And in case of falling in with any squadrons of the enemy they were not to quit them for the purpose of giving information until they should have followed them so far on their course as to be certain of their destination. Then they were to make the best of their way to the Admiral to whom in their judgment the intelligence was most material.[3]

Three frigates were all that could be spared for the purpose at the moment, but Cornwallis was directed to keep one of his own cruisers permanently off Finisterre to complete the line. His other cruisers, which he kept normally to the westward, further reinforced it, but at no time do more than six frigates appear to have been employed in the service.[4] It was not strictly, therefore, a cruiser line in the modern sense, but rather a means of securing a proper distribution of cruisers to cover the ground as effectively as possible.

Beyond Finisterre the line was to be continued down to St. Vincent, so as to connect Cornwallis's command with Nelson's, and this extension was undoubtedly the suggestion of Nelson himself. He had been consulted on the question by Barham soon after his arrival in London, and had reduced his opinion to writing in the following letter: —

"'ALBEMARLE,' *Augt.* '29*th*, 1805.

"MY DEAR LORD, — With great deference I venture by Your Lordship's desire to state my opinion of the necessity of a constant succession of frigates and fast sailing sloops being employed for the protection of our Commerce and the destruction of the Enemy's numerous privateers on the Coast of Portugal, from off Cape Ortugal to St. Ubes, many of them small, lurking under the Bayonne Islands and the Burlings. Ships on this service would not only prevent the depredations of the Privateers but be in the way to watch any Squadron of the Enemy should they pass on their track. A frigate belonging to the Mediterranean Fleet must always be off Cape St. Vincent. Therefore intelligence will be quickly conveyed and the Enemy I think never again lost sight of. I was happy to hear from good Mr. Thompson that Your Lordship had thought of extending frigates as much as possible from Cape Finisterre to Ireland. This will effectually protect our Commerce and in every way greatly annoy the Enemy. — I am ever, my dear Lord, your most faithful Servant, "NELSON & BRONTÉ."[5]

Nelson's views were adopted, and a special squadron was devoted to the service. It was to consist of four sail, and was entrusted to Captain Lobb, who had been Popham's right-hand man off Boulogne — Popham himself being in command of Baird's escort with a broad pennant. This was the first squadron to be got off. An order for Lobb to receive the necessary number of Popham's signal books was made on Sept. 3rd and his instructions were signed the next day. They directed him to keep frequent communication between St: Vincent and Finisterre, with a view to making known intelligence of the enemy's fleets immediately to the Admirals at Ushant, Ferrol, or Cadiz, "or to any other line of cruisers which from time to time you may be acquainted with." If he failed to get touch with any such line the ship entrusted with the intelligence was to make as directly as possible for one of the Admirals, and Lobb was to be careful to keep in constant communication with Lisbon.[6]

With these orders he received a letter covering his copies of the Signal Book. It explained that their lordships were of opinion that it might be used to advantage in communicating between ships at sea. He was to keep one copy himself and give the rest to his captains. On the 9th fifty copies were ordered to be put on board the *Victory* with a similar letter to Nelson. The same day Drury received twenty-five copies, and two days later fifty were ordered for Cornwallis.[7]

Coming as it did together with the establishment of cruiser lines, the issue of the telegraph code to cruisers reveals a distinct advance towards more scientific systems of intelligence and commerce protection; and in view of the fact that Allemand was still at large, both were certainly needed. Such a squadron operating boldly about the terminal area of the great trade routes and on the vital line of communication with the Mediterranean fleet was a serious danger. Until it could be met with and disposed of, the whole situation must be in a constant state of unrest, and it becomes therefore a matter essential to a knowledge of the campaign to trace the motions of the disturbing factor and the efforts that were made to deal with it.

With his formidable squadron, consisting, as we have seen, of the *Majestueux* 120, four seventy-fours, three frigates, and a couple of sloops, Allemand, after finding nothing in Ferrol, had proceeded to the rendezvous off the Penmarcks which Villeneuve had sent to him at Vigo. He reached it by daybreak on August 30th. Cornwallis was of course watching this important landfall, and had cruising there the *Melampus* frigate and two sloops. Allemand chased them all that day without success, the *Melampus* making away for Cornwallis and the two sloops standing by. They were chased again next day and this time only escaped by sacrificing guns and gear. The *Melampus* reported to Cornwallis the following day and the action he took was entirely in the spirit of the tradition as to the functions of the Western Squadron. That function, as we have seen, was to secure the approaches to the Channel for all purposes; the blockade of Brest being only part of the means to effect that object. As has been already explained, this principle had been recognised in the normal distribution of the Home Fleet; that is, a small battle squadron was usually maintained on the south coast of Ireland, either under the Cork Admiral or as a division of the Western Squadron. Owing to the strain on the British naval resources caused by the three-power coalition, this squadron, it will be remembered, had been absorbed into the Western Squadron and Cornwallis had devoted it to the great Biscay blockade. Hitherto this arrangement had sufficed to prevent any battle-ship interference with cruiser control of the Channel approaches; but with the appearance of Allemand's squadron on the scene that control was threatened, and threatened at a most critical time.

It so happened that Popham was in the act of sailing from Cork with Baird's expedition and a vast mass of the East and West India trade. He had nothing but a couple of sixty-

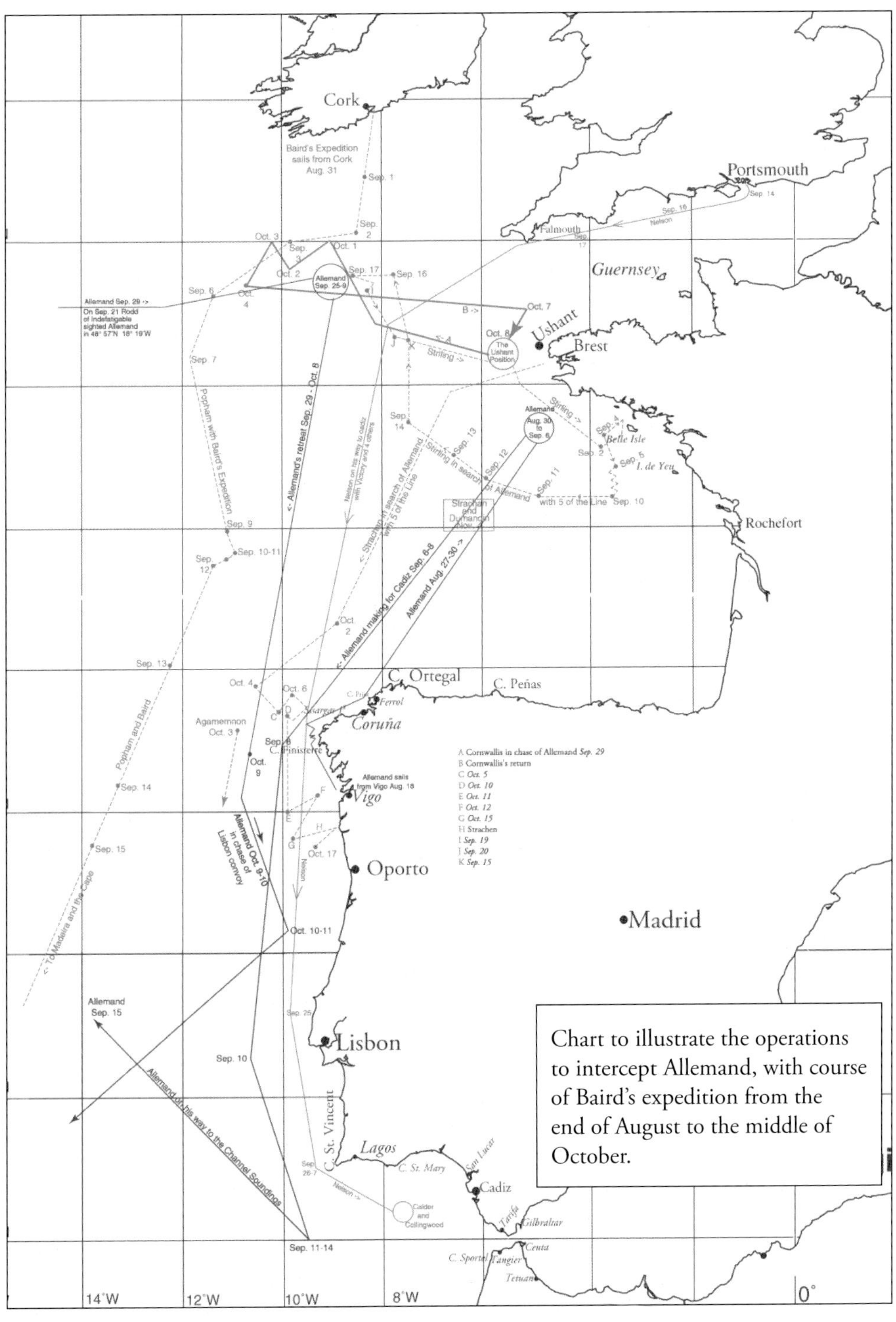

Chart to illustrate the operations to intercept Allemand, with course of Baird's expedition from the end of August to the middle of October.

fours, a fifty, and a few cruisers, and an encounter with such a squadron as Allemand's would have meant a serious disaster.[8] Whether Cornwallis knew the acuteness of this particular danger is not recorded, but there were others of which he had certainly been informed. Only a week before he had received from the Admiralty the very secret despatch already mentioned, informing him that Rainier's priceless convoy was about due, and bidding him have a special regard for its safety if there was any indication that the enemy were making it their objective.[9] Nor was this all. The first convoy from the Leeward Islands was also due, and owing to the suspension of the normal sailings by the irruption of Villeneuve and Missiessy it was unusually large. It consisted of no less than two hundred sail, and so rich was it that it will be remembered Cochrane, anticipating the orders of the Admiralty, had taken upon himself to assign for its escort the *Illustrious*, one of the two fast seventy-fours that Collingwood had detached after Nelson.[10] Finally the Lisbon-Oporto convoy outward-bound was also on the point of sailing.

It was a situation that was causing Barham considerable anxiety. He believed that the next move of the enemy would be to break up their main fleets and "to employ squadrons at sea" for preying on commerce, and this, as we have seen, had actually been Napoleon's intention until the news of Craig's expedition forced his hand. Barham accordingly informed Gardner that he was going to place under his orders a heavy cruiser squadron as strong as circumstances would permit, not only for the annoyance of the enemy's cruisers, but for the protection of the homeward-bound convoys, and also of the western coasts when necessary. "By these means," he added, on the old principle of terminal commerce protection, "much strength will be added to the convoys, when they stand most in need of it."[11]

But if the enemy were likely to send out heavy squadrons this was not enough. Without battle-ship support frigates could not be effective. In the circumstances it was clear the old Irish squadron must be restored in some form or other from the Western Squadron into which it had been absorbed. So long as the Home division of that squadron was kept massed before Brest it could not support effectively the cruiser control of the Soundings. At all reasonable risk it must be divided, and we have seen how, as early as August 27th, Barham had directed Cornwallis to detach four or five of the line to receive the convoys a hundred leagues west-south-west of Scilly, so soon as he was reinforced sufficiently to be able to retain eighteen with his flag.[12] Owing to the extreme difficulty of manning the necessary ships until the Trade came home these reinforcements had been seriously delayed. Yet as soon as Cornwallis had got the report of Allemand's presence from the *Melampus* he did not hesitate a moment. To his broad view of the meaning of his fleet the danger to the trade route overrode the letter of Barham's order. His fleet, as Barham had recently told him, was the mainspring from which all offensive operations must proceed, and in this spirit he decided to make the detachment at once, having little doubt he could contain the Brest fleet with less than eighteen of the line until his reinforcements arrived.

Stirling, who had remained with his flag, was chosen for the command, and the force entrusted to him was just equal to that of Allemand and no more — on the principle perhaps that no squadron can do serious injury to trade with an equal squadron operating against it.[13] His instructions were unfortunate, though in the circumstances, correct.

Allemand's presence off the Penmarcks determined Cornwallis not to send the detachment direct to the station Barham had ordered, for it indicated something different from a direct stroke at the convoys.

Allemand's position, however, was, as we know, a mistake. Napoleon at this time had almost given him up for lost and was raging at Villeneuve for his blunder. "Admiral Villeneuve," he wrote, "has filled the cup at last. On his sailing from Vigo he gives Captain Allemand the order to go to Brest and writes you that his intention is to go to Cadiz. That is absolute treason. Here is Allemand's squadron seriously compromised and he must roam the seas for months. . . . Villeneuve is a wretch we must break ignominiously."[14] But ignorant of these cross purposes Cornwallis could only interpret Allemand's inexplicable position as indicating an intention to seek supplies in L'Orient or Rochefort, and he decided to fling the division at him at once. Stirling was therefore directed first to look into both those ports, and if he found the enemy in either to blockade it. If, on the other hand he ascertained they had not gone in, he was "immediately to proceed to the northward to protect the homeward-bound convoys and see them into the Channel."[15]

With these instructions Stirling parted company on August 31st, and proceeding along the Breton coast looked into L'Orient on September 1st. No attempt was made to spread and for this perhaps Stirling is not to be blamed for it was incredible Allemand would be cruising so close to Cornwallis. So without any suspicion of the enemy's being so near, Stirling had passed inshore of him, and finding nothing in L'Orient he worked down with light and baffling airs past Belleisle and the Morbihan to look into Rochefort. But in vain; gales succeeded the calm weather and baffled his purpose. For a week he was hovering on the coast within fifty miles of Allemand, and yet neither got wind of the other.[16]

All this time the adventurous French commodore had been cruising about fifteen leagues from the Penmarcks trying to pick up news of Villeneuve. On the 5th he spoke a Portuguese who had recently sighted the Combined Squadron at sea to the north-westward of Ferrol, and had also seen Calder off Finisterre. The natural inference was that Villeneuve had found it impossible to proceed to the northward and was being forced to retire to Cadiz. In the circumstances it was worse than useless for Allemand to hold the rendezvous longer. On the morrow, moreover, he found that one of the sloops which he had chased off had picked him up again, and there and then he decided to get away to the southward immediately. He was only just in time. Two days later Stirling ascertained from neutrals that the evasive squadron was not in Rochefort, and he held away under a press of sail for his station off Scilly, passing on his way over the very ground which Allemand had just vacated.[17]

Narrow as was the escape it was complete. Stirling with all the speed he could make was going as wide as possible from his chase. It was nearly a week before he reached the entrance to the Channel, and here he found Parker in the *Amazon*, whom Cornwallis had sent away the day before Allemand was reported, to cruise to the westward.[18] He had been a fortnight on the station doing his best to protect the stragglers of the Jamaica convoy which had just passed in, and two days before meeting Stirling had been rewarded by capturing the *Principe de la Paz*, a fine new Vigo privateer of twenty-four guns, commanded by a famous French skipper; but of Allemand he had found no trace.[19] Stirling, however, continued to hold the position. He had heard the Jamaica convoy was safe, but nothing of Rainier's

East Indiamen, although in fact they had all anchored safely in the Downs, as Stirling was leaving the French coast to cover their entrance into the Channel. On September 19th, as he was thus engaged, he was gladdened with the sight of a strange squadron. It closely resembled the one he sought, and clearing for action he gave chase. But the strangers proved to be Nelson with his four consorts, struggling against southwesterly winds on his way to Cadiz. He of course could report that nothing had been heard of Allemand Channelwards, and that Rainier was in safety. Moreover, while they were still together, the *Decade*, appeared from the southward bringing home Admiral Bickerton on sick leave. She also had nothing to report. Nelson accordingly proceeded on his way, and Stirling, instead of continuing to hold the position, turned back to rejoin Cornwallis.[20]

No decision could have been more unfortunate; for it so happened, as we shall see directly, that on that very day Allemand by a remarkably bold stroke was taking up a cruising station not forty-five leagues to the west of him. With all the facts before us it is easy to condemn the movement — not so much as a stroke of ill-luck as an error of judgment — the only one that can be laid at Cornwallis's door during his admirable conduct of the station. Seeing that all the convoys were not yet in and Allemand was still unlocated, it will probably be thought that he should at least have sent Stirling back the moment he rejoined. But it must be remembered the situation was by no means easy. The probability was that Ganteaume, now if ever, would make a desperate attempt to break out and join Villeneuve at Cadiz, and any weakening of the Brest blockade except for high cause was to be avoided. In the view of the Admiralty, Allemand must have returned to port, and even before Rainier had been heard of, they had actually informed Cornwallis he was at liberty to reconsider the necessity of making the detachment they had ordered.[21] It was on these amended instructions he decided to keep his squadron massed for the present.

And how, in fact, did Allemand come to be where he was? If ever squadron bore a charmed life it was his. After miraculously escaping Stirling off the Penmarcks, as above related, he had made for Cadiz fair into the lap of Calder. There seemed no possibility of his return, yet again a happy accident was to keep him out of harm's way. This time, however, it was his characteristic mixture of daring and caution that earned its reward. On his way down the coast of Portugal he heard for certain that Villeneuve was in Cadiz, and he pushed on under every stitch he could carry, but not direct for the port. After passing St. Vincent on September 11th he warily held on to the southward till he reached the latitude of the Straits. Here he would be certain to fall in with something that could tell him how things stood, and sure enough the same day a British brig came gaily into his squadron thinking he was Nelson, who was daily expected.[22] She, of course, had to strike, and from her crew Allemand learnt that Cadiz was blockaded by twenty-six of the line and Cartagena by five. His position was now of extreme difficulty. To break the blockade by force was impossible. A lucky flaw of weather might enable him to run it, but then if he failed, so he argued, his retreat would almost certainly be cut off by Nelson as he came down the coast. He had, therefore, to recognise that his courageous attempt to join Villeneuve had failed, and he ran out into the ocean to consider what he was to do.

The result was worthy of him and of the best traditions of the French service. Calling his captains to council, he read them the passages in his instructions which seemed to meet the case. "You will consume your provisions in cruising wherever you can do the enemy most harm, and you will not return to port till six months after sailing." The place where he could do most harm was the mouth of the Channel, but he did not disguise from himself not only that the West Indian and American convoys then due came home under strong escort, but that in all probability a battle squadron would be sent out to meet them. Now, as we have seen, Stirling at the moment was hurrying with all speed to take up the station, as Allemand feared. Still he read on: "Your instructions will clearly inform you of the spirit of your mission and its object. . . . Use all your audacity to do harm to the enemy — that is the pith of what the Emperor commands." "Then," says the intrepid commodore, "I hesitated no longer, and I lay my course to take up a station to the westward of the Lizard."[23]

It was a bold resolution, and it came within an ace at the outset of winning him a resounding success. To the northward Popham was passing down with his vast convoy and Baird's expedition, and the course, which Allemand was steering to make his westing in the usual way, would take him right athwart Popham's track. As things stood, it was almost inevitable they should clash, Popham's noon position on the 9th was about 200 miles N.N.W. of Finisterre, and on the 11th Allemand started from the Straits' mouth to the north-west. Had Popham held on there is no saying what might have happened, but by good luck it so happened that he met baffling winds, and in three days made little more than thirty miles on his true course. Thus it happened that Allemand must have crossed his track certainly not more than three days ahead of him, and probably much less.[24] Recent writers have commented on the ease with which we passed military expeditions to their destinations in the height of the Trafalgar campaign, but it is submitted such complacency is wholly unwarranted. Both Craig and Baird had run the gravest risk of destruction. In Craig's case the danger arose by no fault of the Admiralty, for the most scientific arrangement had been made to cover his passage. But Baird's sailing was based on a supposition — a supposition for which there was no direct evidence — that Allemand had returned to port, and the best opinion will hardly regard the movement as a fair risk of war. Luck, and luck alone, saved him.

But now Fortune, having dealt so kindly with Baird, had a smile for Allemand. After so narrowly missing the glorious chance, which his audacity and enterprise had earned him, he was making almost exactly for the position which Barham had told Cornwallis to occupy — that is, about a hundred leagues west-south-west of Scilly. It was about one hundred and fifty miles to the westward of the position Stirling had taken, and we have seen how Allemand reached it the day Stirling and Nelson met. By what reasoning or intuition Barham divined that this position would not be far enough to the westward we cannot tell, nor why it was Stirling did not carry out Barham's instructions. It is possible, of course, that Cornwallis compromised with a nearer position, since he was going beyond the letter of his instructions in detaching Stirling at all before his reinforcements arrived. All that we can say is that, had Barham's strategy been followed to the full, Allemand's squadron almost certainly must have been rendered incapable of further cruising. But, as it was, while Stirling moved away to rejoin Cornwallis, Allemand sat down undisturbed in the midst of the great trade fairway, coolly shifting spars and refitting his worst ships with such means as he had at his disposal. There he lay for four days with his cruisers and fastest seventy-fours spread, and on the 24th he found about a dozen sail in sight all round him making for the Channel. He gave chase, but next day his leading ship came back to report a squadron of eight of the line, and it was not till the following morning that he discovered the real nature of the chase.

It was, in fact, a small convoy from St. Helena, consisting of a single Indiaman, three South Sea whalers, two other merchantmen, and a damaged straggler from the West Indian convoy that had sought its protection. The escort was the *Calcutta*, an old East Indiaman that had been converted into a fifty-four, and she was then in command of Captain Woodriff, whose conduct richly deserves recording. Finding his pursuers were gaining, he ordered his convoy to disperse to the north and east, while he held back to engage the leading frigate. As the action began Woodriff held to the southward to try to draw the enemy away from his convoy. In this he was entirely successful. The frigate held off at long range to let a seventy-four come up, and Allemand, enraged to see how things were going, impetuously chased with his whole squadron. About sunset the seventy-four got in range and Woodriff furiously engaged her, but as she fired entirely at his rigging he was quickly disabled, though it was not till ten o'clock that he hauled down his flag, surrounded by the whole of Allemand's squadron.[25]

By this brilliant conduct Woodriff had led his pursuers into the area Stirling had just left. Had Stirling only remained where he was Allemand's daring cruise must still have been cut short, but as it was Woodriff had done enough. Not only had he saved all his convoy except the uninvited guest, but he had also saved the West Indian convoy which the *Illustrious* was bringing home. On the previous day Allemand's cruisers had fallen in with some of its stragglers, and brought in four of them richly laden the morning of the action. But Allemand, in his eagerness to capture the *Calcutta*, had chased far out of the convoy's real track. On the three following days four more stragglers were brought in, but the mass of the convoy, thanks to Woodriffs cunning, got safely home. Allemand's chief reward was the *Calcutta*, which he added to his squadron. Woodriff was, of course, court-martialled for his loss, but his trial was a mere excuse to give him and his company a kind of triumph.

Meanwhile Allemand, without perceiving it, had been watched. The *Moucheron*, one of the cruisers Cornwallis had sent to the westward, heard the firing. It was dead calm, but she made for the sound of the guns with her sweeps. During the night she got close to the squadron, and in the morning stood by and quietly counted them while Allemand was refitting the *Calcutta*. The *Moucheron* was apparently flying American colours. At all events Allemand took no notice of her, and having completed her reconnaissance she made off to Cornwallis.[26]

But this was not all. One of Woodriffs whalers in escaping had fallen in with the Portugal convoy of thirty-three sail outward-bound, under escort of Commander Hawes in the *Aimable*. He immediately hauled off his natural course to give the enemy a wide berth, and pass nearer to Cornwallis. The admiral must be warned, but he had nothing to send him but the *Diligent*, a valuable storeship for the Gibraltar garrison. Yet he determined to take the responsibility of detaching her, and so it was Cornwallis got the first news of what was going on.[27]

At the moment she arrived, Cornwallis, finding everything quiet in Brest, and some of the ships refitting, was preparing to take his fleet into Falmouth to refresh, and he had just formed an inshore squadron of four of the line to remain on guard in his absence under Sir Richard Strachan.[28] Like Barham, he was still under the belief that Allemand must have made for some port to replenish. If so there would be plenty of time to blockade him, when he was located; and he had contented himself with detaching frigates to watch Rochefort, L'Orient, and Ferrol, besides those he had looking out to the westward.

It was early on September 29th that the storeship came in. Cornwallis immediately sent her on to Strachan to tell him to go in search of the enemy's squadron to the southward and escort the storeship across the Bay. No sooner, however, had he done so, than the *Moucheron* appeared to report that she had located the enemy, had fixed the squadron beyond doubt as Allemand's, and that she had left him lying quietly in the fairway, repairing rigging, and picking up everything that came by.

To be flouted in so impudent a manner in the heart of his own station was more than old "Billy-go-tight" could endure. So strongly did his paramount function now assert itself, that he boldly determined once more to leave Brest open and do himself what his detachment had failed to achieve. Ganteaume, or no Ganteaume, the control of the Channel approach must be secured. Strachan's orders were allowed to stand, and away he went for Finisterre, while the Admiral, leaving a single frigate to keep an eye on Ganteaume, made a dash for the phantom squadron with all the rest of his fleet.

Heading straight for the point where the *Moucheron* had located it, he hunted up and down upon the scene of Allemand's depredations, but not a trace of him was to be had. After three days' work Cornwallis was convinced the wary French commodore must have got wind of him, and on the fourth day, having fallen in with the homeward-bound Portugal convoy, he decided to escort it into the Channel out of harm's way. This he did, and by October 8th was back again on his station off Ushant, and next day was reinforced up to his full strength.[29]

The truth was that, by the time the *Moucheron* reached Ushant, Allemand had recognised that he had made the ground too hot to hold him. It was then four days since Woodriff's convoy had got away. Two days, he calculated, would see the news in England — two more would bring a squadron down upon him. He dared not linger another hour, and so with just judgment the very day Cornwallis began his dash at him, he was flying away to the southward for Vigo. Again he had struck his blow and was gone, with nine prizes for his reward.[30]

The whole episode is worthy of note as representing probably the utmost effect that can be hoped from raiding squadrons operating against trade. The only theatres in which such operations can count on making a real impression on the course of the war are the home terminals, and in a lesser degree, the oversea terminals and focal points. Allemand with a squadron, with which no amount of cruisers could hope to deal, had boldly chosen the home terminal and with every advantage in his favour. Our cruising system was still so imperfect, that it was a full week before he was located, and our home battle squadrons were fully occupied. And yet their mere presence in home waters made it impossible for him to hold his ground long enough to do vital damage. It was on this immutable principle that our trade protection had always been founded. It sprang from our geographical position, and must endure so long as that position endures. It goes to the root of our whole system of naval defence, and exposes the fallacy that any strength of military defence would alter it. If a battle fleet were not required in home waters to control the passage of a foreign army, it must still be there to control the home trade-terminals. No other sure system of trade protection has ever been devised — no patrolling of the seas can ever supply its place. The seas are wide — the trade routes are many, and so long as the point of convergence is safe, nowhere upon the high seas can an enemy hope in war time to encounter enough trade to make commerce destruction an adequate object for her battle squadrons.

The audacity and judgment with which Allemand had acted left nothing to be desired, and yet as a strategical operation his cruise had wholly failed in its object. Napoleon had designed it with confidence as a means of disturbing the British dispositions and forcing them to break their concentration; but so sure was the grasp of the essentials under Barham and his admirals that it had not availed for one moment even to loosen their grip. The raiding squadron had been ignored until the conditions permitted operations against it without prejudicing the security of the main positions. The whole affair, indeed, will serve to demonstrate the futility of seeking to entice our fleets away, so long as a sound strategical tradition remains green in the service.

Let us follow the intrepid and resourceful Allemand a little further, and see how his extraordinary luck pursued him. He was now making for Vigo to renew his water and secure his prizes, and at the same time Strachan was racing across the Bay to cut him off at Finisterre. Strachan was there first. On October 4th he was some sixty miles north-west of the Cape, and thence he cast to and fro, always nearing the land. Nothing could have been more scientific than the means which Cornwallis had adopted to catch the elusive squadron, and yet again it escaped. How it happened we cannot tell, but it would seem that Allemand must have passed Strachan to seaward. At any rate, on the morning of October 9th Allemand sighted the *Agamemnon* 64. She was following Nelson down and was then about sixty miles due west of Finisterre, while Strachan at the same time was hovering about twenty-five miles to the north-north-west.[31] Allemand at once gave chase and pressed her so vehemently with his flagship that it was only by starting her water she escaped. So desperately, indeed, did Allemand push her that he was carried to leeward of his port.[32] Still nothing would hold him. Just as he abandoned the *Agamemnon* he saw to the southward the *Aimable* with the Portugal convoy which had eluded him in the mouth of the Channel. Regardless of consequences, he chased again still further to leeward of Vigo. The *Aimable* was within an ace of being captured. She too had to start her water, cut away her boats, and heave overboard a quantity of shot. Once she was on her beam ends with the press of sail she tried to carry, but at last she got away. The bulk of the convoy also escaped, and Allemand had nothing for his pains except three stragglers and a small letter of mark.[33]

While the Rochefort squadron was thus brilliantly raiding Nelson's line of communications, Strachan was still hovering off Finisterre in ignorance that his chase had passed. Allemand was in fact lying-to nearly two hundred miles to the southward — trying to rally his scattered squadron and wondering what to do next. Scurvy had possession of his crews, and speedy relief was essential. To beat back to Vigo would take ten days at least, even if it were still open. An exaggerated report of Strachan's squadron had reached him. It was said to be ten of the line, and to be waiting for him off Ferrol.

He suspected the *Agamemnon* when she escaped him had made for this squadron, and that he would find it had come down to bar his way to Vigo. Here again he showed his usual sagacity. Strachan had indeed got wind of him, though not from the *Agamemnon,* and that very day, October 10th, was moving down to Vigo, confident of bringing him to action as he returned. But Allemand was not so easily handled. There was still one more chance for him, and that was to run to the Canaries. This course he boldly took next day, leaving Strachan in hopeful patience covering the approaches to Vigo, while he himself sped southward without knowing he was on the heels of Popham and Baird.

CHAPTER XXI

The Deadlock At Cadiz

It was on the evening of September 28th that Nelson reached the fleet off Cadiz, and on the morrow — his birthday — he took over the command. On his way down the Portuguese coast he had communicated with Lobb's cruiser line, and off Lisbon had issued directions that his arrival was to be kept secret. His mind, as usual, was occupied with making good the ground behind him, and guarding himself against the interruption of his line of communication by an escape of the Brest squadron. The possibility of such an escape during the equinoctial weather was a long-established strategical factor, and in view of the importance of securing the flow of his promised reinforcements, Nelson could not ignore the danger. Off St. Vincent he stopped a cruiser that was going home with Collingwood's despatches, and in accordance with the system he had recommended he ordered her to remain there to continue Lobb's line. Her instructions were to direct new arrivals to look for him "between Cape St. Mary and Cadiz," the rendezvous he had chosen. If they should find him gone in pursuit of the enemy, new orders would be found off Cape Spartel. "Should the enemy's fleet from Brest make its appearance," so the instructions concluded, "I desire you will join me with an account thereof with the utmost despatch." In this significant remark we probably have a reflection of the prevailing anxiety which had crippled Cornwallis's freedom of action, and by holding him to Ushant had given Allemand his opportunity.

From this point, moreover, Nelson sent forward an order by Blackwood that no notice was to be taken of him when he joined by salute or otherwise. His main preoccupation was still the difficulty of forcing Villeneuve to action, and his first precaution was, if possible, to conceal his arrival. He even begged General Fox at Gibraltar to forbid the publication of the news in the local press. "For I much fear," he wrote, "that if the enemy know of our increased numbers, we shall never see them out of Cadiz." On seeing how the Combined Fleet lay not in the bay, but crowded up in the harbour, he had hopes that possibly Colonel Congreve and his rockets might prove effective, if other means failed, "Even should no ships be burnt," he wrote to Castlereagh, "yet it should make Cadiz so very disagreeable that they would rather risk an action than remain in port."

But the pressure on which he had most faith was famine. This, however, could only be effected by a rigorous blockade of all the Andalusian ports into which Danish vessels had been pouring supplies from France. Now the Government for political reasons had a strong antipathy to these blockades. They never failed to have the effect of exasperating neutrals, and so strongly was this objection felt that only a short time since Lord Keith had been absolutely forbidden to close the North Sea ports through which Marmont's corps and the Dutch squadron and flotilla were being supplied.[1] Collingwood, however, had boldly taken the matter into his own hands, and established a blockade of the whole coast. Nelson resolved to continue it, and begged Castlereagh to support him and see that naval officers did not suffer for the execution of his order. Neutrals, he made free to hint, would take it quietly enough if Ministers at home would only stop the abuse of granting licences for British vessels to enter the blockaded ports.

On starvation, then, and on concealing his force he relied principally for bringing Villeneuve to a decision. From the pressure of Craig's expedition he had no hope at all. He even yet did not know its object. When he sailed the situation at Naples was still too obscure for Ministers to say anything definite; but his ignorance of what it really portended was about to be enlightened. On September 17th, as Nelson was leaving the Channel, a courier arrived late at night at the Foreign Office with despatches that at last cleared the uncertainty. In his bag was Elliot's despatch from Naples announcing that Craig had reached Malta in safety, and that conferences for co-operation between him and the Russians were in full swing. Despatches from Craig were enclosed to say he would have at least 6,000 men ready for action without denuding the Malta garrison. There was also a despatch from Vienna in which the ambassador said that as Cobenzl expected, Napoleon had refused the offer of mediation, his counter demands had been firmly rejected, the whole, Austrian army had been placed on a war footing, and at any moment the Archduke Charles might strike a blow in Italy. For the Austrians were still persuaded the initiative would be theirs, and to the Archduke had been committed their main offensive movement against Napoleon's new kingdom.[2]

Nothing could have been more opportune for Pitt. Exhausted by the strain of the recently-closed session, in which the opposition of Fox and his friends had been more implacable than ever, he felt unable to face Parliament again on the same terms, and conduct the war as well. The only chance he saw was to form such a coalition with Fox, as his father had done so triumphantly with Newcastle in the crisis of the Seven Years' War. Party must cease for a time and a true national government take its place. Full of this idea, he had gone down to Weymouth, where the King was taking his accustomed spell of sea air guarded by two or three precious cruisers. But the stubborn old monarch proved as obdurate as ever. Nelson's friend Rose came down to help. "I told his Majesty," he wrote in his Diary, "that considering our situation in the House of Commons, I was perfectly persuaded, if Mr. Pitt should be confined by the gout or any other complaint for two or three weeks there would be an end of us." But it was no good. The King was so much upset by the bare idea of Fox in the Cabinet, that another attack of insanity was feared. They had to desist, and Pitt was left to face the prospect of yet another session, in which he would have to fight Fox all day and Napoleon all night.

In these circumstances news that held out a hope of striking a brilliant blow before the new session opened was in the highest degree inspiriting, and in ten days the necessary action was decided on. On September 21st Castlereagh informed the Admiralty that in the event of hostilities on the Continent (which were now certain), Craig's force might be employed on the coast of Italy. He desired them, therefore, to call Nelson's attention to what was in the wind, and to direct him, "after providing effectually for the blockade of Cadiz, to keep in view the object of covering such operations as Sir James Craig may undertake from any interruption by the enemy's naval force in the Mediterranean," and to keep in constant communication with him.[3] Accordingly on the same day, secret instructions to that effect went forward for Nelson with a copy of Craig's orders enclosed.[4]

It will be seen that the ideas of the Government did not quite coincide with those of Nelson. In Pitt's eyes the function of the fleet was fulfilled if it succeeded in sealing up Villeneuve's fleet so that it could not interfere with his combined flank attack on Italy, and Nelson's orders had been drawn in this sense. It will be remembered that they gave him practically a free hand, but with the express proviso that he was to blockade Cadiz so as to prevent the Combined Fleet putting to sea. Nelson's preoccupation, on the other hand, was to force it to sea and destroy it, knowing full well the precariousness of a long winter blockade on the capricious Andalusian coast.

Barham must have shared the Nelsonian view. As soon as it was known that Napoleon had abandoned the invasion, the Government had set their hearts on destroying the demobilised flotilla by a combined attack on Boulogne. The moral effects of the operation, if successful, would be invaluable for securing the position of the Government and for reconciling the country to the sight of their army being sent overseas to act offensively on the Continent. From this point of view it may be taken as justifiable for ministers to press the operation whatever its purely strategical defects. These defects, however, the Admiralty had regarded as prohibitive, ever since Nelson's failure in 1801. But Colonel Congreve's invention was thought by Castlereagh to have made a difference. Sir Sidney Smith, with characteristic self-confidence, was sure it could be done, and had been charged to make the attempt. A closer view quickly brought him round to the Admiralty view, that it was impossible without the support of a military force. This Pitt was wise enough not to sanction without a special report from Sir John Moore, and that great master of war was now ordered to make the necessary reconnaissance. Barham, who believed as little in the rockets as he did in Sidney Smith, threw cold water on the scheme. If a military force was available he saw a far better objective against which it could be employed, and that was Villeneuve's fleet. He therefore submitted that if troops went at all they should go to Cadiz. Moore, however, reported privately to Pitt that the Boulogne enterprise was not a feasible military operation, and there it ended.[5]

In the meantime, as we know, the problem of getting a decisive blow at Villeneuve, in which Barham and Nelson were absorbed, had been solved for them by Napoleon himself. As Nelson appeared at Cape St. Vincent the order directing the Combined Fleet to sail forthwith for Naples reached Cadiz. On hearing of it Gravina went on board Villeneuve's flagship, the *Bucentaure*, and announced that his fourteen ships were ready for sea. At Villeneuve's request he gave instructions that the Spanish dockyard was to render the French every possible assistance in completing their stores, while Villeneuve issued a stirring order. By the following Monday all troops necessary to fill up the ships' companies were to be on board, for on that day he meant to go forth and "to strike down England's tyrannical domination of the seas." The same evening, however, the signal stations reported that a three-decker and two seventy-fours were joining Collingwood from the westward. "That makes thirty-one," wrote Villeneuve, in a lower tone, "well known to be in the offing." Still it was not yet ascertained that it was Nelson who had come, and the embarkation of the troops proceeded. By October 2nd it was complete, but towards evening Gravina received two expresses from Lisbon by which the tone of confidence was severely shaken. They told that Nelson had arrived "with four of the line and great projects for attacking, bombarding, and burning the Combined Squadron." The effect was startling. At the cost of interrupting the preparations for sea a defence flotilla of gunboats, bomb-vessels, and anything that could be handled in bad weather was hastily organised and manned with officers and men from the fleet.[6] Moreover, instead of being able to get the ships out into the bay as they were ready, the fear of Nelson's doing something desperate made it advisable to keep them still crowded up in the harbour out of harm's way. Still Villeneuve proclaimed his intention of sailing the moment he had a fair breeze.

At Cadiz in fine autumn weather there is a land wind at night from the east, fair for coming out, while outside in the morning is found a westerly breeze fair for entering the Mediterranean. On the evening of the 7th an easterly breeze sprang up, and signal was made to prepare to weigh but it was almost immediately annulled, for the wind increased so rapidly as to threaten a real Levanter "diametrically contrary to the course they had to make" Such is the story Villeneuve told officially[7] But the truth would seem to be that Nelson's arrival had once more dominated the spirits of the French Admiral and most of his colleagues. Ever since he had joined nothing had been seen of the fleet from the signal stations except an inshore squadron of five cruisers, with an occasional glimpse of communicating ships of the line. Nelson must be there but what he was doing and what his strength no one could tell. "I could not close my ears," wrote Villeneuve in reporting to Dècres his arrested attempt to sail "to the observations which came to me from all sides on the inferiority of our force compared with that of the enemy who have now certainly from thirty-one to thirty-three of the line, of which eight are of three decks, and a large number of frigates. To go out in such circumstances is stigmatised as an act of desperation beyond the power of the two Courts. Accordingly he says he decided to call a Council of War. Escaño, who was still Gravina's Chief of the Staff, gives, however, another version of the calling of the Council which rings more true. According to him on October 6th Villeneuve informed Gravina that by superior orders he must put to sea the moment supplies were complete, and requested him to have his squadron ready "The Spanish Admiral," says Escaño, "confined himself to replying that he considered it necessary before weighing to hold a Council to hear the opinion of all the Staff officers of both nations, but without further discussion he gave orders to demobilise the flotilla and for its officers to return to their ships."

On the following morning, therefore, a Council was held on board the *Bucentaure*. Villeneuve opened the proceedings by communicating the Emperor's secret orders, "that the Combined Fleet was to sail at the first favourable opportunity, and that wherever it found the enemy in inferior strength it was to attack him without hesitation in order to force him to a decisive action." On these instructions, so Escaño says, Villeneuve put it to the Council whether they should go to sea or remain at anchor in hopes the enemy would attack them, in which case they would probably be able to destroy them and obtain a free passage out. The Spanish officers had been careful to discuss the question previously, and they unanimously supported Gravina's opinion that in view of the superiority of the British fleet Napoleon's orders did not bind them to seek an action at the moment, and that they ought to abide an attack at anchor. The Frenchmen, however, had not taken the same precaution, and a violent debate was the result, some of them hotly insisting that there could be no doubt they should go out and fight immediately. Captain Prigny, however, Villeneuve's Chief of the Staff, pointed out that even if there were no more than twenty-five of the enemy outside, still the Combined Fleet was not superior to them.

"They," he said, "have kept the seas without intermission since 1793, while most of their own fleet have scarcely weighed anchor for eight years." He therefore urged the success that might be obtained with a well-organised defence flotilla, and concluded with the maxim that no superior order could bind them to attempt the impossible. Admiral Magon at once sprang up to refute the Chief of the Staff and the opinion of the Spanish officers, and expressed himself so hotly and in language so violent that a scene ensued. General Galiano, one of the brigadiers of the Spanish troops, got up to protest. The behaviour of the Frenchman was more, says Escaño, than his nice and lofty sense of honour could endure, and he demanded that Magon should be called upon to withdraw his offensive expressions. The Council was at once in a storm. Higher and higher it raged, till Gravina quelled it by moving suddenly that the question be put without further discussion. Thus it was he stated it: "Ought or ought not the Combined Squadron to put to sea, seeing that it was not in such superiority of force as to balance its inherent inferiority?"A vote was taken, and the result was a decision to remain at anchor. It was further agreed to re-establish the defence flotilla with contingents from the fleet till a favourable opportunity for going out should occur.[8]

Thus it was the Admirals tried to save Napoleon from his reckless determination to hurl his fleet upon Craig and the Russians; and it so happened that while the resolution of inability was being taken Nelson received from home the communication which for the first time explained to him the meaning of the expedition at Malta. The effect of the despatch was finally to clear his mind and to enable him at last to form a definite idea of the shape the campaign would thenceforth assume. It is certain at least that on receiving the news he changed his view of the enemy's probable action and fixed a plan of operations from which he never again swerved. To appreciate the point, it is necessary to grasp clearly the information he had previously and the dispositions he had made.

Newspapers of September 20th had already reached the fleet announcing that the Continental war was certain. There were also local rumours that Napoleon had ordered the Cadiz fleet to sea, and that in Council of War they had decided to disobey. Villeneuve, it was said, was to be superseded in consequence by Dècres.[9] Though the news could only strengthen the expectation that the Combined Fleet would soon put to sea, it gave little light on its objective. It was quite as likely it would be used for a diversion to the north or west as that it would act directly in the Mediterranean. Nelson, indeed, had been absorbed in arranging for the cruiser command of that sea, while his battle fleet was held to Cadiz, and had just sent home a memorandum of the minimum cruiser force that was required for the whole of his station.[10] Between writing this despatch, however, and the receipt of the new instructions concerning Craig, he made a significant change in his arrangements.

His first step on taking over the command had been to send Blackwood to recall Admiral Louis from before Cadiz. Collingwood had stationed him close in with an inshore squadron consisting of the *Queen* 98, the *Canopus* 80, and three seventy-fours. It was a normal feature of blockade, as it was then practised, of which Nelson did not approve, unless there were exceptional circumstances to justify it; and in this case the danger of a sudden westerly squall to an inshore squadron was a special reason for not employing one. The inherent advantage of the blockader is his power of concealing from the enemy his actual strength, position, and movements, and in Nelson's eyes full use should be made of this advantage. He had therefore decided to remove the whole of his battle fleet out of sight and to watch the port with a cruiser squadron only, which Blackwood was to command. The new disposition is significant. For it emphasises the growing expectation that the exigencies of the situation would force the enemy to sea if only they were given an apparent chance of escape. There was reason enough to believe they might make the attempt any day, for Blackwood from his inshore position had already reported that the troops were being embarked. Yet at the same time Nelson set about preparing for a long and exhausting watch. It was mainly a question of supply. A certain amount of the work could be done in fine weather on the spot from transports, but it was only by sending his ships away in batches to Gibraltar and Tetuan that he could rely on keeping his stores and water up to the mark. To this embarrassing necessity he was no doubt reconciled and even bound by his instructions. For so long as there was an active squadron in Cartagena he must have something to watch it. He must guard against its interference up the Mediterranean or on the trade route through the Straits, to say nothing of the possibility of its slipping into Cadiz while the main British fleet was kept wide of the port. Accordingly on October 2nd, Louis, much against his will, was ordered to the Straits with his squadron and a small convoy which had arrived for Malta.

The position which Nelson himself decided to occupy was from sixteen to eighteen leagues west from Cadiz. In order to keep touch with the enemy he gave Captain Duff of the *Defence* an advanced squadron of four seventy-fours with which he was to maintain signal communication with Blackwood's cruiser squadron without getting in sight of the Spanish signal stations. "In fresh easterly breezes" he wrote to Blackwood, I shall work up for Cadiz, never getting to the northward of it, and in the event of hearing they are standing out of Cadiz, I shall carry a press of sail to the southward towards Cape Spartel and Arrache."[11]

Such were his ideas and intentions before he received the information about Craig, that is, he expected the enemy to sail with the first easterly wind. On the 5th the wind did come easterly, and in view of Louis's detachment Nelson began to be seriously anxious for his promised reinforcements from home, and in writing to Barham to explain what he had done he urged the importance of annihilating the enemy and not merely "spoiling their voyage." To Rose he wrote next day more strongly. "I am very very very anxious, he said, "for its arrival, for the thing will be done if a few more days elapse. . . . It is, as Pitt knows, annihilation that the country wants. . . . Numbers can only annihilate (*sic*). Therefore I hope the Admiralty will send the fixed force as soon as possible."[12]

Blackwood's information that the troops were embarking was at the bottom of Nelson's anxiety, and he sent it on to Collingwood together with his own doubts as to what the enemy meant to do. Collingwood, with his fresh experience of the station, seized the opportunity to hint to his chief that his appreciation was incorrect and his anxiety premature. "Now, my lord," he wrote, with a striking penetration of Villeneuve's mind, "I will give your lordship my ideas on the subject. . . . If they are to sail with an easterly wind, they are not bound for the Mediterranean, and your lordship may depend upon it the Cartagena squadron is intended to join them. If they effect that — and with a strongly easterly wind they may — they will present themselves to us with forty sail. If by any good fortune Louis was to fall in with that squadron I am sure he would turn them to leeward . . . and a French ensign might bring them to us. Whenever the Cartagena people were expected they lit the light-house. Captain Blackwood should look to that as a signal."[13]

Now it was on the following day that Nelson received the news of Craig's intended operations in Italy. The despatch came out in the *Royal Sovereign*. She joined on October 8th, spick and span after her refit for Collingwood's flag, and though the easterly wind continued to blow. Nelson's immediate anxiety passed away. With Craig's instructions in his hand it is clear he had no longer any doubt that Villeneuve was destined for the Mediterranean, and Collingwood's appreciation had convinced him the enemy would not sail with the wind at east. This view he now adopted, and the characteristic tenacity and singleness of mind with which he clung to it was evinced at once. It so happened that the day after Louis parted company, Blackwood informed him by signal that the enemy's troops were embarked, and that they intended to sail on the first easterly wind. As the wind had then come east Louis decided to send on his convoy with two of his squadron and to return to Nelson with the rest. "But Lord Nelson," so James tells us, "conceiving the whole to be a stratagem to draw him nearer to Cadiz for the purpose of obtaining a more accurate knowledge of his force, ordered the Rear Admiral to proceed in the execution of his orders."[14]

Louis, therefore, much to his own and his captain's disgust, had again to part company, and in accordance with Nelson's new view of the situation fresh instructions were sent to Blackwood. His squadron had just been made up with new arrivals to its full strength of five frigates and two sloops. "Those," Nelson wrote to him, "who know more of Cadiz than either you or I do, say that after these Levanters come several days of fine weather — sea breezes westerly, land wind at night — and if the enemy are bound for the Mediterranean they will come out at night . . . run to the southward and catch the sea breezes at the mouth of the Gut and push through while we have little wind in the offing." He was therefore to take measures to ensure detecting any such movement, and was furnished with special long-distance night-signals to give warning.

As for the battle squadron, Nelson was now quite clear what to do with it. "At present," he wrote to Collingwood, "I am sure the Mediterranean is their destination. . . . Should the enemy move. . . it is then probable that I shall make the signal to bear up and steer for the entrance of the Straits."[15] At the same time all arrangements were completed for the expected action. It was now he issued his order of battle and the famous plan of attack — the "Nelson touch" as he called it — which hitherto he had only explained verbally to his captains when they assembled to greet him on his taking over the command.[16]

Then for a week all was quiet, save for the painful duty of sending Calder home for his trial and the passing disturbance which Allemand created. On the 13th Sir Edward Berry joined in the *Agamemnon*, bringing news of his narrow escape, and the same evening Calder parted company. The belief was that Allemand was still to the northward about Vigo, and Nelson was in some anxiety lest Calder should fall into his hands. To have such a squadron on his communications with home was far from pleasant. He had full particulars of Allemand's force and its proceedings from a French officer who had been taken in a recapture by one of the ubiquitous Guernsey privateers. Further intelligence was brought in by the *Diligent*, the store ship which had informed Cornwallis of Allemand's presence in the Soundings. Strachan had escorted her well to the southward till she was safe in Lobb's hands, and he was now quietly cruising off Vigo for Allemand's superior squadron, under the belief it was somewhere close to him and about to make the port.[17] Nelson was naturally far from easy about him. "I wish he were stronger," he wrote to Blackwood on the 14th, "but I am sure he will spoil their cruising;" and again to Collingwood on the 17th, "I wish he had a good three-decker with him."[18]

For the rest he was busy with the problem of controlling Italian waters, difficult enough in itself without the disturbance on his communications. The *Agamemnon* had brought out a repetition of his instructions for co-operating with Craig, and the expedition was much in his mind. He had already informed the Admiralty he must have three cruisers besides those he originally asked for, if he was to keep up communication with the expeditionary force. He was now very anxious to send a squadron of ten of the line to his own old station, but till Villeneuve was dealt with this was impossible, and all he could hope for — and that not immediately — was a strong cruiser squadron which he intended to place under Keats of the *Superb*. Still, so deeply was he concerned with the importance of supporting Craig that he did take the extreme step of sending Louis an order to escort the Malta convoy past Cartagena before he rejoined.[19] At this time he seems to have had little expectation of the enemy's putting to sea. He was preparing bomb-vessels and looking for the arrival of fire-ships, as well as Congreve and Francis with their rockets and torpedoes to force things to an issue.[20] But his hope of a decision rested mainly as before on the slow pressure of famine and little on the stimulus of the Anglo-Russian threat in South Italy. There is no reference to it in Nelson's correspondence, though he must have discussed it with Collingwood. We know at least that on this ground Collingwood regarded Villeneuve's continued inaction as inexplicable. "It is very extraordinary," he wrote to Nelson on the 18th, "the people in Cadiz do not make some movement. If they allow the war to begin in Italy, they cannot hereafter make up for the want of assistance they might give in the first instance."[21]

Once more Collingwood showed his power of penetration. His vision of what was stirring inside Cadiz could not have been more just. As he wrote the hour had come.

The resolution which the Council of War had first taken was just the kind of thing that Napoleon expected, and the precautions he adopted to meet it, acted even more promptly than he planned. On October 12th, four days after the Council of War, Admiral Rosily reached Madrid on his way to supersede Villeneuve. The posting system had broken down, the roads beyond Cordova were infested with brigands, and the French Ambassador warned him not to proceed till arrangements could be made for his travelling in safety. It was ten days' journey on to Cadiz, but in half that time word came to Villeneuve that Rosily had reached the capital. Guessing in a moment what it meant, and without saying a word to any one, on the 18th, as Collingwood was writing the letter just quoted, he suddenly ordered Magon with seven of the line and a frigate to proceed to sea at dark and endeavour to capture Blackwood's squadron and find out what was behind it. Before, however, the order was executed, word came in by telegraph of Louis's detachment at Gibraltar. The news was that the convoy which had been waiting there for escort, had sailed eastward in charge of four of the line, and that two others were said to be in the port.[22] Villeneuve's inference was that Nelson must be six of the line short. Now if ever was his time. There was no wind and little sign of it, but he was desperate, and without consulting any one he made the general signal to prepare to weigh.[23]

CHAPTER XXII

The Main Fleets In Contact

"ENEMY have their topsail yards hoisted." At six o'clock in the morning of October 19th the signal fluttered from the *Sirius*, the nearest frigate inshore; and then at seven the long-awaited No. 370. It meant "The enemy's ships are coming out of port or getting under sail." In ten minutes Blackwood passed it on to the *Phœbe*, which he kept to the westward. As the light grew, they got it through to the *Mars*, Duff's easternmost ship, and by half-past nine Nelson had it. He was then nearly fifty miles to the westward of Cadiz. Without a moment's hesitation or waiting to form order of sailing he gave the word for "General chase, south-east," and shortly afterwards made the signal to prepare for battle.[1]

Meanwhile Blackwood had despatched one of his two sloops to the *Victory* and the other to warn Louis, while he himself watched the enemy struggling to get out of the harbour on the faint land breeze. By three o'clock a signal came through from him that the enemy's fleet was at sea, though in truth it was only Magon's division that as yet was outside. Nelson held on his way. The movement to cut off Villeneuve from the Straits was that which he had settled from the time he had learnt from the Government how much rested upon Craig's operations, but he had also in view an immediate object of his own. The recent easterly wind let him hope that he might find Louis coming out of the Straits to give him his whole fleet in hand for the final decision.[2] As evening closed down, in order to ensure his purpose as far as possible he formed the "Advance Squadron," for which in accordance with Mediterranean practice his tactical Memorandum provided. A division of eight two-deckers was placed under Captain Duff of the *Mars*, five of them to look out ahead and the rest to continue to keep signal touch with Blackwood's cruisers.[3] The rest of his fleet, according to the regular practice, were to observe the Admiral's motions closely during the night, as he would probably manœuvre without signals. At the same time he superseded "General chase" by signalling for the order of sailing; but as during recent exercises three of his seven three-deckers, *Britannia*, *Prince*, and *Dreadnought*, had proved very bad sailers, he directed them to take station as convenient.[4] The point should be noticed as the first step in the process of disintegration which his "Order of battle "and "Plan of attack" were to suffer, as the actual tactical conditions of the occasion developed themselves to his elastic mind.

At one o'clock in the morning, having attained his desired position, he hove-to, and at dawn found himself in sight of Gibraltar between Capes Trafalgar and Spartel, that is, in the entrance to the Straits. In the growing light every eye was strained for a sight of Louis's squadron, but not a sign of it was to be seen. The truth was that his return to Nelson after he had first started and the prevailing easterly winds had prevented his reaching Gibraltar for five days after he received his orders, and it was not till the 15th that he was able to complete his water and victuals at Tetuan. This done he hurried away to rejoin Nelson, but meeting a westerly wind, was forced back to Tetuan, and there on the 17th, before he could sail again, the order reached him to see the Malta convoy forward. The result was that he missed Blackwood's sloop, and when Nelson was looking for him between Spartel and Trafalgar he was two hundred miles away and still going to the eastward. Nor was it till the 21st of famous memory that in accordance with the usual practice he dismissed the convoy off Cape Tenez and stood back towards Cartagena to cover its further progress.[5] Thus after all the practically inert Cartagena squadron, though it failed to make any movement which Napoleon had designed for it, did avail in the hour of crisis to break the vital British concentration. A more significant instance could not be found of how much more difficult to deal with is a purely expectant attitude at sea than on land. It is a radical and far-reaching difference between naval and military strategy, due mainly to the exigencies of commerce protection.

Disappointing as it was to Nelson's men that Louis was nowhere to be seen, there was a worse trouble to disturb them. An action had been expected confidently at dawn, but Villeneuve was nowhere to be seen. The sun rose stormily; the fine weather had passed; it was thick and wet, with a very short range of visibility. In breathless impatience they scoured the mist, but look as they would there was not a sign of the enemy anywhere. What had become of them? "All our gay hopes are fled," wrote Codrington to his wife that morning, "and instead of being under all sail in a very light breeze and fine weather, expecting to bring the enemy to battle, we are under close-reefed topsails in a very stormy wind with thick rainy weather and the dastardly French we find returned to Cadiz." This belief must have been a mere inference from their not being in sight. "Had they persevered," he added, "we should certainly have come up with them from the decisive dash we made for the Gut of Gibraltar."[6] Where could they be if not in Cadiz? One thing at least was clear. In such foul weather as was blowing up, the fleet could not stay where it was. "I must guard," Nelson had written to Barham, "against being caught with a westerly wind near Cadiz, as a fleet of ships with so many three-deckers would inevitably be forced into the Straits."[7] Accordingly, so soon as it was light enough to be sure how things stood, he decided to make use of the stiff south-south-west wind to get back towards his old station.

Scarcely had he made the decision when one of Blackwood's frigates hove in sight flying the welcome signal that the enemy bore to the north. Nelson immediately signalled for the order of sailing, and about an hour later hove the *Victory* to and summoned Collingwood on board to consult him. Collingwood, it is said, was for making an immediate attack, but this was not to Nelson's mind. We can only guess his reason. It may have been that he felt Collingwood's plan would mean engaging too late in the day and too near Cadiz to ensure a decisive battle, and yet the wind was fair to carry him rapidly into action. What he did was to reform order of sailing and to stand on again north-west under easy sail as though to entice Villeneuve to attempt to pass him inshore.[8]

At the same time he summoned Duff and two of his captains, and instructed them to keep contact with Blackwood and the enemy. Then without recalling the rest of the Advance Squadron into the line, he held on the course he had chosen, presumably to avoid premature contact or a premature disclosure of his force. By noon it had brought him some twenty miles south-west of Cadiz. Blackwood's second sloop by this time had communicated, and informed him that she had seen forty sail coming out the previous evening, but this still left the enemy's conduct a mystery. In the afternoon, however, Blackwood telegraphed a message which put a clearer aspect on the situation, and seemed to account for the enemy's not having been caught at the Strait's mouth. It was that they appeared determined to go to the westward. "And that," wrote the Admiral in his diary they shall not do, if in the power of Nelson and Bronté to prevent them." The course he was steering, whether by intention or not, was exactly what was wanted. He therefore held on as he was till two o'clock, when the fleet was taken aback by a sudden shift of wind into the west-north-west. The sailing order was thrown into confusion, and all movement was checked till he could restore his formation.

If the mystery of Villeneuve's intention was hard to fathom, it was no wonder, for the true explanation of his not having been found in the Strait's mouth lay in circumstances beyond his control. Blackwood was understood to have reported that the whole allied fleet had got to sea on the evening of the 19th, but in fact its seamanship had proved unequal to the task in the light airs that prevailed. It was not till nearly noon on the 20th that Villeneuve had the whole of his force well under way. His intention, as Nelson divined, had actually been to make direct for the Mediterranean, but outside he had met the southerly wind shifting to the south-west on which Nelson under easy sail was reaching back from the Straits, and he had been compelled, as Blackwood had reported, to stand to the westward. On this course he began laboriously to form his order of sailing.

His organisation was based on the old tactical idea of "equalising the line," and using the surplus units as a *corps de reserve*. Believing that after Louis's departure Nelson would have only twenty of the line with his flag, he formed a *corps de bataille* of that number, in three divisions under his immediate command. With the remaining twelve he constituted an *escadre d'observation* in two divisions, which, like Nelson's Advance Squadron, was to be employed as a reserve. Gravina was in command of it, and his instructions on the time-honoured plan were to keep somewhat ahead and to windward, so as to be able to succour any part of the fleet upon which the enemy should concentrate. Seeing that Villeneuve was convinced that Nelson would adopt the principle of concentration, the organisation was well conceived for dealing with it, had only the power of execution been equal to the design. But in the shifting squalls that prevailed, the lack of cohesion in the allied fleet and its defects in seamanship became more and more apparent. So unhandy was the manœuvring that for three hours the cumbrous fleet laboured in vain to attain its formation. About four o'clock the wind came westerly. The sailing order was still far from being formed, but regardless of consequences Villeneuve felt compelled to seize the opportunity of getting to the southward, and he signalled to wear together. The confusion that ensued was almost hopeless, and after wearing the effort to form the order of sailing continued more laboriously than ever. The evolution was only possible by forming on the ships furthest to leeward, so that although Villeneuve tried to keep close-hauled on the starboard tack and steer to the west-south-west as though to weather Nelson or get a good offing for entering the Straits, his mean course must have been about south, and he was reported thus by the British frigates about nightfall.

If Villeneuve was in trouble with his fleet, it was little wonder, for after the shift of wind Nelson himself took two hours to restore his order of sailing.[9] He did it by coming to the wind on the starboard tack, so that the fleet was now heading about south-west. But towards four o'clock — that is, when Villeneuve was wearing his fleet — Nelson was doing the same, but on the opposite or port tack. Whether he knew the enemy had gone about is doubtful. There is no trace of the movement having been reported to him. The *Euryalus* had run down to the battle squadron and was signalling direct to the *Victory*, but was not in sight of the enemy; and the last signal she had made was that their leading ship bore to the north of him.[10] The effect of the British movement was to give the fleet a course very little west of north, so that Nelson must have known he was steering direct to meet his enemy. Indeed, the weather had cleared so much with the westerly wind that before sundown several of the enemy could be seen from the mast-head close in to Cadiz.[11]

Is it possible after all that he was thinking of engaging that evening? It is not probable. An officer present tells us, that the general impression in the fleet was that the enemy did not mean to go back into Cadiz, but that, seeing they had remained at sea in face of the blustery weather, it was evident they were going to attempt to escape at the risk of an action. True, it was at this time that Nelson finally concentrated his fleet. At sunset the whole of the Advance Squadron, except the two or three connecting ships, were reabsorbed into the order of sailing.[12] He was also in the most favourable position for delivering the attack which the Memorandum laid down, and we know it was a favourite idea of his to approach directly end-on, so that the enemy could not tell whether he meant to engage to windward or leeward.[13] If he did contemplate engaging, it must have been in a night action, and this was what Villeneuve was expecting. But he cannot in fact have had any such intention. For when he absorbed the Advance Squadron into the fleet, he telegraphed to Blackwood that he relied on him and his cruiser squadron to keep touch during the night, and at eight o'clock, just as Villeneuve in fear of an immediate attack was signalling for the line of battle as convenient, he wore away again seawards — that is, to the south-west.[14] He must therefore have been bent on encouraging the enemy to make their expected attempt to escape, and by keeping to windward of them to ensure it should not succeed.

This movement was accurately followed by all the fleet except one vessel, a chance that was to have a curious effect for good on the coming battle. The *Africa* 64 apparently did not take in the signal, and held on to the northward till she lost touch.[15] For eight hours Nelson held this course under easy sail, Blackwood keeping, him hourly informed of the enemy's position through the connecting ships of the line. At four o'clock in the morning, with the wind at west-north-west, he wore again "to the north-east," he himself says, but the *Victory's* Log gives the course more accurately as north by east, and this was maintained through the night.

The effect of these movements had been to annul the Order of Sailing. Indeed, it would seem that in those days when fleets were not accustomed to cruise in regular formation, the sailing order was seldom preserved after dark, and especially as in this case when there had been any manœuvring during the night. At daybreak accordingly the fleet was in no regular formation. Collingwood was apparently about the van of his division, but Nelson was not. Most of his ships had stretched ahead of him, and what the French saw when it was light enough was a confused mass of vessels "in no particular order" stretching about south-east and north-west, with the two flagships near each other about the centre.[16]

The fleets were now bearing from one another about south-west and north-east, and some eight or nine miles apart. Shortly after six it was light enough for each to see the other, and what Nelson made out was the Combined Fleet in no distinguishable formation steering for the Straits. The moment of his life and of the campaign had come. What should he do? Should he carry out the attack, as he had laid it down, or should he not? What in these first minutes of the waxing light was the thought that held uppermost in his mind? Death has robbed us of the answer. We can only glean the fragments that lie scattered upon those hallowed waters and bid them tell us, if they will, the golden secret.

CHAPTER XXIII

Nelson's Plan Of Attack

The old and much-disputed question, whether Nelson did or did not attack in accordance with the Memorandum, dates from the morrow of the action. Some officers, in every way equipped for a right judgment, held that he did; others equally well equipped assumed the contrary as a fact beyond dispute.[1]

Collingwood passes shyly over the question, and leaves it practically untouched. All he says in his official despatch is that — "as the mode of attack had been previously determined on and communicated to the flag-officers and captains, few signals were necessary," and yet it is certain many were made. Two months afterwards, in a private letter to Sir Thomas Pasley, he wrote that the plan which Nelson had determined to adopt was executed well and succeeded admirably. But what did he mean by the plan? Earlier in the letter he explains it thus: "Lord Nelson determined to substitute for exact order an impetuous attack in two distinct bodies. The weather line he commanded, and left the lee line totally to my direction. He had assigned the points to be attacked." But no one will assert that this is an adequate summary of the plan of the Memorandum. It conveys little more than the impression of an attack by divisions in "General Chase." The distinctive idea is barely indicated, and it entirely ignores the subtle method of engaging by which Nelson intended to realise that idea. Collingwood therefore was saying at most that the general intention of an attack in two independent divisions was carried out. It need not, however, be assumed from this that Collingwood did not appreciate the niceties of the Memorandum. The chivalrous loyalty of his nature would not in any case permit him to say more, and in everything he wrote of the action we can read between the lines a lofty determination to ignore any detail which might be turned even remotely to detract from the glory of his dead friend or to suggest in any degree that the victory was not entirely Nelson's.

Captain Harvey of the *Téméraire*, who was Nelson's second in the line, is equally general, and yet the Log of the ship shows that he was by far the most detailed and methodical observer of the action. "It was noon," he wrote, "before the action commenced, which was done according to the instructions given us by Lord Nelson." Whether by "the instructions" he meant the written "Plan of Attack," or the verbal instructions passed down the line during the approach, every one must judge for himself. It is certainly impossible to assert beyond the possibility of contradiction that he meant the "Plan of Attack." The other two witnesses for the affirmative are equally vague. Thirty years after the event, Codrington said he could remember calling the attention of his first lieutenant to Nelson's movements as he came into action, remarking, "How beautifully the Admiral is carrying his design into effect;" but a week after the action he wrote to a Lord of the Admiralty, "We all scrambled into battle as soon as we could."[2] Lastly, there is the fact that Captain Hope of the *Defence* endorsed on his copy of the Memorandum: "It was agreeable to these instructions that Lord Nelson attacked the combined fleets of France and Spain." This appears to exhaust the affirmative evidence such as it is, and so far as it is known at present.

The negative testimony is richer and far more explicit. Captain Moorsom of the *Revenge*, in Collingwood's division, said: "A regular plan was laid down by Lord Nelson before the action, but not acted on;" and again, "Admiral Collingwood dashed directly down, supported by such ships as could get up, and went directly through their line. Lord Nelson did the same, and the rest as fast as they could." In his opinion, then, there was no difference in the way the two divisions engaged. Both made an almost perpendicular attack — that is, the two lines went "directly down" instead of getting into the designed position parallel to the enemy's line and then hauling to the wind.[3] His son, Admiral Constantine Moorsom, who earned himself a rare reputation as a scientific student of tactics, went further. In his *Principles of Naval Tactics*, the only original treatise on the subject which the service had produced, he wrote, that "there was an entire alteration both of the scientific principle and of the tactical movements."[4]

The only fully reasoned criticism which we have from the pen of an officer who was present is to the same effect. It was written about 1820 by Admiral Sir Humphrey Senhouse, who served in the battle as a lieutenant in Israel Pellew's ship, the *Colossus*, an officer who highly distinguished himself in the later years of the war and was afterwards flag-captain, both in the Channel and the Mediterranean.[5] His criticism was based on the then undisputed fact that the British Fleet bore up in succession and attacked in two lines ahead, and his argument is that it would have been better "if the regulated plan had been adhered to." "The attack of this almost infallible Admiral," he says, "was different from that laid down in his instructions, substituting a line-ahead for a line-abreast in his division"; and he holds that the change sacrificed both simultaneous impact and superior concentration of attack. He assumes the form of engaging in two lines ahead end-on as a fact that no one present at the action would dispute, and indeed no one did. "You are to understand," wrote Captain Harvey of the *Téméraire*, "that we bore down on the enemy in two columns," and every one who touched the point said the same thing.

Sir Charles Ekins, who had every opportunity of knowing, proceeds on the same assumption without a shadow of doubt. "It is known," he wrote, "to all the captains of the fleet that the plan of attack from to windward was, by previous concert, to have been of a different and still more formidable nature."[6] Indeed, it is believed that every categorical statement on the point by officers who were present or directly concerned — that is, setting aside rough generalisations, and what is only inferential or an *obiter dictum* — asserts that the attack as delivered differed in important particulars from the plan of the Memorandum.

For those accustomed to weigh historical evidence there cannot be serious doubt of what the departure was, in the deliberate judgment of the Naval Staff of the time. On this we have evidence that no inferential argument can shake: for it lies in the next edition of the Signal Book. There, beyond all dispute, is a new Signal for a form of attack purporting, as the "Signification" explains, to embody the experiences of Trafalgar and the principles of the Memorandum. It is to "cut the enemy's line in order of sailing in two columns."

It is accompanied by a diagram showing an almost vertical attack in two lines ahead without previous deployment, and a long instruction explaining the method of engaging in succession and its tactical advantages, such as they were, over simultaneous impact.[7]

The best foreign criticism took precisely the same view. Here, for instance, is the appreciation sent to the Spanish Government some six weeks after the action by Escaño, Gravina's accomplished Chief of the Staff. "Nothing," he concludes, "is more seamanlike, or better tactics, than for a fleet which is well to windward of another to bear down upon it in two separate columns, and deploy into line at gunshot from the enemy. But Admiral Nelson did not deploy his columns at gunshot from our line, but ran up within pistol-shot and broke through it. . . . It was a manner in which I do not think he will find many imitators."[8]

How, then, in the face of these uncompromising and authoritative statements, can we reconcile the view — and it undoubtedly prevailed — that the plan of the Memorandum was carried out? The explanation is not far to seek.

On analysis the famous document, like others of its class, will be found to be composed of two groups of ideas — the first relating to major tactics, and the second to minor. The origin of the first group may be traced back to a conversation which Nelson had with his faithful counsellor Keats at Merton, while he was waiting for his call. "No day," said Nelson, "can be long enough to arrange a couple of fleets and fight a decisive battle according to the old system. . . . I shall form the fleet into three divisions in three lines. One division shall be composed of twelve or fourteen of the fastest two-decked ships, which I shall keep always to windward, or in a situation of advantage. . . . I consider it will always be in my power to throw it into the battle in any part I may choose. . . . With the remaining part of the fleet formed in two lines I shall go at them at once, if I can, about one-third of their line from their leading ship. . . . I think it will surprise and confound the enemy. They won't know what I am about. It will bring on a pell-mell battle, and that is what I want." Setting aside the third division — a point to be dealt with later — this scheme coincides with the action much more closely than it does with the Memorandum. Indeed, the expressions "go at them at once," and "pell-mell battle," suggest that Keats's memory, by a familiar psychological process, was coloured by what actually occurred. Still here we have three of the four major ideas — attack in separate divisions instead of one line — concentration on the rear — and concealing the nature and point of the attack till the last moment.

The Memorandum itself is much more subtle. It contained a fourth idea that was entirely Nelson's own. Calder's main conception had also been concentration on the rear, and he too had not formed his battle order or disclosed his attack till he was very close. But Calder's attack had been parried by the enemy's van coming down to the assistance of the rear. It is in the craft with which the Memorandum provides against such a move that lies its most brilliant and original feature. Nothing else is entirely Nelson's. Duncan at Camperdown had attacked in two divisions; Clerk of Eldin had suggested the principle of approach in echelon on which Nelson's intended formation was based, while from Calder's action he got the warning of what he had to expect from the enemy.

Nelson's Memorandum opens with a recital of the delay inseparable from forming a large fleet in one line, and his consequent determination to organise his fleet in such a way that the order of sailing will be the order of battle, but with this proviso. The order of sailing was to be the order of battle, "with the exception of the first and second in command." This neglected point is important. It meant that in order of sailing the two admirals would as usual lead their respective divisions, but in order of battle they would not. Some other station would be assigned to them. Assuming a fleet of forty sail, the organisation would be in two lines of sixteen ships, with an advance squadron of eight (or one-fifth) composed of the fastest two-deckers — but as this last factor eventually disappeared it can be discarded for the present.

The next point is new — the second in command is to have entire direction of his line after the Admiral's intentions are made known to him. The wording of the paragraph does not make it quite clear at what time this independent direction was to begin. What did Nelson mean by "after the Admiral's intentions are made known to him"? A later paragraph defines it, at least for the attack from to windward, which was the attack actually delivered. In this case Nelson himself will conduct the approach until the whole fleet is "nearly within gunshot of the enemy's centre." He will then signal to Collingwood the manner in which he is to attack. The signal that will probably be made is specified, and he is also warned what he may be wanted to do in case certain counter-movements are made by the enemy. Then Nelson repeats that the entire management of the lee line will be left to the second in command "after the intention of the Commander-in-chief is signified." This could only mean that the independent direction was to begin directly Nelson had given his colleague the signal to engage, and not before. In other words, his obvious and natural intention was to conduct the approach himself and then to leave his colleague a free hand to do his special part of the work.[9]

Having got thus far with his major tactics he breaks off into the minor, dealing successively with the two conditions of finding the enemy to windward or to leeward. In engaging from to leeward — he will attack in three lines, in line-ahead. Collingwood will lead through as near as he can at the twelfth ship from the rear, so as to concentrate on about three-fourths of his own number.[10] Nelson's line will lead through about the centre; and the advance squadron, a few ships ahead of it, "so as to ensure getting at their Commander-in-chief, whom every effort must be made to capture." This idea of enveloping the enemy's Commander-in-chief was a return to the central idea of medieval tactics. Indeed, nothing is so remarkable in this immortal Memorandum than the way in which it seems to gather up and co-ordinate every tactical principle that had ever proved effective.

He then falls back again into major exposition. The principle of the attack is concentration of the entire fleet upon the enemy's rear as far forward as their Commander-in-chief and the units immediately ahead of him. This would leave some twenty sail untouched and free to act as Gravina had done in Calder's action, but he considers his form of attack provides sufficiently against any section of his fleet being doubled on by the unengaged ships of the enemy. "It must be some time," he says, "before they could perform a manœuvre to bring their force compact to attack any part of the British fleet engaged or to succour their own ships, which indeed would be impossible without mixing with the ships engaged." His meaning clearly is, that if the worst comes to the worst, there will be a mêlée, which must result in a decisive action. "I look with confidence," he adds, "to a victory before the van of the enemy can succour their rear, and then the British fleet would most of them be ready to receive their twenty-sail." He concludes this part of the Memorandum by a return to minor tactics, in which he explains exactly what is to be done if the van does tack, but as the attack was not made from to leeward these details may be discarded.

From this point onwards the document is concerned entirely with the minor tactics of an attack from to windward — the form which he hoped to and did adopt. The section is headed, "Of the intended attack from to windward. The enemy in line of battle ready to attack." In this case he says "the divisions of the British fleet will be brought nearly within gunshot of the enemy's centre," and a diagram is given to illustrate the intended position.[11] The signal would then most probably be made for the lee line to bear up together upon the twelve rearmost ships of the enemy — that is, as before, upon three-fourths of its own number.[12]

From the position in which Nelson intended to place him, the second in command would be able to deliver Howe's attack through the intervals of the enemy's line, going down with every stitch of canvas set in the regular line of bearing, obliquely, as Byng tried to do at Minorca, with his broadsides bearing. "Some ships," wrote Nelson, "may not get through their exact place, but they will always be at hand to assist their friends, and if any are thrown round the rear of the enemy, they will effectually complete the business of twelve sail of the enemy."

Such an attack made from to windward was open to two well-known parries, with which Nelson proceeds to deal. The enemy might wear together so as to make the rear their van, or they might execute the manœuvre of the old French text-books, by bearing up together and running to leeward, so as to get the attacking force between two fires and avoid being raked. In either case Collingwood was to persist in his attack on the twelve ships assigned to him and press it home, "unless otherwise directed by the Commander-in-chief, which is scarcely to be expected." The remainder of the enemy's fleet was to be left to Nelson, but of what he intended to do he says no more than "that he will endeavour to take care that the movements of the second-in-command are interrupted as little as possible." In short, his major function was to contain the van, and the minor tactics would depend on circumstances.

From the approach which he contemplated it would be open to him either to cut the line at one point in line-ahead, or, like Collingwood, to cut it at all intervals; while the Advance Squadron, to which in the weather attack no special function was assigned, would be always in reserve to support either Admiral as circumstances required. But there are clear indications that he relied mainly on the former manœuvre, risky as it was. The danger which had caused it to fall into disuse since the old Dutch Wars was, firstly, that the leading ship was likely to be overpowered by a concentrated fire as she approached; and the second was, that if any ships did succeed in getting through they were liable to be cut off and surrounded. Nelson, we are often told, never measured risks. Nothing is really further from his character than such folly. In this case he faced the risks, measured them with consummate tactical insight, and provided a means of discounting them that was without precedent. His highly original and scientific idea was a combination of two principles — high speed, and massing guns to the utmost at the point of shock. For the first time on record the attack was to be made not under "fighting sails "as usual, but under every stitch the spars would carry. He would gather the highest attainable speed and so bring his momentum to the maximum, and the danger period to the minimum.

The second expedient was still more remarkable. It was obtained, as will be shown directly, by massing his three-deckers in the van of his line. This was a method of concentration which had been suggested originally by Bigot de Morogues in his *Tactique Navale* in 1763, as the only one that was really effective. Rodney had introduced a signal for it, but it had never been used till Nelson now set his seal upon it, to overcome the almost insuperable difficulties of the manœuvre for which his tactical scheme called most loudly. There was no case in which a well-formed line of battle had been broken successfully by the old method in line-ahead, but Nelson must have thought that in the French theory he saw his way where no one before him had dared to tread. He would arm the head of his line for the fatal shock with a mass of fire that nothing could resist, and would overpower the time-honoured defensive formation by sheer weight of metal and momentum. He would form his van of a group so powerful that even if it were cut off and surrounded it could hold its own against any concentration that could be brought to bear upon it. Thus it was that at the supreme crisis he called to his aid the theory of the great French tactician — the theory of concentration of gun power in the fewest possible units and in the shortest possible length of line. And so in the culminating hour of sailing warfare the theorist and the man of action were at one.

Morogues' solution of the problem of concentration may have been in Nelson's mind for some time. We have seen how the idea of massing heavy ships in the van is to be detected in the two orders of battle which he had issued during his chase of Villeneuve.[13] In both cases, however, the arrangement may have been accidental or due to other considerations. Be that as it may, the Trafalgar order places it beyond doubt that Morogues' suggestion was the fundamental idea on which he disposed his ships. By a curious chance no copy of the order actually used in the action has come down to us. Indeed, it is most probable he never prepared one for the reduced fleet with which he eventually had to engage, since he did not anticipate fighting without Louis's division.

The latest and only one he is known to have drawn up was issued with the Memorandum on October 10th. Calder was still with him at the time, and it includes his ship as well as those of Louis's division and one or two that were daily expected, leaving blanks for the rest. The original signed and dated copy, issued "Off Cadiz, Oct. 10, 1805," is in the museum of the United Service Institution, with the fleet pennant-board attached. It is on a form designed for the forty sail that had been promised him, as given below, the ships not present at the battle being printed in italics with the causes of their absence appended in brackets.

ORDER OF SAILING

VAN SQUADRON

Vanes at the main
First Division

1. Téméraire 98.
2. *Superb* 74 (*not arrived*).
3. Victory (flag) 100.
4. Neptune 98.
5. ————
6. *Tigre* 74 (*with Louis*).
7. *Canopus* 80 (*Louis's flag*).
8. Conqueror 74.
9. Agamemnon 64.
10. Leviathan 74.

Van or Starboard Division
Second Division

11. *Pr. of Wales* (flag) 98 (*home with Calder*).
12. Ajax 74.
13. Orion 74.
14. Minotaur 74.
15. ————
16. *Queen* (*with Louis*) 98.
17. *Donegal* (*at Gibraltar*) 74.
18. *Spencer* (*with Louis*) 74.
19. ————
20. Spartiate 74.

REAR SQUADRON

Vanes at the fore
First Division

1. Prince 98.
2. Mars 74.
3. R. Sovereign (flag) 100.
4. Tonnant 80.
5. ————
6. Bellerophon 74.
7. Colossus 74.
8. Achille 74.
9. Polyphemus 64.
10. Revenge 74.

Rear or Larboard Division
Second Division

11. Britannia (flag) 100.
12. Swiftsure 74.
13. Defence 74.
14. ————
15. *Kent* 74 (*not arrived*).
16. *Zealous* 74 (*with Louis*).
17. ————
18. Thunderer 74.
19. Defiance 74.
20. Dreadnought 98.

Apart from the striking concentration of powerful units in the van of each line the document presents other remarkable features. It will be observed that the organisation is quadruple in two squadrons and four divisions, each with its flag-officer. This was an innovation, but whether Nelson's or not cannot yet be said with certainty. The normal organisation since the reforms of Howe and Kempenfelt had been threefold, that is, in three squadrons, and for a fleet of this size each squadron would be in two divisions. It had become usual also to provide for a dual formation in two "Grand Divisions" by splitting the centre squadron, and attaching its two divisions to the van and rear squadrons respectively. It will further be noted that no provision is made for the Advance Squadron which the Memorandum contemplated, as had been done in earlier Mediterranean orders.[14]

It is incredible that if Nelson issued an order of battle subsequent to this, no copy of it should have survived. We may assume, therefore, with some certainty that the order used in the action was that issued with the Memorandum, modified only by the exigencies of the case. Judging by the various extant lists purporting to show how the ships went into action the actual battle order must have been formed by simply closing up the intervals left by missing units, but with one important alteration. *Britannia* was certainly in Nelson's squadron, and in her own list and two others she is shown sixth. We may assume then, as was only natural, that when Calder went home, Lord Northesk was brought over to take his place at the head of Nelson's second division. His place would naturally have been taken by Louis, who was now the fourth flag-officer, but as he was away, the head of Collingwood's second division seems to have been assigned temporarily to the *Dreadnought*, from which ship Collingwood had just shifted his flag to the *Royal Sovereign*.[15]

On these indications we get the actual battle order of the reduced fleet as follows: —

PROBABLE ORDER OF BATTLE AT TRAFALGAR
As modified from that of October 10 for the ships actually present.

Van or Weather Squadron
1st Division

1. Téméraire 98 (Harvey).
2. Victory 100 (Hardy).
3. Neptune 98 (Fremantle). .
4. Conqueror 74 (J. Pellew).
5. Leviathan 74 (Bayntun).
6. Africa (?) 64 (Digby).

2nd Division

7. Britannia 100 (Bullen).
8. Ajax 74 (Brown).
9. Orion 74 (Codrington)
10. Agamemnon 64 (Berry). .
11. Minotaur 74 (Mansfield).
12. Spartiate 74 (Laforey).

Rear or Lee Squadron
1st Division

1. Prince 98 (Grindall).
2. Mars 74 (Duff).
3. R. Sovereign 100 (Rotherham).
4. Tonnant 80 (Tyler).
5. Belleisle 74 (Hargood).
6. Bellerophon 74 (Cooke).
7. Colossus 74 (Morris).
8. Achille 74 (King).

2nd Division

9. Dreadnought 98 (Conn).
10. Polyphemus 64 (Redmill).
11. Revenge 74 (Moorsom).
12. Swiftsure 74 (Rutherford).
13. Defence 74 (Hope).
14. Thunderer 74 (Lechemere).
15. Defiance 74 (Durham).

This order, it is true, does not coincide exactly with any of the extant lists of how the ships came into action. But no two of them agree, none have any certain authority, and all are demonstrably incorrect in detail.[16] But taken with the official order of October 10th, it affords the best indication of the organisation that was in Nelson's mind. In that order we have a concentration in the van of the weather line of three three-deckers broken only by the *Superb*, a powerful seventy-four under his special favourite Keats, whom he had promised to be his second if he arrived in time.[17] Possibly a fourth three-decker was intended, as he was expecting two more, and the fifth place was left vacant. Similarly in Collingwood's line we have in the leading four units, two three-deckers, an eighty, and another powerful seventy-four, with the fifth place again left vacant. It was given to *Belleisle*, an exceptionally heavy two-decker, when she arrived.[18]

A further important feature to note in the arrangement of the two vans is that neither Nelson nor Collingwood were to lead their lines in order of battle, but only in the normal order of sailing. In the Memorandum, Nelson wrote, "My line would lead through," not "I should lead through," and Captain Harvey says that in consequence of a signal made at the last moment he went into action astern instead of ahead of the *Victory*, implying that Nelson's station was second in order of battle, as we should expect in the absence of the *Superb*. As to Collingwood's place, we have a distinct statement that it was third, as in the official order of battle.[19]

There is one more point in the order that was actually used, and which must be noticed as a departure from the Memorandum. The various lists agree that in the action the two squadrons were not equal. In all of them Nelson is shown with twelve units, and Collingwood with fifteen. The numerical inferiority of Nelson's column was no doubt partly due to the absence of Louis's squadron, since all but one of his ships belonged to the weather line in the official order. But the inferiority is more apparent than real, for if three-deckers are counted as two units, Nelson has sixteen against Collingwood's eighteen. For the purpose of containing by breaking the line in line-ahead Nelson's numerical inferiority was of small moment, while if Collingwood was to attack twelve of the enemy, it was essential to keep his division as nearly as possible one fourth superior in number.

Such an allocation of force was all the more necessary owing to the absorption of the Advance Squadron into the two main divisions, and the consequent change from a triple to a dual organisation. This fundamental alteration has never been clearly explained, and is worth consideration. By recent Mediterranean practice the Advance Squadron had been nothing but an Observation Squadron, but it is clear that Nelson had in his mind a step forward which would give it a real tactical function. In the Memorandum he treats it not merely as an Observation Squadron, but as a kind of reserve. On the assumption that his fleet would reach the promised number of forty sail of the line, he gives it in the Memorandum, though not in the Order of Sailing, an organisation in two grand divisions of sixteen ships each, with an Advance Squadron of eight of his fastest two-deckers, that is, one-fifth of his battle squadron and not the one-third which, as we have seen, he had been using on the eve of the engagement. Its purpose he explains by saying that, "It will always make, if wanted, a line of twenty-four sail on whichever line the commander-in-chief may direct." Now, so far as we know, no such organisation was ever carried out, but owing to the circumstance that we have no "Organisation"of the fleet later than the 10th, it is almost impossible to say what was done.

An Observation Squadron had existed from the first. On taking over the command and before the Memorandum was issued, Nelson gave Duff four ships, namely, the *Mars* (his own), *Colossus*, *Defence*, and *Ajax,* two being from each squadron according to the original Order of Sailing. After the issue of the Memorandum, *Belleisle* and *Agamemnon* arrived and were added to the connecting line, being again one from each squadron. This detachment Nelson called his Advanced Squadron. "I have," he writes to Ball ten days before the battle, "an Advanced Squadron of fast-sailing ships between me and the frigates."[20] If Codrington is correct it must by this time have received its full organisation. Eight units, he says, were detached for this service after the Memorandum was issued, of which his own ship *Orion* was one. But he was obviously in some confusion as to what Nelson said he was going to do with them. He understood generally that the attack was to be made upon the enemy's rear in two lines, Collingwood making the main attack, while Nelson prevented the van from interfering, as it had done in Calder's action. He would effect this by cutting the line in rear of the allied Commander-in-chief, while the Advance Squadron cut it ahead of him so as to isolate and surround the enemy's flagship and her seconds. But Codrington was by no means clear, and naturally enough; for this form of engagement was enjoined by the Memorandum for the special case of an attack from to leeward only. In the other part of the document, which explains the intended attack from to windward, no independent attack is assigned to the Advance Squadron, though its existence is clearly shown in the diagram. We can only assume that in this case the general reserve clause relating to it would operate, and that it would be used to reinforce either line as necessary.

Brilliant as the Memorandum is as a tactical conception, a certain obscurity in its exposition must be admitted. It bears throughout marks of the haste with which it was drawn up when Nelson believed that the shift of wind into the east would bring Villeneuve out in a few hours. Its arrangement, as we have seen, is without logical order or system; it is full of repetitions; the diction in places ignores grammar; and the order of battle which it predicates differs radically from that which was issued. The meaning consequently is often far from clear without careful interpretive study, and the actual conditions on the eve of the battle can only have increased the captains' uncertainty.

As the situation stood, it was obvious the attack must be made from to windward. The diagram in the Memorandum clearly showed the existence and position of the Advance Squadron for such an attack, and yet the Advance Squadron had been absorbed the night before and had ceased to exist as a separate organisation. Up till the last moment there was nothing to tell Nelson's captains that he had departed from the organisation he had laid down in the Memorandum. In the voluminous evidence that is extant there is no hint that he explained to the officers concerned that this tactical alteration had been made. If he had issued any fresh instructions, Codrington certainly could not have forgotten the circumstance or omitted to mention it. Long afterwards he dealt with the point, but the only impression left in his mind was that the arrangement had not been cancelled, and that Nelson had said that the eight ships were to draw out of the line if the enemy's van should threaten to come down to the assistance of the rear. But this is hardly possible. The Advance Squadron, as constituted on the night before the battle, consisted, as we have seen, of the five ships sent ahead, and four connecting with the cruisers. But of these no less than six belonged to the division which Collingwood led into battle, and they could not possibly have been called out of the line without paralysing the main attack.

Two conclusions, then, seem to be inevitable. The first is, that so long as Nelson had hope of recovering Louis's squadron, the idea of an Advance Squadron was still in his mind; but when that hope failed he abandoned the triple organisation altogether. The second is that no fresh tactical instructions were given to the fleet after his decision was made.

Such, as nearly as they can be ascertained, are the facts which are relevant to the problem of Nelson's real intentions. By the light of them we must seek to penetrate the meaning of his changing movements. They are all we have to reveal what was working in his mind, and by their aid alone can we reach any right appreciation of the tactics he actually employed.

CHAPTER XXIV

The Battle Of Trafalgar

As the morning of October 21st broke in soft serenity, Nelson, as we have seen, found himself with his fleet in disorder and a section of it absent, in presence of a superior enemy to leeward — not as he had pictured them "in the line of battle ready to attack," but apparently in no regular formation. The body of them bore from the flagship a little south of east, some nine miles away as estimated in the *Victory's* Log; and with Gravina's squadron to windward of the van they appeared to stretch north-north-east and south-south-west, with their heads to the southward as though making for the Straits.

The apparent lack of formation was due to the fact that Villeneuve was trying to change from the "order of battle as convenient" which he had hastily ordered at night-fall, to the regular order (*ordre naturel*). His organisation had been further disturbed by the discovery that the British fleet was stronger by five ships than he expected. Instead of being, as he had calculated, just equal to his *corps de bataille*, it outnumbered it, and thus at the last hour he found his whole tactical design was upset. To meet the case there was only one thing to do. The *corps de bataille* must be strengthened; his well-designed dual organisation must be sacrificed, and instead of having Gravina's advanced squadron as an independent unit, he was forced to order him to take station ahead of the *corps de bataille*. Thus after all his care and forethought, there was fixed upon him a single unwieldy line, the very formation which he knew to be the worst for meeting English tactics.

To be compelled on the eve of engaging to abandon the only arrangement which could have availed to baffle Nelson's intended attack was bad enough, but it was by no means the end of the trouble. The squally weather had passed in the night, and had been succeeded by light airs very variable in the north-west quarter. The British had it at first fairly fresh about north-west, but the Combined Fleet had it lighter, and shifting between west-south-west and west-north-west. There was also a heavy swell rolling in from the same quarter which made manœuvring still more difficult, and the result was that, as the allies began to execute the new movement, the confusion increased and all semblance of order disappeared.[1]

In these conditions it has been assumed that the proper and natural thing for Nelson to do was to restore his order of sailing and bear up together, or at least to form the line of bearing so as to get the fleet into the position the Memorandum depicted.[2] He did neither. It would have been contrary to the established practice. Fleets in those days rapidly lost order and cohesion if they tried to move any distance in line-abreast or line of bearing, and it had been one of the most useful reforms of Howe and Kempenfelt to abolish the clumsy method of the old order of sailing. On their improved system, adapted from the French, a fleet in sailing order always moved in two or more lines ahead, and nothing was held to have increased tactical mobility so much as this happy innovation.[3] No Admiral would have thought of reverting to the discredited system at such an hour, and least of all Nelson, whose plan depended on holding the fleet in his hand in the highest attainable state of flexibility and cohesion till the moment came to fling it upon the enemy in the manner that the moment should require.

What he did was to signal at once for the Order of Sailing, and a few minutes afterwards — that is, probably as soon as the first signal was answered — "to bear-up and sail large" with the compass signal east-north-east. Now this was a signal not intended for a formed fleet, that is, a fleet in sailing or battle order. It was used only to an unformed fleet, and the effect, therefore, of the two hoists was an order to bear-up one after the other in turn as they happened to be sailing and take their regular stations in the wake of their respective flagships as they steered east-north-east.[4] The plain evidence of the Signal Book is endorsed by the Master of the *Neptune*, who expressly records that they bore up in succession.[5] Moreover, under Nelson's own hand we have exactly what he intended. In the last entry in his Private Diary he wrote, "At daylight saw the enemy's Combined Fleet from east to east-south-east; bore away; made signal for order of sailing." There can therefore be no shadow of doubt that he regarded "bearing away" as a preliminary to forming the order of sailing, and that he meant the fleet to form upon him as he bore away east-north-east.[6]

Now this is precisely what the enemy saw. The first impression as the British fleet bore up in the distance was that it was forming line-abreast or line of bearing or groups disposed abreast.[7] As the movement went on, however, it was seen to be dividing into two groups or "pelotons," which would be the natural effect of the various ships cutting their corners to get into the Admirals' wake. Finally in about two hours it was evident that these two groups were developing into two columns with the heavy ships leading.[8]

Villeneuve's first idea was that Nelson was coming down upon his rear in a mass of groups with the double intention of securing a superior concentration and cutting him off from Cadiz.[9] To meet such an attack there was a special signal in the French book. It ran, "The fleet of the Republic being in order of battle and in any line whatever to leeward, the enemy in group formation (*en peloton*) or in any line whatever or even in several lines, endeavouring to engage the rear of the fleet — order to all the vessels to wear together."[10] Villeneuve's fleet being in the process of carrying out his last signal for *ordre naturel* was in no condition to manœuvre. It was indeed in so much disorder that in many places it was *en pelotons* instead of in line. Nevertheless he determined to make the signal, and thus for the second time tried to wear his unformed fleet together, regardless of the consequences.

Did Nelson expect this when he made his undisguised threat upon Villeneuve's rear? Blackwood, who had been called on board the *Victory* about this time, says "he appeared very much to regret it."[11] Yet the Memorandum anticipated such a movement. Should the enemy wear together, Nelson had written, the original rear was still to be Collingwood's "object of attack." It is clear, however, that he had not looked for the movement so soon. He was providing for its being made when the attack was fully developed. Still that Villeneuve wore sooner than he expected is hardly enough of itself to account for his annoyance. There is, moreover, a further difficulty about what was in Nelson's mind at this time. How could he possibly have attacked as he intended, on the course he was steering for the rear, if Villeneuve had held on to the southward? The only way, without interchanging the positions of the two squadrons, would have been to stand for the enemy's van as it then was, and then haul to the wind in succession on the opposite tack and so bring his fleet in echelon abreast their centre. But even this would have been very awkward, and in the light wind would have taken too much time. When Villeneuve reversed the order of his fleet the situation was much more favourable, since the position of the Memorandum could have been obtained, when Nelson thought fit, by simply throwing the two divisions into the larboard line of bearing. Why then did Nelson regret it? The answer is that he did not yet realise that Villeneuve was in order of battle. To him the allied fleet in the distance appeared to be like his own in cruising order — the *route libre* of the French. "At seven," he wrote in the last entry in his Private Diary, "the enemy wearing in succession. May the Great God whom I worship grant to my country and for the benefit of Europe in general a great and glorious Victory." He must have thought, like Cromwell, that the Lord had delivered them into his hand. As we know they were not "wearing in succession" but "together," and if Nelson had realised they were in order of battle he could not have mistaken the manœuvre. It must have seemed to him that they were performing another manœuvre — in fact the one he himself had just executed. In his eyes it was not a line of battle being inverted, but an unformed fleet in which the ships were wearing in turn one after the other in the now obsolete sense of "in succession."[12] It could only mean that he had caught them unawares, and that to save themselves from an attack in chase they were hurrying *en route libre* for Cadiz.

At that time, indeed, the British fleet had all the appearance of threatening the old vehement attack of Hawke and Boscawen — attack in general chase with the leading ships forming line as they chased. In some of the British ships the impression seems to have been that this was actually Nelson's intention. "The signal was made to chase," wrote a lieutenant of the *Royal Sovereign* in his Journal. "Bore up and made all sail in chase," says the Master of the *Conqueror*[13] It is then quite possible and indeed the best explanation of all the circumstances that this idea was at first uppermost in Nelson's mind — to fling his fleet upon the unformed enemy at the earliest possible moment, or as Collingwood told Pasley, to deliver "an impetuous attack in two distinct bodies."[14]

Whether or not this was actually his first impulse, it is certain it did not last long. However much the inversion of the enemy's line annoyed him, it quickly became apparent he was adhering to the principle of his plan of attack. So soon as he realised their intention to head to the northward he again made the signal to bear up, this time with the compass flag "East." He did not, however, steer that course, but as the Logs of the leading ships show, from half a point to a point north of east, direct for the enemy's centre. It was just what the Memorandum provided, and would bring the whole weight of his attack upon their new rear.[15]

But before proceeding further, it is necessary to clear the expressions "centre" and "rear" from the ambiguity which has been so fertile in error. Owing to the change in the allied formation much confusion arose both in their own and the British reports in specifying the various parts of the fleet. When Villeneuve decided to invert the line, he ordered Gravina to form the squadron of observation in the rear of the *corps de bataille*. This, the main body of the fleet which was Villeneuve's immediate command, consisted

PLAN OF
TRAFALGAR
attached to the report of
Captain Prigny,
Villeneuve's Chief of the Staff
(Archives de la Marine BB[4] 232)
from
Desbrière's Trafalgar

Note: This Plan was also adopted by Dumanoir

■ French and Spanish Fleet

□ English Fleet

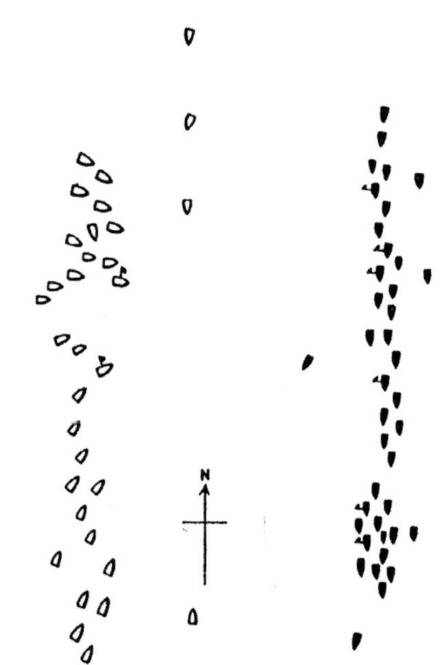

About 6:30 after Nelson's first two signals. British lines beginning to form.

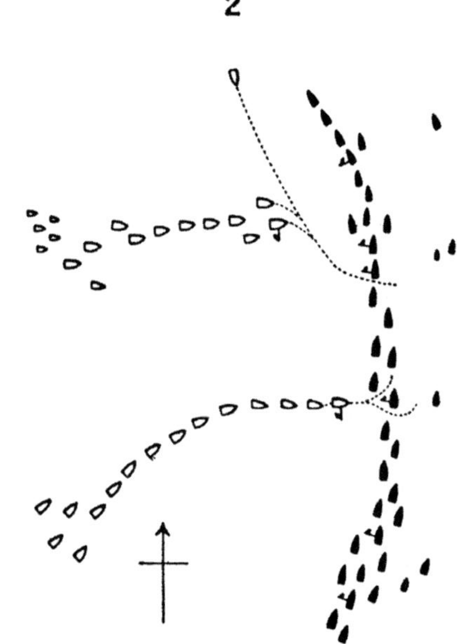

About 11:30. Nelson steering to pass ahead of S. Trinidad and his subsequent turn to starboard.

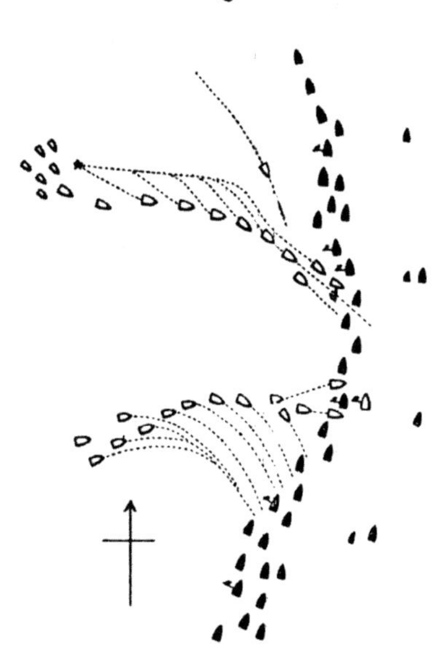

About 12:30. Shewing the ships of Nelson's division edging into his wake after his turn to starboard.

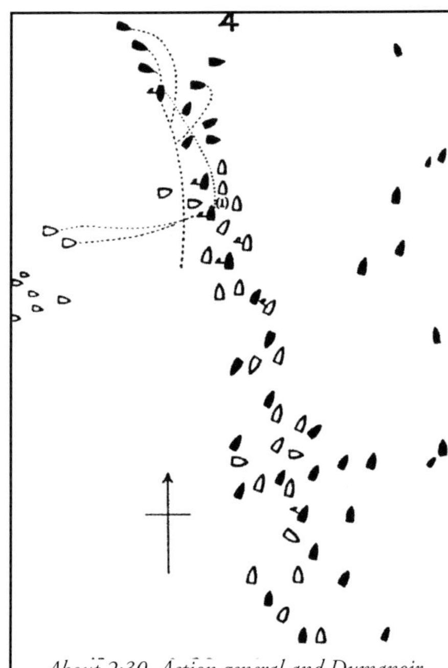

About 2:30. Action general and Dumanoir wearing. This note is attached: "(1) Course which the commander of the van should have taken."

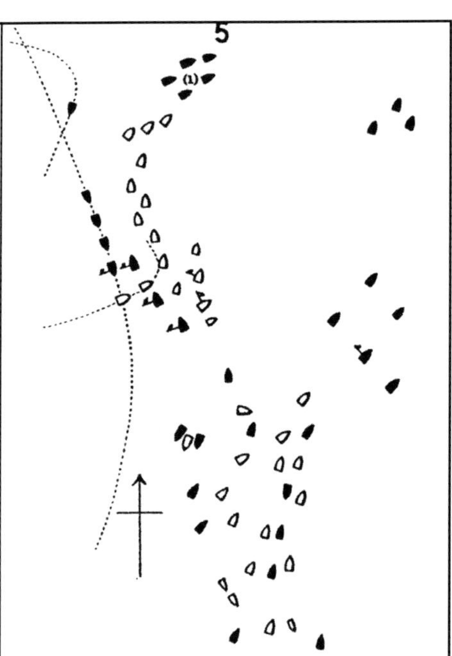

About 3:00. This note is attached: "(1) These ships did not run for Cadiz. They came into action: for instance the Intrépide amongst others."

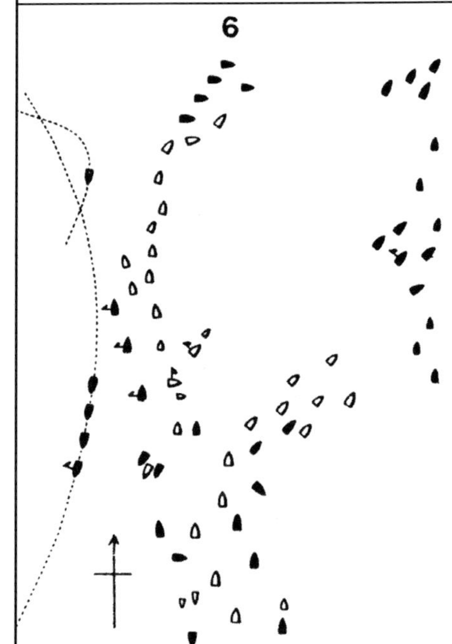

About 3:30. Dumanoir's attempt on the rear. The new British line is not shown.

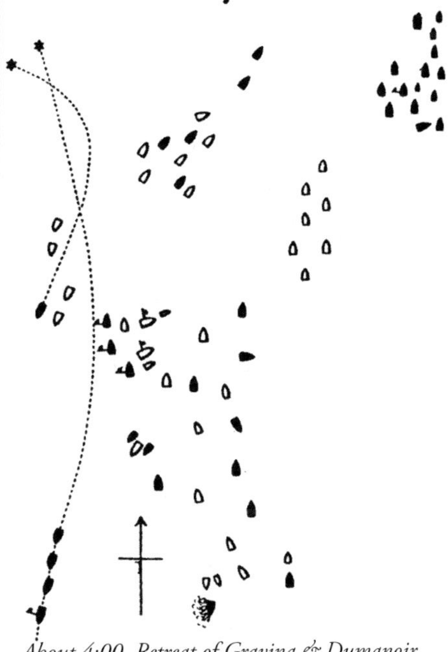

About 4:00. Retreat of Gravina & Dumanoir. The Neptuno isolated.

of three squadrons, which were designated "Van," "Centre," and "Rear." The new disposition, however, upset the old designations. Some officers in their reports kept to the original nomenclature, and used "Rear" as meaning the rear of the *corps de bataille*; while others gave it up and used "Rear" to designate Gravina's observation squadron, which was now the true rear of the fleet. So also with the "Centre." In some reports it means the old "Centre"; that is, the centre of the *corps de bataille*. In others it means the centre of the complete line; that is, the new "Centre"comprising the original "Rear" and part of the original "Centre," while the rest of the original "Centre" became part of the actual van. As a consequence of this ambiguity it happens that in some reports both Nelson and Collingwood are said to attack the centre, while in others Nelson is said to attack the van and Collingwood the rear. To clear up the confusion the French Staff prepared for Napoleon the lucid table [on the following page], which it is well to grasp at the outset:[16] —

It must be taken, then, for all tactical purposes that as soon as it was seen that Villeneuve was inverting his order, both the British columns steered for the centre, or if we regard the Combined Fleet as having fallen into two grand divisions, as in effect it actually did, then Nelson steered for the rear of the van and Collingwood for the van of the rear.

By Nelson's signals, as we have seen, the approach was being made on the true centre in sailing order, that is in two columns line-ahead, but it was almost immediately modified in a remarkable manner by the independent action of Collingwood, By the text of the Memorandum, it will be remembered, the Second-in-command was to have entire control of his division "after the intention of the Commander-in-chief had been signified," but no such intimation was to be expected till Nelson had brought both divisions "nearly within gunshot of the enemy's centre."

They were nowhere near such a position, yet as Collingwood read the Memorandum he must have thought that the time for the free hand which Nelson had promised him had already come, and within half-an-hour of Villeneuve's making the signal to invert the order of battle, Collingwood signalled the lee division "to form the larboard line of bearing," thereby actually overriding Nelson's signal for the Order of Sailing.[17]

This startling fact has escaped notice apparently because it has always been assumed that Collingwood made his signal at the last hour. It has further been taken, as a matter of course, that he made it in consequence of the fact that a concavity which developed in the allied line had brought Gravina's division almost parallel with Collingwood's approach. But if this were so the larboard line of bearing is not the formation he would have required The truth is, it had nothing to do with the concavity. Collingwood gave the order nearly two hours before Villeneuve made the signal which, as we shall see, produced the malformation.

LINE OF BATTLE

As issued to all the ships of the fleet on Oct. 6

Inverted Order

Squadron	Division	Ship	Guns
Third Squadron		Neptuno	84
Third Squadron		Scipion	74
Third Squadron		Rayo	74
Third Squadron		Formidable (flag)	80
Third Squadron		Duguay Trouin	74
Third Squadron		San Francisco de Assisi	74
Third Squadron		Mont Blanc	74
First Squadron		San Augustin	74
First Squadron		Héros	74
First Squadron		Sma. Trinidad (flag)	130
First Squadron		Bucentaure (flag)	80
First Squadron		Neptune	80
First Squadron		Leandro	64
First Squadron		Redoutable	74
Second Squadron		Intrépide	74
Second Squadron		San Justo	74
Second Squadron		Indomptable	80
Second Squadron		Santa Anna (flag)	120
Second Squadron		Fougueux	74
Second Squadron		Monarca	74
Second Squadron		Pluton	74
Squadron of Observation	*Second Squadron*	Bahama	74
Squadron of Observation	*Second Squadron*	Aigle	74
Squadron of Observation	*Second Squadron*	Montañes	74
Squadron of Observation	*Second Squadron*	Algeçiras (flag)	74
Squadron of Observation	*Second Squadron*	Argonauta	84
Squadron of Observation	*Second Squadron*	Swiftsure	74
Squadron of Observation	*First Squadron*	Argonaute	74
Squadron of Observation	*First Squadron*	San Ildefonso	74
Squadron of Observation	*First Squadron*	Achille	74
Squadron of Observation	*First Squadron*	Pr. de Asturias (flag)	112
Squadron of Observation	*First Squadron*	Berwick (flag)	74
Squadron of Observation	*First Squadron*	Nepomuceno	74

LINE OF BATTLE

With the changes indicated in M. Prigny's report and in the Journals

9 vessels for some time out of action	Neptuno	
9 vessels for some time out of action	Scipion	
9 vessels for some time out of action	Intrépide	
9 vessels for some time out of action	Rayo	
9 vessels for some time out of action	Formidable	
9 vessels for some time out of action	Duguay Trouin	*To leeward of line*
9 vessels for some time out of action	Mont Blanc	
9 vessels for some time out of action	San Francisco	*To leeward of line*
9 vessels for some time out of action	San Augustin	*To leeward of line*
8 vessels attacked by 1st Column	Héros	
8 vessels attacked by 1st Column	Sma. Trinidad (flag)	
8 vessels attacked by 1st Column	Bucentaure	
8 vessels attacked by 1st Column	Neptune	*To leeward of line*
8 vessels attacked by 1st Column	Rédoutable	
8 vessels attacked by 1st Column	Leandro	*To leeward of line*
8 vessels attacked by 1st Column	San Justo	*To leeward of line*
8 vessels attacked by 1st Column	Indomptable	*To leeward of line*
16 vessels attacked by 2nd Column	Santa Anna (flag)	
16 vessels attacked by 2nd Column	Fougueux	
16 vessels attacked by 2nd Column	Monarca	
16 vessels attacked by 2nd Column	Pluton	
16 vessels attacked by 2nd Column	Algeçiras	
16 vessels attacked by 2nd Column	Bahama	
16 vessels attacked by 2nd Column	Aigle	
16 vessels attacked by 2nd Column	Swiftsure	
16 vessels attacked by 2nd Column	Argonaute	
16 vessels attacked by 2nd Column	Montañes	*To leeward of line*
16 vessels attacked by 2nd Column	Argonauta	*To leeward of line*
16 vessels attacked by 2nd Column	Berwick	
16 vessels attacked by 2nd Column	Nepomuceno	
16 vessels attacked by 2nd Column	Achille	*To leeward of line*
16 vessels attacked by 2nd Column	San Ildefonso	
16 vessels attacked by 2nd Column	Principe de Asturias	

Note. — "The positions in the Squadron of Observation are uncertain."

AB. Nelson's division in larboard line of bearing.

A′B′. Collingwood's division in larboard line of bearing

CD and C′D′. The two divisions hauled into line of battle.

EF. Combined fleet *en ligne de plus près*.

Note. — The line of the British approach is taken as E.N.E., as directed by Nelson's first signal.

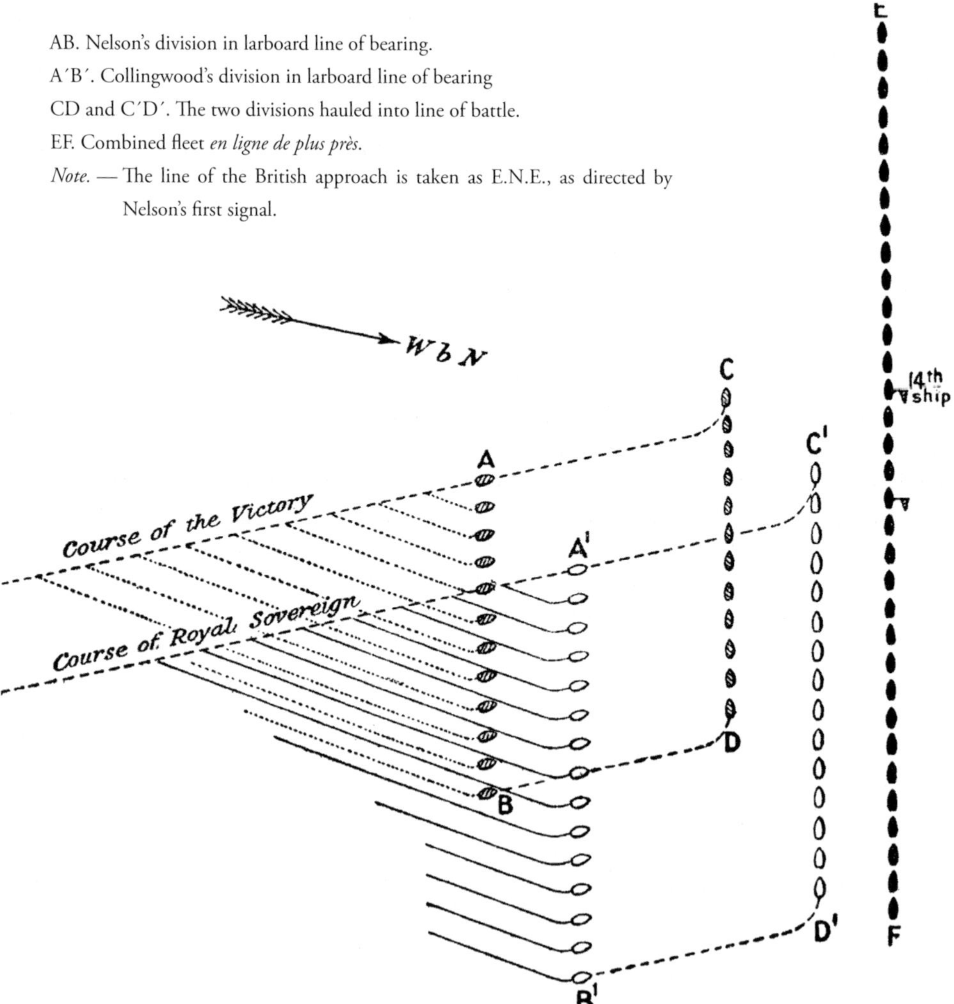

Diagram To Illustrate The Intention Of Collingwood's Signal For The Larboard Line Of Bearing

Why, then, did Collingwood make the signal? Its tactical purpose, as laid down in the Signal Book, leaves little room for doubt. A note to the signification explains it somewhat obscurely as meaning that the ships were "to bear from each other on the point of the compass on which they would sail, keeping a point from the wind, if formed in a line-ahead on the larboard tack." This survival of Howe's crabbed style is unintelligible until we know that by "keeping one point from the wind" was meant one point from the true close-hauled line, that is, seven points from the wind instead of six, which was the true close-hauled line or *ligne de plus près* of the French. The phrase therefore merely embodies the British practice of keeping a point in hand for contingencies.[18] The instruction then may be translated thus: "The line of bearing is to be formed in such a way that when the ships haul together into line of battle their line will be seven points from the wind or one from the true close-hauled line." In short, it was the ordinary evolution to bring a column from the approach into a line of battle parallel to and on the same tack with the *ligne de plus près* which the French were trying to form.[19] The explanation of Collingwood's conduct is that he believed he was doing what Nelson would naturally expect him to do, in order to get the fleet into the position of the diagram, and that as soon as his own manœuvre was fairly advanced, Nelson would commence it in his turn. It was in fact the obvious evolution to bring the two divisions into echelon nearly abreast the enemy's centre, as the Memorandum distinctly laid down for the windward attack.

Nelson, however, had a subtler idea, and made no corresponding move. Still, although, as we shall see, he did not yet consider Collingwood in full control of his division, he must have seen no harm in what his second was doing. At any rate he raised no objection, and permitted the evolution to continue as best it could. But it is to be observed that by his conduct he made it practically impossible for it to be carried out. It is obvious that when a fleet is going large in line-ahead, the close-hauled line of bearing cannot be formed unless the leading ships shorten sail. Nelson did not shorten sail and Collingwood, who was to commence the attack, had to conform and keep his speed. But although *the* line of bearing was thus put beyond his reach *a* line of bearing was still possible. Collingwood's division had not had time to get into line-ahead astern of him, and most of the rear ships were to starboard of his wake and already partly in position for a bow-and-quarter line. After about half-an-hour Collingwood seems to have recognised the situation. His chief continued to hold on without any sign of deploying or shortening sail, and either because Nelson did not conform or because he saw the line of bearing parallel to the enemy was impossible, he abandoned it for a bow-and-quarter line such as he could hope to achieve.

Accordingly he signalled to *Belleisle*. whom he had just ordered to take station astern of him, since his true second *Tonnant* could not keep up, to take station to the southwest of him, as though he intended to substitute a southwest bow-and-quarter line for the larboard line of bearing. Five minutes later he signalled to the *Revenge*, the fastest ship about his centre, to keep a line of bearing from him; but the point on which she was to bear is not stated. We might assume it was south-west also, were it not that immediately afterwards he made a signal to the *Belleisle* and also to the *Achille*, a ship midway between her and the *Revenge*, to alter course one point to starboard together the signification of the signal was, "Alter course *together* one point to starboard or to the course pointed out by compass signal, the ships preserving their relative bearing from each other;" and the instruction attached provides that "when a line of bearing has been formed the ships are to preserve that relative bearing from each other whenever they are directed to alter course together."[20] Now, no compass signal was made, nor was it possible the line of bearing had been formed in the seven minutes that had elapsed since the previous signal. On the evidence of the signals, therefore, the only conclusion is that Collingwood had seen that even a south-west line of bearing was impossible without his shortening sail, that he had consequently overridden his south-west signal by that for one point to starboard, and had found himself forced to be content with a line of bearing only one point from the line-ahead.

This conclusion has all the more weight since it is the only way of reconciling his various signals for line of bearing with the fact that he himself, in his official despatch and in his tactical explanation to his friend Pasley, says he attacked in column. Of a line of bearing he says not a word in either place. An irregular ill-formed bow-and-quarter line one point from the line-ahead was of course in the circumstances tactically indistinguishable from a column, and this is why Collingwood's own official statement that the fleet attacked in two columns is endorsed by Harvey and Senhouse, as well as by Moorsom himself, who was captain of the *Revenge*, and indeed by every eye-witness and contemporary writer who touched the question.

It is of course possible, by selecting fragmentary passages from the ill-kept Logs and Journals and by calculations based on the various times at which ships alleged they engaged, to infer that possibly a real line of bearing was formed; but the rigour of historical science absolutely forbids such fragile web-spinning to obscure a question which is illumined by direct and unimpeachable evidence to the contrary. Not only have we the categorical positive of the signals and of the very best authorities present, but there is the irrefutable negative that in all the mass of contemporary description there is absolute silence as to the lee line having approached in the manner suggested; For historical scholars such silence on a matter of the highest importance, even if it stood alone, would be conclusive. But it does not stand alone, and the weight of direct evidence behind it leaves no room for doubt that, however anxious Collingwood may have been to form a line of bearing he found that, as Nelson held on as he was, it was perhaps contrary to his wish and certainly impossible to achieve.

What Nelson thought of it all is difficult to fathom. His mind at this time is impenetrable. He was still steering for just ahead of the centre under a press of sail with his division forming in his wake as best it could, as though he was still bent on delivering Hawke's attack in chase to prevent the enemy escaping.[21] "His great anxiety," wrote Moorsom, "seemed to be to get to leeward of them, lest they should make off into Cadiz before he could get near." But as he advanced it became evident that Villeneuve did not mean to avoid him. To his surprise the Combined Fleet, after wearing, had boldly hove-to to form their line of battle and await his attack.[22] For such a condition of affairs Hawke's attack was singularly ill-adapted, unless he could get up before their battle order was complete. The bold attitude of the enemy certainly upset Nelson's calculations. "About ten o'clock" says Captain Blackwood, "Lord Nelson's anxiety to close with the enemy became very apparent." He must have been in a high state of nervous tension, for he kept saying to Blackwood that they put a good face on it, but always added quickly, "I'll give them such a dressing as they never had before." Still he made no sign of deploying in conformity with Collingwood's signal, but he did begin interfering with his colleague's line, as though he did not yet regard him as in charge of it, and a passage of some humour took place between the two old friends.

Both of them, in breach of the established order of battle, were still leading their divisions. Neither showed any inclination to get back into his proper station, and Nelson's officers, in extreme anxiety for his life, were worrying about it. Blackwood at last undertook to approach him, and after trying in vain to persuade him to direct the battle from the *Euryalus*, he begged him to let the three ships astern — *Téméraire*, *Neptune*, and *Leviathan* — go ahead of the *Victory*. With difficulty Blackwood got permission to carry the order to the *Téméraire* to pass if she could, and the necessary signals were made.[23] But if Nelson consented to get into his proper station, "Coll" must do the same. The *Prince*, which should have been leading the lee line, was falling far astern. There was no chance of her ever getting into her station, and Collingwood was seen coolly pushing on right ahead of his division, regardless of support. Such a challenge was more than Nelson's fighting instinct could endure. But even so he could not bring himself to use his authority by a direct order. So like any schoolboy he began to try to jockey him out of the lead. Collingwood had just made the signal for *Belleisle* to take *Tonnant's* place, but without regarding it Nelson signalled the *Mars*, which had been one of the connecting ships and was now coming up fast, to take station astern of the *Royal Sovereign*, with what intention soon appeared. Collingwood paid no regard. On the contrary it was now he made his final signal for a point to starboard together, and it is possible that Nelson's obvious anxiety to keep him back had not a little to do with his determination to abandon the attempt to form even a south-west line of bearing. Without his shortening sail it could not be done, and shorten sail he would not unless Nelson set him the example, or gave a direct order. Still Nelson would not do either, but a quarter of an hour later he tried again. This time he went a step further and actually signalled *Mars* to lead the lee division. In the absence of the *Prince* it was her proper station by the order of battle, and no hint could have been broader for Collingwood to fall back astern of her. But this attempt was even less effective than the last. Collingwood, it is clear, had no intention of getting back into his station short of a direct order, which he must have known his old friend would not have the heart to give. He at least had the justification that there was now no three-decker but his own to lead his line, and his defiant reply was to set all his studding-sails.[24] Then Nelson gave it up, and thenceforth there was little chance of *Téméraire* being allowed to obey his last order.

The story goes that at this time Nelson caught sight of some one resetting one of his studding-sails, and thinking it was being taken in without his orders, he delivered himself with a heat that seemed beyond the occasion. Away to leeward Collingwood, with his division in an irregular bow-and-quarter line disposed steeply on his starboard quarter, was still pressing on in his newly coppered ship and drawing gradually more and more ahead of his second astern. It was no wonder, then, that when Blackwood got back to the *Victory* he found Nelson in a peppery humour doing all he could to increase his speed and prevent *Téméraire* carrying out the order that had been wrung from him. But for his colleague's disobedience he had nothing but admiration. "See," he exclaimed half-an-hour later, "how that noble fellow Collingwood carries his ship into action!"

Meanwhile the situation had been crystallizing. It was now perfectly evident that, far from running away, the enemy were defiantly abiding his attack. Welcome as Villeneuve's attitude was, it had its drawbacks. It brought the shoals of Trafalgar under his lee, so that it would be difficult to push home the attack, and it opened Cadiz as a point of retreat. On the other hand it greatly facilitated the plan of attack which Nelson had in mind. The need to hurry was obviously not so great as he had supposed, and it might have been thought that now if ever he would attempt to deploy and bring about the situation which the diagram in the Memorandum had prescribed. There was, however, a difficulty about it which did not exist in Collingwood's case. Most of Nelson's division were coming into line from his larboard quarter,[25] so that they were very badly placed for forming a line of bearing such as Collingwood had been attempting. It would take much longer, and moreover, Nelson had conceived a subtler and more effective way of performing the function that he had set himself in the Memorandum. He was to contain the van, and, as we shall see, his infallible eye for a situation told him that by far the best way of concealing his intention from the enemy and holding them in uncertainty was to keep on as he was in line-ahead. This at least is what he did, and accordingly, about this time, Villeneuve began to see that the two British *pelotons* were developing into two lines ahead, directed, the one about his own flagship, the other at his own rear squadron, which, since Gravina was forming the true rear, was now in fact part of the centre.[26]

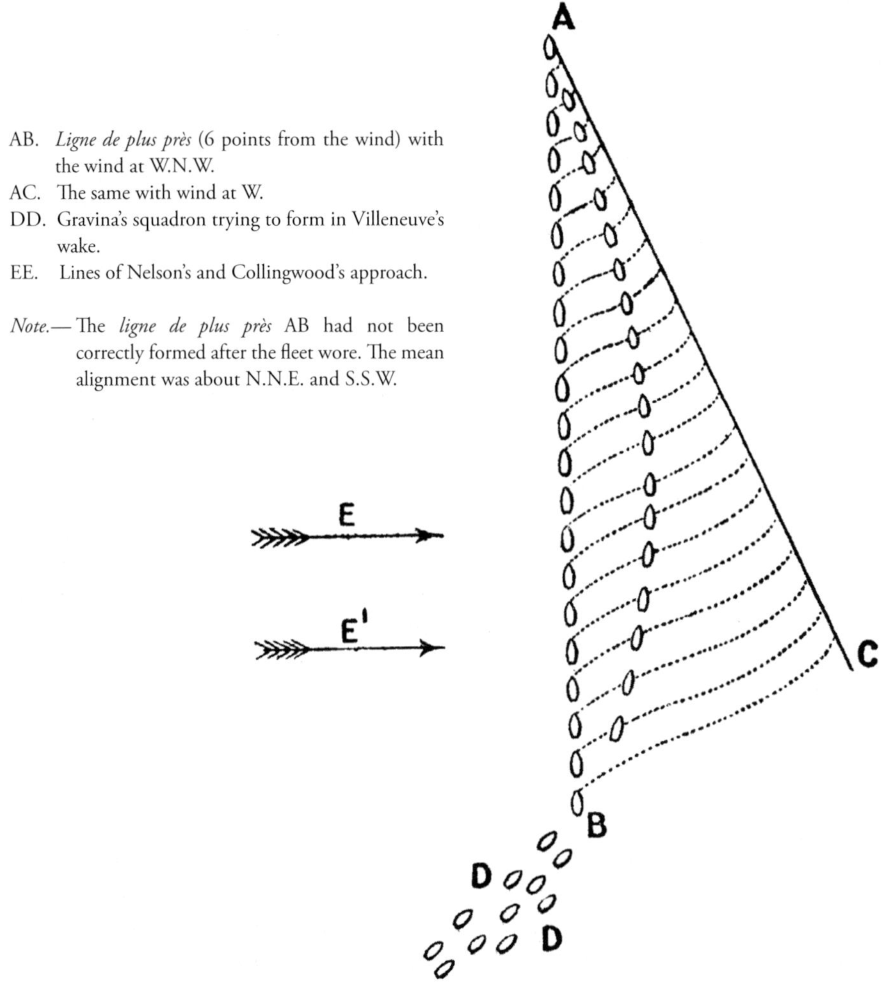

AB. *Ligne de plus près* (6 points from the wind) with the wind at W.N.W.
AC. The same with wind at W.
DD. Gravina's squadron trying to form in Villeneuve's wake.
EE. Lines of Nelson's and Collingwood's approach.
Note.— The *ligne de plus près* AB had not been correctly formed after the fleet wore. The mean alignment was about N.N.E. and S.S.W.
A
C
B
D
D
E
E'

Diagram To Show How The Allied Line Became Convex In Trying To Re-form For The Shift Of Wind

The relative alignment of the two fleets was now becoming what it remained till the moment of impact. The two British lines, owing to the manner in which they were being formed, had the appearance of converging slightly upon the enemy's centre, their mean direction being now about east. The extremities of the allied fleet bore from each other roughly about north-north-east and south-southwest, with an increasing sag to leeward. The wind had settled at about west, varying sometimes a little north of it, and sometimes south,[27] and as the van ship hauled up to it and her successors edged into her wake, the general alignment of the van half of the line was about north and south, but a little west of north in the extreme van as it is shown in all the French official plans. The rest of the fleet would have had an alignment curving gradually from the centre to almost south-west in the extreme rear. As the British lines were approaching on a mean course about east, their general direction to all tactical intent was perpendicular to the central portion of the enemy at which they were aiming.

For Nelson this fortuitous malformation of the enemy's line was very opportune. It went far to remove the main difficulties of carrying out the fundamental ideas of the intended attack. But he cannot have foreseen it, for it arose from a chance shift of wind. Nor can it have influenced him in the first hours of his approach. The signal which produced it was not made by Villeneuve till ten o'clock, and even when the dislocation commenced Nelson was too far away to be able to realise its effect at once. By eleven o'clock, however, after the movement had been in progress an hour, it must have become pronounced, and by that time Nelson was not more than three miles from the enemy's centre.[28] We cannot therefore place his recognition of the crescent formation later than that hour nor much before. In any case it is impossible to trace any influence it had on the British attack. There were no fresh signals and no alteration of course. Both Nelson and Collingwood held on as they were with every stitch of canvas set, and making with their utmost effort between two and three knots.[29]

Collingwood's division continued to struggle for the formation he had last signalled, but certainly without undue attention to accurate stations. Indeed, in the unformed rear at least his captains interpreted their chief's succession of signals with characteristic freedom as an intimation that he wished them to get into action as quickly and simultaneously as possible. It was the true spirit of the British service in its later manifestations, and as Codrington frankly says, "We all scrambled into battle as soon as we could."[30] As for Nelson's division, it continued to trail after him, swarming roughly into line as best it could.[31] No check was made. As they approached the fire zone, where the utmost impetus was vital, the speed was even increased. Collingwood signalled for more sail, and Nelson promptly responded still more emphatically with "Make all sail possible with safety to the masts" Laggards were left far behind, and the two old friends in exultant rivalry seemed bent on nothing but to see who could be first into the furnace that awaited them.

Nelson apparently had not yet made up his mind exactly what he was going to do, and probably, as the Memorandum suggests, did not intend to decide till he saw what the situation called for at the last moment. He was still steering steadily for the centre just ahead of the *Santisima Trinidad*, the largest ship in the allied fleet.[32] The functions he had assigned himself, it will be remembered, were not only to contain the van but also to envelop the Commander-in-chief. But as yet the Commander-in-chief could not be found. He had not shown his flag and Nelson's main anxiety at this time seems to have been to ascertain his position. "Although," says James, "every glass on board the *Victory* was put in requisition to discover the flag of the French Commander-in-chief, all the answers to Nelson's repeated questions on the subject ended in disappointment."[33] James must have had this from an eyewitness, and it affords a perfectly simple explanation of why Nelson made for the *Santisima Trinidad*. He was then under the belief that Decrès had come to take the chief command over Villeneuve's head, and it was natural to seek him in the largest ship in the fleet which was also a new comer.[34]

A different explanation, however, related to his function of containing the van, has come of late years to confuse our appreciation of Nelson's tactics. Because he made for a point higher up the line than the one he eventually attacked, it is said he was making a feint on the van in order to hold it inactive. The sole contemporary evidence of this is in entry in the Master's Log of Codrington's ship the *Orion*. "The *Victory*, after making a feint of attacking the van, hauled to starboard to reach the centre." This in itself contains no actual assertion that Nelson altered his course to port before turning to starboard. But when questioned on the point by Nicolas in his old age Codrington said, "He was under the impression that he was expressly instructed by Nelson that he himself would probably make a feint of attacking the van" (instead of using the Advance Squadron for that purpose, as he had intended originally). "I have no doubt," he added, "of the *Victory* having hauled out to port for a short space." He also said he remembered calling his First Lieutenant's attention to it at the time, which would account for the isolated entry in *Orion's* Log. Then, after giving some corroborative details about Nelson's studding-sails, he went on to say that it was this movement to port which occasioned the *Victory* to suffer so severely from the raking fire of several ships ahead of the centre. Evidently then his memory was failing him, for the ships that raked Nelson were those for which he had been steering all along and which he eventually attacked.[35] No one who was at Nelson's side knew anything of such a manœuvre. Besides his own staff, he had three frigate captains on his quarterdeck, and not one of them says a word about it. Nor does it appear from any of the enemy's reports. Like the original entry in the *Orion's* Log they duly record the turn to starboard, but not the alleged one to port. It is impossible indeed to believe it ever took place, and till better evidence is forthcoming it must be dismissed as a by-product of Codrington's enthusiastic admiration of his chief.

Nor does this conclusion rest on negative evidence alone. We have the direct testimony of Blackwood that what Nelson had in his mind at this time was not a feint on the van but a real attack, and that this attack involved if anything a preliminary turn to starboard and not to port. In fact it was well before the time of Codrington's alleged feint that Nelson made up his mind what he was going to do, and it was one of the curiosities of the oft-told story that this remarkable decision has been almost ignored. Yet there can be no doubt about it. The *Euryalus* records that at 11.40 she repeated a telegraph message from Nelson to this effect: "I intend to push or go through the end of the enemy's line to prevent them from getting into Cadiz."[36] It is obviously not entered verbatim. James, who also knew of it, and was told it was made to Collingwood, gives it thus: "I intend to pass through the van of the enemy's line to prevent him from getting into Cadiz."[37] Such a signal is certainly startling. No other ship records it, and yet it is impossible to believe it was not made when it appears in the Log of the senior repeating frigate. Whatever its actual words, it can only have meant that Nelson had abandoned his plan of attack on the rear half of the enemy in favour of that recommended by Howe and Kempenfelt for engaging a numerically superior fleet.[38] It is possible that the signal which Villeneuve had just made to his van to make more sail had renewed Nelson's abiding apprehension that his enemy meant to avoid a decisive action by slipping back into Cadiz. To thwart the movement he would attack the van, as he had told Collingwood to attack the rear, and would leave the centre — on Torrington's plan — unengaged.

Such a sudden and complete variation of his plan — though characteristic enough of Nelson's genius and expressly foreshadowed by the Memorandum — is difficult enough to believe of itself. But there is the further objection that it involved the abandonment of another cardinal point of his plan. The new attack sacrificed entirely the idea of enveloping the Commander-in-chief. This consideration, however, so far from throwing doubt on the signal which *Euryalus* records, goes far to corroborate it. For it so happens that Nelson had at the moment good reason for not seeking the Commander-in-chief in the centre. Collingwood had just telegraphed to him "that the enemy's chief appears to command in a frigate."[39] Collingwood then must have read in Nelson's message a natural answer to his own. If Villeneuve was not in the centre it was not there a decision was to be sought, but in the van, and for this reason. The most serious change which Nelson's new idea made in the plan of attack was the apparent abandonment of his own containing function on which the success of Collingwood's attack depended. But, in truth, it involved no real abandonment. The natural consequence of his altered form of attack was that the enemy's centre would stand on at once to relieve the van. Indeed this was the inherent weakness of all attempts to concentrate on the van. Nelson would probably be doubled on, but that would bring on a mêlée and Collingwood would be left free to "complete the business of the rear."

There seems, then, to be no sufficient reason to reject the explicit statement of *Euryalus's* Log. It was just at this time that Nelson revoked his permission to *Téméraire* to pass ahead of him and ordered her to take station astern.[40] In other words, at the last moment he strictly re-formed his column as though he intended to break the line in line-ahead, and this we know from an unimpeachable source was actually his intention. The enemy's van was just opening fire on him at long range, and he dismissed his three frigate captains to inform the ships in his rear exactly what his intentions were. Blackwood went straight alongside the *Neptune*, in his boat and informed Captain Fremantle that Nelson's intention was "to cut through the enemy's line about the thirteenth or fourteenth ship, and then to make sail on the larboard tack for their van."[41] Now, about the thirteenth ship we know a wide gap had opened in the enemy's line owing to ships to leeward not being able to get into station.[42] Nelson clearly intended to seize the opportunity of this break in the line to pass through it and then to run up the van and engage it from to leeward, crippling each unit as he passed with his massed three-deckers, and leaving them a prey to his weaker following.

It was a conception entirely worthy of him and entirely in accord with the fundamental principle of his plan. It fully and worthily explains his neglect to deploy — his persistent clinging to his line-ahead, which so much effort has been made to explain away. For the purpose of containing the van it served admirably. Till the last moment it was impossible for the enemy to tell whether or not the van was his objective, for to the last he himself had not decided. Both van and centre were equally threatened. For a regular feint there was no need, and certainly none was made. If, as several witnesses clearly record, he was steering for the *Santisima Trinidad*, his intended movement for the gap a ship or two astern of her would mean a short turn to starboard before hauling to the wind on the opposite tack; and so far from being a feint on the van, it would if anything amount to a feint on the centre. But the whole meaning of the decision is this. At the last moment his unmatched eye for a battle had seized a weakness in the enemy's position and with perfect mastery he meant to deliver his attack accordingly. It was only by keeping his division in line-ahead that such a sudden stroke was possible. Surely it needs no excuse. Leadership could not well rise higher.

This then was undoubtedly the last order which Nelson conveyed to his fleet before engaging. But no sooner were the frigate captains away with it than he saw reason to change his resolution. As the fleets drew together Villeneuve had signalled to engage as soon as they were in effective range, and then, as the rear opened fire on Collingwood, he and all the other Admirals displayed their flags. The commander-in-chief was confessed. He was for Nelson and Bronté, and no one else. His station was tenth in the actual line, and in an instant Nelson, instead of making for the gap astern of her, was heading to pass between the *Bucentaure* and *Trinidad*, her second ahead.

For the moment at least it would seem he had abandoned his project of attacking the van, for the original plan of the Memorandum. The little *Africa* was coming in from the northward and he signalled her to engage the leading ship of the enemy, as though he felt he must sacrifice her to keeping the van quiet till he had settled the business of the enemy's two flagships. But this was not so easy. His sudden reversion to his original idea of enveloping the commander-in-chief was as suddenly foiled. Villeneuve seeing his purpose, hauled to the wind, and drawing ahead into a line of bearing on the *Trinidad*, closed the interval which Nelson had chosen. He had to stand on down the line for the next opening exposed to a terrific concentration of fire from the group round the *Bucentaure*. It was too warm work to last long, as Nelson said. The enemy were looking every moment to see both him and Collingwood crushed by the mass of fire. The wind had nearly dropped. Astern of the *Bucentaure* was the gap through which he had originally intended to lead the line for his attack on the van, but now there was no more than a regular interval as difficult as the other. The *Redoutable*, to avert the threatened attack on the flagship, had devotedly forced her way close to Villeneuve's quarter. There was no possibility of passing clear between the two ships, but if Nelson was to have the commander-in-chief it must be this or nothing, and in desperation he put up his helm and crashed in under the *Bucentaure's* stern.

That was the end of his tactics. If he still retained his purpose of engaging the van from to leeward, the bold move of the *Redoutable* had completely foiled him. Though magnificently supported by *Téméraire*, who almost touched his stern, he failed — in the tactical sense at least — to break the line. Running hard aboard the *Redoutable* he simply stuck in the enemy's formation, incapable of leading the movement if he had had a mind, or indeed of any further manœuvre. *Neptune*, it is true, followed *Téméraire* through the line astern of *Bucentaure*, raking her as she passed; then hauled her wind to the northward in accordance with Nelson's last directions by Blackwood and settled down with the *Santisima Trinidad*. But the movement went little further, and the weather column, as it surged up against the enemy's clubbed formation, simply flattened itself out with the impact.

In intention, risk, and daring, it was in the end an unprecedented vertical attack in line-ahead upon a closely formed and even reduplicated line of battle. To some slight extent, it is true, its perpendicular character was at the last moment modified. So closely did *Téméraire* and *Neptune*, follow their chief that his sudden movements forced them upon his port and starboard quarters to avoid running foul of him.[43] In the rear, moreover, the line had never been formed accurately, and his captains hurried up to port and starboard of him more like a pack of wolves than a formed fleet. Still in tactical principle no attack could have been weaker — none could have offended more seriously against the principle of simultaneous impact. To all tactical intent it ended as it had begun, by both columns making the onslaught which Hawke had devised for a flying enemy.

Hazardous, even desperate, as seemed Nelson's use of it, it was in truth the outcome of heroic judgment and insight. Both risk and advantage had been accurately weighed. The enormous mass of gun power at the head of Nelson's line dominated the counter-convergence of fire, and brought on the mêlée round the French Admiral which Nelson required, while the rear of his division as it stretched on into action made it impossible for Dumanoir to come down directly without submitting himself to a crossing of the T.

In Collingwood's case the risk and daring of the attack was even greater than with Nelson. He had no mass of three-deckers in his van, and the speed of his ship and the steepness of his line of bearing left him to suffer the first shock with even less support than his chief received. Not content, moreover, with the dozen ships which Nelson had allotted to his division, he took more than half the original allied rear as well as Gravina's advanced squadron — sixteen ships in all. Three of them were so far to leeward as to be out of the line, and all were so much crowded that the twelfth ship was not easy to distinguish. Somewhere about the right place was a Spanish three-decker, flying a Vice-Admiral's flag, and under such temptation a man of Collingwood's spirit could scarcely be expected to count with scrupulous exactness. The result was that he too struck the actual centre where the enemy's formation was practically at right angles to his line of advance. "About noon," he says, "the Royal Sovereign opened a fire on the 12th, 13th, 14th, and 15th ships from the enemy's rear and stood on with all sail to break the enemy's line. A quarter past twelve altered course to port;" that is, at the last moment he changed his direction higher up the line and ran through under the stern of the Spanish Vice-flagship *Santa Anna*.[44]

For all his prompt attempt to deploy he was unsupported for a quarter of an hour. So far from establishing a concentration on the enemy's rear, he himself was exposed to the concentrated fire of four powerful ships, but in the exhilaration of having beaten his chief in the wild race he could only cry to his flag captain, "What would Nelson give to be here!" He was first into action and the rest mattered not. *Belleisle*, with *Mars* close at hand, was first to bring him relief. Then he was left alone with the *Santa Anna*, while his consort was cut to pieces and dismasted by a powerful concentration in her turn.

Apart from Collingwood's refusal to check his onset, the advance had been too nearly vertical for the line of bearing to produce anything like unity of impact behind him.

POSITION of the COMBINED FORCES of FRANCE & SPAIN,

at the commencement of the Action 21st Oct. 1805, with **LORD NELSON**, Cape Trafalgar, bearing E.S.E. 4 Leagues.

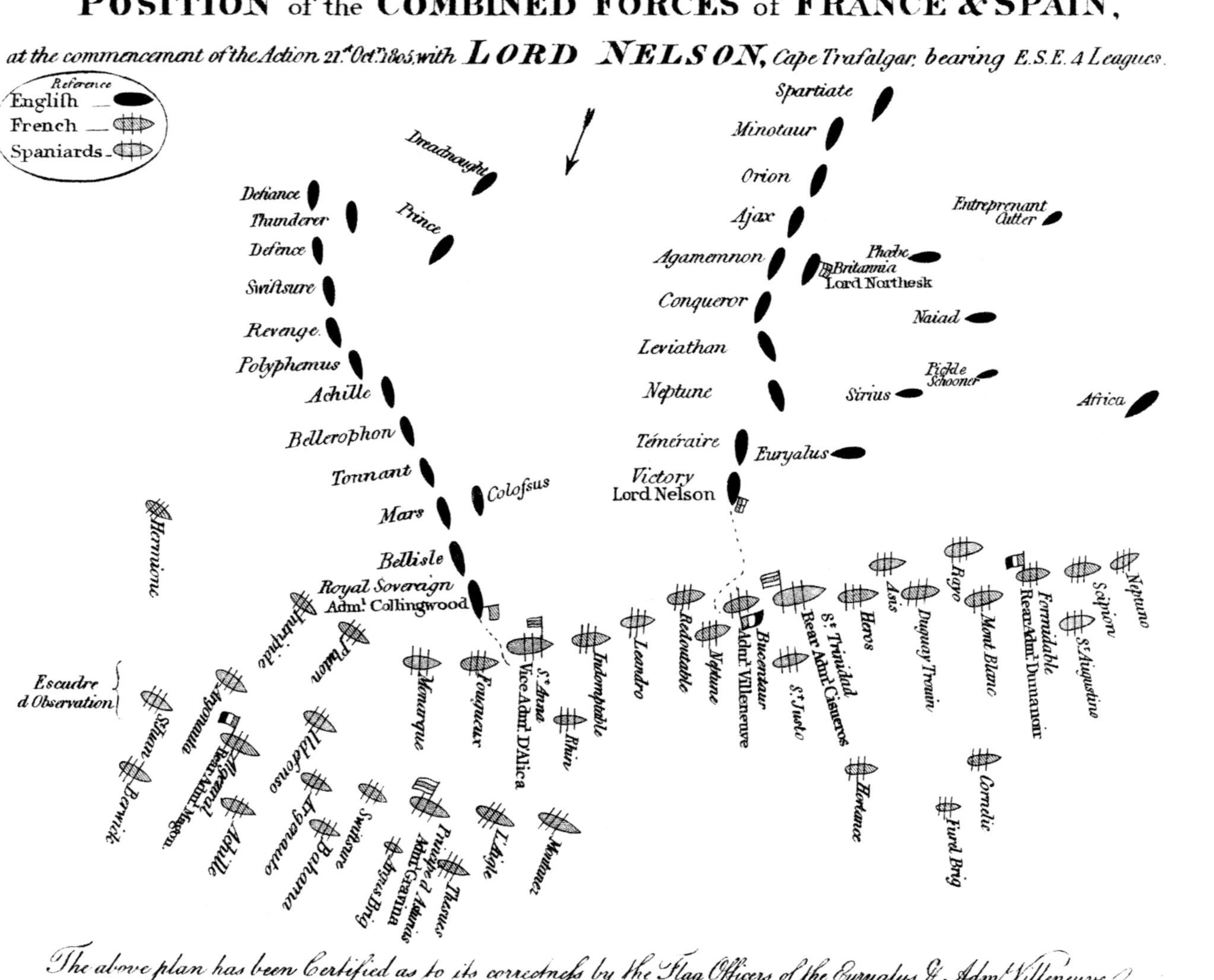

The above plan has been Certified as to its correctness by the Flag Officers of the Euryalus, & Adml. Villeneuve.

Almost every ship in the first half of his division met with a similar reception. "Instead of doubling on the enemy," says Senhouse, who was in the *Colossus*, the sixth ship of Collingwood's line, "the British were on that day themselves doubled and trebled on; and the advantage of applying an overwhelming force collectively it would seem was totally lost. The *Victory, Téméraire, Sovereign, Belleisle, Mars, Colossus*, and *Bellerophon* were placed in such a situation at the onset, that nothing but the most heroic gallantry and practical skill with the guns could have extricated them. . . . The position of the Combined Fleet at one time was precisely that in which the British were desirous of being placed; that is, to have part of an opposing fleet doubled on and separated from the main body."[45] The same could be said of other ships astern of the *Colossus*, such as the *Revenge*. What Codrington saw from Nelson's line — and he says he was placed so as to have a specially clear view — was the ships of the lee division coming up one by one and attacking the remainder of the enemy's rear in succession.[46] Owing to differences of speed and the fact that Collingwood's squadron was still unformed when he ordered the line of bearing, the ships came into action not only one after the other, but at irregular intervals — so irregularly indeed that the enemy thought they were being attacked by distinct groups. One was Collingwood's own, another seemed to follow the *Revenge*, while a third was headed by the *Dreadnought* and *Polyphemus*. So closely clubbed was the allied formation by Gravina's pressing on to support the centre, that though the line was penetrated in all parts there still remained yet another group to double on the extreme rear.

It was nearly an hour before the action became general, and things were reduced to a more equal footing. By that time some twenty-two British vessels must have been in action with the twenty-two French and Spanish that had been cut off. It was a mêlée at pistol-shot all along the line, in which the captains on both sides supported and relieved one another with brilliance and devotion, and with as much skill of manœuvre as mangled rigging, the clouds of hanging smoke, and that almost breathless afternoon permitted. Each side extorted bursts of admiration from the other. It was a fair fight against foes worth fighting, and with no advantage on either side, except in the superior sea training and gunnery of the British. It was only gradually by sheer hard fighting that Nelson's and Collingwood's men redressed the disadvantage of the impetuous attack. In an hour or so they began to reap its fruits, and to establish a domination over the raging fire into which they had flung themselves one by one.

All this time the enemy's van had made no movement to intervene. There some ten or eleven ships, practically untouched save for the little *Africa* as she ran down from the northward to get into her station, were held inactive by Rear-Admiral Dumanoir, in spite of what every one regarded as his plain duty. The censures that he earned may rest in the grave of acquittal which his court-martial awarded him. We are only concerned with what he did — and deeply concerned, for here is the measure by which we must gauge the value and effectiveness of the "containing"element in Nelson's plan.

It was not for more than two hours after the action had begun — one hour after it had become general — that, in response to Villeneuve's repeated signals, Dumanoir began to tack. Till then Nelson's bewildering method of engaging held him in uncertainty of what the weather division was going to do. But when it was clear that the strange tactics meant an attack on the centre in column, he saw, so he says, the possibility of cutting off Nelson's rearmost ships — a danger to which the line-ahead attack obviously exposed them. It was a risk Nelson had calculated and taken with a light heart. "It must be some time," he wrote in the Memorandum, "before they could perform a manœuvre to bring their force compact to attack any part of the British fleet," and so it proved.

The wind was so light that it was only by using boats that Dumanoir's ships could get round at all, and it was nearly three o'clock before they were standing down. By that time the back of the Allies' splendid resistance was broken. Not a mast was left in the flagships which Nelson and Collingwood had attacked, and all three of them had struck. Still there was a chance; for the British ships which had borne the brunt of the struggle were for the most part dismasted hulks, and Nelson was lying mortally wounded. In the extreme rear at any rate, if not in the centre, there were possibilities of effective interference. Here the action was comparatively fresh, and Gravina was desperately holding his own against a concentration that was steadily increasing. He himself, like Nelson, had been laid low with a wound that was to prove mortal, but the chief of his staff was maintaining the struggle with obstinate courage, and there was nothing to tell that Villeneuve's right hand was not still strong to save the situation. The promise of this hope, and the danger of the honoured Spanish Admiral were so great, that when Dumanoir led down to windward only four units followed him — three French and the Spanish *Neptuno*, the headmost ship. Nearly all the rest made for Gravina to leeward, and one, the *Intrépide*, went straight into the mêlée that was dying round the *Bucentaure*. This, in the opinion of Villeneuve's staff, was the course all should have taken.[47] It was the most direct and the surest way to renew close action while there-was yet a ray of hope. But as it was, the daring *Intrépide* was checked by the little *Africa*, which had run the gauntlet of the enemy's van successfully, and had now reached the centre. The gallant Frenchman was thus held unsupported, and was quickly captured by some fresh ships — *Ajax* and *Orion* being two of them — which Nelson's Rear-Admiral Lord Northesk seems to have led up in the *Britannia*.[48]

By the time Dumanoir was well set on his course there were only the last two ships of Nelson's column, *Spartiate* and *Minotaur*, not in action, and it was these vessels the French Rear-Admiral thought he could cut off. They saw the danger, but it was not their own they saw. It was the critical position of the flagships and the *Téméraire*, as they lay almost helpless wrecks and cumbered with their prizes. Captain Mansfield in the *Minotaur*, the slower ship of the two, was leading, for the principle of the line-ahead had been preserved to the end. Seeing there was not a moment to lose, Sir Francis Laforey, in the *Spartiate*, begged leave to pass her, and so the two devoted men held straight on across Dumanoir's bows, raking him at pistol-shot as they passed, and then hove-to to leeward between him and the British Admirals. And there they held their ground, engaging the four French ships as they passed and forcing them to keep their wind. It was a splendid bit of work, two seventy-fours standing up to three seventy-fours and two eighties, and it was done on their own initiative in the true spirit of the Memorandum.

No moment in the action, except the first, was more critical. The *Victory* and *Royal Sovereign* had each but a single mast standing, and were both unmanageable. The *Téméraire* was a hulk absolutely helpless. The *Britannia* had passed through to engage the ships to leeward and could not have returned, and only the *Neptune* and a couple of crippled two-deckers remained in a case to resist Dumanoir's attack. But this was far from the worst.

Collingwood had already been warned that Nelson was dangerously wounded, and now in the strain of the crisis, when no one could see how it would end, Blackwood came on board the *Royal Sovereign* to break the terrible news that he was dead. The soul of the battle had sped, but, acute as was the shock to Collingwood, not for one moment did he lose head or heart. He was now in command. In his hand it rested to save his friend's imperilled victory.

The *Thunderer*, one of the last of his own squadron, was looming up out of the smoke with all standing. Her part in the action serves well to illustrate the kind of concentration which the attack in succession was now producing. She began firing her starboard guns at the extreme rear at 1.15; at two she was alongside a two-decker that had been already engaged; and in a quarter of an hour she had brought down all her masts and forced her to strike. In another quarter of an hour she had served a second crippled two-decker in the same way. Next was Gravina's shattered flagship, that after getting rid of the *Dreadnought* was hotly defending herself against the *Revenge*. Bearing up she passed under her stern, and raked her so severely as to force her finally to run to leeward out of action. She then hauled her wind and passed up the line as she saw the enemy's van about to come down.[49] At the same moment *Minotaur* and *Spartiate* were coming up into action, and Collingwood's first signal as commander-in-chief was to these three ships to tack and engage Dumanoir's five that were coming down to windward upon the centre and were then barely three-quarters of a mile away. "Set every sail we were able," says the *Thunderer*, who naturally had not come off unscathed. "In passing cheered the *Victory*." *Minotaur* and *Spartiate*, as we know, were anticipating the order, and were already engaged with Commodore Valdez in the *Neptuno*[50] By a desperate effort both *Victory* and *Royal Sovereign* got some guns to bear, and so did some of the two-deckers. *Neptune*, too, was soon ready, and Dumanoir, finding how much bite was left in the apparently helpless centre and that *Bucentaure* had struck, held on as he was to see what could be done in the rear, abandoning the *Neptuno* to the mercies of *Minotaur* and *Spartiate*.

But in the rear, too, Collingwood was ready for him. His hand was as steady on the action as ever. Seeing what Dumanoir was threatening, he made the general signal to come to the wind in succession on the larboard tack.[51] The consequence was that by the time Dumanoir was in a position to attack the rear he saw half-a-dozen ships hauling out to form a new line to windward. To sink his spirit still further, he could see Gravina's flagship clearly bearing away out of action and flying the signal for the fleet to rally round her. Here at least was a good reason for Dumanoir to hold on and try to join her to leeward round the British rear. But again his heart failed him. The response to Collingwood's signal had assumed so threatening an aspect, and Gravina and the ships rallying round him were soon so far on their way to Cadiz, that he dared not make the attempt, and giving up the action for lost, he held on to the southward for the Straits. As for the rest of his squadron that had tried to get down to leeward, they were quickly headed off by the *Britannia* and her consorts, who pursued them towards Cadiz, capturing one and crippling others. Then came Collingwood's signal to haul to the wind, and it amounted to a recall.[52]

But for this more might undoubtedly have been done. Gravina's flagship would certainly have been taken, for she was now unmanageable and in tow. But to say nothing of the grand prizes, the situation of the dismantled British ships on a leeshore and with signs of a coming gale, was far too critical for anything more to be attempted. Every ship that could steer or make sail was required to assist them, and in Collingwood's judgment the limit of risk had been reached. He did not even deem it possible to anchor, though Nelson had made the preparatory signal before the action began, and it was his last wish that it should be executed. Firing had now everywhere ceased except where the *Neptuno* was making her last effort. Shortly after four she struck, and the most decisive naval action in our history had come to an end.

The enemy's commander-in-chief and two of his flag officers were prisoners in the British fleet. Of the thirty-three of the line which had left Cadiz the day before, only nine got back that night to safety; four were flying for the Straits; leaving no less than twenty on the field of battle, of which seventeen were totally dismantled, thirteen actually in possession of prize crews, and one in flames, while every British flag was still flying.

Thus whether the Plan of Attack was acted on or not, Nelson's tactics were justified. His forecast of their containing capacity was fully realised. The van had not been able to move till too late, and when it did it had failed, as the Memorandum foretold, to bring its force compact upon any part of the British fleet. For the rest we cannot do better than take the deliberate summary of the Spanish Staff, drawn up when all the circumstances were known and after making all allowances for inaccuracy of detail. "The attack," they say, "was upon the centre and rear of our line, and by concentrating their force upon it, they involved the rearguard in a regular action, line to line, doubling our extreme rear and leaving the van out of action."[53] The words give an accurate estimate of the action as it eventually developed. They are also a correct summary of the main idea of the Memorandum. In the eyes of the Spanish Staff that idea was carried out entirely. On the other hand their reports, as well as those of the French, are full of bewildered astonishment that an attack made so recklessly and so regardless of established principle — made in column without any regular deployment — was not crushed in the bud. No ingenuity of deduction can answer this criticism. The approach up to the moment of impact was in tactical effect an end-on approach in line-ahead. Neither the irregularity of Nelson's line nor the accidental broadening of his front at the last moment will alter the fact, nor will Collingwood's well-meant but unexecuted signal for the line of bearing remove it even in his case. In neither line was there any developed deployment before the leading ships were in contact, nor, taking the fleet as a whole, was there any such unity of impact as Nelson had designed in his diagram.

If, then, these were the facts, as all the contemporary evidence agrees, was the battle fought in accordance with the plan of attack or was it not? The answer surely is plain and simple enough, for all the casuistry with which it has been inwebbed. In major tactics it was; in its minor tactics it was not. The main ideas, as the Spanish Staff saw, were fully and triumphantly realised, but the actual method of realising them was not the one Nelson had indicated. Possibly he had discussed the method he used verbally, but of this we know nothing. All we can say is that in the culminating hour of his unmatched experience he flung away the security of scientific deployment, and in its place he staked all on the moral and material advantage of speed and momentum against an enemy apparently unformed and seeking to escape him. The risk he took of having the heads of his two columns isolated by a loss of wind or crushed prematurely by the concentration to which he exposed them naked, almost passed the limits of sober leading. Its justification was its success and the known defects of his opponents. Yet it may be permitted to doubt whether, if he had realised how much higher was the spirit of his enemy than he expected, he would have dared so greatly. Blackwood lets us see how acutely nervous he was when he recognised how good a face they put upon it, but it was then too late to alter. To check the impetuous attack at the last moment in order to substitute one of lower risk would have been an error of the gravest kind.

Then surely he was right. The lack of training and sea experience in his enemy on which he relied saved him and justified the heroic risk he had taken. Some capable officers, reviewing the tactics afterwards in cold blood, believed, it is true, the hazard was unnecessary, that an hour or so of delay in attaining the position he had designed would have left time enough "to complete the business" and have given even more decisive results. It is a point on which no one can now pass judgment, seeing that it depends on the niceties of a dead art. All we can say is that the risk he took was great — that it was not one he intended to take when he made his plan, nor one that his captains expected. And yet when all is said and done, that final resolution remains as the stroke that above all others touches his leadership with divinity. Such flashes of genius will not submit to reasoned criticism, they are beyond rule or principle, and every effort to measure them by scientific standards can only be lost in the final comment — "It was a glorious victory."

CHAPTER XXV

End Of The Naval Campaign

The decision which Pitt's policy required had been obtained. Napoleon's attempt to use his fleet in the Mediterranean had been crushed, but not without cost. Small as it was compared with the results obtained, it was heavy enough to prevent Collingwood from following up at once the instructions which he had inherited from Nelson to support the military operations of the Coalition in Italy.

In the night after the battle the threatening gale came up, and in the two following days increased to such violence that had it not shifted a little to the southward not a single prize nor one of the dismasted victors could have escaped wreck. Three of the vessels which had engaged Nelson and *Téméraire* most hotly went down — *Redoutable*, *Fougueux*, and *Bucentaure* herself. Prisoners had to be released, and with friend and foe working resolutely hand in hand it was only by the most desperate exertions that many of the others could be kept afloat and off the rocks.

To increase the difficulty, on the second day Cosmao, one of the finest captains in the French service and the senior officer left unwounded in Cadiz, boldly put out with five of the line and seven cruisers to rescue such of the prizes as were drifting towards the bay. Believing that Dumanoir as well as Gravina had got into Cadiz with ten of the line, Collingwood ordered an equal number to cast off their prizes and form battle order.[1] The French frigates managed to rescue the *Santa Anna* and *Neptuno*, both of which were little better than wrecks, but it was only at a cost which made Nelson's victory more decisive. For in returning to port the *Rayo*, a three-decker, together with one eighty and a seventy-four of Cosmao's squadron, went ashore. Next day the *Donegal*, which just before the battle Nelson had been forced to send into Gibraltar for her needs, rejoined, and together with some of Collingwood's least injured ships began a wholesale destruction of the prizes. There was nothing else to be done. Several that had gone ashore were burnt; even the splendid *Santisima Trinidad* had to be sacrificed. Of the nineteen vessels captured four were recaptured and eleven wrecked or destroyed, and in the end only four were brought into Gibraltar.

By the 24th the gale had abated and Collingwood was able to re-establish the blockade of Cadiz — more for the moral effect than anything else, for he now knew that Dumanoir was not there and that there was almost nothing seaworthy left in the port to blockade. Having got things in hand, one of his first cares was to send away a sloop with the news to Elliot at Naples. His despatch admirably presents the situation and his intentions. "As it is of great importance," he wrote, "to the affairs of Italy and Europe in general that the events which have lately taken place on this coast should be known as soon as possible at the Court at which you reside, I lose no time in informing you. Sir, that on the 19th instant the Combined Fleet sailed from Cadiz, their destination certainly for Italy. On the 21st . . . the action began at noon and after a most severe conflict for three hours the enemy gave way and Admiral Gravina retired with nine ships towards Cadiz; four others (French ships) escaped under Rear-Admiral Dumanoir to the southward and are supposed to have got into the Mediterranean; leaving to his Majesty's squadron twenty sail of the line captured. . . . The most decisive and complete victory that ever was gained over a powerful enemy. Eighteen of the enemy's ships were left without a mast in them, and I will venture to say had the battle been fought in the Ocean far from land and unembarrassed by the rocks and shoals of Trafalgar, there probably would not one of the enemy's ships have escaped. On the 22nd a gale of wind arose which continued for three days, sometimes blowing with extreme fury, dispersed the fleet in all directions, driving most of the captured hulks ashore and two or three were driven into the port of Cadiz. The rest so entirely disabled that I have been under the necessity of burning and sinking them. . . . The Combined Fleet is annihilated. I believe there are not more than four or five ships in Cadiz which can be made ready for sea. . . . I understand there are neither masts, sails, nor cordage to refit them — a shattered fleet and empty magazines. But what has raised their admiration and excited their dread too of the British Flag beyond anything, is the keeping our station before their port after so severe an action, which I have done to convince them that we are not to be removed by their utmost efforts from a station that is necessary to be kept. As soon as I can make the necessary arrangements, I propose coming into the Mediterranean, and if the Spanish squadron of Cartagena is in motion and at sea, to use my utmost endeavours to destroy them also and send to the Italian coast such a force as will check any operations the enemy may have in contemplation there."[2]

There were some who believed he would have been better employed in making his demonstration at Naples without the loss of a day instead of off Cadiz, but after the terrible strain of that exhausting week he probably did all that was humanly possible. "In short," he wrote to Cornwallis, "my strength is exhausted."[3] From the Cartagena squadron or Dumanoir's, wherever it might have gone, there was really little to fear as Louis was still somewhere about the Straits, and even if Dumanoir entered the Mediterranean and eluded him, he would certainly have to make for Toulon to refit before he could do anything at Naples.

As a matter of fact he had not entered the Straits. On the 22nd the southerly gale had struck his crippled squadron, and it was found impossible to stand up to it. Towards evening, moreover, he saw sails in the Gut which he believed to be Louis's squadron, and he decided to reach to the westward in hopes of falling in with Allemand. For two days he hunted for him, doing the best he could to refit and stop his leaks, and then on the 25th decided to go northward. On the 29th, as Louis was coming out of the Straits to rejoin Collingwood, he doubled Cape St. Vincent. Neutrals were questioned, but not a word of Allemand could be had, and he stood on for Rochefort in ignorance that Strachan was ahead of him still waiting patiently in eager hope of intercepting the squadron Dumanoir was seeking.

Strachan had remained as we left him in constant touch with Lobb's cruiser line about Vigo till the day of the battle. Then hearing that the ships which Villeneuve had left in Vigo were ready for sea, he had moved away to let them out, and on the 24th had taken station off Finisterre convinced that with Nelson off Cadiz they would try to get north.[4] He was thus excellently placed. Dumanoir's flagship and some others were making so much water that he felt forced to keep near the coast. After passing the latitude of Finisterre early on November 2nd, he was actually in sight of Cape Villano, and though he had stolen past Strachan inshore without being seen, he was at the point of junction of the two British cruiser lines, and as a matter of course quickly found he was being observed.

Two frigates, the *Boadicea* 38 and *Dryad* 36, which seem to have formed part of the Ushant-Finisterre line and must have been on the Finisterre rendezvous, were to the westward, while a third had just passed inshore of him, and was a little to the southward. It was Baker again in the *Phœnix*, with his genius for being in the right place, and another highly interesting piece of cruiser work ensued. After his hairbreadth escape with the *Didon* from Allemand he had nearly been caught by the Combined Fleet as he was trying to get his prize to Gibraltar. Eventually he had stood north again and taken her safely home, to be rewarded for his feat, as the custom was, with a cruise. On October 29th he had left Falmouth for a station to the westward of Scilly, where he was to open sealed orders.

On the second day he fell in with a Dane who said he had been detained by Allemand from the 13th to the 15th. He had been released in latitude 37° 51′ and longitude 14° 3′, that is, about 250 miles west-north-west of St. Vincent, and his captors then steered north-west.[5] As we know that Allemand was then on his way to the Canaries, this was a false course to drown his scent. Baker, of course, could not know this. It was the ordinary track to reach the French Atlantic ports, and the inference was that Allemand was somewhere down the Bay making for Rochefort. Baker had not yet reached his allotted station, but so eager was he to let Strachan know his news that he decided to break the seal. He found nothing but a handsome order to proceed to a very profitable cruising ground. Then he did not hesitate a moment. Prize money was flung to the winds and away he went for Ferrol, where he expected to meet with Strachan. Not finding him there he made for the Finisterre rendezvous, with the result that at daylight on November 2nd he found himself, as we have seen, passing inshore of what he believed to be Allemand's squadron.

Dumanoir, who was then sailing east-north-east, promptly detached the *Duguay-Trouin* to chase him; but Baker, instead of trying to escape, held on south-west for the regular rendezvous, where he was sure to hear of Strachan. In vain the Frenchman tried to cut him off. By five o'clock he had passed across her bows to windward, and Dumanoir signalled the recall. During the last two hours of the chase Baker had been firing signal guns, as Dumanoir naturally believed, to the other two frigates, but in fact he had not seen them. What he had sighted was part of Strachan's squadron to the southward. Dumanoir, with all Allemand's luck, must have passed close by him the night before, unseen, for all that Strachan had his squadron widely spread, and but for Baker's activity the fugitives might well have got away. The other two frigates by a strange chance did nothing. It was nearly nine and quite dark before they made out the *Phœnix*, and as they were between her and the enemy, she mistook their recognition signals as coming from Dumanoir's squadron. A little later they saw the squadron for which the *Phœnix* was standing, but again their signals were mistaken, and making sure they were alone between two divisions of Allemand's squadron they stood clear away and were seen no more.[6]

Even the *Phoenix* was fired upon before she could make Strachan understand. Luckily it was his flagship, the *Caesar* 80, that was nearest to her, the rest being scattered far astern. Baker reported he had just been chased by Allemand's squadron, and that they were close by to leeward. "I was delighted," wrote Strachan, "and told him to tell the captains astern I meant to engage at once." So away went the *Phoenix* again to rally the squadron, while Strachan held on after the chase. He could see them in the moonlight standing away in line abreast, but when the moon set he lost them. Dumanoir, in fact, in order to throw him off, altered course to the south-east so soon as it was dark, but Strachan was not deceived. He merely shortened sail till he was joined by two of his seventy-fours, *Hero* and *Courageux*, and one of his frigates, *Æolus* 32, with Lord William Fitzroy still in command. Of the rest of his squadron the *Namur* 74, and *Santa Margarita* 36, were still astern, and his fifth ship of the line, *Bellona* 74, as well as the *Indefatigable* had unfortunately just parted company.

But weakened as he was and though he had lost sight of the chase, he had no doubt what to do. As though he saw clearly into Dumanoir's mind he made straight east-north-east for Cape Ortegal. It was for that point also that Dumanoir was steering to get a departure, and possibly with the hope of slipping into Ferrol. But Strachan had cleverly cut him off. At daybreak on the 3rd, with his other frigate *Santa Margarita* added to the units in company, he had Ortegal in sight, and by nine o'clock the chase appeared again in the north-east. A couple of hours later the *Phoenix* and *Namur* were seen coming up, and behind them a stray frigate they had picked up. She proved to be the *Révolutionnaire* 38, a heavily armed cruiser, that went some way to make up for the loss of the *Bellona*. The force at his disposal thus amounted to four of the line and an equal number of what we should now call first-class cruisers, and here lies the main interest of the encounter. For the first time in anything that could be classed as a fleet action the fighting power of cruisers was about to be used directly to influence the issue, and that not in line with the battleships in the primitive style, but as a detachment with separate functions in accordance with the most recent ideas of our own time.

All day on the 3rd the weary chase went on towards Rochefort with the British slowly gaining, but when darkness fell the two fleets were still far apart. So fine was the night, however, that the chase was easily kept in sight, as it stood on in line of bearing, and when morning broke the *Cæsar* was barely six miles from the *Scipion*, the last of Dumanoir's four ships. Ahead of the British squadron and just within gunshot were the frigates that had been leading, and before six they had taken hold of the French rear. The power of heavy cruisers to stop a flying battle fleet was never better shown. In an hour or two the *Margarita* and *Phoenix* got near enough to keep yawing and giving the *Scipion* their broadsides. Dumanoir was still hoping to avoid an action. He had had to jettison a score of his eighty guns to keep his flagship afloat, and was in no condition to fight even an inferior force. But by eleven o'clock, finding it impossible to shake off the frigates with his stern-chasers, he was forced to haul to the wind in line of battle, and an action became inevitable.

Strachan still had but three of his squadron up, and in accordance with the then favourite plan he hailed his captains to say he meant to attack the rear. He himself led into action with his flagship, she being the most powerful vessel in the squadron. The most approved method of engaging for a fleet coming up from astern of an enemy in line of battle and

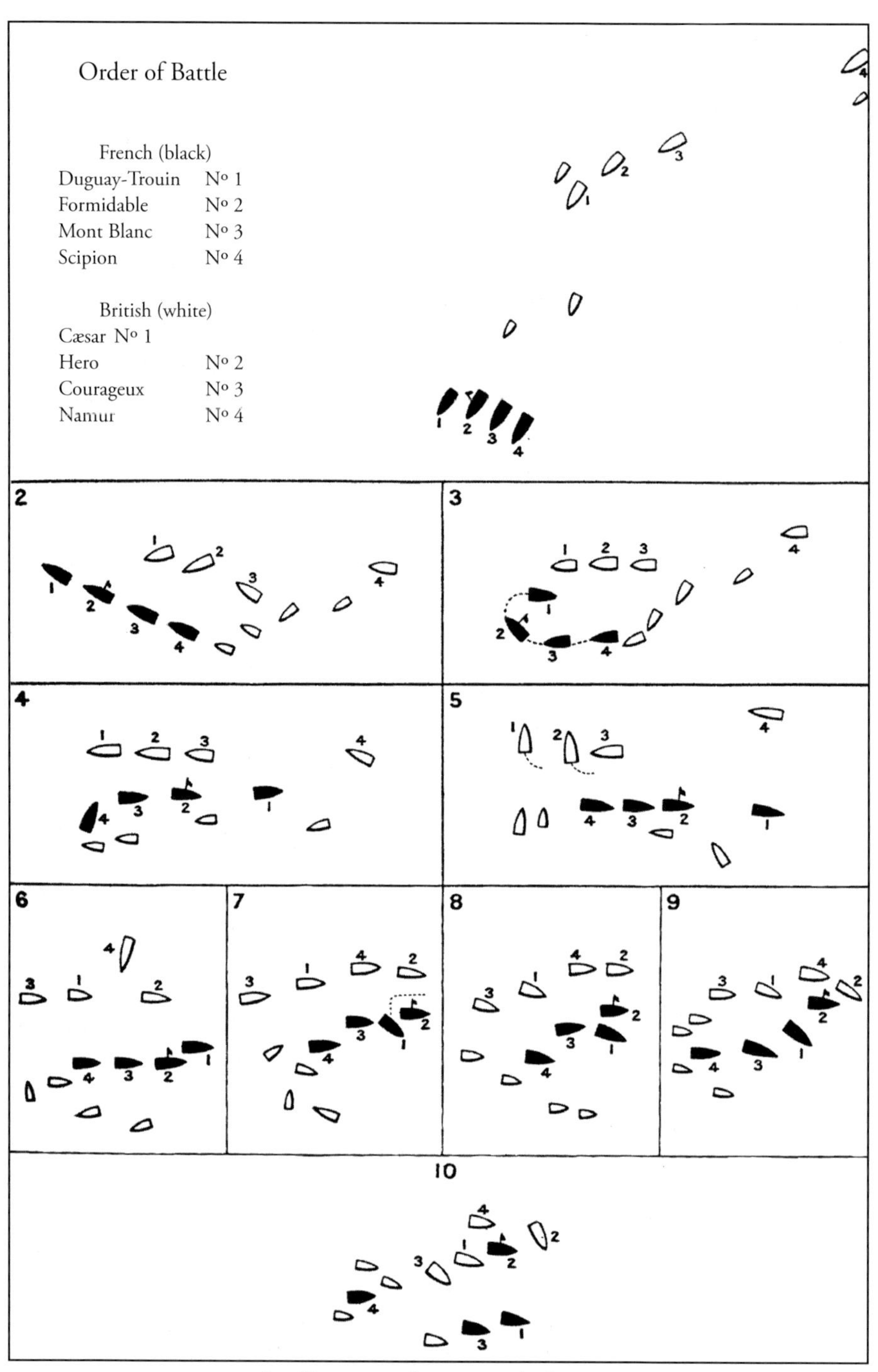

Sir Richard Strachan's Action

From a plan attached to the Report of Rear-Admiral Dumanoir le Pelley (*Archives de la Marine BB*[4] *237*). *Desbrière's Trafalgar.*

from to windward was by inverting the line, that is, for the leading ship to engage the enemy's rearmost and her second astern to pass on under cover of her fire and take the next ahead, and so on. But this Strachan did not do, probably because Dumanoir was second in the French line, and he wanted to bring the two flagships together. In any case he himself, like Nelson, led the line, engaging the two sternmost ships as he passed and hauling up abreast the French flagship. No attempt was made to break the line and engage from to leeward, as Nelson had laid down in his Memorandum of 1803, and this perhaps is explained by the interesting action of the cruisers. Instead of taking the orthodox position to windward of their own line and away from the enemy, they got into position on the lee and weather quarters of the rearmost ship and continued to engage her.

Strachan thus secured a concentration on the rear, and left the van ship, the *Duguay-Trouin*, out of action. Dumanoir promptly signalled to tack in succession, with the intention of covering his two rear ships and cutting off the *Namur*, which was now seen to be coming up. It was a bold move, for it had to be done under a destructive fire from the *Caesar* and her second the *Hero*, and it brought the French down within pistol shot of the British line. And not only this. The other two heavy frigates had come up, and it brought them all four in line to leeward. Dumanoir was thus doubled on and deprived of the possibility of bearing up to get out of action. It was, therefore, unnecessary for Strachan to attempt the hazardous manœuvre of breaking the line in order to secure a decisive action, and indeed Dumanoir evinced no desire to avoid one.

The effect of the French move was that the two lines passed on opposite tacks. Then, instead of tacking again, Dumanoir held on to isolate the *Namur*, who was keeping her wind to weather them, and for more than half-an-hour the action ceased. Strachan was, of course, trying to get round. The obvious move was to tack, but his rigging was so badly injured that he was forced to wear. The result was confusion, and seeing the French were getting away and threatening to weather him he signalled to the *Namur*, as Nelson had done to the *Africa*, to bear up and engage the van. To save time, as the *Hero* had got round first, he ordered her to lead, and formed a new line on her. In this formation the action was renewed with a fresh attack on the French rear, the frigates retaining their position astern and to leeward. At the same time the *Namur* came into line astern of the *Hero*, and the *Duguay-Trouin* being out of action, Strachan's four ships could concentrate on Dumanoir's other three. "The French squadron fought to admiration," wrote Strachan in his despatch, "and did not surrender till their ships were unmanageable," but by four o'clock the business was done and all had struck.

It was not till Strachan had the French Admiral on board that he discovered what he had done. "Judge of my surprise," he wrote, "when I found the ships we had taken were not the Rochefort squadron, but four from Cadiz." He had not been fighting Allemand after all, but a mere remnant that had escaped Nelson's hands. The elusive Allemand was, of course, far away, and to the end he maintained his reputation.

The day before the battle of Trafalgar, finding no European port open to him, he had resolved to run for the Canaries. In a fortnight he was close to Teneriffe, where he learned from a Portuguese schooner fresh from Madeira that a British expedition, consisting of eight of the line, as many frigates, and 130 transports, had recently demanded shelter there and had been refused. It was, of course, Popham and Baird, whom he had so narrowly missed a few weeks before. They were said to be destined for a distant expedition, and were to take the Canaries on the way. If it were true, Allemand was in a terrible plight; but he decided to hold on in hopes the British squadron had passed forward, and that he would be able to retake the islands if he found a hostile garrison in occupation. On the morrow, the day Strachan and Dumanoir met, he made Teneriffe and cleared for action. But it was a false alarm. Baird and Popham had passed on to the Cape of Good Hope without touching the Canaries, and Allemand was received with open arms by the Spanish Governor. Here he stayed for a fortnight to land his sick, revictual, and sell his prizes, which realised not far short of £20,000, and this, of course, was all over and above the value of the numerous less valuable captures he had sunk. But, as usual, the damage he had done to British trade cannot nearly have covered the cost of his expedition.

Still this indefatigable officer was far from regarding his campaign as finished. As yet he had not had a word of the Combined Fleet. He believed it was still blockaded in Cadiz, and he laid his plans accordingly. Having obtained three months' victuals and recruited his companies, he would cruise for a while about Madeira for the British colonial trade and reinforcements, and then would proceed off the coast of Portugal to sit on the communications of the squadron that was blockading Villeneuve. With this intention he sailed on November 19th. The very next day he sighted seven sail, which he believed to be one of the British squadrons in search of him. It was reported to be inferior, and he formed battle order and gave chase. In the night, however, the strangers eluded him. There was, in fact, no British squadron near him.

The strangers were probably a convoy, and they must have had a narrow escape. Three days later, about Madeira, he captured a British West Coast vessel outward bound, and learned from her skipper that before leaving Portsmouth he had heard a great battle had been fought, in which Nelson had been killed, but he did not know the particulars. With no further captures Allemand passed on from his Madeira station, but it was not till the middle of December that he reached the coast of Portugal. Here on the 18th and 19th he took and sunk three British vessels, and from them he learned that there was a squadron about on the look-out for him, and that the Combined Fleet had been annihilated by Nelson and Strachan. "The indiscretion," he says, "of those who brought me the news struck consternation aboard and aroused keen anxiety to get into port." At last the heart was beaten out of him and his squadron, and he resolved to seek shelter in Rochefort. One last stroke of luck still awaited him. It came with a westerly gale and thick weather that drove up at the right moment and carried him on at ten knots to the latitude of Rochefort, and there unseen he ran in in safety on Christmas Eve. So his brilliant Odyssey had ended. "On the 3rd (Nivôse)" he concluded his report, "I anchored in the Road of Aix Island after 161 days' absence, of which 148 were under sail, bringing back, with the squadron His Majesty entrusted to me, the enemy's ship of the line *Calcutta*. If, my lord, His Imperial and Royal Majesty and your Excellency condescend to approve the dispositions I made in the various difficult and embarrassing circumstances I met with, I shall feel highly recompensed for the pains I have taken to this end."[7]

Oh si sic omnes! If Craig's expedition had not forced Napoleon's hand, if, as he first intended, he had been able to wait till winter loosened the blockades and had been able to split up his fleet into cruising squadrons under young officers of Allemand's stamp, what infinite trouble they might have caused to our colonial and commercial interests! But that at least Nelson's crushing victory had prevented. Pitt's offensive policy had undesignedly forced Napoleon to expose his fleet to annihilation, and all hope of effective action at sea was gone.

CHAPTER XXVI

Conclusion

By universal assent Trafalgar is ranked as one of the decisive battles of the world, and yet of all the great victories there is not one which to all appearance was so barren of immediate result. It had brought to a triumphant conclusion one of the most masterly and complex sea campaigns in history, but in so far as it was an integral part of the combined campaign its results are scarcely to be discerned. It gave to England finally the dominion of the seas, but it left Napoleon dictator of the Continent. So incomprehensible was its apparent sterility that to fill the void a legend grew up that it saved England from invasion. That legend grew green till the present generation, unsupported as it was by the plain succession of events. Under the dry glare of modern historical methods the legend has withered, and in its place springs up the question, why was it that the consequences of Nelson's last achievement fell so far below his confident expectation, and why did Pitt die believing himself defeated?

The fault, it is certain, cannot be laid to his door. Not a moment had been lost in following up the blow. So soon as Napoleon's change of front was known, the War Office threw itself into bringing forward the disposable force for immediate action, and by the first week of October Castlereagh had settled the first step of the continental campaign. Bernadotte, in conformity with Napoleon's vast movement, had withdrawn his corps from Hanover, and was *en route* to join the Grand Army for the invasion of Austria, leaving nothing behind him but a small garrison in Hameln, on the Weser, to secure a re-entry from Westphalia.

The opportunity of driving the French from Northern Europe in Napoleon's absence was too promising to be resisted. A Russian force was on its way to join the Swedes at Stralsund, and Pitt decided that without waiting till the whole disposable British force could be mobilised, the king's German legion should sail at once to co-operate with the allies.[1] In view of the approach of winter and the closing of the northern seas with ice, the operation was extremely hazardous, but the risks were faced. To minimise them it was decided to send the expedition not to the Baltic, but to the Elbe, where from Cuxhaven and Stade it could rapidly join hands with the Swedes and Russians from Stralsund, at Lauenberg on the Weser. Accordingly Lord Keith was placed in direct communication with the War Office and ordered to get the troops across as quickly as possible, while Cornwallis covered the operation before Brest.

The Legion, with two British brigades which formed the advanced force under General Don, numbered about 11,000 men, and they were to be followed as soon as transport was ready by the rest of the disposable force, which Castlereagh hoped would eventually bring the whole up to sixty or seventy thousand.

It was not, of course, on this force alone that Pitt relied for success. The British expedition was only one element in a grand combined movement on Napoleon's left flank, and the backbone of the combination must be Prussia. Her attitude to the Coalition was still uncertain. At Berlin the War and the Peace parties were still at grips, and it was to stiffen and embolden her that Pitt had hastened the despatch of his first contingent. If Prussia could only be enheartened to take a hand it was calculated that in the spring, with the Swedes and Russians from Stralsund and various contingents from the minor German States, the combined army would reach a hundred thousand men. Such a force threatening Holland and the northern French frontier could not be neglected. It must at least act as a powerful diversion and cover an advance of the main Prussian army which it was proposed should move at once through Moravia against Napoleon's left. Such was the stroke which Pitt endeavoured to play — so it was he meant to use his command of the sea — on the well-tried lines his father had followed with so much success to save Frederick the Great. It is a bypath of the Austerlitz campaign that is now long forgotten. Yet it was nothing but the incalculable rapidity of Napoleon's heroic change of front that condemned it to failure and oblivion.

The incapacity and blindness with which the great soldier directed his naval campaign was only equalled by the astounding brilliance and certainty of touch with which ashore he snatched himself free from Pitt's toils. It was one of the many dramatic strokes of the campaign that on the day that Trafalgar was fought, as Nelson and Collingwood were contending in their snail's race to be first in the hour of reckoning, Napoleon was issuing from the camp of the Grand Army at Elchingen in Bavaria his famous Ninth Bulletin. It told how, two days before, General Mack, in accordance with Nelson's prophecy, had surrendered at Ulm with 30,000 men. The effect, taken together with that of the actions which led to it, was that the Austrian home army had almost ceased to exist. By a last stroke of irony it had happened just as Villeneuve was being driven out of Cadiz by his master's ruthless treatment and there was no longer need for the fleet to be hazarded to almost certain destruction.

Staggering as was the blow which Napoleon had delivered, it by no means involved the end of the Coalition. It had been obtained only at the cost of sinning against a high strategical canon which condemns operations calculated to raise up fresh enemies. In order to out-manœuvre Mack Napoleon had violated Prussian territory, and the insult gave the War party at Berlin the upper hand of the vacillating king. Advances were made to the other Powers engaged, the nebulous threat on Napoleon's left flank began to materialise rapidly, and on November 3rd, as Strachan was in the heat of his chase after Dumanoir, the Treaty of Potsdam was signed. By its terms Prussia accepted the British proposals, and agreed that if within four weeks Napoleon did not accept her mediation she would join the Coalition with 180,000 men.

At last Pitt's great idea seemed to be realised, and Lord Harrowby, a member of the Cabinet, was hurried off to Berlin on a special mission to push things forward into action. There he arrived in the middle of November, just as the news of Trafalgar was flashing over Europe and as Don was landing in the Weser.[2] Harrowby carried full powers to arrange for a complete alliance, to define the common objects and to concert a plan of campaign. The main object was to secure prompt action, and Prussia, like Austria before her, was timidly bent on wasting time with an armed mediation. Harrowby was authorised to go even beyond what England had already offered. He was to promise a magnificent subsidy for all her troops and the command of the auxiliary army on the Weser if she would begin operations in Moravia at once. He was also empowered to deal with Sweden, Denmark, and certain of the Westphalian States, and to undertake that by the spring England would provide 70,000 men for use on the Continent or in maritime expeditions as the Allies desired. To mark England's disinterestedness he was to say that if the Coalition forced Napoleon to a general peace she was willing to give up without compensation all her conquests excepting only Malta and the Cape. Amongst the military experts consulted was Sir Arthur Wellesley, who had a brigade in the expeditionary force. He threw cold water on the whole plan — not for any inherent strategical defects — but because, with the same sure military insight that had prompted Nelson to protest against Mack, he was certain the Prussian army could not be mobilised in time to do any good. The situation indeed was gone too far to leave much hope of saving it. If Napoleon's first blow had stirred up a hornet's nest on his left flank, on his right its effect had been all he could wish. In view of the threatening aspect of affairs in Italy he had been compelled to withdraw St. Cyr from the south and to use his corps to reinforce Masséna on the Adige. To Masséna had been committed the task of holding back the superior army of the Archduke Charles, whose mission was to drive the French out of Italy and put an end to Napoleon's new kingdom. Masséna's function was, in fact, defensive, but the moment he knew of Ulm he sprang forward and made a rough attack on the Austrian camp. The Archduke hurled him back, but seeing how desperate was the condition of Austria, it was impossible to follow up his success. All that it secured him was a safe retreat, and he rapidly fell back out of Italy to try to save the situation at home.

With that retreat all hope of effective action by Craig and the Russians was gone. It was on October 30th, the day of Masséna's unsuccessful attack on the Archduke's camp, that Craig finally received his summons to meet the Russian expedition. Syracuse was to be the point of concentration. But so perverse was the weather that it was ten days before he even lost sight of Malta. Tired of waiting, the Russians passed on, and eventually the two expeditions concentrated off Cape Passaro, where a century and a half before the elder Byng had struck one of the many blows which England had delivered to save Sicily from falling into the hands of a first-class naval power.

Craig had brought his force up to 8,000 men, but the promised Russian reinforcement from the Black Sea had not arrived, and all told the combined force numbered not more than 20,000. As the King of Naples had just broken down under Napoleon's pressure, and had signed in despair a treaty of neutrality, there was some doubt as to what to do. The Russian envoy, however, had little difficulty in persuading the high-spirited Queen to denounce the treaty, and to join the Coalition, promising that the kingdom would be defended. Elliot always said he opposed so flagrant a breach of faith, and believed no good could come of it. He was certainly no party to the arrangement, but under it both the Russian and British troops were invited to land. It was not till November 20th they anchored in Naples Bay, and then it was only to hear the staggering news of Mack's capitulation and the Archduke's retreat.[3]

What was to be done? To Craig at least it was obvious that the French could return whenever they liked, and invade the Neapolitan dominions in such strength as it would be impossible for the local forces and their allies to resist. Elliot was of Craig's opinion that any further attempt to defend Naples could only end in disaster. His diplomacy, he knew, was powerless in face of the Russian ascendancy, but he trusted that the British General's influence over General Lacy was such that the British view would prevail.[4] But even if it did, the difficulties of the situation were far from solved. Simply to re-embark the troops was to leave the unhappy Queen to the extremity of Napoleon's vengeance which their reception would have earned her. True, there was a valid and urgent excuse for a re-embarkation. A message had come from the Archduke begging that the expeditionary force should be brought to Venice to act on Masséna's rear and stop his pursuit; but this was equally out of the question. Not only was the operation beyond the strength available, it was also too late, and was certainly beyond Craig's instructions. The two Generals agreed, therefore, to go into cantonments and collect transport and horses for their cavalry and guns, and to watch developments till further orders.

They had not long to wait. The situation indeed had been developing with rapidity. On November 3rd, the same day that the Treaty of Potsdam brought Prussia into the Coalition, Castlereagh issued final orders for the whole disposable force of the kingdom to prepare for foreign service. By the end of the four weeks on which Prussia insisted for her armed mediation all would be ready, but things were not going quite smoothly. Prussia was showing herself difficult about the ultimate settlement to be achieved. Hanover was her Naboth's vineyard, and amongst other things she wanted England to agree to its cession in exchange for Frisia and part of Westphalia. This proposal, however, the Cabinet refused even to communicate to the king. As for the mediation it mattered little. It was now understood to be nothing but a dilatory device to gain time for mobilisation. Before the end of November, Pitt had not only seen the full terms of the treaty, but Harrowby had also received a comprehensive plan of campaign from the German Staff which was all that could be desired, and fitted nicely with the ideas of the British Cabinet. England was specially to charge herself with securing the mouths of the Elbe, Weser, and Emms, which would be the lines of supply for the Combined Army of the North, and to further as much as possible the flow of stores from Russia to the King of Prussia's magazines. Since the overthrow of Napoleon's fleet it was a duty which presented no difficulties. As for the operations of the Allies ashore the general plan of campaign was based in full accordance with the traditions of the elder Pitt's time on defensive action upon the Emms and Weser to cover the main operations till events justified something more drastic. All was going well except for the Swedes, who refused to advance till Prussia had committed herself by an act of war. Operations were amicably concerted between the Duke of Brunswick, who was commanding in chief, Tolstoi, who commanded the Russian contingent, and Blücher, who was Chief of the Staff in a Prussian corps commanded by the Grand Duke of Hesse. Hameln was already invested by Tolstoi and Don; and Lord Cathcart, with the main body of the British expeditionary force, was at Yarmouth only waiting for a wind.[5]

Clearly, then, Napoleon's position was one that could not be maintained for long, and certainly not over the winter. Some of the remnants of Mack's army had succeeded in joining the Prussians, while others had escaped through the Tyrol and come down in rear of Masséna. At all costs, then, another blow must be dealt, and Napoleon, in spite of the danger that was brewing on his left rear, staked everything on a rapid forward movement to meet the advancing Russians still further from his base. His rapidity and daring were triumphant. At Austerlitz, on December 2nd, the fatal blow was delivered, and Pitt's grand fabric was in ruins. Though at first the truth was not realised, the Third Coalition had ceased to exist.

The respite on which Prussia insisted had just expired, but instead of keeping her word and immediately taking advantage of the desperate position into which Napoleon had pushed himself, she began to weaken at once. Harrowby, fearing the worst, had to warn Don not to commit himself too far. He was then at Verden on the Weser, and so sure had seemed the position that he had recently ordered the empty transports to return for further duty. Now he had to recall them in view of a retreat, and he himself had to stand fast as he was. This was the situation which greeted Cathcart, when on December 15th he reached Cuxhaven, and which staggered the anxious Generals in their cantonments at Naples.

Elliot was in despair. The day after the news of Austerlitz reached the Neapolitan Court, he sent home a hopeless despatch reviewing the situation. The misfortunes and blunders of the Austrian Generals, he said, had in their fatal consequences passed all calculation. In the interval between the embarkation of the troops at Corfu and Malta and their arrival at Naples, the formidable power of the Austrian monarchy had melted away. "I am tempted," he wrote, "to say with Shakspeare, 'It has vanished like the baseless fabric of a dream.'" Vienna, the Tyrol, and Venetia were in the hands of the enemy, and the Archduke Charles, who had the only Austrian army still in existence, was said to be retiring into Hungary. There were even rumours that a French army was already in movement for Naples.[6]

It was not quite true, but true enough. The day before Elliot wrote Napoleon had informed Prince Eugène, his viceroy in Italy, who was getting nervous, that he was about to send back St. Cyr with 5,000 men. But it was not so easy to find the troops. An armistice with the Austrians had been signed and negotiations for peace were commencing, but Vienna was showing an unexpectedly stiff front. Talleyrand had strict orders to keep Naples out of the treaty, but Napoleon was doubtful whether he would be able to insist on its annexation. The Archduke was in Hungary, drawing near to Vienna, and it was found necessary to absorb Masséna's corps into the Grand Army. Clearly Austerlitz had not finished the business unless Prussia could be frightened out of the path on which she had set her timid foot. To this end Napoleon was exerting the whole force of his personality, and by the middle of the month it was done. Haugwitz, the Prussian envoy, suddenly collapsed, and on December 15th set his hand to an abject desertion of the allies. Still the end was not yet. The king refused to ratify what Haugwitz had done, and Austria was still holding out.

Meanwhile British troops were still pouring across the North Sea. Including the recruits that had flocked to the German Legion, Cathcart had some 25,000 men and was already stretching forward to the Emms with intent to seize Holland while it was still denuded of French troops.[7] But a despatch from Harrowby announcing that the armistice which followed Austerlitz had been signed, brought all to a standstill. Russia, it is true, had been no party to it, but the Czar was on his way back to St. Petersburg, and Prussia was begging that no offensive movement should be made. Our arrangement with her had provided for Cathcart's retreat in case of need into Prussian territory. No promise had yet been given, and clearly she was no longer to be trusted without one. Leaving his troops where they were, Cathcart at once went up the Weser to Nienberg to hold a conference with Tolstoi.

The Russian General had been given to understand that his master had hope of continuing the war in concert with Prussia in the spring; but for the present it was agreed there must be a general falling back to a defensive position. The investment of Hameln was raised, Cathcart stopped all the last arrived transports, recalled his advanced posts from the Emms, and began to concentrate on the lower Weser round Bremen. Still he had no thought of abandoning his loyal Russian allies without express orders from home. To complete his position he prepared to seize Bremen, as the best means of securing his retreat and of defending himself if the ice should shut him in.[8] There was indeed little hope of a successful issue, and he warned the Government not to send on the third division of his force, which, after sailing, had been driven back by a gale with some loss. It was inexpedient, he thought, in the circumstances, to lock up more of the disposable force in North Germany. But the transports were already at sea, and things were going from bad to worse. They had sailed again on December 22nd, and next day all was over. Prussia had given in; Austria had agreed to terms of peace; and the main Russian army was sullenly retiring.

It was at Naples that the reaction was first felt. On the morrow of the preliminaries of peace being agreed, St. Cyr received orders to march. On the 25th the Peace of Presburg was signed between France and Austria, and without waiting a day Napoleon issued a bulletin to his army announcing that the Bourbon dynasty at Naples, for its crimes and treason, had ceased to exist. By the end of the month the Emperor's brother Joseph had received orders to reign in his stead, and Masséna had been sent down to command the army that was to put him on the throne.

At the urgent entreaty of the doomed Queen, Lacy and his staff were engaged in a reconnaissance of the Neapolitan frontier to see if resistance were in any way possible before giving in to Craig's views. On January 3rd he was back, and a full council of war was held for a final decision. Lacy was there with three of his staff, and Craig with Stuart his second in command, and Campbell his second brigadier, as well as the Russian Commodore Greig and Captain Sotheron of the *Excellent*, whose year-long vigil was still unended. The unanimous decision was that with the force available the frontier was indefensible. As to the alternative, there was a difference of opinion. The question was whether any part of the kingdom could be held or whether the allied forces should re-embark. The Russians were decidedly in favour of abandoning the capital and retiring the whole of the troops — Russians, British, and Neapolitan, into Calabria, which they were convinced could be retained. They were supported by Stuart and Bunbury against the British commander-in-chief. Craig took a different view. His instructions enjoined that whatever he could or could not do, he was to make sure of Sicily. So soon as it was in danger he was to occupy Messina, if possible by consent of the King; if not, then without it. Since neither he nor Elliot had been any party to the recent convention by which Russia had undertaken the *Defence* of Naples, they did not regard the British honour pledged like that of the Russians. Nevertheless Craig, as a soldier, did feel bound to Lacy, just as Cathcart did to Tolstoi. His position was extremely difficult. He was firmly of opinion that, under his instructions, the hour had come to secure Sicily, that he ought at once to place Messina beyond Napoleon's reach, but, at the same time, he could not permit his view to carry him so far as to decline to be bound by the decision of the majority, Accordingly he entered a separate written opinion, in which he pronounced strongly against the idea of holding Calabria, as a measure that could do no good either to Naples or the common cause. Nevertheless, he said he considered himself bound in honour not to desert his Russian colleague, and solely on that consideration he consented to share the risks and dangers which, in his eyes, the proposed operation promised.[9]

The decision was immediately conveyed to the Court. They were in despair, but worse was yet to come. Into the midst of their distracted protests broke an aide-de-camp of the Czar. He had come in hot haste from Austerlitz, and he handed Lacy a peremptory order to evacuate Italy.[10] On a smaller scale it was a betrayal as barefaced as that of which Prussia had been guilty. Its sole and sufficient excuse was hard necessity. Craig's conscience at least was clear, his hands were free, and he hesitated no longer to carry out his plain instructions. His troops were marched down again to their landing-place at Castellamare, while the Russians returned to Baia. In vain the Court entreated for a delay while they attempted to avert Napoleon's vengeance through the Pope. It was a hopeless expedient Mercy was as much out of the question as resistance, and after a few days' hesitation the Russians returned to Corfu and Craig on January 20th anchored his force before Messina.

On the North Sea the same unhappy scene was being enacted. As Craig marched down to Castellamare news reached London that Prussia was certainly intending to desert the Coalition, and to make the best terms she could for herself. To complete the general perplexity, Pitt was on his death-bed, stricken down by the shock of Austerlitz. He had just come back from Bath, worse rather than better for the change, and was in no condition to transact business. But the crisis was acute. The troops had been sent in the first instance mainly in the hope of stiffening Prussia's attitude to Napoleon, and she was obviously becoming again like wax in his hands. The Ministers had to face the possibility that at any moment she might accept the bribe of Hanover and declare for Napoleon. In that case half of our whole disposal force, which was now with Cathcart, would be in serious jeopardy. On January 3rd he had occupied Bremen, and had concentrated everything in its immediate neighbourhood. But with Prussia hostile the position was scarcely tenable, even with the rivers open. It was obvious that Cathcart must be either reinforced or withdrawn at once before winter locked him in.

Still to reverse Pitt's policy, as he lay helpless, was more than the Ministers had the heart to do without his consent. Castlereagh and Hawkesbury therefore took the responsibility of going to his bedside. The interview was the last blow. Till then there had been fair hope of recovery, but on the morrow it was obvious he was dying. It was the last piece of business he did for his country, and to the end he strove against the wreck of his heroic policy. The last shred of hope must be clung to. Orders went out to General Cathcart not to withdraw at once, but that he was to hold himself in readiness to re-embark the whole force the moment he got the word from Berlin. He had not long to wait. A despatch from

Lord Harrowby almost immediately quenched even the last spark of hope; and as Craig was anchoring at Messina definite and urgent orders went off to Cathcart to re-embark forthwith, and to Keith to cover the retirement.

So fell the last fragment of all the dying Minister had hoped of his great Coalition. If the British position were to be secured it must be done single-handed. Pitt's wisdom had foreseen it, and provided the means in the two little forces of Craig and Baird. They still remained to close the chapter with a welcome gleam of success.

With Craig's transports before Messina, Sicily was safe. He could secure his point at any moment, and was content to hold his hand till the consent of the Neapolitan Court to an occupation was obtained, or till need arose to act without it. His action was not stayed for long. Three days after he arrived, as London was hushed in its waking with the news that Pitt was dead, the *Excellent* was weighing anchor; St. Cyr was in motion; the hour for which Nelson more than a year before had bidden her stand-by had come, and the King was on board. He landed at Palermo, where Acton was waiting for him, and with his old adviser at his side there was little doubt how things would go for Craig. The *Excellent* went back for the Queen, and she too sought the refuge Nelson had provided. A day or two later he was with the King again, and all was settled. An invitation came at once for Craig to land, and on February 16th Messina was occupied.

It was the last stroke of the Trafalgar campaign — and fitly so; for it was the central point around which it had turned. Little as seemed the gain in the midst of the vast continental struggle, it was enough; and Napoleon knew it, as was quickly confessed, although for a while he believed that the removal of Pitt's firm hand from the helm would enable him to do with England what he would.

The tragic death of the great War Minister forced on the King a change of Government. Amidst the ruins of the Coalition he had no choice but to place himself in the hands of the Opposition. With the rest of the old servants who had shaped the campaign went Barham. Without honour or recognition the great sailor, who had handled the fleet with a mastery never equalled since Anson's days, retired into the obscurity from which Pitt had called him in the hour of need.

Not a word can be found to show that the country recognised in the least the perfection of his work. His rigid determination to permit none of the old evil influences to prejudice the efficiency of the machine with which Pitt had entrusted him; his ruthless attitude to family influence and his sparing reward for plain duty done had set against him those who make reputations — the self-seekers in society and the service. "The present Admiralty, I hear," wrote the wife of Cornwallis's Captain of the Fleet, "are making their arrangements of *congé*. . . . In no case do I believe they would have remained in, for the cry is violent among the Navy against them, and they have really treated Baker, Sir Richard Strachan, and others like delinquents, Lord Barham, as I hear, holding the language 'that it was his duty to make other people do theirs, because it was their duty.' This sounds *very fine*, *magnificent*, and let us add nonsensical. . . . Lord Townshend wrote to Lord Barham to ask him to make him (Lord James Townshend) a lieutenant. What would you say if I assert that this was refused? When you consider Lord Townshend's services, his respectability, is it not incredible? Lady Townshend is very indignant, but likewise hurt to death about it!"[11] Trivial as is the letter, it goes far to explain how the reputation of one of the greatest of our strategists and administrators suffered so complete an eclipse. Such an attitude as he assumed in such an age, however high the motive or the occasion, was not to be forgiven; and his solitude and silence did the rest. No one perhaps except Pitt really knew what he had done.[12]

At the Foreign Office the change was as complete as at the Admiralty, and here lay Napoleon's chance. In the desperate condition of affairs the King had at last to accept the services of Fox. The office he selected was that of Foreign Secretary, and, as was only to be expected, no sooner was he fairly seated than he tried to snatch a peace. Napoleon seemed equally willing. Within a fortnight of Pitt's death Fox was in direct communication with Talleyrand. By May regular negotiations were established on the basis of *uti possidetis*. But the rock they split upon was Sicily.

Fox, it is true, in his fanaticism for peace, did his best to throw it away. There was a period when Napoleon might have had it on excellent terms, but he let the chance go by in the intoxication of his success, and then it was too late.[13] It was a piece of mad perversity. But for Napoleon, at the zenith of his power, the one fragment of success that was left to England in Europe was unendurable to the pride which had been so completely humbled at sea. His first orders to Joseph on his accepting the crown of Naples had been that he was immediately to seize Sicily. He had merely to throw troops across in the confusion that reigned, and the thing would be done. Apparently Napoleon's own failure had taught him nothing. So far from being able to carry out his brother's order, Joseph had not yet succeeded in possessing himself of Calabria. Supported by a squadron under Sir Sidney Smith, Gaeta was still flying the Bourbon flag, and the "brigands" were holding out in the hills. Napoleon kept urging more energetic measures, but though General Reynier was operating in the mountains with 7,000 men, little solid progress was made.

In view of the secret negotiations with Fox, the delay was exasperating, and the pressure on easy-going Joseph grew stronger. "The English," wrote the Emperor in the middle of June, "are willing to recognise you as King of Naples, but without Sicily they will refuse to recognise you. Peace could be made if you were master of Sicily." Joseph's answer must have been galling in the extreme. Craig had gone home on sick leave, and Stuart, left in command, suddenly threw some 5,000 of his men across the straits, and assisted by a naval brigade from Sidney Smith's Squadron, inflicted a severe defeat upon Reynier at Maida. It was the first time Napoleon's troops had crossed bayonets with the British army, and they had been beaten by an inferior force.

To add to the vexation of it and the loss of prestige, the whole of Calabria was immediately in flames. A strong counter-movement set in against Joseph, and so far from his being able to seize Sicily, it looked for a while as though he were to lose his crown as suddenly as it had been gained. From that day till the end of the war in 1814, every effort of Napoleon's to win the heart of the Mediterranean was fruitless. It remained in British hands till the last to mark the justness with which Pitt's great campaign had been conceived. He had failed to save Europe, but he had secured the British Empire. Beside the vital outpost in Sicily he had won another as valuable in the south. By the middle of January Baird was in full possession of the Cape. These two positions were the solid return of the unmatched work which Pitt's Admirals had performed at sea, and together they rendered the Empire impregnable.

That and no less was what the campaign of Trafalgar achieved. It was not merely that it secured the British Isles from invasion. The ramparts it built stretched to the ends of the earth. It was not merely that it destroyed the French naval power. By securing bases in the Mediterranean and towards the East, it made it impossible for any partial revival of Napoleon's navy to place any part of our overseas possessions in serious jeopardy. Against any other man than Napoleon, with any other ally than Prussia as she then was, it might well have done much more. As it was, the sea had done all that the sea could do, and for Europe the end was failure.

APPENDIX A

Pitt's Instructions To Lord G. Leveson-Gower

[*Foreign Office. Russia.* 58.]

DOWNING STREET, *June* 7, 1805.

My Lord, — In addition to the contents of my Dispatch No. 15 of this date, in which I treat of the proposal that His Majesty should consent without reserve to an offer to be made, in the last resort, to Bonaparte by Monsieur de Novossilzoff of the evacuation of Malta, as a condition of the immediate adoption of the arrangements proposed in the Treaty signed on the 11th of April at St. Petersburgh, it appears expedient, at this crisis, that, in order to place in their true light the great and extensive sacrifices already consented to by the King, I should declare more at large to your Excellency the sense which His Majesty entertains of the comparative situation of Great Britain and of the nations on the Continent of Europe, with respect to the power and views of France, lest those liberal sacrifices which are the result of a great and comprehensive view of general Policy, should be misconceived as the effect of impending danger or of anxious apprehension. It cannot, however, have escaped the observation of the Cabinet of St. Petersburgh that, whilst the energies of the Continental Powers are held in suspense between the danger of submission and the apprehended consequences of opposing resistance to the uninterrupted course of insults or encroachment on the part of France, Great Britain has disproved the vainglorious boast of the French Government by a contest maintained, with advantage, single-handed.

The immense and expensive preparations for the invasion of this country have been blocked up and confined by the British Navy within the range of the protecting batteries which line the enemy's coast, and valuable Colonies have been conquered from France and her Dependent Allies. During this period of successful events, the Naval and Military force of Great Britain have progressively increased, and the financial resources of the country have continued unimpaired.

But notwithstanding the means which His Majesty has proved that he possessed of providing for the immediate security of his own Dominions, he has never lost sight of the policy by which their permanent interests are connected with those of the Continent. On this principle His Majesty has declined entering into any negotiation with France except in concert with other Powers, and especially with the Emperor of Russia. On the same principle he has offered great and extensive sacrifices for the purpose of obtaining, if possible by Treaty, a general arrangement for the security of Europe, and, in the other alternative, the most liberal co-operation towards the vigorous prosecution of a Continental war. His Majesty in proposing these extensive sacrifices for stipulated conditions of general security, in undertaking to provide such ample contributions for the support of war, if that alternative should be resorted to for the general advantage, stated at the same time the degree of security which he deemed essential, and the outline of the provisions by which alone it appeared to His Majesty such security could be ensured to the different States of Europe. The King observes, with the highest satisfaction, that, in the event of war being found to be the only course by which a state of security to Europe can be established and preserved, the views of the Emperor of Russia are in perfect conformity to those of His Majesty. But, in estimating the conditions proper to be offered to Bonaparte with the intent to avert the calamities of War by proposing the most moderate provisions for the future Safety and Independence of the Powers of the Continent, His Majesty observes, with regret, that the modifications introduced into the Treaty, as signed by your Excellency, fall, in many essential points, far short of the stipulations stated as necessary in His Majesty's original proposal.

In Italy the intended arrangement by no means gives effect to the principle, the importance of which is recognized in the 10th Separate Article of the Treaty, that the frontiers of France should, on one side, be confined within the Alps; for it cannot be contended that, in effect (whatever may be expressed in terms) France will be confined within the Alps, if a sovereign of the family of Bonaparte should be established in Piedmont. The uninterrupted influence of France over the councils and conduct of Spain from the period of the accession of the Duke of Anjou to the throne of the latter kingdom, affords a sufficient example of the consequences which must inevitably follow from the proposed distribution of the North of Italy, connecting, as it will, France and Lombardy under the Government of the family of Bonaparte. The sovereignty in that case provided for the King of Sardinia would not, either in strength of frontier, in extent of territory, or in the amount of its revenue or population, be capable of maintaining a state of independence against France, even with every support which might reasonably be hoped for from Austria, though the latter Power should be put in possession of Mantua, which however is not made an absolute condition under the terms of the Treaty.

On the side of Holland and the North of Germany the provisions for security and independence are not more solid. Although the establishment of a powerful state in that quarter is specified as the surest mode of providing for the security of the United Provinces, such an arrangement is relinquished as hopeless. In the present instance, the additional Barrier proposed for Holland, inadequate as it is, is not to be insisted upon, and even the ancient line of their territory is not positively stipulated. It is evident upon this cursory statement of the inadequacy of the modified terms which compose the conditions of the Treaty as signed by your Excellency, that the view with which His Majesty proffered the sacrifice of all his conquests made during the present War has not been adhered to. Yet His Majesty is fully sensible of the benefits which may be derived from any improvement of the present state of Europe, and from any arrangement of territory which may afford some additional means of resistance, especially if this improvement is accompanied by that confidence which is the result of successful opposition to encroaching ambition, and which may lead to future exertion, it increased means of such future exertion are held forth; and above all by a system of co-operation and concert among the leading Powers. His Majesty therefore, however disappointed in the expectation of a more adequate provision for the immediate and effectual security of Europe, is ready, on his part, to agree to the modifications proposed by His Imperial Majesty. The Treaty has accordingly been ratified with the exception of that part of the 10th Separate Article which relates to the evacuation of Malta by His Majesty's troops; and with certain verbal alterations in the same Article, where the expression of sentiments attributed to the King, is carried somewhat beyond the real opinion and feelings of His Majesty. These alterations however in no degree affect either the principles or the object of the Concert. There is also an alteration in the 7th Separate Article which becomes necessary in consequence of the terms on which His Majesty has expressed his readiness to admit of a substitute for Malta in the Mediterranean.

Having stated to your Excellency the view which His Majesty has of the probable degree of efficacy of the conditions provided by the Treaty, if they should be accepted by Bonaparte, I trust your Excellency will be able to convince the Russian Cabinet that the evacuation of Malta by Great Britain under such a state of things, would not be consistent with the future security and permanent tranquillity of Europe. If the continent should be left (as stated above) open to the future aggressions of Bonaparte, and that the restraint on the naval operations of France in the Mediterranean should be removed by the surrender of the British Establishment in that sea; the coasts of Italy, Turkey, Greece, and Egypt would be exposed to the unrestricted enterprizes of the common enemy; and would soon be subject to his absolute control.

It would exceed the limits of a dispatch to state (and would indeed be superfluous and unnecessary to your Excellency, who are so well informed of them) the long course of historical events, in which the protecting influence of the British Navy in the Mediterranean has been exerted for the advantage of Europe. It is however essential to draw your Excellency's attention to the particular circumstances which, at the present time, render a British station in that quarter of peculiar importance. To prove this position it is sufficient to observe the earnest and unremitting exertions of the French Government to secure to itself the command of every port in the Mediterranean. Already in possession of Toulon, of Corsica, and of many of the ports of Italy, and with an entire influence over the ports of Spain, Bonaparte has arbitrarily annexed to France the Island of Elba, and, if he had succeeded in the attempt which he made subsequent to the Treaty of Amiens to place Malta in the hands of the Knights of St. John of Jerusalem, deprived as they were even of the benefits of the provisions of that Treaty, and of all means of maintaining their independence, he might again, at pleasure, have either purchased or seized that Island, and have thereby secured the absolute control of Sicily and Naples, and the means of effecting his designs against the Ottoman territories. In the absence of a British fleet, what power could check the progress of French ambition to these ends? Would Malta, in the hands of Russia, operate that check, without a British fleet? No; but it may be said that Malta, with the flag of Russia flying on its ramparts, would still afford that salutary station to the British fleet. That question certainly forms a part of the discussion of this great subject, and merits consideration.

The just and enlightened views of the present Sovereign of Russia neither are nor can be doubted, and create a perfect reliance on the present system of Russia; but, in forming a final arrangement, it is necessary to secure permanence to the system on which that arrangement depends — past experience gives no assurance of that security. I am unwilling to recall the painful recollection of the moment at which Russia was on the point of exerting, in conjunction with France, all the powerful means of that great Empire. Had such a Confederacy been actually established and brought into action, and the fleets of Great Britain at the same time excluded from the Mediterranean, all the calamities which still threaten to overwhelm Europe, unless prevented by resistance, would, in that case, have been at once effected and irretrievably confirmed. The danger which then existed may, by possibility, again recur, if the same disposition should, in any future reign, misguide the policy, and misapply the powerful influence of the Russian Empire. But without looking forward to possible contingencies, which it is painful to contemplate, your Excellency will perceive that, even under the present system, so congenial to the character and disposition of the reigning Emperor, the continuance or renewal of the weakness and apathy of the other Powers of Europe, might again necessarily prevent the Emperor of Russia from taking an active part in any future war between England and France; in which case Malta would become a neutral port, open indeed to the commerce of both belligerents, but receiving only a limited number of the ships of war of either nation; a circumstance indifferent to France, with the possession of ample and convenient ports, but capable of operating, under certain situations of Italy and the other maritime stations within the Mediterranean, as an absolute prohibition on any naval operations by Great Britain in those seas.

The wise and generous policy of the Emperor of Russia has led him to feel, in common with the King, the importance of supporting the Ottoman Empire. With this general object equally in view, Great Britain and Russia have obviously a more near and pressing interest in distinct and different parts of the possessions of the Porte, and they are respectively, at this time, in possession of the stations, which can afford the most immediate and effectual support to the quarter most essentially interesting to each. Corfu is at once the bulwark and key of Greece, as Malta is of Egypt; but as the latter would not be equally effectual to that object in the hands of Russia, neither could it be expected, if the Ottoman Dominions should be threatened and endangered by France, that Russia would divert her attention from the object more immediately interesting to itself, to provide for the security of that which is more particularly and pointedly connected with the interests of Great Britain. It will also be remembered that, by the Treaties which have been concluded with the Porte, the assistance of a British fleet has been deemed indispensably necessary for the security of the Turkish Dominions. This aid His Majesty cannot effectually afford without the possession of Malta, and the command which it gives in those Seas. Russia cannot keep up a garrison in Malta and supply the place without infinite difficulty and expense, especially if there be not a superior Russian fleet in the Mediterranean, for, without that protection, the supply from Sicily might, at the pleasure of France, be cut off, and even the Island itself might consequently be reduced by famine; or perhaps the vicinity of France might even afford the opportunity of besieging its extensive fortifications with so superior a force as to preclude an effectual resistance during the long period which must elapse before the arrival of reinforcements.

It must also be recollected that the active intrigues of France might prevail upon the Porte suddenly to prohibit the passage of the Dardanelles, for the purpose of preventing either naval or military reinforcement, or, if intrigue should prove ineffectual, the fleets of France, triumphant in those seas, might shut the passage by force. If such would be the ineffectual and precarious possession of Malta by Russia, it seems to be for the general interest of all the Powers of Europe, but more especially of Russia, that the Island should not be separated from His Majesty's Dominions, by exchanging it for any other naval station in the Mediterranean. Before I quit this part of the subject, it is necessary that I should observe upon an argument which has been dwelt upon as being of considerable weight in discussing the question of the evacuation of that Island. It has been said that Great Britain having once consented to evacuate Malta on the condition of being secured against the repossession of it by France, His Majesty cannot, at this time, be justified in insisting upon the retention of that place. In this mode of reasoning a variety of answers immediately present themselves. It is a received and undisputed principle that a state of war not only puts an end to the absolute provisions of all existing treaties, but of course, also to all conditional concessions, which, under particular circumstances previous to the existence of war, might have been deemed expedient or admissible. In the Present case it is further to be observed that the unconditional and unrequited evacuation of Malta is now proposed; whereas, at the period alluded to, other stipulations favourable to Great Britain attended the condition annexed to Malta — important Colonies were retained and confirmed to her by treaty as the price of peace, and engagements entered into by France for the independence of different states in Europe. Subsequent to the conclusion of peace great encroachments had been made by the French Government, and some of the very countries which, according to the terms to be now proposed under the 10th separate Article of the Treaty would remain in possession of France, were annexed to that Republic, subsequent to the provisions made with respect to Malta at the Treaty of Amiens. Piedmont has since that period been incorporated into France; Elba has been seized and appropriated to the French Republic; the stipulated independence of Holland has been violated by arbitrary changes of its form of Government, and by the despotic control exercised over the commerce and resources of that country; Switzerland, instead of enjoying the covenanted choice of its own form of Government and the independence of its national existence, has been controlled, degraded, and oppressed. The Kingdom of Naples has been menaced and invaded; and in one word, every condition has been violated, which appeared at that time to afford a semblance of security to Europe. It is obvious, upon these grounds, that His Majesty cannot be called upon, in point of consistency or justice to recur to stipulations which were provided under a state of things in every respect distinct and different from the present, and which have been rendered impracticable by the subsequent conduct of the French Government.

Impressed as His Majesty is with all these powerful considerations, nothing could now induce him to entertain in any shape or on any conditions, the idea of relinquishing this possession, but an extreme desire to meet, if possible, the wishes of the Emperor of Russia, and to show his anxiety to facilitate, as much as possible, any general and solid arrangement for the security and interests of Europe. But in no case, can it be consistent with those very interests (independent of those of Great Britain), even if any circumstances should render the evacuation of Malta admissible, that His Majesty should be left without some secure and adequate station in the Mediterranean.

The result, therefore, of what I am to state to your Excellency by His Majesty's command is, First, That it is impossible for His Majesty to consent to relinquish the possession of Malta in return for such inadequate provisions for the security of the Continent as those arising out of the modifications proposed to be admitted by the 10th Article; and, Secondly, that however favourable might be the conditions obtained for the Continent, he could in no case listen to such an arrangement without obtaining in exchange for Malta some Naval Station in the Mediterranean, which, though in many respects inferior, might afford a competent security against the attack of an enemy, and be in its nature and position effectual to some of the principal naval objects of Great Britain in that quarter.

The condition on which His Majesty would be induced to consent to such an arrangement can only be that of more effectual provisions being concluded for the general security of Europe — and more particularly for that part of it in which the interests of Great Britain are most immediately involved — by the establishment of a firm and solid Barrier for the protection of The United Provinces.

The following conditions, in His Majesty's view of the necessary measures to be pursued, ought to be insisted upon: —

First: The absolute re-establishment of the King of Sardinia in Piedmont, with such a line of defence in the Alps as may be deemed sufficient for the security of his dominions.

Second: The present and permanent independence of Switzerland, secured by the uninfluenced choice of its own form of Government, and by the undisturbed construction of the fortresses necessary for the perfect security of its territory, as stated in the 10th separate Article.

Third: A substantial Barrier to Holland, and further effectual means for the future preservation of that country against the attempts of France, by the interposition and co-operation of some great Military Power interested in its defence. His Majesty, on the fullest consideration, is confirmed in the opinion that, in the present state of Europe, that essential object can be assigned to Prussia alone. But to induce and enable that Power to make effectual exertions for that important purpose, it will be necessary to give to Prussia such a military line of frontier as shall connect advantageously with that of Holland, together with such an acquisition of territory as shall amply supply the means of supporting the necessary charges of maintaining and defending that frontier.

The King entertains an earnest desire to conform his proposals for effecting this purpose, to the views entertained by the Emperor of Russia, in as much as may be consistent with the objects for which alone His Majesty would feel himself justified in admitting any exchange for Malta. His Majesty is disposed, therefore, to state the acquisitions to be assigned to Prussia considerably short of the extent of those originally suggested in the dispatch to Count Woronzow of the 19th of January, as expedient to be given in the event of Prussia becoming a party to the concert.

Although at that time the evacuation of Malta was not in discussion, and certainly not in the contemplation of His Majesty, Your Excellency will observe that the territory proposed as an inducement to Prussia to join in the concert consisted of the whole of the Netherlands (not within the line to be drawn from Antwerp to Maestricht) together with the whole of the Duchies of Luxembourg and Juliers, and the other territories between the Meuse and the Moselle; and further (if no insuperable objection should be stated) the whole of the country acquired by France on the left bank of the Rhine, eastward of the Moselle; but in consideration of that arrangement having been in contemplation, as the result of successful war, and that the present proposals are to be made with a view to prevent that extremity, the King is disposed to assent to the offer of lower terms, even for the evacuation of Malta, which His Majesty cannot, however, but consider as, on his part, giving an advantage; which could not otherwise be obtained by the enemy, except as the consequence of the most successful war. His Majesty, under the circumstances of the present moment, will be contented that the proposal to be made to France shall not exceed what, to His Majesty, appears the least which can afford either sufficient means, or sufficient temptation to induce Prussia to undertake, and effectually provide for, the safety of the United Provinces, and which was stated in the dispatch of the 19th of January, as the least that could afford security.

For this object, therefore, His Majesty would deem it an adequate arrangement if Prussia should be put in possession of the fortress of Luxembourg, together with such proportion of that Duchy as will form an effectual military line from thence to Maestricht, with the fortress necessary to be constructed, and the whole of the country included within that line, the Meuse, the Moselle, and the Rhine; trusting, however, that any necessary increase for the sole and obvious purpose of rendering more effectual the military line of defence will not be objected to by His Imperial Majesty.

His Majesty is the more disposed to flatter himself that the Emperor will be inclined to acquiesce in this proposal as he perceives with pleasure, not only that the principle of securing the Barrier of Holland by the interposition of a Great Power is recognised by His Imperial Majesty; but that after stating in the first instance, the restoration of the former Prussian territories on the left of the Rhine, as a fit offer to be made to Prussia, it is proposed to make in certain cases an addition (the extent of which is not defined) to those territories, and to carry their limits to whatever frontier may ultimately be assigned to France in that quarter. His Majesty is indeed aware that this extension of territory is suggested only in the supposed event of successful war. But the same degree of security in this most essential quarter, which is meant in that case, to be obtained by war, His Majesty thinks himself reasonably and justly entitled to insist upon in the first instance as a condition of negotiation, in return for such an additional sacrifice of strength and security as he is now called upon to make with a view to pacific arrangement.

The King, however, on his part, is not disposed tenaciously to adhere to any precise view of this question which he may have adopted, though it has by no means changed since the original exposition of the subject in the dispatch above alluded to; but His Majesty will be well satisfied to give his consent to any different or more limited arrangement to which the King of Prussia would consent as sufficient to induce and enable him to undertake the protection and co-operate in the future defence of the United Provinces.

The security of Holland, the ancient and important ally of Great Britain, being so far provided for, and the different States of Italy being placed in a situation to repel the hostile attacks of France, the King will be satisfied to place after a time to be limited, the harbour of Malta under the protection of a Russian garrison, due provision being at the same time made for the civil government of the Island, in a way satisfactory to the inhabitants, provided an arrangement can be made by which His Majesty shall be put in possession of the Island of Minorca as the substituted Naval Station for the fleets of Great Britain, although the relative security of that Island against invasion and capture, can bear no comparison with that of Malta. But His Majesty considering the advantages to Europe of the improved stipulations under which he engages to make such exchange, is satisfied in this, as in other instances, to relinquish considerations peculiar to himself, for the solid advantages to be procured for his allies; and for the better and more certain establishment of general and permanent tranquillity. With a view to compensate Spain for the transfer of Minorca His Majesty would be ready to concur in any reasonable arrangement which might be made in Italy for the benefit of the King of Etruria, and he trusts that, by the interposition of His Impl. Majesty the Court of Spain might without much difficulty be reconciled to this proposal. The period to be limited at the expiration of which this arrangement can take place, must not be less than three years; in order to afford His Majesty a reasonable time for completing such works as may be necessary for the defence of Minorca; and also to afford an opportunity of making a considerable progress in the essential work of strengthening the Barriers of Holland, Germany and Switzerland.

His Majesty thinks it necessary also expressly to declare, that, in agreeing to make this last sacrifice for the purpose of obtaining security for the Continent by negotiation rather than war, he can consider this offer as binding only in the event of a pacific arrangement, and that if the negotiation should not take place, or should not prove successful, it shall at no future time be made a claim, that this important possession shall again become matter of negotiation. Although the King has every reason to be convinced, that this disposition on his part to concur in the views of His Imperial Majesty, will be met in every respect with a corresponding sentiment on the part of the Emperor of Russia, — His Majesty has nevertheless especially commanded me to repeat to Your Excellency in this confidential dispatch, his firm determination not to concur in any proposal that can countenance the slightest expectation of a revision of the Maritime Code, — and to express His Majesty's confident hope, that His Imperial Majesty will not persevere in the idea of a measure, which however contrary to the intention of His Imperial Majesty, will nevertheless bear the appearance of a disposition unfavourable to the rights and interests of Great Britain, and which can lead to no practical result.

[*Endorsed.*]

DRAFT
To LORD G.L. GOWER,
June 7th, 1805.
No.16.
By the Messenger Elsworth.

APPENDIX B

Further Instructions To Lord G. Leveson-Gower

[*Foreign Office. Russia.* 58.]

DOWNING STREET, *July* 1805.

My Lord, — The information received by a courier just arrived from Berlin is in some respects so decisive, and in every point of view so important, that I lose no time in addressing some observations to Your Excellency on the present state of affairs, and on the course which it may in consequence become expedient to adopt in conjunction with Russia. At the same time that His Majesty's Government learned that the arrogant usurpation by Buonaparte of the obvious objects of the proposed negotiation, had determined the Emperor of Russia to put an end to the mission of Monsr. Novossilzoff, and that His Imperial Majesty had ordered the French passports to be returned into the hands of the Prussian Minister, information was also received that Prussia is decidedly averse to any exertion for its own independence, or for the deliverance of Europe, and that Austria, though more directly threatened, and more immediately in danger, has not manifested any disposition to accede to the proposed concert, or to enter into any more active alliance with Great Britain and Russia than that which she had contracted with the latter Power in the defensive Treaty concluded in November 1804.

This disposition of the two powers renders the stipulated force of 400,000 unattainable, and the general deliverance of Europe at the present period impracticable. The object and the means proposed by the concert concluded between His Majesty and the Emperor of Russia being thus, for the time at least frustrated, it becomes a subject of important deliberation to determine how far it may be practicable for Great Britain and Russia, without the assistance of Prussia or Austria, to check the progress of France in any particular quarter, or to afford security against her meditated attacks to any of those powers, which, having manifested a just sense of the conduct and views of the French Government, are thereby become the more immediate and particular objects of its enmity. Sweden and Naples are the States which obviously come under the above description, they are also respectively more or less open to the aggressions of France; Naples indeed is not merely threatened but already in part occupied by the troops of the French Republic. On the other hand also the line of Prussian guarantee has been so uniformly contracted as the councils of French encroachment have been extended, that no reasonable expectation of security for Swedish Pomerania can be founded on the professed protection of the North of Germany by Prussia.

In considering therefore the expediency and probable effect of the employment of Russian troops, unsupported by Austria and Prussia, the points which first present themselves as important and as, upon the whole, most likely to be occupied with security and effect, are 1st the Kingdom of Naples and 2nd the tract of country in the North of Germany lying between the Elbe and the Baltic. The importance of security to those points, if attainable, will be immediately obvious to Your Excellency. The occupation of the Kingdom of Naples (especially if a sufficient army should be collected to clear it of St. Cyr's army, and to establish the line of defence in the Province of Abruzzo) must be productive of considerable advantage to the common cause. A force so stationed would in the first place afford the most effectual check to any projects which Buonaparte may entertain on the side of Greece; the deliverance of Naples would manifest to the Ottoman Porte, and to all the powers of the second order, that a steady adherence to the good cause will be followed by powerful exertions and efficient measures of protection and defence on the part of Great Britain and Russia. The entire security of the Kingdom of Naples by the vigorous defence of an extensive frontier, might also (it is to be hoped) operate as an encouragement to Austria, to act with energy on the side of Venice and the Tyrol for the recovery of a security against France in that quarter, of which she has been entirely deprived by the stipulations of the Treaty of Lunéville. Should Austria, by the example of the Russian operations in Naples, be brought into action, not only would the South of Italy at least to the Arno, be immediately delivered, but the great objects of the concert would thereby at once be revived, and the estimated number of 400,000 men might be collected and employed for the general deliverance of Europe. The occupation of the district between the Elbe and the Baltic would not indeed hold out so early or such extensive prospects of any general influence on the course of events. The occupation however of that district would, in the first instance, have the effect of checking the progress of French ambition, and of counteracting any secret negociation which may be on foot for the occupation and partition of those countries. Further advantages might by contingent events be derived from such a position, if securely maintained, a force might ultimately be collected from Hanover, Denmark, and Sweden, which, reinforced by a powerful army of Russians, and assisted by demonstrations and co-operation on the side of Flushing, might, if the Dutch nation should manifest a disposition to throw off the yoke of slavery with which they are oppressed, effect the deliverance of the United Provinces especially if the collection of such a force and the temptation of the acquisitions to be offered to Prussia should at length induce that Government to consult its true interest and adopt a firm, wise, and dignified line of policy.

Such being the immediate and possible advantages to be derived from the secure occupation of the two points in question, there arise three other heads of consideration necessary to be discussed before those measures can be determined.

1st. Upon what grounds the occupation of those countries is to be assumed.

2nd. How great a force, and at what expense, it will necessarily be employed, how long and with what expectation of a favourable result this defensive system can be continued; and lastly, how far it has been ascertained that either or both the lines of frontier above alluded to, are capable of such a defence as may defy the undivided exertions of the French power.

Upon the first head perhaps no great difficulty may exist: there is little doubt that with respect to Swedish Pomerania Mecklenburgh, Lubeck, &c., the respective Sovereigns of those districts would readily invite or receive the security offered by Great Britain and Russia. At Naples there probably exists an equal disposition to invite the assistance of a united British and Russian army, if such a force should present itself within reach of affording immediate protection to those Kingdoms; indeed the recent threat of Buonaparte that he would consider Naples as in a state of war with France if his title of King of Italy should not be acknowledged on a given day, would be sufficient, in any consequence of that threat, to justify the occupation of Naples by the allies of his Sicilian Majesty. If the threat should be followed by war, the assistance will of course be invited and accepted, if it be followed by a compelled acknowledgment of a title, which implies in terms the annihilation of the Sicilian Monarchy, the King of Naples can no longer be considered in a situation to give the consent or refusal of an independent Sovereign, and his deliverance may be lawfully undertaken without requiring his assent.

With respect to the second consideration, it has undoubtedly been a question frequently agitated, whether an absolute defensive in war were admissible in principle; or possible in practice, with a general conclusion against the adoption of such a state of war; in the present instance, however, it is worthy of consideration how far such a system may operate to the effectual injury of the particular enemy against whom it shall be employed. There is every reason to expect that the command of the sea and the resources of the countries within the reach of the two proposed points of operation, would enable the Allies to supply their armies at a much cheaper rate, and in greater abundance, than could the enemy acting against those lines of frontier, and drawing his supplies from the country immediately behind him. The consideration of relative numbers may also make an important difference in the expense of the warfare, if, from the nature of the country, a comparatively small army should be found sufficient to occupy the exertions of a very considerable force of the enemy. A long and unsuccessful series of efforts would tend, more than any thing, to lower the military estimation of Buonaparte, and thereby to overturn his usurped dominion. This however must depend upon the answer to the second head of consideration, which I have not materials to ascertain, and which must depend upon the numbers proposed to be employed. This also depends upon the solution of the question in the 3rd and last head: "How far it has been ascertained that either or both of the lines of frontier alluded to, are capable of such a defence as may defy the undivided exertions of the French power." This question requires an earnest and attentive consideration. It is in all cases difficult to decide upon the expediency and practicability of military operations, without having first received very detailed information from intelligent officers well acquainted with the local circumstances and military resources of the countries in which a campaign is to be conducted. This difficulty must be felt even on an enlarged scale of active operations, where much may be trusted to contingent circumstances, and to the skilful conduct of combined and active military movements. But, in the occupation of a limited frontier, upon a system merely defensive, it is of indispensable necessity to be minutely informed of the grounds upon which a rational expectation of success, little short of absolute security, may be rested. Impressed with this view of the subject, His Majesty's Ministers are desirous of learning from the Russian Government the nature of the information it has received with respect to the most effectual mode of employing its forces without any assistance from the other great military Powers of the Continent, either on the points of which I have been treating, or in any other quarter which may have occurred to the Cabinet of St. Petersburgh.

An extensive diversion of the French force to operations on the Continent, even independent of the great and decisive results which are in contemplation of the concert concluded between His Majesty and the Emperor of Russia, must evidently be an object of interest and advantage to this country; but His Majesty has too just a feeling of the nature and extent of the cordial union which so happily subsists between His Majesty and the Emperor of Russia to be desirous of such a diversion, at the hazard of any important failure which might either be injurious to the interests and influence of Russia, or which might in any degree affect the high military reputation of that Empire. It is therefore the wish of His Majesty's Government to learn from the details collected by Russian officers how far the defence of the frontiers of the Kingdom of Naples or of any given line in the north of Germany could be undertaken with a prospect of baffling the utmost efforts of France by the opposition which Russia, unsupported by Prussian or Austrian co-operation, could present in both or either of those quarters respectively.

The desire expressed by the Russian Court of the re-establishment of peace between this country and Spain induces me to mention to Your Excellency the possibility of another course of operations, more distant indeed in prospect, and certainly less likely to be adopted with effect, than that which I have already opened.

The Kingdom of Portugal is at this moment in an uneasy and precarious state of purchased neutrality, and there is great reason to apprehend that both the military and pecuniary resources of that country are in a worse state than the Government is willing to avow. I have hitherto in vain represented to the Portuguese Minister the necessity for procuring from his Court an accurate statement of the means which it possesses, and of the assistance it would require to enable Portugal to hold the language of independence, and, at the same time, to provide such means of defence as would secure that character to the country.

The Chevalier de Souza has indeed stated in conversation that 15,000 auxiliary troops for a twelvemonth would give such protection to the country, and so much energy to the Government, that they would be enabled to place the native force on such a footing as should render it after that period sufficient for its own defence. I doubt, however, whether any energy could be created in the Portuguese Government unless the Prince Regent could be induced to commit the administration of affairs to different Ministers, who should not either from the operation of their fears or their prejudices appear so entirely devoted to France. The recall of Messrs. de Souza and d'Ameida, or the appointment of any other persons of energy and decision of character, might possibly restore Portugal to such a state of exertion as might place that country out of the reach of French aggression. That point being established, it might be worth consideration whether the present disposition of the Spanish nation, of a great proportion of its ancient nobility, and of the Prince of Asturias, assisted by Portugal and the auxiliary forces employed in that country, might not at once deliver the King of Spain from the control of France and the domineering influence of the Prince of Peace, and once again firmly establish the barrier of the Pyrenees between Spain and France. I am aware that such an event might more reasonably be expected as the consequence of a general confederacy of the great military

Powers of the Continent, than as the partial operation of a more limited concert, but in suggesting even less probable subjects of discussion, I am fulfilling the disposition of His Majesty's Government to comply with the desire of the Russian Cabinet that the means of acting against France without the assistance of Austria and Prussia should be amply discussed and fully considered.

[*Endorsed.*]

DRAFT
To LORD G.L. GOWER,
July, 1805.

APPENDIX C

The Trafalgar Signal, 1816

Signal No. I. 7. Cut through the Enemy's Line in the Order of Sailing in Two Columns

The Admiral will make known what number of ships from the Van Ship of the enemy the Weather Division is to break through the enemy's line, and the same from the rear at which the Lee Division is to break through their line.

To execute this signal the fleet is to form in the Order of Sailing in two columns, should it not be so formed already; the leader of each column steering down for the position pointed out, where he is to cut through the enemy's line.

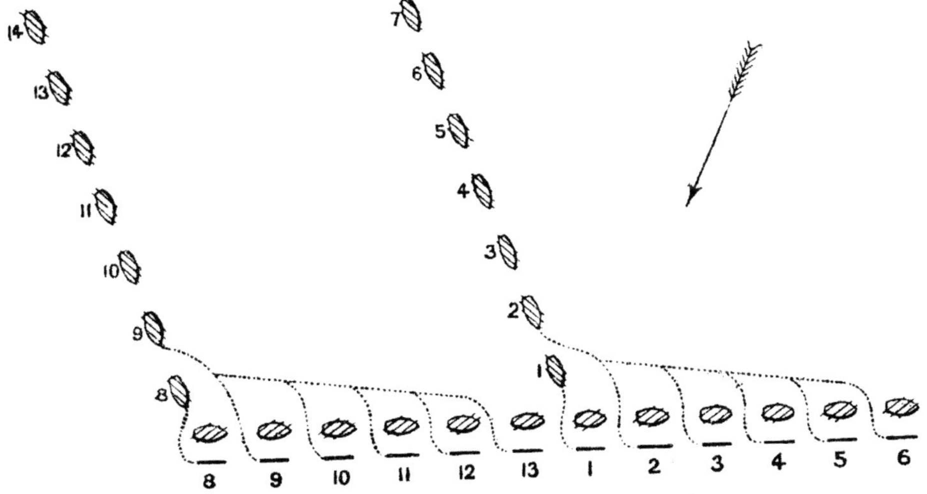

Diagram Of The Trafalgar Signal
From the *Signal Book* of 1816

If the Admiral wishes any particular conduct to be pursued by the leader of the Division in which he happens not to be, after the line is broken, he will of course point it out. If he does not, it is to be considered that the conduct of the Lee Division, after breaking the line, is left to its commander.

In performing this evolution, the second astern of the leader is to pass through the line astern of the ship next ahead of where her leader broke through, and so on in succession, breaking through all parts of the enemy's line ahead of their leaders, as described in the Plate.

By this arrangement no ship will have to pass the whole of the enemy's line. If, however, in consequence of any circumstance, the rear ships should not be able to cut through in their assigned places, the captains of these ships, as well as the ships which are deprived of opponents in the enemy's line by this mode of attack, are to act to the best of their judgment for the destruction of the enemy, unless a disposition to the contrary has been previously made.

It will also be seen that by breaking the line in this order the enemy's van ships will not be able to assist either the Centre or the Rear without tacking or wearing for that purpose.

NOTE. Owing to the diagram in the plate being apparently incomplete, the significance of the signal and its instruction is somewhat obscured. The diagram shows an attack end-on in two divisions upon an equal number of ships, all of which are engaged. But the first and last paragraphs of the instructions make it clear that a concentration on the rear and centre of a superior fleet is intended as at Trafalgar, and we must assume that the unengaged van of the enemy is not shown. The intention then becomes clear. It is a device to reduce the risk which was so widely recognised in Nelson's attack. So far as the weather column is concerned, the exposure of the leading ship to a dangerous concentration remains. But in the lee column it is avoided. Instead of leading for the van ships of the section which she is to cut off, she leads for the rearmost, and is thus less exposed to a concentrated fire. The rest of her division then engage in succession and in reverse order till the assigned interval is reached.

Another advantage of this modification of the attack is that every enemy's ship is doubled on by the British ships as they pass to their proper stations. Thus in the lee line No. 8 fires her starboard guns on the ship which No. 9 is engaging to leeward, and reserves her larboard guns to rake her proper opponent as she passes through the line under her stern. Similarly the British No. 10 would double on the two ships engaged by Nos. 8 and 9 in succession, and so on. If the leading ship in each division survived the first shock, as they did at Trafalgar, the attack is obviously very formidable, but in a commanding breeze it could easily be parried or avoided by the irregular French methods.

Its interest, however, remains, viz., that being clearly founded on Nelson's Memorandum, it represents an end-on attack in line-ahead, and seeks by an ingenious modification to minimise its obvious tactical defects.

APPENDIX D

Lord Nelson's Memorandum

[*Holograph draft in Nelson's hand, unsigned; amended in that of his chaplain, Dr. Scott. Two sheets* (*eight pages 4to*), *British Museum*][1]

Mem°.[2]

Memorandum

Victory, off Cadiz, 9th Oct. 1805.[2]

Thinking it almost impossible to bring a fleet of forty sail of the line into line of battle in variable winds thick weather and other circumstances which must occur, without such a loss of time that the opportunity would probably be lost of bringing the enemy to battle in such a manner as to make the business decisive —

I have therefore made up my mind to keep the fleet in that position of sailing (with the exception of the first and second in command) that the order of sailing is to be the order of battle, placing the fleet in two lines of sixteen ships each with an advanced squadron of eight of the fastest sailing two-decked ships *which*[2] will always make if wanted a line of twenty-four sail, on whichever line the commander-in-chief may direct.

The second in command will[3] after my intentions are made known to him have the entire direction of his line to make the attack upon the enemy and to follow up the blow until they are captured or destroyed.

If the enemy's fleet should be seen to windward in line of battle, and that the two lines[4] and the advanced squadron can fetch them[5] they will probably be so extended that their van could not succour their rear.

I should therefore probably make the second in command's[6] signal, to lead through about the twelfth ship from the rear (or wherever he[6] could fetch, if not able to get as far advanced). My line would lead through about their centre and the advanced squadron to cut two three or four ships ahead of their centre so far as to ensure getting at their commander-in-chief on whom every effort must be made to capture [him].[7]

The whole impression of the British fleet[8] must be to overpower from two to three ships ahead of their commander-in-chief supposed to be in the centre to the rear of their fleet. I will suppose[9] twenty sail of the enemy's[10] line to be untouched, it must be some time before they could perform a manœuvre to bring their force compact to attack any part of the British fleet engaged or to succour their own ships, which indeed would be impossible, without mixing with the ships engaged.[11] Something must be left to chance;

nothing is sure in a sea fight beyond all others. Shot will carry away the masts and yards of friends as well as foes but I look with confidence to a victory before the van of the enemy could succour their rear[12] and then that the British fleet would most of them be ready to receive their twenty-sail of the line, or to pursue them, should they endeavour to make off.

If the van of the enemy tacks the captured ships must run to leeward of the British fleet, if the enemy wears the British must place themselves between the enemy and the captured and disabled British ships and should the enemy close I have no fears as to the result.

The second in command will in all possible things direct the movements of his line by keeping them as compact as the nature of the circumstances will admit. Captains are to look to their particular line as their rallying point. But in case signals can neither be seen or perfectly understood no captain can do very wrong if he places his ship alongside that of an enemy.

[13] Of the intended attack from to windward. The enemy in the line of battle ready to attack.

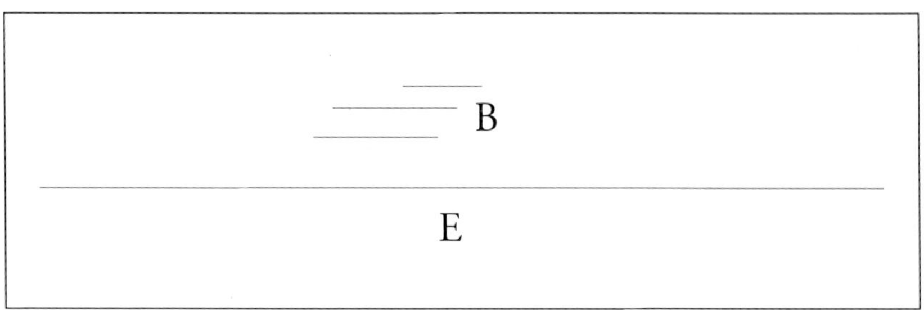

The divisions of the British fleet will be brought nearly within gunshot of the enemy's centre. The signal will most probably then[14] be made for the lee line to bear up together to set all their sails even steering-sails[15] in order to get as quickly as possible to the enemy's line and to cut through, beginning from the 12 ship from the enemy's rear. Some ships may not get through their exact place but they will always be at hand to assist their friends and if any are thrown round the rear of the enemy they will effectually complete the business of twelve sail of the enemy.

Should the enemy wear together or bear up and sail large still the twelve ships composing in the first position the enemy's rear are to be *the* [16] object of attack of the lee line, unless otherwise directed from the commander-in-chief which is scarcely to be expected as the entire management of the lee line after the intentions of the commander-in-chief is [17] signified is intended to be left to the judgment of the admiral commanding that line.

The remainder of the enemy's fleet 34 sail are to be left to the management of the commander-in-chief, who will endeavour to take care that the movements of the second in command are as little interrupted as possible.[18]

APPENDIX E

Lists And Plans Showing The Manner Of Engaging At Trafalgar

1. A list attached to Collingwood's official despatch. Nicolas, vii. 215.

2. *The Britannia list,* — From the Journal of Lieutenant John Barclay of that ship. *Great Sea fights* (N.R.S.), ii. 215.

3. *The "Naval Chronicle" Plan.* — Published in the *Naval Chronicle*, December 31, 1805 (vol. xiv. p. 495), and reproduced in Mr. Newbolt's *Year of Trafalgar*, p. 98. This was the earliest plan printed. It represents three stages of the approach as in the official French plan, namely, the first "At daylight," and the second "At 9 o'clock," showing the British fleet in process of forming sailing order as it bore up; and the third "At 12 o'clock at noon," showing the actual moment of contact with the columns almost vertical to the enemy's line, but slightly converging. In the accompanying note we are told it was engraved from a drawing furnished "by a gentleman who copied it from the original in the possession of the Admiralty." . . . It further states that "The situation, as here represented, has been vouched to be correct by Admiral Villeneuve in the original sent to the Admiralty." Several errors, and particularly in the order of the allied ships, suggest that the work was hurriedly and carelessly done by the anonymous gentleman.

4. *The Craig Plan.* — This little-known plan is a hand-coloured copperplate engraving from the design of the famous William Marshall Craig, drawing-master to the Princess Charlotte, and miniature painter to the Duke of York (*Dictionary of National Biography*), who was the most fashionable designer of his time. It was published on January 9, 1806, by Edward Orme, "Printseller to the King," a well-known naval and military publisher. It contains the noon position only; that is, the actual attack, and bears the inscription: "Position of the combined forces of France and Spain at the commencement of the action," &c. At the foot is this note, "The above plan has been certified as to its correctness by the Flag-officers of the *Euryalus* and Admiral Villeneuve." From this it would appear that it was taken from the same original as the *Naval Chronicle* plan, though it is more carefully done. That this was its origin is certain, for at the top half of the plate is a picture purporting to represent Nelson explaining his plan of attack to his officers, and on the table before him is a plan showing the attack as it was delivered, with all three positions as in the *Naval Chronicle*. The inference, then, from what we learn from these two sources, is that shortly after the battle, while Collingwood and Villeneuve were on board the *Euryalus* with their staffs, a plan was prepared in concert between them, and that it was forwarded to the Admiralty in the *Euryalus* when she went home with despatches and Villeneuve. It must be doubted, however, whether the plan was regarded as authentic for anything but the disposition of the Combined Fleet, which, indeed, is all the inscription claims. Clarke and M'Arthur state, on what they regarded as very

high authority, that "the British fleet was certainly not in the position stated in the plan sent to the Admiralty, and signed Magendie, captain of the Bucentaure." (*Life of Nelson*, vol. ii., *Continuation*, p. 167.) Clearly, then, "the plan sent to the Admiralty" must have been the original of that signed by Magendie, which is given by Colonel Desbrière in his *Trafalgar*, *Appendix*, p. 186. By "Flag-officers of the *Euryalus*," therefore, the Craig print may mean not Collingwood and his staff but the French "flag-officers" only; but as Villeneuve is specially mentioned as the French authority, it is equally likely that the British "flag-officers" are meant.

In any case it must have been considered that the delineation of the British fleet was not quite correct in detail. Nothing seriously wrong is suggested. Clarke and M'Arthur imply only that Magendie's plan made the lines too regular, not that the general disposition or manner of approach was wrong. It is evident, then, that it was the order and position of the British ships which left room for improvement and not the general line of the attack. This is placed beyond doubt by comparing the plans of Craig and the *Naval Chronicle*. It will be seen that in Craig's design a number of alterations had been made in the British fleet, but the general plan of attack, in two lines ahead almost vertical, remains the same in both. The alterations given to Craig were in details of the order and positions of individual units only. *Britannia*, for instance, instead of being fourth in Nelson's line, as she is in the *Naval Chronicle* and Magendie's plan, is shown hauled out to windward, with the seventh ship, *Agamemnon*, passing her, approximately as in the Harbin plan (*Frontispiece*). Moreover, the *Neptune* and *Leviathan*, instead of being in accurate line (as Clarke and M'Arthur complained), are represented also hauling out to windward as though to pass ahead of the *Victory* in accordance with the signals that had been made, certainly to the *Leviathan*, and probably to the *Neptune* as her next ahead.

On the whole, then, from the above hints and the standing of the designer and publisher, we may take it that the Craig engraving is the most authentic plan we have. True, it does not show the line of bearing in the lee division, but this was only natural, since Collingwood did not regard it as of sufficient importance for mention in his dispatch, and neither Villeneuve nor Magendie could have seen it.

5. *The Magendie Plan*. — From Colonel Desbrière's version of the original in the *Archives de la Marine* (Paris). It may be doubted if this is identical with the plan sent to the Admiralty, for the British lines are not shown accurately formed as Clarke and M'Arthur imply they were originally. It is possible that Magendie altered this on the representations of British officers. This appears to have been the foundation of Prigny's final plan, and also of the one Dumanoir exhibited at his court-martial, both of which are given by Desbrière.

6. *The Harbin Plan* (*Frontispiece*). — This hitherto unpublished plan is in MS., coloured. It is said to have belonged to a petty officer called Harbin, who was present at the battle, and to have been handed down in his family, till it recently came into the author's possession. Its value is that it is clearly independent, and not founded on any other known plan, and especially that it alone shows Collingwood's line of bearing, and shows it exactly as would be expected from the signals that were made. For Nelson's line it is of no value, except for the position of *Britannia*, since it does not give the irregularity which Nelson's sudden changes of intention created in his van.

7. *The Nicolas Plan.* — Published by him in the *Nelson's Despatches* (vol. vii. p. 301), 1846, without any indication of its origin. This also is clearly not based on the Admiralty plan, for Gravina's squadron is shown prolonging the rear, and not passing up to leeward, as in Magendie's; while in the British fleet *Britannia* is fourth in Nelson's line, and *Dreadnought* is leading Collingwood's second division. Moreover, it shows the irregularity in Nelson's van, but not quite in the same way as the Craig plan.

In endeavouring to prove that Nelson's attack was not practically vertical, some writers would discard the testimony of the existing plans. A letter of Captain Moorsom's is quoted, in which he says: "I have seen several plans of the action, but none to answer my ideas of it. Indeed, scarce any plans can be given. It was irregular, and the ships got down as fast as they could and into any space when they found the enemy, without attending to their place in the line." On this three remarks arise. 1. The letter was written from Spithead on December 4th, before the Craig plan was published. 2. He is clearly referring not to the general plan of attack, but to the positions of individual units in action. 3. In a previous letter from Gibraltar, November 1st, he himself gave a rough diagram showing the British fleet "going down in two columns pointing towards the centre," and only slightly inclined from the perpendicular. (See *Great Sea Fights*, ii. p. 242, where the diagram is omitted. The original is in the possession of Lady Longmore.)

APPENDIX F

Schedule Of Signals Made At Trafalgar

For the tactics of any battle the primary authority must always be the signals actually recorded. An attempt, therefore, has been made below to tabulate the whole of the signals entered in the logs and journals of the ships, with their signification, number, ship by whom made, and ship or ships to whom made. To each is appended the particular log or logs in which it is found, with the time of making as recorded by the different ships.

With regard to these "logs," it should be remembered that the official record of a ship's movements and of the events that transpire on board is the *log book*. At the time of Trafalgar the ship's *log book* was kept by the master, who was the navigating officer. It is therefore known as the *master's log*. The master, in common with the other officers, was also required to keep "an exact and perfect journal." When the ship was paid off he had to deliver a copy of the *log* and of the *journal* to the Navy Office. As a rule the *masters' journals* were simply copies of the log, made solely to comply with the regulations. In certain cases, of which the *Téméraire* is the most striking instance, the *log* contains many important signals omitted from the *journal*. Both have been denoted by the letter "M."

The captain and lieutenants were also bound to keep journals, and deliver signed copies at stated intervals. The *lieutenants' journals* have not as a rule been preserved. The *captains' journals*, which, together with the logs, are now in the Public Record Office, are denoted by the letter "C." The letter "N," which will be found in two cases, signifies that the entry is taken from logs given by Nicolas in his *Nelson's Despatches* (vol. vii.), the originals of which have not been found in the Record Office. The schedule only extends to mid-day, when the action became general.

Signals Extracted From The Logs And Journals For 21st October 1805

Signal		By Whom Made	To Whom	Authority		Remarks
Signification in Signal Book	Number			Log	Time Logged	
Form the order of sailing in two columns	72	Victory	General	Belleisle M & C	5:40	
				Bellerophon C	?	
				Ajax M	6:00	
				Orion C	6:00	
				Defiance	6:00	
				Mars M & C	6:09	

Signal		By Whom Made	To Whom	Authority		Remarks
Signification in Signal Book	Number			Log	Time Logged	
When lying-to, or sailing by the wind, to bear up and sail large on the course steered by the Admiral or that pointed out by signal	76 E.N.E. flags	Victory	General	Belleisle M & C Bellerophon C Ajax M & C Mars M & C Orion M & C Defiance M	6:00 ? 6:10 6:14 6:15 6:15	
Prepare for battle.	13	Victory	General	Belleisle C Bellerophon C Ajax C Defiance M & C Conqueror M Naiad M Neptune M Euryalus M	6:00 6:20 6:20 6:30 6:35 6:40 7:00 7:00	
When lying-to, or sailing by the wind, to bear up and sail large on the course... pointed out by signal.	76 E. flags	Victory	General	Bellerophon C Ajax C Achille M [1] Naiad M [1] Defence M & C [1] Euryalus M	6:42 6:45 6:50 6:50 7:00 7:00	[1] Do not mention compass flags
The ships may take such stations as are most convenient at the time without regard to any established order of sailing.	265	Victory	Prince Dreadnought	Téméraire M Téméraire M	7:23 7:25	
For captain to come on board Flagship.	—	Victory	Euryalus Sirius Sirius Phœbe Naiad Naiad	Téméraire M Euryalus Sirius N Téméraire M Téméraire M Téméraire M Naiad M	7:40 8:00 7:45 7:46 7:46 7:46 7:50	
The ships may take such stations as are more convinient at the time, &c.	265	Victory	Britannia Prince Dreadnought	Belleisle M Belleisle M Belleisle M	8:00 8:00 8:00	
When lying to, &c., to bear up and sail large on the course steered by the Admiral...	76	Victory	Prince [2]	Téméraire M Naiad M	8:33 8:40	[2] "Hauled to port to give room for the line to form. Answered signal to bear up."—Prince M

Signal		By Whom Made	To Whom	Authority		Remarks
Signification in Signal Book	Number			Log	Time Logged	
For the ships of the Fleet to be kept on the larboard line of bearing from each other though on the starboard tack.	50	Royal Sovereign	Larboard Division [3]	Defence M & C Agamemnon M	8:45 ?	[3] Agamemnon notes it as a "General" signal.
Form the larboard line of bearing, steering the course indicated. *The ships to bear from each other on the point of the compass on which they would sail, keeping a point from the wind if formed in a line ahead on the larboard tack.*	42 [4]	Royal Sovereign	Larboard Division	Defence M & C Téméraire M	8:46 8:47	[4] This signal annulled the previous one, which was probably hoisted in error.
Make more sail. The leading ship first, if in the line of battle or order of sailing.	88	Royal Sovereign	larboard Division	Belleisle M & C Defence M & C Téméraire M Revenge M	8:45 8:46 8:47 9:00	
Alter the course (? together) one point to port.	82 (?) [5]	Admiral	General	Belleisle M & C	9:00	[5] This appears to be an error. No other ship mentions such a signal, nor does any ship's log record such an alteration of course.
Interchange places in the line of order of sailing. *The ships which are to change will have their signals shown at the same time.*	46 with Bellisle's & Tonnant's pennants	Royal Sovereign	Belleisle Tonnant	Bellisle M & C Téméraire M	9:20 9:23	
Make more sail.	88	Royal Sovereign	Belleisle	Belleisle M & C Téméraire M	9:20 9:35	
A particular ship, division, or squadron to take a station bearing from the Admiral as pointed out by compass signal.	267 with S.W. flags	Royal Sovereign	Belleisle	Belleisle M & C Téméraire M	9:30 9:35	

Signal		By Whom Made	To Whom	Authority		Remarks
Signification in Signal Book	Number			Log	Time Logged	
Take a station astern of the ship whose distinguishing signal will be shown after this signal has been aswered. *The ships are to act as circumstances may require to make room for the ship to take the station pointed out for her.*	269 with Téméraire's pennants	Victory	Leviathan	Téméraire M	9:36	
A particular ship…is to take a station bearing from the Admiral as pointed out by compass signal. (This is the signification as amended in the "Appendix" of 1804)	267 [6] ?	Royal Sovereign	Revenge	Téméraire M	9:40	[6] Also recorded by Captain Moorsom of the Revenge (see *Logs of Great Sea Fights*, ii. p. 244). In neither place is a compass signal mentioned.
Make more sail.	88	Royal Sovereign	Revenge	Téméraire M Revenge C	9:40 ?	
Take a station astern of the ship whose distinguishing signal will be shown…	269 with Royal Sovereign's pennants	Victory	Mars	Téméraire M	9:41	
Alter the course *together* one point to starboard… ; the ships preserving their relative bearing from each other.	81	Royal Sovereign	Belleisle Achille	Belleisle M & C Téméraire M	9:40 9:42	
Lead the Fleet or a particular column pointed out by signal. *If the line of battle be formed, or forming when this signal is made, the ship to which it is addressed is to be considered as the leading ship of the five.*	97 [7] with larboard divisional flag	Victory	Mars	Téméraire M Mars M (Log) Conqueror	9:58 10:05 10:10	[7] Not answered. Mars (C) also enters it, but at 9:05, which, presumably, is an error for 10:05.
Prepare for battle.	13	Victory	General	Minotaur M Pickle M	10:00	

Signal		By Whom Made	To Whom	Authority		Remarks
Signification in Signal Book	Number			Log	Time Logged	
Come to the wind together on the larboard tack. *This signal also implies wearing, if necessary, from the starboard to the larboard tack.*	102 [8]	Defence	Phœbe	Defence M & C	10:40	[8] Probably a mistake for 107, 108, or 109, "To close," &c.
Make more sail.	88	Defence	Orion	Defence M & C	10:41	
Lead the Fleet, or a particular column…	97	Victory	Mars	Mars M (Journal)[9]	10:45	[9] "Answered signal and crowded on stunsails." (Similar signals are recorded in the Log and Journal of Orion as having been addressed to Mars and Leviathan respectively at 12:15, but it is obviously impossible for such a signal to have been made at the moment when the heads of the columns were just engaging.)
Make all sail possible with safety to the masts. (*Appendix*)	307	Victory	Defence	Téméraire M	11:02	
Make all sail possible with safety to the masts. (*Appendix*)	307	Victory	Africa	Africa M Naiad M Orion M Orion C Téméraire M	10:53 11:05 11:15 11:25 11:25	
Alter course *together* one point to port, &c.	82	Defence	Orion	Orion M & C	11:32	
Make more sail.	88	Royal Sovereign	General	Mars M Bellerophon	11:40 ? [10]	[10] By Bellerophon this was after No. 63, "Prepare to anchor." She also enters it as "80" by error.
I intend to push or go through the end of the enemy's line to prevent them from getting into Cadiz.	Telegraph message [11]	Victory	? Royal Sovereign	Euryalus M	11:40	[11] See Nicolas' *Nelson's Despatches*, vol. vii. pp. 148, 186.
Keep in close order.	56	Royal Sovereign	Belleisle	Belleisle M & C	11:50	
Make all sail possible with safety to the masts.	307	Victory	General	Téméraire M	11:55	

Signal		By Whom Made	To Whom	Authority		Remarks
Signification in Signal Book	Number			Log	Time Logged	
England expects that every man wil do his duty.	Telegraph message	Victory	General	Orion C	11:25	
				Naiad M	11:35	
				Neptune M	11:40	
				Defence M & C	11:48	
				Euryalus	11:56	
				Defiance M & C	12:00	
				Revenge M	12:10	
Prepare to anchor after the close of day.	8 Preparative with 63	Victory	General	Africa C	11:32	[12] Log quotes "62" in error.
				Neptune M	11:46	
				Bellerophon M	12:00	
				Naiad M	12:00	
				Orion M & C	12:00	
				Euryalus M	12:00	
				Dreadnought M	12:00	
				Ajax M	12:05	
				Téméraire M	12:10	
				Conqueror M [12]	12:10	
				Defiance M	12:15	
Take a station astern of the ship whose distinguishing signal will be shown…	269 Victory's pennants	Victory	Téméraire M	Neptune	11:50	
				Téméraire M L	12:00	
				Conqueror M	12:15	
Engage the enemy more closely.	16	Victory	Africa	Africa M	12:00	
				Conqueror M	12:25	
Engage the enemy more closely.	16	Victory	General	Belleisle C	11:55	
				Neptune N	11:56	
				Téméraire M	12:10	
				Ajax C	12:10	
				Bellerophon C	12:13	
				Orion M & C	12:15	
				Achille M	12:15	
				Africa M	12:15	
				Ajax M	12:18	
				Naiad M	12:20	
				Euryalus M	12:20	
				Conqueror M	12:30	
Make all sail possible with safety to the masts.	307	Victory	Africa	Conqueror M	12:25	
				Téméraire M	12:26	
				Achille M	12:30	
				Naiad M	12:30	

CHAPTER 1

1. For the recent French recognition of Napoleon's responsibility for the renewal of the war, see P. Coquelle, *Napoleon and England*, translated by G.D. Knox. 1904.
2. Fortescue, *County Lieutenants and the Army*, p. 10.
3. Colonel Henderson, when head of the Staff College, used to lay down the rule that "the first duty of the British army was to assist the navy in getting command of the sea." And in this case the assistance wag real and enduring.
4. J. Holland Rose, *Select Despatches relating to the Third Coalition* (Royal Historical Society, 1904), p. ix.
5. Warren to Harrowby, July 24, 1804: Rose, *Select Despatches relating to the Third Coalition* (Royal Historical Society, 3rd Series), vol. vii. p. 25.
6. *Ibid.*, p. 32, August 14.
7. Harrowby to Gower, October 10: Rose, *Third Coalition*, p. 45.
8. Nelson to Marsden, October 10, 1804: Nicolas, vi. 227. See also Earl Camden to Nelson, August 29 (*Ibid.*, p. 228*n*), informing him that the threat of invasion will prevent their sending an expedition to the Mediterranean before winter, and that meanwhile they are despatching an officer to Sardinia to report.
9. Leveson-Gower to Harrowby, November 28: Rose, *Third Coalition*, p. 72.
10. Amongst other measures that were adopted at this time was the erection of the Martello Towers on the threatened coasts, not in a spirit of passive defence, but in order to set free an effective striking force. Another was the digging of the Hythe Military Canal. This work, which seemed to be designed to stop an army which had crossed the Channel, came in for much ridicule by the "blue water" men of the day. Writing in September 1805, from Hythe to the Viceroy of Ireland, Charles Yorke says his regiment is "at work in the mud of a large ditch called the Royal Military Canal, which is said to be intended to prevent the French penetrating into the country . . . when they shall have crossed another ditch somewhat wider and rather more difficult to pass" (Rt. Hon. Charles Yorke to Earl of Hardwicke: *Add. MSS.* 37506). Military opinion would probably regard this criticism of the work as superficial. It was, of course, intended to delay the advance of a force that had landed, and give time for the concentration of the territorial forces which had been arranged, just as the Martello Towers were intended to delay the landing.
11. The original arrangement was: Margate Roads, 1 or 2 of the line; Queen's Channel, 2; King's Channel, 2; Goldamore Gate, 1; Buoy of Rough, "a frigate to communicate" (*i.e.* by semaphore telegraph); Hoseley Bay, "a ship of force." Eventually they were done away with, and their crews devoted to a number of hired cruisers. — *Admiralty Sec. In-letters*, 537.
12. Barham to Cornwallis, August 15: *Cornwallis Papers, Hist. MSS. Com., Various Collections*, vi. p. 411.
13. Pitt had offered this command to Lord St. Vincent, "which," he says, "I spurned at, unless Mr. Pitt unsaid all he had said in the House of Commons against me." —*Cornwallis Papers, Ibid.,* p. 418.
14. Melville to Cornwallis, July 29, 1804: *Blockade of Brest* (Navy Record Soc.), ii. 38.
15. The leading cases were the Armada in 1588, and the French attempt to invade from Dunkirk in 1744. In both cases the intruding fleet was only saved from destruction by the weather and a *sauve qui peut*.
16. Draft, "Instructions to Admiral Cornwallis: Secret, Aug. 24, 1804," signed by Melville, Gambier, and Colpoys. — *Barham Papers*. For Cornwallis's own precis of the long document, see *Blockade of Brest*, ii. 48.
17. The final return of the state of the Grand Army on the coasts, and its flotilla (Aug. 1-15) was as follows:—

Ports	Flotilla			State of Army Ready	
	Units	Capacity			
		Men	Horses	Men	Horses
Étaples	365	27,000	1390	20,000	1200
Boulogne	1153	73,000	3380	45,000	1500
Wimereux	237	16,000	769	13,000	—
Ambleteuse	173	15,000	673	15,000	—
		131,000	6212	93,000	1700

Desbrière, *Projets et Tentatives de débarquement aux Iles Britanniques*, v. 465.

18. The authority for this is the *Memoires de Miot de Melito*, ii. 244, which the French Staff accept, as trustworthy. See for this and an admirable summary of the whole situation, Desbrière, *Projets et Tentatives de débarquement,* iv. 336 *et seq*.
19. Rose, *Third Coalition*, p. 90.
20. De Martens, *Recueil des Traités*, vol. ii, pp. 110-111. For the whole negotiation, see *Ibid*; pp. 75 *et seq*.
21. He was an officer of Irish extraction. He signed his name "Lacy." (See his letter of July 8th, enclosed in Elliot's despatch of August 9th, *F.O. Sicily*, 25.) foreigners spelt it "Lasci" or "Lascy."
22. Rose, *Third Coalition*, pp. 110, 143, 151. Pitt's views on the military situation as it stood without Prussia, and his ideas as to how the British army should be used, were explained in detail in a despatch to Leveson-Gower drafted in July.
23. Rose, *Dumouriez and the Defence of England*, p. 260.

CHAPTER II

1. *Blockade of Brest* (N.R.S.), ii. 158-166. Desbrière's *Projets et Tentatives*, iv. 306.
2. *Admiralty Secretary, Out-letters* (*Secret Orders*), 1363.
3. Nelson to Marsden, Dec. 26, 1804: Nicolas, *Nelson's Letters and Despatches*, vol. vi.
4. Nelson to Orde, Dec. 29.
5. Nelson to Ball, Feb. 11th, and see also same to Melville, Feb. 14th.
6. Villeneuve to Decrès, Jan. 21 : Desbrière's *Projets et Tentatives*, iv. 299. An instance of an officer's neglecting Nelson's principle was Admiral Sampson's almost fatal attempt to intercept Admiral Cervera at Puerto Rico in the Spanish-American War. It was this immutable principle, "so imperturbably followed," as Colonel Desbrière says, which rendered futile all attempts to entice our fleet away from the time-honoured covering position at the mouth of the Channel.
7. Napoleon to Decrès: Desbrière, iv. 325. *Correspondance de Napoléon*, x. 117.
8. See Desbrière, *Projets*, vol. v., part iii., chap. 4.
9. Desbrière, *Projets*, v. 371.

CHAPTER III

1. *Dreadnought* 98, *Tonnant* 80, *Mars*, *Illustrious*, and *Minotaur* 74: *Blockade of Brest*, ii. 203.
2. Desbrière, v. 473.
3. To Fouché, August 9, 1805: *Correspondance de Napoléon I.*, xi. 72.
4. In 1805 there were two types of the 98-gun second-rates. The newer or 18-pounder type were over 2100 tons, with a broadside of about 1050 lbs. There were only three in commission — the *Dreadnought* and the

Neptune and *Téméraire*, Nelson's two seconds at Trafalgar, but two new ones still larger were completed that year. They averaged 2277 tons. The rest, of which there were eight in commission, were of the 12-pounder type, that is, they carried thirty "twelves" instead of "eighteens" on their upper deck. They ranged from 1870 to 2000 tons. These figures do not include carronades.

5. Bigot de Morogues, *Tactique Navale*, p. 27. The defensive power of three-deckers was strongly shown in the *Victory* at Trafalgar. In an unpublished letter of the Rev. A. T. Scott, dated October 27 (of which Major Marsh, R.A., has kindly given me a copy), he says: "On the quarter-deck, poop, and forecastle the slaughter was immense; on the other decks comparatively nothing; on the lower deck only two wounded, and, strange to tell, by musket-balls."
6. *Life of Nelson*, ii. 333.
7. Ganteaume to Napoleon, July 14th: Desbrière, v. 640. The calculation works out in this way: 30 of the line with 12 three-deckers = 42 units. Ganteaume's 21 with 3 three-deckers = 24 units. The Admiralty finally fixed the minimum force for Cornwallis at 18 of the line. The three-deckers varied normally from 5 to 8. Taking the average number as 6, we again get 24 units, as against Ganteaume's 24. Similarly when, on Missiessy's return to Rochefort, Gardner detached Graves to blockade him, he left himself with 8 three-deckers and 7 others, or 23 units to watch Ganteaume's 24; but Gardner's flagship was the newly-launched *Hibernia* of 120 guns, the largest ship in the navy. When Stirling from Rochefort joined Calder in order to intercept Villeneuve and Gravina coming back from the West Indies, they had together 15 of the line with 4 three-deckers, or 19 units. The *Curieux* had reported the allies to be 17 of the line, but they were really 20 with six 80-gun ships. Gardner before Brest at the end of May had 10 three-deckers and 12 others = 32 units, including Collingwood's squadron of 2 three-deckers and 8 others, or 12 units. Under his discretionary power, therefore, he only detached half Collingwood's squadron, which left him with 26 units, of which, however, 3 were only sixty-fours. — *Blockade of Brest*, ii. 27. Many similar instances will be noticed in the course of the campaign.
8. See particularly "Barfleur," *Naval Policy*, p. 212.
9. Many of the smaller 18-pounder seventy-fours also carried twelve 32-pounder carronades, *e.g.* the *Dragon* (1815 tons) had twenty-eight 32-pounders, thirty-four 18-pounders, and twelve 32-pounder carronades.
10. Napoleon to Decrès, March 13, 1805: *Correspondance*, x. 221.
11. Napoleon to Decrès, *Ibid.*, June 2, 13, 22; July 5, 19.
12. Bunbury, *Passages in the Great War*, p. 183. *W.O.* (6), 56, March 28.
13. *Admiralty Secretary, In-letters* (*Secret Orders*), vol. 1363, March 27.
14. *Admiralty Secretary, In-letters* (*Secret Orders*), vol. 1363, April 6 and 15.
15. Cotton had 6 three deckers, 2 eightys, and 9 others, against Ganteaume s 3 three-deckers, 2 eightys, and 16 seventy-fours. Cotton in his despatch (as printed in *Blockade of Brest*, p. 217), says he had 7 of the line. Coll&gwood says 17 (*Ibid.*, 223). Gardner was about to join in another three-decker, *Hibernia* 120, which would give him 25 units against 24.
16. Ganteaume to the Emperor: *Desbrière*, v. 473. Cotton to Admiralty: *Blockade of Brest*, ii. 217.
17. From various references in his letters it appears that Palmas was Rendezvous 98. The position south of Toulon was No. 102. No. 97 was "under Cape St. Sebastian," just north of Palamos in Catalonia. A list of Mediterranean Rendezvous in use at this time is yet to seek. In *Add MSS.* 34950, p. 49, there is such a list issued by Nelson in September 1805. It was the official list which was used throughout the rest of the war, but its numbers differ from those of the earlier list: *e.g.* "Off Toulon" was No. 93 in the new, list.
18. Nelson did apparently have a cruiser on Rendezvous 97, "off Cape St. Sebastian," and this perhaps he thought was enough to locate Villeneuve if he tried to steal down the coast of Spain. But as the Toulon squadron started south to pass outside the Balearic Islands, Rendezvous 97 was not approached.

CHAPTER IV

1. For Nelson's "Order of Battle and Sailing "issued here, March 26th, see Hubback, *Jane Austen's Sailor Brothers*, p. 132. It is for twelve ships, including the *Excellent*, in two divisions.

2. Auriol, *La France, l'Angleterre, et Naples*, vol. ii. pp. 33-6.
3. *Ibid.*, chap. v. and p. 222 (Alquier to Talleyrand, March 29th); and Nicolas, vi. 377.
4. The new cruiser distribution was as follows — one at Galita, one on the coast of Africa, and one between Galita and the shore, with instructions to get information from Tunis. These three were to stop Villeneuve stealing to the eastward by hugging the African coast. Then there were two between Nelson and Toro, besides one to ascertain if the enemy had passed the Straits of Bonifaccio, another to Naples, and a fifth to hark back and see if the enemy had returned again to Toulon. — Nelson to Ball: Nicolas, vi. 399.
5. Orde to Lord Melville, March 27: Nicolas, vi. 383 *n.*
6. Strachan to Nelson, April 30: *Nelson Papers, Add. MSS.* 34929.
7. This curious movement is recorded in the Log of the *Glory*, Orde's flagship, but not in any of his despatches. The despatch he sent off after making it merely records, that he had not yet been able to double St. Vincent owing to adverse weather.
8. Orde to Nelson: *Add. MSS.* 34929, April 11.
9. For Orde's despatches and cruiser orders, see *Admiralty Secretary, in letters*, 410, March 19, April 10, 11, 12, 15, 17, 19; and for his flag-captain's report, which entirely confirms them, Ralfe, *Naval Biography*, ii. 75.
10. Log of the *Glory*. For the *Melampus*, see her *Log*, and Gardner to Marsden April 22 : *Blockade of Brest*, ii. 236.

CHAPTER V

1. Stanhope, *Life of Pitt*, i. 377.
2. Middleton to Pitt, Feb. 8 and March 15, 1790: *Chatham Papers, Bundle* 111. He left in Pitt's hands a long and detailed memo. on the reorganisation of the Board.—*Ibid.* and *Bundle* 245.
3. Stanhope, *Life of Pitt*, iv. 287, and Wilberforce's *Life*, iii. 223. In the *Barham Papers* there is also a "Note for Mr. James," the historian, in which it is stated, "Mr. Pitt coming to power, it was decided by Mr. Pitt and Lord Melville to consult Sir Charles Middleton in all matters connected with the restoration of the fleet."
4. Woronzow to Czartoryski: De Martens, *Recueil de Traités*, xi. 109.
5. Stanhope, *Life of Pitt*, iv. Appendix, p. xxiii.
6. To Lord Hardwicke, Viceroy of Ireland, April 26: *Hardwicke Papers, Add. MSS.* 35706.
7. He had just returned from escorting Nelson's victual and coal ships to Rendezvous 97, that is, under Cape San Sebastian, on the Catalonian coast. Nelson to Capel: Nicolas, vi. 409.
8. Lord Mark Kerr to Nelson, April 9: *Nelson Papers, Add. MSS.* 34929.
9. This, according to the Signal Book (1808), in which the rendezvous were printed for the first time, was No. 52, "six leagues due N.W. of Finisterre," but James says it was at this time 38 leagues N.W. (vol. iv. p. 452). The two cruisers actually met 5 or 6 leagues S.S.W. of Finisterre.
10. Kerr to Gardner, April 23: *Blockade of Brest*, ii. 237.
11. *Out-letters* (*Secret Orders*), 1363, April 25.
12. *Hardwicke Papers*, April 30 : *Add. MSS.* 35706.
13. *Admiralty Minutes*, 152, April 27.
14. *Ibid.*, April 27.
15. *Secret Orders*, 1363, March 6. Saumarez sent the *Cerebus* away on March 27. *In-letters*, 223, July 15.
16. *Secret Orders*, 1363, April 27.
17. Bertrand, *Lettres inédites de Talleyrand à Napoleon*, 1800-9, p. 118 : Lyons April 10.
18. To Cambacérès, Lyons, April 13th: *Correspondance*, x. 315.
19. *Correspondance*, p. 317.
20. "Secret Intelligence from Paris," March 29th, April 17th: *Admiralty In-letters* (*Secretary of State*), 4198, April 30th.
21. Sir John Barrow, *Autobiographical Memoirs*, p. 264.
22. *Admiralty Minutes*, 256, April 25th. This was a minute requiring Marsden the Secretary to furnish him

with a detailed memorandum on the organisation and Staff of the Admiralty, and the distribution and course of work. The reorganisation Barham founded on it will be dealt with later.

23. *Out-letters* (*Secret Orders*), 1363, April 30th.
24. *Admiralty Minutes*, 153, May 1st.
25. *Trafalgar*, p. 3.
26. *Admiralty Minutes*, 256. The memo. is signed and corrected in Barham's hand and dated "May."
27. *Autobiographical Memoirs*, p. 277. Barrow was a member of the Board, having been appointed Second Secretary by Lord Melville in May 1804. He did not write the *Memoirs*, however, till he was quite an old man, after forty years' service at the Admiralty. His memory failed him at times in matters of detail, but otherwise the book seems trustworthy. The Second Sea Lord was Vice-Admiral Philip Patton, a man who had made a special study of the personnel of the Navy and had foretold the great mutinies. The Third Sea Lord was Captain Lord Garlies. Besides the two Secretaries there were three Civil Lords, including two former Secretaries of exceptional ability and experience. One was the veteran Sir Philip Stephens, who had begun his official life as Lord Anson's secretary, and had been Admiralty Secretary from 1763 to 1795; the other Sir Evan Nepean, a Navy clerk, who, after serving as Under-Secretary successively at the Foreign and War Offices, had succeeded Stephens at the Admiralty until 1804. — (Sir J. K. Laughton in *Dictionary of Nat. Biog.*).

CHAPTER VI

1. Craig's orders with instructions to co-operate were contained in a despatch to Nelson, dated March 27th (*Out-letters, Secret Orders*, 1363), but there is no trace in his correspondence with the Admiralty of his having received it till May 1st. It was not until April 15th that he received the Admiralty bag of February 16th. — Nicolas, vi. 404.
2. *Journal*, April 10 and 16. In the revised list of rendezvous used in September, No. 71 was Tarifa, No. 80 was Formentera west end.
3. Phillimore, *Life of Sir William Parker*, i. 281. The *Decade* had reached Naples by the 9th. She must therefore have left England on March 22nd or 23rd, that is, three or four days before the 27th, the day on which Nelson's instructions to co-operate with Craig were issued. See also Nicolas, vi. 406 *n.*
4. Nicolas, vi. 406 *n.* The letter is dated April 9th, the same day the *Decade* arrived. She had been therefore nearly six days beating out to Nelson.
5. Nicolas, iv. 406.
6. Nelson to Thomas, H.M. Bomb *Ætna*, April 16th : Nicolas, vi. 404 ; and *Nelson's Journal*, April 16th.
7. Phillimore, Life of *Sir William Parker*, vol. i. 284. Parker to Nelson, April 18th: *Nelson Papers, Add. MSS.* 34929, f. 170.
8. Nelson to Capel, April 18th: Nicolas, vi. 408.
9. Phillimore, *Sir William Parker*, i. 284.
10. Nelson to Otway, April 26th: Nicolas, vi. 415.
11. To Marsden, May 1st: Nicolas, vi. 418.
12. Clarke and McArthur, *Life of Nelson*, II. Part, iii. 94.

CHAPTER VII

1. FitzGerald to Mulgrave, April 13th and 14th: *State Papers*, Foreign (*Portugal*), vol. 47.
2. FitzGerald to Mulgrave, May 3rd: *S.P. Foreign* (*Portugal*), 47.
3. FitzGerald to Mulgrave, May 5th: *S.P. Foreign* (*Portugal*), 47. Log of the *Orpheus: Captains' Logs*, P.R.O.
4. Fitzgerald to Mulgrave, May 8th.
5. Allen, *Life of Captain Sir William Hargood*, p. 110. Clarke and McArthur, ii. 489.

6. To Rear-Admiral George Campbell, May 10th: Nicolas, vi. 431. Nelson in addressing the letter seems to confuse Donald Campbell with Captain George Campbell, who had been commanding the *Canopus* under him.
7. Hardy to Mansfield, May 10th: *Nelson's Hardy*, p. 127.
8. Phillimore, *Sir William Parker*, p. 292.
9. Nicolas, vi. 430, and *note*.
10. Nelson to Earl Camden, May 14th: Nicolas, vi. 438. His instructions to Knight are *Ibid.*, p. 433.
11. Phillimore, *Life of Sir William Parker*, i. 289.
12. Hardwicke to Charles Yorke, June 1st: *Hardwicke Papers, Add. MSS*, 35706. Nelson was partly reconciled to the loss of the *Royal Sovereign* because she wanted docking badly and was therefore slow. But the *Superb* was in the same condition and he took her on. He informed the Admiralty that his reason for detaching the *Royal Sovereign* was to render it impossible for all the force at Cartagena to make any impression upon Knight's force. Here then we have further evidence of the value Nelson placed on three-decked ships. The Cartagena squadron consisted of six two-deckers, and he considered he had enabled Knight to deal with it by leaving him with two three-deckers and one seventy-four.

CHAPTER VIII

1. For the *Beagle's* movements see Burn's Report: *Captains' Letters*, 1535, April 12 and 25; and *Captains' Logs*, 1530; and Chart.
2. *Admiralty Minutes*, 153, May 2nd. Admiralty to Admiral Young, Commander-in-chief at Plymouth, May 2nd: "Captain Burn has omitted to say how the wind was when he met the squadron, supposed to have sailed from Toulon on 9th or 10th ultimo." Villeneuve does not record having been observed.
3. *Out-letters* (*Secret Orders*), 1363, May 2nd.
4. To Gardner and Collingwood: *Ibid.*, May 4th. These are the first orders actually signed by Barham.
5. Admiralty to Collingwood, Postscript: *Out-Letters* (*Secret Orders*), 1363, May 4th.
6. *Ibid.*
7. To Gardner: *Ibid.*, May 9th.
8. *Ibid.*, May 9th.
9. Gardner to Marsden, May 9th: *Blockade of Brest*, iv. 255.
10. Same to same. May 11th: *Blockade of Brest*, iv. 258.
11. *Out-letters* (*Secret Orders*), 1363, and Gardner to Marsden, May 15th: *Blockade of Brest*, ii. 260.
12. *Secret Orders*, 1363, May 14th.
13. *Secret Orders*, 1363, May 15th and 16th.
14. Mulgrave to Gower, June 7th: Holland Rose, *Third Coalition*, p. 165. *F.O. Russia*, 58.
15. De Martens, *Recueil de Traités*, xi. 109.
16. Mulgrave to Woronzow, May 7th: Rose, *Third Coalition*, p. 145. For the whole argument see same to same, June 7th, in which despatch it was repeated and developed.
17. De Martens, *op, cit.*, xi. 111.
18. *Secret Orders*, 1363. To Hood, April 5th. To Captain Woodriff of the *Calcutta*, (East Indiamen's escort), April 29th. To Collingwood and to Nelson, May 17th.
19. Gardner to Marsden, May 7th: *Blockade of Brest*, ii. 278.
20. Gardner to Marsden, May 19th, with enclosures: *Blockade of Brest*, ii. 266.
21. See Gardner to Marsden, May 22nd: *Blockade of Brest*, ii. 275; and Maitland's report; *In-letters*, 128. Maitland saw them on the 11th in "lat. 43° 44' and long. 20° 48' W. (by chronometer 20° 16')." With a westerly wind they were steering E. by S.½S. This must be magnetic, the variation being about 22½ degrees W. True E. by S.½S. would have brought them below Finisterre, an impossible course for Missiessy to be steering on a fair wind. The practice of French fleets returning from the West Indies to the Bay seems to have been to make the latitude of Ortegal about 500 miles W. and then run down it for a landfall.

The knowledge of this practice accounts for Calder's advanced cruiser being where she was. To his other precise information Maitland added coloured representations of the signals Missiessy had made.

22. Gardner to Marsden, May 22nd, enclosing Calder to Gardner, May 15th; *Blockade of Brest*, ii. pp. 275-7.
23. Gardner to Marsden, May 22nd: *Ibid.*, p. 275. The ships he detained were *Foudroyant* 80 (Graves's flag), *Windsor Castle* 98, *Warrior* 74, *Repulse* 64, *Raisonnable* 64.

CHAPTER IX

1. *Naval Chronicle*, xii. 205, and ix. 201, where there is a sketch of the Rock.
2. Desbrière, v. 507.
3. Napoleon to Decrès, April 12th, and to Lauriston, Cambacérès, Talleyrand, Murat, Pino, and Decrès, April 13th: *Correspondance*, x. 312-320.
4. Napoleon to Lauriston, April 13th, and to Villeneuve and Decrès April 14th: *Ibid.*, pp. 314, 321.
5. Decrès to Villeneuve, April 17th: Desbrière, vol. v. p. 513.
6. For this, see Desbrière, v. 517.
7. Desbrière, v. 518.
8. Napoleon to Talleyrand, and same to Decrès, April 23rd: *Correspondance* x. 338-9. Same to same, May 4th: *Ibid.*, p. 375.
9. Napoleon to Decrès, April 23rd: *Correspondance*, x. 339 341 and Desbrière, v. 522.
10. For all the above orders, see Desbrière, v. iii. chapters 7 and 9.
11. For a typical example of what would happen should such co-operation be attempted, see the case of Badiley, Appleton, and Van Galen at Leghorn in 1653: *England in the Mediterranean*, i. 265 *et seq.*
12. Beurnonville (French ambassador at Madrid) to Talleyrand, May 14th and 16th: Desbrière, v. 578-81.
13. *i.e.* the Lesser Antilles, in English official parlance the "Leeward Islands." See *England in the Seven Years' War*, i. 352.
14. Napoleon to Decrès, May 25th and June 8th. Napoleon wrote: "Ces combinaisons de mouvements du continent, fondées sur des détachements de quelques 1000 hommes, sont des combinaisons de pygmies."
15. For the above letters of May 25th to 28th, see *Correspondance de Napoléon*, x. 441-454. The salvo was probably fired on news of Prevost's repulse of the attack on Dominica.
16. Desbrière, v. 596. Decrès quotes the *Morning Chronicle* of May 9th and the *Sun* of the 16th. The May-June number of the *Naval Chronicle* (vol. xiii. p. 484) also published Napoleon's intention to "balayer la Manche" with sixty of the line and fight our fleet, while his frigates covered the passage of the troops.
17. Desbrière, v. 596. This document is an unfinished draft.
18. *Ibid.*, p. 599. Colonel Desbrière observes on this remarkable paper, "In all but what concerns the gross error in appreciating the character of Nelson, we cannot admire too much this letter whose forecasts were realised with almost absolute precision." Colonel Desbrière would seem therefore to take Decrès' remarks on Nelson seriously; but it is submitted that there really seems no reason to do so. It is almost impossible to believe that a man who could expose in so masterly a manner the strategical fallacies of Napoleon and penetrate so acutely the British intentions, could really be so bad a judge of the main personal factor. The awe in which Napoleon's officers stood of him, seems quite enough to account for Decrès' preferring not to contradict the Emperor's shallow view of Nelson's capacity, if there was another and safer way of attaining the end which be had in view.
19. Beurnonville to Talleyrand, June 13th and 17th: *Ibid.*, p. 622.
20. To Decrès, June 14th: Desbrière, v. 612.

CHAPTER X

1. *Out-letters* (*Secret Orders*), 1363, May 30th.
2. *Ibid.*, June 4th. He was told they had intelligence of the Toulon squadron having left Cadiz on April 10th, and that "though very imperfect it increases the probability of its destination being for the East Indies or the Cape of Good Hope." An earlier warning to the same effect had been sent him.
3. To Decrès, June 16th.
4. *In-letters*, 410, Bickerton to the Admiralty, May 14th and 16th. Knight to same, May 15th. Bickerton's last letter is minuted, "Approve his proceedings under the circumstances he describes."
5. Craig to Lord Camden, May 16th: *W.O.* (1), *In-letters*, 280. All Craig's despatches go to confirm the judgment of his enthusiastic young admirer. Ensign Charles Boothby. "The name of my new chief I had long known; for his fine person and dark flashing eye had been pointed out to me when a boy as belonging to the finest officer in the service." — *Under England's Flag*, p. 3.
6. Bickerton to Admiralty and Collingwood to same, May 27th, off Finisterre: *In-letters*, 410.
7. *Secret Orders*, 1363, June 8th.
8. Collingwood to the Admiralty and Bickerton to same, June 24th: *In-letters*, 441. Bickerton had the *Queen* 98, the *Tonnant* 80, *Bellerophon* 74, and *Minotaur* 74. The Cartagena squadron was reported to be two first-rates, three 74's, and one 64. Bickerton never called the *Excellent* to his flag. Writing to Nelson on July 30th he says: "I have not removed the *Excellent* from Naples, for besides the uncertainty I was under where to order her to meet me, I was unwilling to take a step which might have defeated your lordship's measures": *Nelson Papers, Add. MSS.* 34930. The *Excellent*, except for occasional spells under sail for drill and gunnery practice, remained at her moorings from Jan. 17, 1805, to Feb. 11, 1806. — *Log of the Excellent.*
9. Knight to the Admiralty, June 17th, enclosing Fox and Craig to Knight, June 13th, Fox's information, and Craig to Knight, June 15th: *In-letters*, 441. Craig to Lord Camden, June 17th: *W.O.* (1), *In-letters*, 280. Boothby, *Under England's Flag*, p. 20. Bunbury, *The Great War*, p. 189. Knight to Nelson (enclosing his journal), July 16th: *Nelson Papers, Add. MSS.* 34930.
10. Beurnonville to Talleyrand, Madrid, June 18th: Desbrière, v. 625.
11. Bickerton to Admiralty, July 28th: *In-letters*, 411.

CHAPTER XI

1. To Marsden, April 14th: Nicolas, vi. 437.
2. *Ibid.*, p. 139.
3. Phillimore, *Life of Sir William Parker*, ii. 289.
4. Clarke and McArthur, ii. 427 (4th edition), for the reasons for assigning the St. Vincent Memorandum to 1803, see Laughton, *Nelson's Letters and Despatches and Fighting Instructions* (*Navy Records Society*), 280-1. The fact that it was found amongst Lord St. Vincent's papers raises in itself a strong presumption that it was written while he was still First Lord, that is, before May 1804. In 1805 he was playing Achilles in his tent, and Nelson was not in correspondence with him.
5. Allen, *Memoirs of Sir William Hargood*, p. 111.
6. Cochrane to the Admiralty: *In-letters*, 326. April 5, 8, 9, 14, 17.
7. Desbrière v. 539-5. Confusion has arisen by Villeneuve's being supposed to have written "Barbade" instead of "Barboude," as though he meant to attack Barbadoes, which was in the opposite direction and far to windward. It is clear from his later despatch that by "Barbade" he meant the island adjacent to Antigua. With the experience of the Diamond Rock before him he could not have hoped to beat to Barbadoes and do anything there in less than a month, and his stores permitted of no such delay. "If," wrote Nelson afterwards, "Barbadoes is the object . . . a fleet could get there on the average in four or five days from

Martinique. Therefore why should they make a passage of at least fifteen or sixteen days by going to the northward." — Nicolas, vi. 458. Spanish prisoners taken in Calder's action said the objective was Antigua. — *Blockade of Brest*, ii. 323.

8. For this interesting episode see *Life of Sir William Parker*, i. 294, who says Maurice had only 90 men, and that the French lost 800! Desbrière, v. 541, gives Villeneuve's and Reille's accounts. The *Naval Chronicle*, xv. 123, gives Maurice's reports to both Nelson and Cochrane, and the French commander's report to Villaret-Joyeuse, Captain-General of Martinique, with other official documents and comments of the local press. The original of Maurice's report to Nelson is in *Admiralty In-letters*, 411, June 6th.
9. A copy of the intelligence General Brereton had sent from St. Lucia was given to Nelson, and at the foot of it he wrote in his own hand, "Wrote by Major Myers, Sir William Myers' secretary, extracted from the General's letter, and Major Myers has no doubt the intelligence may be relied on" (Signed) Nelson and Bronté, June 4th: *Adm. Sec. In-letters*, 411, and Nicolas, vi. 446.
10. This order of battle was printed in Hubback's *Jane Austen's Sailor Brothers*, p. 138, from Louis's copy, but with some obvious inaccuracies. The following is from Keats's copy, preserved in the Record Office, *Greenwich Hospital Miscellanea* (*Various*), No. 141. It was drawn up apparently on an official form which provided for a fleet of thirty sail.

ORDER OF SAILING AND OF BATTLE.

Van Squadron.	1.	*Canopus* 80 (Rear-Adm. Louis).	*Starboard Division.*
	2.	"	
	3.	"	
	4.	*Superb* 74.	
	5.	"	
	6.	*Victory* 100 (Nelson).	
	7.	*Donegal* 74.	
	8.	"	
	9.	*Spencer* 74.	
	10.	"	
Centre Squadron.	1.	"	
	2.	"	
	3.	*Tigre* 74.	
	4.	"	
	5.	*Northumberland* 80 (Cochrane).	
	6.	"	*Larboard Division.*
	7.	*Leviathan* 74.	
	8.	"	
	9.	"	
	10.	"	
Rear Squadron.	1.	"	
	2.	"	
	3.	"	
	4.	"	
	5.	"	
	6.	*Belleisle* 74.	
	7.	*Conqueror* 74.	
	8.	*Swiftsure* 74.	
	9.	*Spartiate* 74.	
	10.	"	

The *Superb* was a very powerful ship of a new type which was copied from the *Pompée*, captured at Toulon. With her carronades she threw a broadside of 1000 lbs. The *Canopus* (a prize taken in 1798) had a broadside of 1092 lbs. The *Victory's* original armament (*i.e.* without carronades) gave a broadside of 1068 lbs. The *Donegal* was also a French prize of 1798, even larger than the *Superb*. After her re-armament with carronades she was sometimes classed as an 80-gun ship. The *Tigre*, which brought up the rear of Nelson's division, was also a heavy French prize captured in 1798, and equal in force to the *Superb*, as were also *Belleisle* and *Spartiate*. The rest were small 74's. The unequal distribution of ships in the squadrons shows that the divisional and not the squadronal organisation was to be used. In actual sailing Nelson did not occupy his station, but, as the practice was, led the starboard line. Under June 5th he enters in his Journal, "Directed *Canopus* to take her station astern of the *Victory* and the *Northumberland*, to lead the lee line agreeable to the order of battle and sailing issued to the Fleet." With our knowledge of what happened at Trafalgar it may well be doubted whether Nelson would ever have got back into his place if the enemy had been met with.

11. To Lord Seaforth, June 8th.
12. Desbrière, v. 679. Colonel Desbrière again reads the word "Barbade." But his text shows the letter has been incorrectly transcribed in other places, and it ia certain that Villeneuve wrote or meant to write "Barbude" or "Barboude." See notes below.
13. The transcript which Colonel Desbrière used reads "*débarquer entre Antigoa et Mont-Serrat*," but he has kindly informed me that the word should certainly be "débouquer," Anglice "disembogue." This course would not lead anywhere but to Barbuda.
14. Desbrière, v. 680. The *Journal de Reille*, as Colonel Desbrière's transcript reads it, has "*à 10 heures du matin, étant sous le vent de Barbade, les vigies ont signalé un convoi de quinze voiles.*" Here "Barbade" must clearly mean "Barbuda."
15. Captain Nourse of the *Barbadoes* to the Admiralty (*In-letters*, 2231), enclosing the merchants' memorial and the governor's request.
16. Carr to Nelson, June 13th, enclosed in Nelson to Marsden, June 14th: *In-letters*, 411. James gives the name of the *Netley's* commander as Richard Harward and says Nourse was with him. There seems no authority for either statement. — Vol. iv. p. 351. Carr was still in command of the *Netley* in 1807 when she was captured by a French frigate and brig.
17. *Journal de Reille*: Desbrière, v. 681.
18. Letter from an officer on board one of Lord Nelson's ships: *Add. MSS.* 3430, June 19th; Nelson to Marsden, June 14th: *In-letters*, 411. Nicolas missed this letter and it seems never to have been printed. It runs: "*Victory* at sea, June 14th. The *Netley* schooner joined me yesterday morning about an hour after the fleet got under weigh (sic) from St. John's Road, Antigua, when Lieutenant Carr came on board and showed me the accompanying despatches from Captain Nourse of the *Barbadoes*, addressed to you (which in his hurry to return to the *Netley* he omitted to take with him). I therefore judge it proper to forward them to you in the state they were left, and also beg leave to transmit you for their Lordships' information a letter from Lieutenant Carr giving his reasons for having opened the said despatches." The letter was not holograph, but signed by Nelson.
19. The authority for these observations is not known. Clarke and McArthur give it as the purport of his remarks (without mentioning their source of information) on one of the occasions when during the chase he assembled his captains on board the *Victory*. There is another traditional story on the point which has never been published. It was related by Elliot, afterwards Governor of St. Helena, to Lieutenant A.H. Hoskins, R.N., afterwards Admiral Sir Anthony Hoskins. He repeated it to his flag-lieutenant, now Captain Mark Kerr, who has kindly given it to me as he wrote it down at the time as follows: "On the way back from the West Indies Nelson was walking up and down the quarter-deck talking to the officer of the watch, who said 'I wish we could fall in with Villeneuve, sir.' Nelson: 'Yes, it would be very satisfactory to know where he is.' The officer: 'What a glorious fight we should have, sir!' Nelson: 'I don't think I should fight him.' Officer: 'Not fight him! Why all the way out you were dying to get at him.' Nelson: 'All the way out he was getting stronger and I was getting weaker. All the way home I am getting stronger and he is getting weaker. If we

fell in with him now and fought him, I don't doubt we should beat him, and it would be a great thing for my personal glory; but I should be doing my country a great wrong. I know that in a week's time I shall get reinforcements, and he will get none, and then I must annihilate him.'" The moral of the story is obvious, but as it stands it is in some details difficult to understand. By Villeneuve's growing stronger on the outward voyage, he presumably referred to his fleet shaking down by being at sea; but Nelson's growing weaker is curious, since we had a squadron in the West Indies and the allies had nothing.

20. *In-letters*, 326, June 25th.
21. *In-letters*, 326, July 13th and 17th; *Admiralty Minutes*, 154. The minute enjoining the return of the two ships with any convoys that were ready is dated July 11th, that is, in the same week that Cochrane decided to return them on his own responsibility.

CHAPTER XII

1. From Bologna, June 22nd: *Correspondance*, x. 556.
2. To Marmont and to Decrès, Parma, June 27th: *Correspondance*, x. 566-8.
3. To Decrès, Milan, June 6th; *Correspondance*, x. 482.
4. June 14th: *Ibid.*, p. 563. Lacour-Gayet, *Louis XVI.*, p. 661,
5. Gourdon to Beurnonville, July 7th: Desbrière, v. 627. Calder to Gardner July 5th, and Gardner to Marsden, July 6th: *Blockade of Brest*, ii. 298-9.
6. Knight to Nelson, July 16th, and same to Collingwood, August 5th: *Nelson Payers, Add. MSS.* 3430. Napoleon to Decrès, June 22, 25, 27: *Correspondance*, x. 555, 564, 568.
7. To Decrès, June 28th: *Correspondance*, x. 573.
8. *Admiralty In-letters* (*Sec. of State*), 4199, July 1st.
9. *Admiralty Minutes*, 154, July 1st.
10. To Dr. Carlyle, July 2nd: *Blockade of Brest*, ii. 296.
11. *In-letters*, 410, June 8th, endorsed "Approved, July 7th."
12. This unknown document is one of the chief treasures of the *Barham Papers* — a holograph in a volume labelled "Drafts of Orders and Statements in the hand of Lord Barham." It is undated, but as it is specially founded on the information of Collingwood's having detached his two of the line to Nelson, it must have been written on the 7th or 8th. On the 9th, as we shall see, it was cancelled on fresh information.
13. *Barham Papers*. "Orders and Statements, 1805." The last interlineation must have been made before the minute was complete, for the penultimate sentence refers to it. The important change as to the Rochefort squadron must therefore have been made before it left his hands and without any one else's suggestion.
14. *Barham Papers*. The discovery of the text of this order finally disposes of the story that Barham issued it without consulting his colleagues. We now know both Gambier and Lord Garlies signed it in the usual way. The story as furnished officially to James the historian was that Bettesworth arrived "at a late hour at night," that "orders were immediately sent" to Cornwallis to recall Stirling, &c. See "Note for Mr. James," *Ibid.* ("Drafts of Orders and Statements in the hands of J.D. Thompson.") There must, however, have been some hurry and irregularity; for the order does not appear in the series of Secret Orders at the Record Office. It would look as though Barham would not waste half-an-hour to have it copied and that it did not go forward in the usual way through the Secretary. The laconic form in which the orders were drafted bears no trace of the established secretarial manner.

CHAPTER XIII

1. This was not the ship Rodney took in 1782, but a new first-rate built at Chatham in 1795. On her pre-carronade armament she threw a broadside of 1236 lbs. With her 68 lb. carronades it must have been over 1500 lbs.

2. July 13th: Desbrière, v. 639.
3. July 16th: *Ibid.*, 642.
4. Desbrière, v. 640, July 14th. Ganteaume's estimate appears to be based on a list that was afterwards printed in the *Naval Chronicle*, vol. xiv. It is an "Abstract of the British Efficient Naval Force," and purports, as there printed, to be corrected up to July 20th, but is not so corrected. It gives for the "English and Irish Channels" (that is, the squadrons of Cornwallis and Stirling and that of Ireland), 30 of the line, including 11 three-deckers. Those "In Port and Fitting," *i.e.* the Reserve, number 9 of the line, including the *Royal Sovereign*, besides half-a-dozen "guard-ships." The French Intelligence Department probably obtained the list from some other English newspaper. The Irish battle squadron no longer existed as a separate unit. It had been absorbed into the Western Squadron.
5. Here he clearly counts three-deckers as 2 units. Thus 30 of the line with 12 three-deckers would equal 42 units. His own fleet was 22 with 1 three-decker, which would equal 23 units, but only 21 were ready.
6. Saint-Cloud, July 18th: *Correspondance*, xi. 22.
7. Desbrière, v. 465-6.
8. *Appareillage général de la flottille impériale. Dispositions proposées par le chef militaire*, August 3rd (Desbrière, v. 398). Of this the Editor says; "Such a report is past comment; the contradictions and material errors are altogether too glaring."
9. *Ibid.*, p. 466.
10. Cornwallis's *Journal* and *Log of the Ville de Paris.*

CHAPTER XIV

1. *Log of the Glory*. Letters of First Lieutenant of *Egyptienne*: *Blockade of Brest*, ii. 313. At the court-martial Stirling said he could not remember the date, but agreed it must have been the 12th.
2. As the *Guillaume Tell* and the last survivor of the Nile, she had struck to the *Foudroyant* in 1800. The *Malta* by English "Burden" measurement was 2,255 tons against an average of 2,000 of the 98's, but the 98's, of course, had a higher "displacement." When she received her carronades on being brought into the service she threw a broadside of 1,200 lbs., or about 200 lbs. more than the 98's.
3. Court-martial, Calder's defence; *Naval Chronicle*, xv. 164. Lords of the Admiralty to Cornwallis, July 9th: *Barham, Papers.*
4. See the chart in Desbrière, *Trafalgar*, p. 50.
5. Signal 53: "Keep in closer order by closing towards the leading ship or Admiral." The fleet was, of course, cruising at the time and not in order of sailing. In cruising each division followed its flag in no regular formation
6. By the *Signal Book* Instructions of 1799 the intervals in close order were to be from 1½ to 2 cables (*i.e.* 300-400 yards), Art. xix. p. 121. Art. ii., p. 127, gives it at 2 cables, and the distance between the columns as a mile and a half. The diagram (Plate I.), however, which gives a fleet of fifteen sail exactly the same as Calder's shows a mile only between the columns. The practice probably was to vary it with the size of the fleet. (See *A System of Naval Tactics*, 1797, p. 170.) Length of ships of the line averaged about 60 yards. Eight ships with seven intervals of 2 cables gave a column 3,280 yards long — that is, 1.64 mile on sea reckoning of 10 cables to the mile. Calder's fleet in close order must have covered about 1½ square miles. In open order the intervals were from 3 to 4 cables, which with eight ships might give a line of over 3 miles.
7. Galiano, *Revista General de Marina*, 1908, p. 477 *note.*
8. Signal 52: "To keep in closer order." By Instruction xix., p. 121, every time this signal was made the ships closed half a cable.
9. ' The lines of battle were as follows:—

BRITISH

Hero (74)	Alan Gardner
Ajax (74)	Will. Brown
Triumph (74)	Henry Inman
Barfleur (98)	Geo. Martin
Agamemnon (64)	John Harvey
Windsor Castle (98)	Chas. Boyles
Defiance (74)	P.C. Durham
PRINCE OF WALES (98)	V.A. Calder
	V.A. Nugent (Capt.of the Fleet)
	Will. Cuming (Flag-Capt.)
Repulse (74)	A. K. Legge
Raisonnable (64)	Josias Rowley
Dragon (74)	Ed. Griffith
GLORY(98)	R.-A. Stirling Capt. Warren
Warrior (74)	S.H. Linzee
Thunderer (74)	W. Letchmere
Malta (80)	Ed. Buller

FRANCO-SPANISH

Ship	Commander	Division
ARGONAUT (80)	Gravina (flag)	Starboard
Terrible (70)	Mondroyon.	
America (61)	Darrac	
España (64)	Monios	
S. Raphael (80)	Montes	
Firme (71)	Villa Vicentio	
Pluton (74)	Cosmard	Centre
Mont Blanc (74)	Lavillegris	
Atlas (74)	Rolland	
Berwick (74)	Camus	
Neptune (80)	Maistrol	
BUCENTAURE (80)	Villeneuve (flag)	
FORMIDABLE (80)	Dumanoir (flag)	Lee
Intrépide (74)	Déperonne	
Scipion (74)	Bérenger	
Swiftsure (74)	Villemadrin	
Indomptable (80)	Gourreges	Light
Aigle (74)	Hubert	
Achille (74)	Deméport	
ALGEÇIRAS (74)	Magon (flag)	

10. *Signal and Instructions* (*Navy Records Society*), pp, 77, 108, 120, 134,173, 319, 328-9.
11. James says at 3.22 he made the signal "to tack together," which would look as though he wanted to get to windward. It was really hoisted with the preparative and was annulled at 3.30. At 3.33 he made to the Starboard division No. 93, "Make as much sail as can be carried without breaking the order in which the fleet is formed," with compass signal S.S.W. This was the regular movement in forming line of battle to enable weather division to get ahead of the lee. At 3.43 "Line of battle in open order."
12. Duro, *Armada Espa—ola*, viii. 291.
13. The promptitude with which this manoeuvre was executed is attributed to the foresight of Gravina's chief of the staff, Escaño, in a MS. *Elogio de Don Antonio Escaño*, quoted by General Galiano.
14. This meant anything from a cable to half a cable according to the weather.
15. James (vol. iii. 360) says the *Ajax* tacked at 5.45 and immediately bore up to the Admiral instead of supporting Gardner, and he condemns Captain Brown for his conduct. But Brown's Log says he began to engage at 5.35, tacked at 5.50, and hove-to abreast of two two-deckers, one on the weather bow and one on the weather quarter, and there remained "engaging the enemy as they came up out of the fog." He certainly lost more heavily than any ship of his size. The *Ajax's* time must have been ahead of that of the flagship. James did not observe this. He says *Ajax* tacked at 5.45, and that by 5.50 (Calder's time) six ships had tacked!
16. The following returns of casualties will assist in showing where the brunt of the action fell:—

BRITISH	Killed	Wounded
Hero (74)	1	4
Ajax (74)	2	16
Triumph (74)	5	6
Barfleur (98)	3	7
Agamemnon (64)	0	3
Windsor Castle (98)	10	3
Defiance (74)	1	7
Prince of Wales (98)	3	20
Repulse (74)	0	4
Raisonnable (64)	1	1
Glory (98)	1	1
Warrior (74)	0	0
Thunderer (74)	7	21
Malta (80)	5	40
	41	158
Dragon (74)	Not in action 4 wounded by expiosion	

FRANCO-SPANISH	Killed	Wounded
Argonaute (80)	6	5
Terrible (70)	1	7
America (61)	5	13
España (64)	5	10
S. Raphael (80)	53	114
Firme (71)	41	97
Pluton (74)	8	22
Mont Blanc (74)	6	11
Atlas (74)	10	32
Berwick (74)	2	8
Neptune (80)	1	7
Bucentaure (80)	3	3
Formidable (80)	4	6
Intrépide (74)	5	5
Scipion(74)	0	0
Swiftsure (74)	0	0
Indomptable (89)	1	1
Aigle (74)	4	0
Achille (74)	0	0
Algesiras (74)	0	0
	155	341

		Killed	Wounded		
Total	British	41	158		
	Spanish	111	246	155 killed	341 wounded
	French	44	95		

The *Formidable* and *Atlas* both lost their captains killed.

17. By far the best account of the action is that given by James, iii. 360 *et seq*. That which Admiral Ekins attempted (*Naval Battles*, p. 662) is grotesque. He says he could get no very clear or satisfactory account from the captains engaged, except that all agreed it was a very ill-conducted action. Colonel Desbrière, like Ekins, unfortunately thought Gravina tacked instead of wearing, and his diagrams are therefore misleading. General Galiano (*El Combate de Trafalgar*) corrects this error in his diagram. Both he and Desbrière give the invaluable report of Captain Escaño, Gravina's Chief of the Staff, which for the first time renders a trustworthy account of the battle possible (*Trafalgar, Appendix of Documents*, p. 3). Villeneuve's and other accounts are in his *Projets et Tentatives*, v. ch. xiv. Mr. Leyland, in his *Blockade of Brest*, vol. ii. (*Navy Records Society*), prints Calder's account, and two fuller reports by officers in the

Egyptienne repeating frigate. Calder's *Journal* is missing, but the *Logs* of all the ships are in the Record Office. In addition to the documents given by Colonel Desbrière, General Galiano prints the reports of the captains of the two captured vessels *San Raphael* and *Firme*.

18. *Blockade of Brest*, ii. 312.
19. Nelson to Gambier, Oct. 2, in Chatterton's *Memorials of Gambier*, ii. 4.

CHAPTER XV

1. *Nelson Papers: Add. MSS.* 34930.
2. Collingwood to Nelson, off Cadiz, June 18th: *Nelson Papers, Add. MSS.* 34930. Printed in Nicolas, vi. 472.
3. To Marsden, Gibraltar, July 20th: Nicolas, vi. 473.
4. This was not the regular rendezvous No. 52: "North-west of Finisterre, six leagues," but probably that mentioned by James: "38 leagues northwest." The latter position was roughly in the latitude of Cape Ortegal, and about 100 miles to the westward of Ferrol.
5. This rendezvous was also about 30 miles south by west of our own distant Finisterre rendezvous, *i.e.* 38 leagues north-west of Finisterre.
6. August 14th: Desbrière, v. 759.
7. Rapport du capitaine Allemand, July 20th: Desbrière, v. 759. Between this date and August 16th, when he reached Vigo, he saw 91 sail. Of these he sunk 3 English, and no less than 22 neutrals. — *Ibid.*, p. 785.
8. Rapport d'Allemand: Desbrière, v. 759.
9. Instructions pour le commandant de l'escadre de Rochefort, June 9th: Desbrière, v. 606. The second rendezvous was 46° 55′ N 7° 8′ W.; and see *Ibid.*, p. 765.
10. Rapport de la *Gloire* and Rapport d'Allemand : Desbrière, v. 763-5.
11. For the narrow escape of the *Naiad*, see Captain Dundas to Cornwallis: *Blockade of Brest*, ii. 332 ; and Rapport du Capitaine de l'*Armide*: Desbrière, v. 766. The *Naiad* had been detached by Cornwallis to the southward and westward to endeavour to obtain information of the Combined Squadron on August 6th: *Blockade of Brest*, ii. 331.
12. *Ibid.*, p. 766. The *Phœnix* had been sent down by Cornwallis shortly after he returned off Brest to communicate with Calder, according to Barham's general order to keep up communication with Ferrol.
13. See his *General Instructions: Blockade of Brest*, ii. 197.
14. Desbrière, v. 775, August 8th.
15. *Ibid.*, p. 776, August 6th.
16. Desbrière, v. 729, *note* 1.
17. Cornwallis to Marsden, July 29th: *Blockade of Brest*, ii. 328, and *Log of the Phœnix*. Fitzroy's orders are printed by James, vol. iv. p. 451-2, *Appendices* 1 and 2.
18. The report of Captain Milius put the incident on the 8th. James, from the Log of the *Æolus*, puts it on the 7th, in latitude 43° 41′, longitude 10° 11′; that is, considerably to the southward of the point shown in Colonel Desbrière's chart: *Projets et Tentatives*, v. 731. Fitzroy's conduct led to a violent controversy. James, for whom strategical questions had no interest, in his first edition practically accused him of cowardice. Fitzroy answered him in a not too judicious pamphlet. Captain Brenton, in his *Naval History*, supported Fitzroy, and James, in his second edition, returned to the charge at great length and ever greater intemperance. Fitzroy was a tyrannical and unpopular officer, but he does not appear to have been blamed on this occasion by his superiors. Modern naval opinion would now probably be unanimous in confirming the correctness of the behaviour of both Milius and Fitzroy, on the ground that both were charged with definite intelligence duty vital to the campaign. In contrast with Fitzroy's behaviour, James praises the *Niobe's*, who, having no special information, chased a strange sail for three days and three nights with the result that she never found Calder at all; and yet he blames Milius for engaging the *Phœnix* later. For the whole controversy see James (ed. 1902), iv. pp. 54-65.

19. James, who gives a minute account of the action (iv. p. 70), furnishes the following comparative table:—

	Broadside	*Crew*	*Tons*
Phœnix	21 guns, 444 lbs.	245	844
Didon	23 guns , 563 lbs.	330	1091

The Phœnix affords a typical example of the advantage of the carronade armament. Baker had had her re-armed on the new system with 26 short 18-pounders, 4 9-pounders, and 12 32-pounder carronades. The effect was almost to double her weight of metal. Originally her broadside was only 265 lbs.

20. For further details see James, iv. 65 *et seq.*, and Captain Baker to Cornwallis: *Blockade of Brest*, ii. 338.

CHAPTER XVI

1. Intelligence from Holland, July 10th, 13th, and 18th: *Admiralty In-letters* (*Secretary of State*), 4199.
2. Minutes of July 22nd: *Barham Papers.* The ships detailed in the order were *Defence*, *Goliath*, and *Zealous.*
3. Keith to the Admiralty, July 22nd: *In-letters*, 551. Keith at this time had his flag in the block ship *St. Albans* off Ramsgate.
4. *Admiralty In-letters*, (*Secretary of State*), 4199. Received July 26th.
5. Marsden to Cornwallis (two despatches), July 26th: *Barham Papers.* At this time also Hawkesbury from the Home Office was pressing the Admiralty for lieutenants to take charge of a chain of signal stations that was being established on the Irish coasts, and the Admiralty had difficulty in meeting the demand. The stations extended from Pigeon House (Dublin) to Bunmahon in Waterford, clustering closely round the south-east corner of the island. Beyond Cork they began again at Toe Head and continued by Cape Clear and the Great Blasket as far as Brandon Head in Kerry Thence, at wider intervals, they stretched by Galway Bay to Malin's Head in the extreme north. A list of them — twenty-seven in number — is in *Admiralty In-Letters* (*Secretary of State*), 4200, August 5th.
6. Keith to the Admiralty, July 28th: *In-letters*, 551. Keith had under his command at this time four flag-officers: Rear-Admiral Vashon, in one of the Leith guardships; Rear-Admiral "Billy" Douglas, in the *Leopard* 50, watching the Boulogne flotilla; Rear-Admiral T.M. Russell, with the Yarmouth-Texel division; and Vice-Admiral John Holloway, in the Nore guardship for the defence of the Thames. The Admiralty, however, kept a very direct control of the distribution of the ships and the general strategy. Keith habitually submits his proposed instructions for his flag-officers to the Admiralty, and sometimes seems to request that direct orders in accordance with them should be sent to the flag-officer concerned, if the Admiralty approved his suggestion. *In-letters*, 551-2, July 22nd; August 15th, *et passim.*
7. *Secret Orders: Out-letters*, July 21st. For the operations in question see James, iii. 318-323; Desbrière, v. 418-425; Keith to the Admiralty, July 18th-23rd, with enclosures: *In-letters*, 551.
8. *Princess of Orange* 74 (formerly the *Washington*), a Dutch prize; *Ruby* 64, *Polyphemus* 64. Cornwallis to Marsden, August 4th: *Blockade of Brest*, ii. 330.
9. Minute of July 30th: *Barham Papers.*
10. *Admiralty Secretary* (*Secret Orders*), 1363. Shortly afterwards sealed orders, the purport of which is unknown, were sent by Cornwallis to Stirling and Calder, but they never reached them. Some confusion occurred over the reinforcement of Keith. *Goliath* and *Defence* reached the Downs on July 30th, the day Barham ordered them back. On August 6th the other three vessels had arrived, and Keith acknowledged an order to send them back. This was cancelled next day by telegraph, and the ships were sent to Russell off the Texel, with whom they remained. *In-letters*, 551, July 23rd, 30th. *Ibid.*, 552, August 6th, 7th, 8th.
11. Barham to Cornwallis, Aug. 15th: *Hist. MSS. Com.*, *Various Collections*, vi. p.411.
12. Gower to Mulgrave, June 10th: *Foreign Office*, *Russia*, 58. Endorsed, "Received July 3rd." Printed in Holland Rose: *Third Coalition*, p. 174.

13. Gower to Mulgrave, June 29th. Endorsed, "Received July 29th." *Foreign Office, Russia*, 58. Printed in Holland Rose: *Third Coalition*, p. 183.
14. Novosilzow to Worontzow, Berlin, July 18th: Holland Rose, *Third Coalition*, p. 182 and 186-7. This last despatch was not actually communicated to the Foreign Office till August 3rd, but its purport must have been known to Pitt much earlier. See next page, *note* 17.
15. Hawkesbury to the Admiralty, July 27th: *Admiralty In-letters* (*Secretary of State*), 4199.
16. Same to same, June 29th: Rose, *Third Coalition*, p. 185.
17. *In-letters* (*Secretary of State*), 4200, July 25th. This order and that last mentioned of the 27th were anterior to the receipt of Gower's despatches, on which they appear so obviously to be founded. According to the endorsement, the despatches were received at the Foreign Office on July 29th. But it is almost certain Worontzow had received the information they contained some days earlier, and according to his practice he would have communicated it at once to Pitt. Gower explains that he himself had had the information "some days before he had sent it on," but that he had been prevented from writing "by a severe indisposition."
18. Castlereagh to Cornwallis, September 10th. (Copy communicated to the Admiralty.) *Admiralty In-letters* (*Secretary of State*), 4200.

CHAPTER XVII

1. Desbrière, v. 778.
2. Nelson's *Journal*, and *Log of the Victory* (*Hardy*).
3. The number of three-deckers with Cornwallis at the moment is difficult to determine exactly. But counting the *Victory* and *Glory*, he must have had nine or ten. A return in the *Barham Papers*, dated August 20th, shows the Home Fleet with ten three-deckers at sea, and five in reserve refitting.
4. P. Bertrand, *Lettres inédites de Talleyrand à Napoleon*, 120. The French Foreign Office had at this time a department of naval intelligence. Its last report was dated July 20th, and it showed that the British had forty-four of the line on the coasts of Spain and France. In the evening Talleyrand sent the Emperor "une boîte arrangée conformément à l'état présent," *Ibid.*; p. 122. A fortnight later Napoleon wrote to him, "The work that is being done in the Foreign Office on the movement of the enemy's ships of the line is very useful, but it might be more complete." — *Correspondance*, xi. 146, August 27th.
5. August 4th, *Correspondance*, xi. 59.
6. Desbrière, v. 736.
7. Desbrière, v. 739, *note*.
8. See *Ibid.*, p. 749.
9. For this story and the doubts as to its entire credibility see Auriol, v. p. 452 *note* and 493 *note*. He cites *Mémoires de Ségur*, p. 158, where the date is given as August 13th. Thiers puts the incident after the 23rd, but gives no authority for his date (*Consulat et Empire*, v. 464).
10. August 13th; *Correspondance*, xi. 81.
11. Aug. 13th, *Correspondance*, xi. 80.
12. Barham to Cornwallis, Aug. 15th.
13. *Blockade of Brest*, ii. 344, 347.
14. See Captain Hallowell (*Tigre*) to Nelson, August 17th : *Add. MSS*. 34930. According to him Calder reported that Allemand had joined Villeneuve in Ferrol, and Cornwallis calculated the Combined Fleet at twenty-five French and thirteen or fourteen Spanish. See Captain John Whitby (Cornwallis's flag-captain) to Nelson, August 19th: *Ibid.*, "It appears to me nothing could have been more a propos than your junction here, as it has enabled the Admiral to make a large detachment, which the posture of the enemy seemed to make highly necessary — for it the Rochefort squadron have got into Ferrol, the enemy have there thirty sail of the line." Barham also had "no doubt of the Rochefort ships being at Ferrol." See his letter to Cornwallis, *Wykeham-Martin MSS.—Hist. MSS. Com.*; *Various Coll.*, vol. vi. 410.

15. Ganteaume to Decrès, August 23rd: Desbrière, v. 806.
16. To Decrès, August 29th: *Correspondance*, xi. 160.
17. *Influence of Sea Power on the Revolution and Empire*, ii. 176; *Cambridge Modern History*, ix. 226; *Blockade of Brest*, ii., *Introduction*, p. xxxix ; Laird Clowes, *The Royal Navy*, v. 119. It is believed that no naval officer, except Captain Mahan has taken this view. Neither Admiral Colomb, Jurien de la Gravière, nor Desbrière shared it, and it has been distinctly repudiated by Sir John K. Laughton.
18. To Captain Keats, August 24th: Nicolas, vii. 16.
19. *Naiad*, *Nimble*, and *Iris* had been sent down specially after Calder joined. *Hazard*, *Révolutionnaire*, and *Melampus* were already to the southward — *Blockade of Brest*, ii. 337, 345.
20. *Ibid.*, ii. 343, August 16th.
21. *In-letters* (*Secret Orders*) 1363. Signed "Barham, Gambier, Garlies."
22. *Barham Papers*, *Digest of Correspondence*, August 9th; and Barham to Cornwallis, August 10th, *Hist. MSS. Com.*, *Various Collections*, vi. 410.
23. Mahan, *Sea Power* (*French Revolution*), ii. 576. It is only just to the learned and gallant author to note that this criticism was written before he had had any experience of war direction. After he had had such experience he gave a definition of concentration that seems incompatible with his censure of Cornwallis: "Like a fan that opens and shuts, vessels thus organically bound together possess the power of wide sweep, which ensures exertion over a wide field of ocean, and at the same time that of mutual support, because dependent upon and controlled from a common centre. Such is concentration reasonably understood — not huddled together like a drove of sheep, but distributed with a regard to a common purpose and linked together by the effectual energy of a single will."—*War of* 1812, i. 316.
24. Bourchier, *Memoirs of Codrington*, i. 56, October 16, 1805.
25. *Hist. MSS. Com.*, *Various Collections*, vi. 410.
26. On the accepted basis of two two-deckers to one three-decker the tactical coefficient of Cornwallis' fleet was (10 x 2) + 8 = 28 against that of Villeneuve (1 x 2) + 28 = 30.
27. The most moderate and careful of the critics takes a different view of the result of Villeneuve's catching Cornwallis alone. "It seems possible," he says, "that in such circumstances Cornwallis would have had no course but to fly, and that the great concentration of fifty ships in the Channel might have been brought about." — *Blockade of Brest*, ii. xxxix. But there can be no doubt that Cornwallis would have taken the traditional position which Drake had inaugurated and Howe and Kempenfelt had recently adopted, and would have hung to windward of the enemy if they attempted to enter the Channel. He might have refused action except on his own terms, but it was against all tradition and practice that he should have run away.
28. *Barham Papers*, August 20th.

CHAPTER XVIII

1. Lieutenant Delafons to Cornwallis, August 11th: *Blockade of Brest*, ii. 334, and *Log of the Nimble, P.R.O.*
2. Desbrière, v. 730.
3. *Ibid.*, 778.
4. Desbrière, *Trafalgar*, *App*. 38, and see Thiers, *Consulat et Empire*, v. 439.
5. Desbrière, *Trafalgar*, *App*., 106, 108. This letter was not written till August 21st when they were in Cadiz, but it serves to show the general feeling in the fleet. Nelson used the expression referred to in his letter to t^ Admiralty of May 7th. — Nicolas, vi. 428.
6. Desbrière, *Trafalgar*, *App*., p. 105.
7. Thiers, *Consulat et Empire*, v. 442. This is the only known letter of this date (13th). The correspondence of Dècres was destroyed in the Tuileries fire during the Commune after Thiers had worked from it. There are traces however, of another letter. On September 8th, Napoleon wrote to Dècres: "After having had the despatches of Villeneuve, you ought never to have supposed he would come to Brest. He wrote to you,

"I am going to Cadiz,'" and then he refers to Lauriston's letter: *Correspondance*, xi. 183. Dècres, however, in acknowledging Villeneuve's letters on September 1st, implies that they left his destination uncertain. — Desbrière, v. 822.

8. Desbrière, *Trafalgar, App.*, p. 7, and Report of the *Nimble*. Dècres, even in attempting to defend his old friend, took the same view. "On August 10th," he says in his report to the Emperor, the fleet weighed; several vessels collided and suffered damage. Numerous reconnaissances were engrossing the enemy's movements. The Admiral learned that Calder and Nelson had joined; his anxieties redoubled; he had only forty days' victuals. He remained in the bay till the 13th. Finally . . . he puts to sea and steers first W.N.W., and on the 25th decides to make to Cadiz. It would seem from the correspondence of Vice-Admiral Villeneuve, that he had taken this resolution as early as the 11th." — Desbrière, *Projets*, v. 726 *n*.
9. *Ibid.*,v. 786.
10. Captain Edward Brace's report, enclosed in Captain Blackwood's despatch of August 16th: *Captains' letters*, 1534. He gives the course as W. by N.½ N., and the position Lat. 44° 17′, Long. 9° 26′.
11. *Ibid.*, and Phillimore's *Life of Sir W. Parker*, i. 303.
12. Cornwallis to Calder, August 19th: *In-letters*, 129. Endorsed, per *Naiad*, and a duplicate by *Hazard*. See also same to Marsden, August 19th: *Blockade of Brest*, ii. 346. This was the despatch in which he announced to the Admiralty his division of the fleet, which Barham was ordering at the same time.
13. Cornwallis to Marsden: *In-letters*, 129, August 20th.
14. To Decrès and to Ganteaume (by telegraph), August 21st: *Correspondance*, xi. 105-6.
15. His course is very doubtful. He and all the authorities, including Escaño, say it was W.N.W. on a N.E. wind. But Reille says the noon position of the 15th was about 40 leagues W.N.W. of Finisterre, that is, about 55 leagues W. of Ferrol. One means of reconciling this position with the course given is to assume that the positions are "true" and the courses "magnetic." The variation about Finisterre in 1805 was about 22½ west (see *Log of the Victory*, August 13th-16th, where Hardy observed it each day, varying from 22° 35′ W. in long., 118° and 23° 15′ in long., 12° to 22° 49′ in long. 11°). Therefore a "magnetic" course W.N.W. would give a "true" course just about W. A further corroboration that this was the actual course is that it led direct to Allemand's first rendezvous. Villeneuve gives the evening position as 80 leagues W.N.W. of Finisterre; but it is, of course, impossible for him to have covered the distance in the time. Another explanation is, that although he was steering about W.N.W., the combined effects of the leeway and drift of the Portuguese branch of the Biscay current setting strongly S.S.E., may have made his actual course about W. In any case, he cannot have got so far north of the latitude of Ferrol as he is represented in the French staff map (Desbrière, v. 782), for after turning south he was off Cadiz in eighty hours. It was a run of 550 miles from the latitude of Ferrol (say sixty leagues west), giving a speed of seven knots, which is the utmost his fleet could have done, as he had to wait occasionally for laggards.
16. There is no trace of these vessels in the reports of the British cruisers which were then to the north-east of him.
17. Colonel Desbrière is of opinion these eight sail were "certainly Allemand." But Reille says that all of them that were examined were neutrals. At 2 o'clock A.M. on the 14th, Villeneuve was tacking under Cape Prior; at 4 o'clock Allemand saw three suspicious sail to the N.E., and Colonel Desbrière thinks these were some of Villeneuve's cruisers. But Allemand says he was then in 45° 39′ N., 13° 31′ W. (*i.e.* 11° 11′ Greenwich), which was about 150 miles N.W. of Cape Prior: *Projets*, v. 783; *Trafalgar*, 100.
18. In this Captain Griffith may well have been mistaken. It was nearly dark, and he himself apparently was not seen by the fleet at all.
19. *Log of the Dragon* (Griffith's). James (iii. 374) is the authority for Griffith's trick. Lauriston to the Emperor, August 21st: Desbrière, *Trafalgar, App.*, p. 107.
20. Journal de Reille. "A midi . . . 40 lieues Ouest-nord-ouest du Cap Finisterre": Desbrière, *Projets*, v. 785. It is this position that fixes Villeneuve's mean course from Ferrol as due west true.
21. Allemand's Journal: *Ibid.*, 784.
22. Desbrière, *Trafalgar, App.*, p. 108, August 21st.
23. Desbrière, v. 646.

24. Desbrière, *Trafalgar, App.*, p. 7.
25. *Ibid.*, p. 108. Villeneuve in his report says he turned back at a point 80 leagues W.N.W. of Finisterre, but this is impossible. He could not in seven or eight hours run 120 miles from his noon position.
26. *Life of Parker*, i. p. 303. Without anchoring, Dundas carried on to Ushant "with a duplicate of the information, should any unforeseen accident have prevented the *Naiad* reaching Admiral Cornwallis." — *Ibid.* p. 304.
27. For this Drury was reproved by the Admiralty, and told to be more careful how he sent his cruisers on detached service for the future. — *In-letters*, 620, August 2nd, 11th, 14th, 16th.
28. This was approximately accurate, but how Strangford knew is not stated.
29. *S.P. Foreign, Portugal*, vol. 47: Strangford to Mulgrave, August 7th. This letter came to hand on September 9th, and was sent to the Admiralty the same day. Endorsed, "Send copy to Lord Nelson": *In-letters, Secretary of State*, 4200.
30. Blackwood to the Admiralty, August 16th and 18th: *Captains' Letters*, 1534. Logs of the *Iris* and *Euryalus*.
31. *Masters' Logs*, 3673 (*Prince of Wales*). There is no indication of his having had further information when he altered course, but at 11.0 a.m. on the 21st a large convoy of transports was seen, which, being uninjured, was perhaps taken as indication that Villeneuve possibly had turned back. Or his idea may have been to keep more to windward, so as to be able to reach back to Cornwallis if necessary.
32. Allemand actually made Cape S. Adrian (the Sisargas) on August 26th: *Journal*, Desbrière, v. 792.
33. *Log of the Nimble*, Calder to Cornwallis, August 22nd: *In-letters*, 129. Napoleon was at the time trying to organise an expedition to relieve San Domingo which Villeneuve had left besieged by the black insurgents. Napoleon to Dècres, August 5th: *Correspondance*, xi. 63.
34. Calder to Cornwallis, Aug. 24th: *In-letters*, 129, and *Log of the Prince of Wales*.
35. *Blockade of Brest*, ii. 356 *n.*; *Life of Collingwood*, 95.

CHAPTER XIX

1. The connection between these two events is only a matter of conjecture for it is not clear at what time exactly Napoleon heard of Craig's being at Malta. He arrived on July 19th. Elliot heard of it at Naples on August 1st (Auriol, i. 387). On Aug. 8th the French Ambassador at Berlin made the offer of Hanover. St. Cyr wrote on the subject on Aug. 15th, but only as news which he had sent some time before: *Ibid.*, 398. The first reference in Napoleon's correspondence is on Aug. 19th, when he had already ordered St Cyr to be reinforced.
2. To Talleyrand, Aug. 22nd: *Correspondance*, xi. 107.
3. *Correspondence of Castlereagh*. To the Duke of York, July 26th, vol. ii. p. 6.
4. *Correspondance*, xi. 117, Aug. 23rd.
5. August 22nd, Desbrière, v. 814. The occasion referred to must be the great but impotent concentration of the Franco-Spanish forces at Cadiz in the autumn of 1780. D'Estaing put to sea on November 6th and anchored at Brest on January 3, 1781. He spent some time cruising off Cape St. Vincent, and his actual passage thence to Brest was fifty-eight days. See Lacour-Gayet, *Marine sous Louis XVI.*, p. 322.
6. *Correspondance*, xi. p. 134.
7. *Correspondance*, xi. 146, Aug. 27.
8. *Ibid.*, 157, Aug. 28.
9. *Castlereagh Correspondence*, ii. 6. There is a similar undated "Memorandum for moving the disposable force" in the *Pitt Papers* Bundle 243. It shows 45,000 foot, 6,700 artillery, and 12,000 cavalry, requiring 308,000 tons of transport at 1½ tons per man. On Russia's suggestion that peace might be made with Spain, Pitt was already contemplating the possibility of using this force on the Peninsula. See *Appendix B.*
10. *Correspondance*, xi. p. 159, Aug. 29.
11. To Duroc (Postscript), *Corrcspondance*, xi. 157.

12. Blackwood to the Admiralty: *Captain's Letters*, 1534. He submitted a bill for £15, 19*s*. 0*d*. for his journey, which was allowed. The telegraph, of course, could not be used at night or in thick weather.
13. Rainier left Madras with Wellesley on March 10th, and reached St. Helena, the great Southern convoy rendezvous, on June 21st. Here they were joined by the China ships and some whalers, making twenty-nine sail, which were valued at £15,000,000. Varying at his own discretion the Admiralty instructions, he sailed again on July 12th after forcing certain neutrals to remain behind anchored under the fort guns for fear of their betraying his route. — Rainier to Marsden. "Off the Start, Sept. 8": *In-letters*, 176; and *Log of the Trident.*
14. *Secret Orders*, August 27th.
15. Vol. xiv. 157.
16. Clarke and M'Arthur, ii. 116. This copy of the Journal is in the Record Office with its covering letter to Marsden, which appears never to have been printed. It is as follows; "Merton, August (*sic*) 1805. In answer to your letter of the 19th requesting, by direction of the Lords Commissioners of the Admiralty, that I will transmit you a journal of my proceedings for their information, I beg leave to acquaint you that never having been called upon (or understanding it to be customary) as Commander-in-chief to furnish their Lordships with a journal of my proceedings, none has been kept for that purpose, except for the different periods the fleet under my command was in pursuit of the enemy, from the 19th of January 1805 till the 12th of March following, and from the 4th of April till the 20th instant, which I herewith transmit for the information of the Lords Commissioners of the Admiralty."
17. Gower to Mulgrave, July 21st and 22nd, received Aug. 12th: *F.O. Russia*, 58. Printed by Holland Rose, *Third Coalition*, pp. 188-93.
18. Gower to Mulgrave, July 31st (two despatches), received August 23rd: *Ibid.*
19. It was not till Sept. 3rd that the Admiralty informed Ministers that Bickerton had seen him as far as Cape Bona with a fair wind. — *War Office*, i, 712. On Aug. 1st, Elliot had written fully of his arrival and the co-operation of the Russians, but though he specially sent the letter to Rome to be forwarded by post overland it did not come to hand till "Sept. 17th at night." — *Foreign Office, Sicily*, 25.
20. Elliot to Mulgrave, July 9th and 16th, received August 14th and 22nd; *F.O. Sicily*, 25.
21. Nelson to Pitt, 6 A.M., Aug. 29th, and same to Lord Minto, Aug. 31st: Nicolas, vii. 20, 25. Castlereagh to Nelson, Sept. —: *Castlereagh's Letters and Despatches*, 2nd series, i. 88. Nelson to Ball, Sept. 30th: Nicolas, vii. 55.
22. Gower to Mulgrave, Aug. 14th, received Sept. 1st: *F.O. Foreign*, 58. Holland Rose, *Third Coalition*, p. 197.
23. Same to same, August 14th: *F.O. Russia*, 58. Received September 1st.
24. Mulgrave to Gower, September 3rd: *F.O. Foreign*, 58.
25. Clarke and M'Arthur, ii. 117. Nelson's opinion must not, of course, be taken too seriously. Mack was a man who had risen from the ranks, but whether by his ability or, like Ralegh, by "his bold and plausible tongue," opinions differed. The British War Office inclined to believe in him. Napoleon regarded him as a charlatan.
26. To Sir A. Ball, Sept. 30th. Nicolas, vii. 55.
27. Clarke and M'Arthur, ii. 117.
28. Croker, *Diary*, ii. 233.
29. Rose and Broadley: *Dumouriez and the Defence of England*, p. 453, Sept. 11th, citing *Add. MSS*., 34931, f. 160; and see *Ibid*., p. 207, for his letter to Nelson of April 20, 1801: "If you have charge of the Mediterranean Sea we can together deliver Italy and France of the democratic tyranny." Two other letters are *Ibid*., pp. 208-210. For his appreciation, written after he knew Villeneuve was at Coruña and on the false supposition that Calder would blockade him there, see *Ibid*., ch. xiii.
30. Nelson to Keats, August 24th: Postscript, "You see by my writing tackle that I am not yet mounted as Commander-in-chief": Nicolas, vii. 16.
31. *Add. MSS*., 34930.
32. On August 29th there is a Minute ordering the *Victory* to join Cornwallis the moment she is ready to sail, and to tell Nelson she is no longer under his command: *Admiralty Minutes*, 154.

33. Admiral Lord Radstock to Nelson, September 3rd: *Add. MSS.*, 34931.
34. *Admiralty Minutes*, 154, Sept 2nd.
35. This day, Sept. 4th, must have been one of the heaviest known to the Admiralty. There were then seven "Senior Clerks" (£800-£350) and seventeen "Junior Clerks" (£250-£90) to deal with the routine of the enormous number of ships in commission; and only four days before they had memorialised for an increase of salary (*Minutes*, 154, Aug. 29th). In July Barham had made an attempt to reduce this paper work by issuing printed forms for returning "Dispositions" and for acknowledging orders and letters. The latter had three columns: (1) The date, (2) Subject of the letter, (3) Result, *i.e.* the action that had been or would be taken on it. For examples, see *In-letters*, 552, August 2nd and 4th.
36. Admiralty *In-letters* (*Secret Orders*), 1363, Sept. 3rd. It was on the 6th that Marsden the Secretary informed him they were ready and requested him to call for them at the Admiralty. — *Add. MSS.*, 34931.
37. Paget to Mulgrave, August 10 and 17, received September 5th (at night) *F.O. Austria*, 74.
38. Elliot to Mulgrave, July 23rd, received September 5th (at night): *F.O. Sicily*. Printed in Auriol, ii. 368.
39. *Admiralty In-letters* (*Secretary of State*), 4199, September 6th.
40. *Admiralty In-letters*, 552, September 5th. Sent to the War Office next day. — *W.O.* (i.), 712. It is worth noting that at this time every scrap of naval intelligence was forwarded daily to the War Office as soon as it came in.
41. Castlereagh to Nelson: *Letters and Despatches*, 2nd series, vol. i. p. 124. This letter was written the day before the news of Nelson's death reached London.
42. Canning was at this time Treasurer of the Navy, and Rose Vice-President of the Board of Trade and Joint Paymaster-General.
43. Desbrière, v. 823.
44. Napoleon to Dècres, September 1st: *Correspondance*, xi. 170.
45. For the vitality of the legend, see Captain Gabriel Darrieu's *La Guerre sur Mer*, 1907, pp. 63 *et seq.* Writing seven years after the publication of the French Staff History, the Professor of Strategy can still quote the paper and say, "It is a specimen of magnificent strategy; its principles are impeccable and the plan in its grandiose proportions could and should have succeeded." He accepts in their entirety Napoleon's travesty of the facts and his elimination of the enemy; treats Barham's dispositions as matters of pure chance; and then, as his better judgment and conspicuous knowledge of his profession reassert themselves, he proceeds to show that the whole plan was based on the Emperor's profound ignorance of the elements of naval warfare, and had no chance of success.
46. Napoleon to Villeneuve, St. Cloud, Sept. 14th: *Correspondance*, xi. 195.
47. To Dècres, September 15th, and Rosily's Instructions, September 17th: *Correspondance*, xi. 204 and 217.

CHAPTER XX

1. See especially the case of the *Cerberus*. After Missiessy's escape from Rochefort she was sent from Saumarez's squadron, on March 27th, to cruise about Madeira for a month and to return immediately. She did not come back till July 15th, and Saumaurez was directed to express to her captain "the high disapprobation of the Admiralty." — *In-letters*, 223; *Secret Orders*, 1363.
2. Nelson had certainly used it to communicate with his battleship captains (see *e.g.* his letter to Hargood, Aug. 5th: Nicolas, viii. 3). In saying the code had just been improved and enlarged Barrow's memory must have deceived him. According to the Introduction and successive Prefaces to the work, the first edition was privately printed in 1800, and was used by Popham in the Baltic principally for communicating between his ship, the *Romney* 50, off Copenhagen, and Admiral Dickson at Elsinore. Later on he used it in the Red Sea, and by the encouragement of Lord Spencer, then First Lord, he prepared a new edition when he came home, adding two new parts. Part I. (the old edition) had about 1000 words; Part II. added 1000 more, and Part III. a number of sentences and phrases. This edition was in quarto, and issued in 1803. Up till

1809 there were several reprints in a cheaper octavo form, but no additions or changes were made.

3. Gardner to Admiralty, Sept. 9th: *In-letters*, 620. He says the orders were dated Sept. 6th. In the *Barham Papers* is a draft of them undated.
4. Cornwallis, it should be said, did not recognise anything peculiarly new in the arrangement, and perhaps a little resented the reflection on his usual methods. In owning a copy of the Irish Station order, together with his quota of Popham's Signal Books, he says: "The instructions contained in the order are nearly the same as have generally been given. I can therefore only guess why the copy of the order was sent to me." — To the Admiralty, Sept. 28th: *In-letters*, 129.
5. This important letter has hitherto been unpublished. It was presented to the Britannia R.N. College, Dartmouth, on Trafalgar Day, 1907, by Mrs. Scarth (of Bearsted, Kent). Thompson was the First Lord's Private Secretary.
6. *Out-letters* (*Secret Orders*), 1184. For his working of the line see *Captains' Letters*, 2075,
7. *Admiralty Minutes*, 154, Sept. 3rd, 9th, 22th. Drury to Admiralty; *In-letters*, 640, Sept. 9th. A minute of Oct. 5th (*Ibid*., p. 155) shows copies sent to the West Indies and North America, and twenty more copies for Nelson.
8. *Log of the Diadem* (Sir Home Popham), *Captains' Logs*, 1743. He weighed on Aug. 28th, but did not get clear out of Queenstown harbour till the 31st.
9. Cornwallis to Marsden, Aug. 20th: *In-letters*, 129. The route Rainier sailed was about two hundred miles west of the Azores and then for the Lizard.
10. Cochrane to the Admiralty, July 17th: *In-letters*, 326. *Admiralty Minutes*, July 11th, ordering him to send home the *Illustrious* and *Ramillies* with any convoy that was ready. He detained the *Ramillies* for the second convoy.
11. Barham to Gardner: *Barham Papers*, written between August 17th and 23rd. More than a month before, July 11th, he had ordered Dacres at Jamaica to send home four of his heaviest frigates for this purpose. — *Secret Orders* 1363.
12. Secret Orders, 1363. 2
13. Stirling had *Glory* 98 (flag), four seventy-fours (*Repulse*, *Triumph*, *Dragon*, *Warrior*), and the *Crescent* 36. The *Melampus* and other cruisers were already out trying to locate the enemy.
14. To Decrès, September 4th: *Correspondance*, xi 176.
15. Cornwallis to Marsden, September 2nd: *Blockade of Brest* ii 352. His actual orders to Stirling have not been found. It is uncertain, therefore, whether he had instructed him to take Barham's position ÐÐ 100 leagues W.S.W. of Scilly.
16. The failure to locate Allemand seems to have been partly due to bad cruising. On September 6th the *Melampus* came back to say she had been chased by four of the line off the Saints the day before in thick weather. But subsequently it proved that the ships from which she had run were two of Cornwallis's own frigates and two sloops. ÐÐ *Blockade of Brest*, ii. 358, 361.
17. Stirling to Cornwallis, September 16th. "Scilly bearing N.E. by E. 26 leagues," enclosed in Cornwallis to Marsden, September 27th. — *In-letters*, 129.
18. Parker to his mother, August 30th. — "Since writing the above I joined Admiral Cornwallis, who with the best intentions and in the kindest manner has ordered me to cruise three weeks to the westward for the protection of the homeward-bound trade." — Phillimore, *Life of Sir W. Parker*, i. 305.
19. Parker to Cornwallis: *Blockade of Brest*, ii. 359. Her commander was François Beck. She had taken our Lisbon packet and a letter of Marque. The crew of the latter and a considerable sum of specie were on board.
20. *Log of the Glory* (Stirling's flag). *Captains' Logs*, 1544. Cornwallis to Admiralty with Stirling's Report, August 22-27. See also "Proceedings of the Fleet" — *Nelson Papers, Add. MSS.*, 34973, and Nicolas, vii. p. 46. Stirling rejoined on Sept. 22nd.
21. *Admiralty Minutes*, 154, Sept. 3rd.
22. Allemand says she was the *Phœbus*, from Gibraltar to Grenada. She does not appear in any navy list, and must have been a simple trader.

23. Allemand's *Journal:* Desbrière, v. 794.
24. The facts of this episode are taken from the *Log of the Diadem*, Popham's ship (*Captains' Logs*, 1743), and Allemand's *Journal:* • Desbrière, v. 793. When Allemand captured the brig he was in 35° 50′ N and 11° 38′ W. (= 9° 18′ Greenwich). This was at 6 P.M. on the 11th. He then took "la bordée du nord.ouest en attendant une plus mûre reflexion." This course, if he continued it, would take him almost direct to Popham's noon position on the 17th (*i.e.* 39° 32′ N. and 14° 12′ W.), and on an average rate of sailing he cannot have crossed the British track much before the 13th and it may have been later. His Journal, however, gives no entries for these days. Popham at this time had only the *Diadem* 64, *Belliqueux* 64 *Diomede* 50 *Narcissus* 32, and the *Leda* 36. The latter he sent forward to Madeira on the 15th.
25. James, iv. 47. Allemand's *Journal:* Desbrière, v. 795.
26. *Moucheron's* Report, enclosed in Cornwallis to the Admiralty: *In-letters*, 129.
27. Hawes's Report, *Ibid.* He took the precaution of sending in a copy of the whaler's log, for the Admiral's information.
28. *Cæsar* 80, *Hero* 74, *Namur* 74, *Courageux* 74, and two frigates.
29. Cornwallis to Marsden, October 5th, 8th, and 9th: *In-letters*, 129
30. Allemand's *Journal:* Desbrière, v. 795.
31. The situation is by no means certain. Captain Sir Edward Berry, who commanded the *Agamemnon*, says at 3.30 A.M. Finisterre bore S.70.W., meaning probably magnetic. Allemand says he sighted her at 4.0 A.M. "ahead and pretty close," but he also says on the 7th he was 12 leagues from Vigo, that is, much further to the southward. The "12 "must be an error of transcription. If he was so close to Vigo on the 8th he could not have seen the *Agamemnon* on the next day, and moreover he must have passed through Strachan's squadron the previous day.
32. For Captain Sir E. Berry's despatch see Newbolt, *Year of Trafalgar*, p. 40, and Nicolas, vii. 117 *note*. Allemand thought he recognised the *Agamemnon* as the *Dragon*, "England's fastest ship."
33. For an amusing account of the *Aimable's* escape by a newly-joined midshipman, see Newbolt, *Year of Trafalgar*, p. 40.

CHAPTER XXI

1. Keith to Admiralty, July 12th: *In-letters*, 557. Barham minuted the letter that such a blockade as Keith suggested was a question for the Foreign Office, and the Minute was sent there accordingly and disallowed.
2. *Foreign Office* (*Sicily*), 25. Elliot to Mulgrave, August 1st (*via* Rome), endorsed, "Received Sept. 7th at night." Paget to same, August 29th and 30th, "most secret," received the same day: *Foreign Office* (*Austria*), 74. Craig's despatches are in *War Office* (1) 280, July 20-1.
3. Castlereagh to the Admiralty, September 21st: *In-letters* (*Sec. of State*), 4200.
4. *Secret Orders*, 1363, September 21st.
5. Maurice, *Diary of Sir John Moore*, ii. 109. Castlereagh to Moore September 23rd. Barham to Castlereagh, September 25th. Pitt to same, October 6th. *Castlereagh Correspondence*, *2nd Series*, i. 86-117; and Stanhope' *Life of Pitt*, iv. 337: "Walmer Castle, October 6th, 1805. — Dear Castlereagh — You will have learned from General Moore the substance of what passed between him and me, which left me convinced that any attempt at landing is attended with too much risk to justify the experiment. I still entertain considerable hopes of something effectual being done, and I trust you will not have had much further difficulty in overcoming the objections both of Lord Keith and the Admiralty. Your answer to Lord Barham places the subject exactly in the true light. . . . With this wind I am much disappointed not to have heard of anything fresh from the Continent. — Ever sincerely yours, W. Pitt."
6. Escaño (Gravina's Chief of the Staff) to Don Enrique MacDonnell, Captain of the *Rayo:* Desbrière, *Trafalgar*, *App*. 98. There was another MacDonnell, a brigadier, in the fleet, who sat on the Council of War.
7. Villeneuve to Dècres, Oct. 8th: *Ibid.*, p. 96.

8. Procès-verbal du Conseil du guerre, &c.," and Escaño's letter to Captain MacDonnell: *Ibid.*, pp. 97-9.
9. Bourchier, *Life of Codrington*, i. 53. Codrington wrote Duplex instead of Dècres.
10. Nicolas, vii. 85-6,107. For the service of the battle fleet his requisition was for 8 frigates and 2 sloops, of which 2 frigates and 4 sloops were to keep open communication with Gibraltar and Lisbon. For observation and commercial blockade service he required 3 frigates at Cape Spartel, Cape St. Mary and the Salvages, and 2 sloops for Cape St. Vincent, as well as a frigate and a sloop off Cartagena. Besides these the officer in command at Gibraltar required 2 frigates and 3 sloops for the protection of the Straits, while for the rest of the Mediterranean were required 3 frigates and 6 sloops, besides the 3 frigates which formed Craig's escort.
11. According to Lieutenant (afterwards Admiral Sir Humphrey) Senhouse the general idea in the fleet was that Nelson chose his position with the following objects: "In the first place to give the enemy chance of escape; next to prevent our fleet being driven through the Straits of Gibraltar in the winter westerly gales . . . and lastly to be ready to intercept the Brest fleet, should they have endeavoured to form a Junction with the fleet at Cadiz before the latter could arrive to the assistance of the former." — *Macmillan's Magazine*, vol. 81, p.415.
12. To the Right. Hon. Sir George Rose, Oct. 6. In view of the fact that this letter is often cited as evidence of Nelson's preference for a number of units as against individual force, it should be noted that what he is pressing Rose for, is "the fixed force." Now besides the *Victory* and *Royal Sovereign* and the two seventy-fours which he had brought out, the fixed force which he was expecting included the *London* and *Barfleur* 98's, the *Agamemnon* 64, and *Belleisle* 74. Thus of eight units half were three-deckers. (To Blackwood, Oct. 8 and 9, Nicolas vii. 88 and 96.) In his official letter to Barham, he says nothing about "numbers," but only "the ships from England" (Oct. 5, *Ibid.*, p. 75). The expression used to Rose clearly proves nothing either way, if read with its context.
13. Nicolas, vii. 81 *note*.
14. Hubback, *Jane Austen's Sailor Brothers*, p. 149; James, *Naval History*, iv. 380; *Log of the Canopus*. Blackwood had the information from a Swede.
15. Nicolas, vii.110, October 10th.
16. For both these documents, see *Appendix D*. It is worth noting that had Villeneuve come out when Nelson first expected him the Memorandum would not have been ready.
17. *Log of the Cæsar*.
18. Nicolas, vii. 121 and 126-7-9. On the same day, the 18th, we have another ray of light on Nelson's regard for three-decked ships. Collingwood, in discussing what ships should receive water from the water-ships, says, "I suppose your lordship would wish the three-deckers to be filled up well." — *Ibid.*, *note*. This seems to put force before numbers.
19. Hubback, *Jane Austen's Sailor Brothers*, p. 152. Louis received the order by a frigate at Tetuan on the 17th. He also at this time sent the *Donegal* 74 into Gibraltar "for a ground-tier of casks."
20. "Mr. Francis" was the famous American, Robert Fulton. He had invented a torpedo, designed to be fixed to the cable of a ship in a tideway, when it would swing under her and be exploded by clockwork. It had lately been tried with success experimentally.
21. *Nelson Papers*, *Add. MSS.* 34968.
22. One of these was the *Donegal* 74, which Nelson had just sent in there, "being obliged to go into the Mole for two days." Nelson to Collingwood, Oct. 19th: Nicolas, vii. 127. The other may have been the *Zealous* 74, which, with the *Endymion* 40 ("both being crippled ships"), Louis had originally sent on with the Malta convoy.
23. Villeneuve to Dècres, Oct. 18th (two letters): Desbrière, *Trafalgar*, *App.* 101-2.

CHAPTER XXII

1. There has been some confusion about Nelson's exact position when he got the signal. He says in his Diary: "Wind at South, Cadiz bearing E.N.E. by compass (*i.e.* magnetic) 16 leagues." The variation as recorded

in the log of the *Montanes* was 20° West (Desbrière, *Trafalgar, App.* 374). E.N.E. magnetic was therefore about N.E. true. On a south wind he could not sail south-east true, nor from a position 16 leagues true S.W. of Cadiz could he make the Straits on that course. The signal he used was the single flag with two guns and the S.E. compass flag, and it meant "The whole fleet to chase in the S.E. quarter." The course required was a little south of east, *i.e.* in the south-east quarter. Probably, however, Nelson's position is wrong, for the noon position in the *Victory's* log is 36° 36′ N. 7° 30′ W., which makes Cadiz bear about 19 leagues E.S.E. magnetic and about E. true, that is, his regular position. From this point a south-east course led into the Straits' mouth. There is nothing to show Nelson had changed the position of the fleet, and probably therefore he wrote "E.N.E." for "E.S.E." by mistake. According to the *Téméraire's* log the course was first E. by S. and wind S. by E., and afterwards S.E. by E. on a W.S.W. wind.

2. Nelson to Collingwood, October 18th and 19th: Nicolas, vii. 127, 129. No instructions to Louis have been found, but Nelson says he told him "an easterly wind must not be lost," even if the convoy had to wait for the next detachment.
3. An Advance Squadron was established in the Mediterranean fleet as early as 1790. It was not Nelson's idea, and was borrowed probably from the French. See *Signals and Instructions* (*Navy Record Society*), pp. 72-3. The composition of the Division in this case is uncertain. Codrington in a letter to his wife (*Life*, i. 57) says: "The above four *Agamemnon*, *Defence*, *Colossus*, and *Mars*) and as many more of us are now to form an advanced squadron, and I trust by morning we shall all be united [*i.e.* with Louis] and in sight of the enemy." He also says his own ship, *Orion*, and the *Belleisle*, were amongst those that went ahead. *Defence* and *Agamemnon* were nearest Cadiz, with *Mars* and *Colossus* as connecting ships. *Téméraire* records a signal (No. 155) to *Belleisle*, *Orion*, *Leviathan*, *Polyphemus*, and *Bellerophon*, "to keep a look-out ahead during the night at a convenient distance for intercourse by night signals, carrying a light in the stern." — *Masters' Logs*, 3706. Colonel Owen, who then commanded the Marines in the *Belleisle*, also says five were sent forward. — Allen, *Memoirs of Sir W. Hargood*, p. 137. There must therefore have been nine pennants in the squadron — that is, one-third of the force with Nelson's flag — an unusually large proportion.
4. *Private Diary*, Nicolas, vii. 133, and *Téméraire's* Signal Log, *Masters' Logs*, 3706. A curious effect of this order was that the French believed these three ships had been formed into an *Escadre d'observation*.
5. *Log of the Queen*. Hubback, *Jane Austen's Sailor Brothers*, p. 152
6. Bourchier, *Life of Codrington*, i. 58.
7. Nicolas, vii. 75.
8. Dr Beatty says: "At 8 o'clock the *Victory* hove-to, and Admiral Collingwood . . . came on board to receive instructions." Codrington related the incident thus: "On the Sunday morning Lord Nelson, as a compliment to Collingwood, called him on board by signal to consult with him, saying to Hardy jocosely that he should not be guided by his opinion unless it agreed with his own; and upon asking him, Collingwood gave his opinion in favour of attacking the fleet immediately. Lord Nelson, however, kept to his plan of waiting till he could get them farther off, as they did not seem determined to return to Cadiz but to persevere in their original intentions, &c. This was one of the passages which Codrington dictated to his daughter, Lady Bourchier many years later." — *Life of Codrington*, i. 59.
9. Hardy's Journal: *Captains' Logs*, 414.
10. *Log of Euryalus: Great Sea Fights*, ii 167. "At 4.10 to *Victory*, No. 413, north, two guns." This was an MS. addition in the Signal Book. It appears in a copy belonging to Captain Hope, R.N., with this signification: "The leading ship of the enemy's line bears on the point of the compass shown herewith." *Euryalus*' time was about three-quarters of an hour ahead of *Victory's*. By *Victory's* time the signal would have been made about 3.30 *Euryalus*' log gives it as 4.10. *Téméraire* says *Naiad* made it at 3.34.
11. Lieutenant Senhouse to his mother: *Macmillan's Magazine*, vol. 81, p 416 The writer was afterwards Admiral Sir Humphrey Senhouse.
12. See Colonel Owen's letters. Allen: *Memoirs of Hargood*, p. 138.
13. See his earlier Memorandum, *Fighting Instructions*, p. 315. "The other mode would be to stand under an easy but commanding sail directly for their headmost ship, so as to prevent the enemy from knowing whether I should pass to windward or to leeward of him."

14. It was already dark, and he used No. 31 of the Night Signals, and began, after his custom, to burn blue lights to indicate his position: *Téméraire's Signal Log*.
15. See Lieutenant Senhouse to his mother, October 27th: "The *Africa*, who had parted in the night." She was not sent to scout ahead, as is sometimes stated.
16. See Reports of the various commanders in Desbrière's *Trafalgar*, and particularly the plan attached to that of Prigny, Chief of the Staff. The confusion of the British fleet is shown by the entries in the logs of how the enemy bore. *Victory* has E. to E.S.E.; *Royal Sovereign* has E.S.E. to E. by N., and must therefore have been little south of *Victory*; *Britannia* E.S.E., ahead of Nelson; *Téméraire* S.E., still further ahead; *Neptune* E. by S., close to *Victory*. *Dreadnought* of Collingwood's division saw them E.N.E., and was S.W. of *Victory* — that is, to windward instead of leeward. *Spartiate* of Nelson's division saw them N.N.E.; *Conqueror* N.E. — both therefore correctly astern of him, as were also *Minotaur* and *Agamemnon*; but *Ajax* and *Africa* were ahead.

CHAPTER XXIII

1. For the text of the Memorandum, see *post, Appendix D.*
2. To Lord Garlies, Oct. 28th: Bourchier, *Life of Codrington*, i. 60 and 77.
3. Captain Moorsom to his father, November 1st, 1805: *Great Sea Fights*, ii. 242. In this letter he says, "We kept going down in two columns, pointing to their centre nearly in this manner," and then in the original he gives a rough diagram showing the two British columns parallel with one another, and nearly vertical to the enemy's line. See *post, Appendix E.*
4. *The Principles of Naval Tactics, exemplified with Tables for facilitating the several evolutions*. By Captain C. R. Moorsom, R.N. London, 1843.
5. This remarkable paper was communicated to *Macmillan's Magazine* in 1900 by the Admiral's daughter. Miss Senhouse believed it was written between 1827 and 1830, but as it was communicated to Sir Charles Ekins, and printed in part by him in 1824 (see *Naval Battles*, p. 271), it must have been originally written earlier, and possibly at Ekins' request. Miss Senhouse's manuscript, however, is a somewhat amplified form, more careful to repudiate any suspicion of belittling of Nelson, and it may have been written later, possibly even when he was Hotham's flag-captain in the Mediterranean. It contains at least this curious addition: "There is a rising naval power which possesses the germs of a growing equality with the naval power of this country, and which may one day rise nearly to the colossal height its great prototype has obtained." This power he contrasts favourably with that of France and Spain, and regards with such serious apprehension as to deprecate the use of Nelson's tactics against it. He of course is referring to the rising power of Turkey and Egypt, which was broken by Codrington at Navarino in 1827. The manuscript, therefore, was probably produced before that time, but the menace continued to exist for some years after. It was, in any case, the result of mature reflection by an experienced staff officer. At the battle he was a lieutenant of only three years' standing, and knew nothing of Nelson's "Plan" or intentions. (See his letter of October 27th, 1805. *Ibid.*, p. 415.) He says there that the plan of attack had been so well arranged . . . that nothing was requisite but the signal to alter course, but he then believed the plan was for Collingwood to cut through the enemy's line or pass ahead or astern of it as convenient and engage them from to leeward, while Nelson doubled on the part engaged from to windward.
6. *Naval Battles*, 268. Ekins wrote in 1824.
7. *Signals and Instructions for the use of H.M. Fleet*, 1816. Signal I. 7, p. 28. *Post, Appendix C.*
8. Fernandez Duro: *Armada Espa—ola*, viii. 353.
9. This was certainly the view taken by the author of the Signal Book of 1816. The instruction in the "Trafalgar Signal" reads: "It is to be considered that the conduct of the Lee Division, after breaking the line, is left to its commander," *i.e.* in the absence of special instructions. See *post, Appendix C.*
10. In a marginal note he explains that if the enemy are less than forty, only a proportionate number of the rear are to be cut off. "British to be ¼ superior to the enemy cut off."

11. For the original as drawn by Nelson, see *post*, p.274. The diagrams differ slightly in the various copies. In one in the British Museum, for instance, it stands thus: —

Sail	8		Advanced Squadron	
	16	40	Weather line	British
	16		Lee line	
		Enemy		
				46 sail

12. The signal provided was a "Single Flag," not in the printed book. He chose the eighth flag, on p. 17, "Yellow with blue fly," which had not been appropriated as a tactical signal, and gave it this signification in MS.: — "Cut through the enemy's line, and engage close on the other side. *N.B.* — This signal to be repeated by all ships." It stands thus in Hardy's copy of the Signal Book now in the possession of Commander Sir Malcolm Macgregor, R.N. The signal was not made at the action.
13. At Sardinia and Barbadoes.
14. *Signals and Instructions* (N.R.S.), p. 73. An "Order of Battle and Sailing" similar to, but not identical with, the above was printed by Nicolas, (vii. 94). It is not signed or dated though assigned to October 9th, and may be a discarded draft of earlier date. It shows only a van and a rear squadron with no divisional organisation. The fifth station in each squadron is filled up and not left blank as in the Northesk copy. The *Kent* is not mentioned, her place being filled by *Orion* (Codrington), who was finally stationed next astern of *Ajax* in Nelson's squadron.
15. The *Dreadnought* appears in this station in the Nicolas plan (vol. vii. 301). She certainly cannot have remained the rearmost ship, for she was one of the three three-deckers specially ordered to take station as her speed would allow. See *Ibid.*, p. 115.
16. See *post, Appendix E.*
17. Nelson to Ball, Oct. 15th: Nicolas, vii. 123.
18. She was taken in 1795, and when first placed on the Navy List was rated as an 80-gun ship. Her armament was 30 32-pounders; 30 24-pounders;18 9-pounders; 14 32-pounder carronades, and 4 24-pounders. Her complement was 700 men, only 50 less than the 98's.
19. Harvey to his Wife: *Great Sea Fights*, ii. 225, and Senhouse to his Mother: *Macmillan's Magazine*, vol. lxxxi. 417.
20. Nicolas, vii. 111, October 11th.

CHAPTER XXIV

1. The varying directions of the wind are very important, particularly as a recent and very ingenious attempt, based on the wind, has been made to show that Nelson's attack was not perpendicular (Thursfield, *Nelson and Other Naval Studies*). It proceeds on the assumption that the wind was steady at north-west as given in the *Victory's* Log up to noon, though this is contradicted by Collingwood himself, who said in his despatch that the wind was about west. He is abundantly confirmed by the French reports, which are unanimous that the wind was as above stated, and by most of the British Logs. *Prince* (Master s Log) has west to south-west. *Neptune* (Captain's Log) gives 5.0 to 8.0 west; 8.0 to 12.0 west by south; 12.0 to 6.0 west. *Thunderer* gives it at noon, south-west by south. The general testimony is that it shifted from somewhere north of west to west, and was even sometimes south of west *Bellerophon* enters successively "west by north," "north-east by north," "north-north-west," and "westerly." *Dreadnought* has "north-west to west." *Revenge* gives it "variable, calm, variable."

2. *The* line of bearing (larboard or starboard) was a highly technical expression meaning a bow-and-quarter line formed seven points from the wind, so that when the ships hauled to the wind together they would be on the (larboard or starboard) tack in close-hauled line of battle. A line of bearing meant any bow-and-quarter line formed on the point of the compass indicated.
3. See "Instructions respecting the Order of Sailing": *Signal Book*, 1799, article ii. p. 127. "The columns are to be parallel to each other, every ship steering in the wake of the leading ship of her column." Cf. *Signals and Instructions* (*Navy Records Society*), pp. 75-77.
4. No. 72. "Form the order of sailing in two columns." The corresponding instruction in the *Signal Book*, No. 4, p. 101, provides that "when a signal is made for any line or order of sailing" with a compass signal, that signal indicates "the direction in which the line is to be formed." If a compass signal is hoisted after the main signal has been answered "it is to show the course the fleet is to steer." In this case no compass signal was hoisted with the one for the order of sailing. What followed was a separate signal, No. 76 = "When lying-to or sailing by the wind to bear-up and sail large on the course steered by the Admiral or that pointed out by signal." In this case east-north-east was "the course pointed out." It has been assumed sometimes that this meant "bear-up together," but the corresponding instruction (No 14, p. 132) begins, "When the fleet is to bear-up in succession and sail large," and it proceeds to say how each ship is to behave with regard to her seconds ahead and astern. It was a signal Nelson was in the habit of making to an unformed fleet, *e.g.*, "Proceedings of the Fleet, September 30th" (*Add. MSS.*, 34973): "At 1.0 hove-to; at 6.0 made general signal to make sail after lying-'to (*i.e.* No. 76); at 6.35, to tack in succession; at 6.35 to bear-up and sail large (No. 76 again); at 6.42 general, to form the established order of sailing." The corresponding signals for a formed fleet "in line of battle or order of sailing" were Nos. 79 to 82. Nos. 79 and 80 to alter course in succession to port or starboard one point or as directed by compass signal; Nos. 81 and 82 to alter course together. There was no signal for an unformed fleet to bear-up together. Until it was in order of battle or sailing such an order could not be given to it, for the simple reason that it would have thrown the fleet out of cruising order, that is, the loose order that was specially maintained to facilitate a rapid formation of the order of sailing.
5. *Masters' Logs*, P.R.O. This Log unfortunately was not printed either by Nicolas or in the *Great Sea Fights*. Otherwise so careful an historian as Admiral Colomb would never have hazarded his unlucky conjecture that the fleet bore up together (*The Battle of Trafalgar*, 1905, reprinted from the *United Service Magazine*). Senhouse also is perfectly clear on the point. "The British fleet," he says, "bore up in succession . . . and continued in the order of sailing of two divisions in line-ahead until the attack" (*Macmillan's Magazine*, vol. lxxxi. 422). The term "in succession" at that time was used not only for movements in line-ahead, but also for movements in cruising order — meaning that no ship was to tack or haul upon the new course till the ship ahead of her had done so. It was a device to prevent confusion and accident.
6. Nicolas, vii. 137. Collingwood in his Journal clearly states that this is what happened. "6.30, Order of Sailing in two columns. . . . Bore up . . . the British fleet in two columns bearing down on them" (*Great Sea Fights*, ii. 201). At first he bore up south 80 east presumably to open out the correct distance from the *Victory* (*Royal Sovereign*, Captain's Log). See also Captain Moorsom's and Captain Harvey's descriptions and the Logs *passim*, as summarised by Mr. Newbolt, *Year of Trafalgar*, pp. 83-4. "Column" in the *Signal Book* was a technical equivalent borrowed from the French for "line-ahead." "Line-ahead" does not occur at all in the signals relating to order of sailing.
7. Some ships seem to have anticipated Nelson's general signal in order as was usual to get nearer their place. See Logs of *Conqueror* and *Ajax: Great Sea Fights*, ii. 257 and 285.
8. See Desbrière, *Trafalgar*, pp. 184-5 and in his *Appendix*, Report of Villeneuve, p. 129; Dumanoir, p. 150; Magendie, p 178; Lucas (*Redoutable*), p. 197; Philibert (Magon's chief-of-staff), p. 233; Épron (Argonaute), p 249L'Achille, p. 263. Two French vessels, *Neptune* (p. 192) and *Fougueux* (p. 214) report the enemy forming en échiquier (*i.e.* line of bearing) and then in column.
9. Desbrière, *Trafalgar*, p. 129.
10. *Ibid.*, p. 192, *Neptune's* report. See also p. 166, Report of the *Héros*, where the text has "enemi en pelotons."

11. Clarke and M'Arthur, ii. 146, and Nicolas, vii. 138.
12. Gravina's Staff report makes this quite clear: "A las 8," it says, "la se—al de virar en redondo a un tempo (to wear together) arrivando succesivamente (bearing up in succession) para quedar alineados en la mura de babor (in order to get into line on the port tack)."
13. It is a curious fact that of the seventeen ships which record the preliminary signals only seven mention that for the order of sailing.
14. To Pasley, December 16th: Nicolas, vii. 241.
15. *Victory* records the change of course thus: "At 7.0 course east-northeast. At 8.0 (till noon), east by north." *Neptune* has: "At 7.0, north-east by east. At 8.0 (till noon), east half-north." Collingwood's Journal has the signal: "At 7.40 to bear up east." *Royal Sovereign's* Log gives her course generally as "south 80 east." *Tonnant* (her second) "east by south." *Conqueror* (astern of *Neptune*) has "east half-south." Confusion has arisen as to the actual course of the approach, since some vessels record only the first compass signal and some only the second. *Ajax* is the only ship that records both correctly.
16. Desbrière, *Trafalgar, App.*, p. 124.
17. This, the most important tactical order in the battle, has always been placed about 11 o'clock, owing to the careless way the Log of the *Royal Sovereign* was kept. *Thunderer* also has it entered, so that it appears in the afternoon. But there are two signal Logs — *Téméraire* and *Defence* — which fix it exactly, though by a miracle they seem to have escaped the notice of the numerous writers who have dealt with the battle. Téméraire (Master's Log) has "8.47, *Royal Sovereign* to Larboard Division Nos. 42 and 88." *Defence* (both Captain's and Master's Logs) has "8.45 Sig. 50 divisional from *Royal Sovereign;* 8.46, ditto 42 and 88." No. 50 is "to keep larboard line of bearing though on starboard tack." *Agamemnon*, in Nelson's division, answered it, thinking it was general. It was probably a mistake of the signal officer, and was at once annulled by No. 42: "Form the larboard line of bearing, steering the course indicated." No. 88 was: "Make more sail, the leading ship first if in line of battle or order of sailing."
18. See *Signals and Instructions* (*Navy Records Society*), p. 77, and *Signal Book*, 1799, Instruction xv. p. 120.
19. The instruction attached to the signal (*Signal Book*, 1799, p. 149, Instruction vii.) provides that "the ships are to place themselves in such a manner that if they haul to the wind together on the tack for which the line of bearing is formed, they would immediately form line on that tack. To do this every ship must bring the ship which would be her second ahead, if the line of battle were formed, to bear on that point of the compass on which the fleet would sail, viz. on that point of the compass which is seven points from the direction of the wind, or six points, if the signal is made to keep close to the wind.
20. Signal 81, and Instruction viii. p. 150.
21. *Victory's* Log says: "Still standing for the enemy's van," but as he is recorded to have headed for the 14th ship, and he never altered his course from E. by N., it is clear "van" here means "the van half of the fleet."
22. In view of the attempts to show Nelson's approach could not have been vertical owing to the supposed movement of the enemy to the northward, the point that they were motionless is very important. The evidence is conclusive from both sides. Form the logs in *Great Sea Fights* we have: "A.M. The enemy forming the line and waiting our attack" (*Britannia*, p. 211). "A.M. Enemy's fleet lying-to and forming the line" (*Spartiate*, p. 262, two entries). "At 12.10 the enemy's fleet then ahead, lying-to" (*Colossus*, p. 265). "At noon . . . the combined fleet lying to" (*Entrepenant*, p. 320). Walker of the *Bellerephon* says: "While we were bearing down on them they formed line and waited for us with great intrepity" (*Ibid.*, p. 323). Senhouse says they were "lying with their main-top sails to the mast and consequently could not keep accurate station" (*Macmillan's Magazine*, vol. lxxxi. p. 421). From the French accounts it is clear that the only motion was what was necessary for forming the line. "Les vaisseaux de l'arrière-garde ont été obligés de se tenir en panne pendant très longtemps" (Prigny's *Abstract*, Desbrière, p. 285). In the *Corps de Bataille* he says it was the same, "d'autres étaient en panne au moment où le combat a commencé" (*Ibid.*, p. 186, and see the Reports he quotes). The *Bucentaure* herself was hove-to (*Ibid.*, p. 187). We have also the fact that the *Victory* steered all through the approach for the 14th ship from the van and records no change in her course from hour to hour, the presumption is that the *Victory* did not change.

23. Clarke and M'Arthur, ii. ch. xii. p. 148. Dr. Beatty says *Victory* signalled *Téméraire* and *Leviathan* to go ahead. — Nicolas, vii. 146. *Téméraire* (Master's Log) records at 9.36 a signal, No. 269, for *Leviathan* to take station astern of *Téméraire*. *Neptune* was evidently lagging.
24. Log of *Royal Sovereign:* "At 11.0, Set studding sails."
25. All the French plans show this, and it is confirmed by such ships of Nelson's division as give their courses, *e.g. Orion* at 7.0, E. by N.; 8.0, E.; 9.0, E. by S.; 10-11, E. by S.½ S.; 12.0 E.S.E.
26. Villeneuve himself says at 9.0. The official abstract puts it as late as 11.0.
27. *Neptune* gives it W. by S., *Thunderer* (at 12.15) S.W. by S.
28. Lieutenant G.L. Browne of the *Victory* wrote: "At 11.0 we were about three miles from the enemy. — *Great Sea Fights*, ii. 197.
29. The fastest ships were doing a little over three knots, the slower ones about two. *Prince*, a very slow ship, gives her speed at two knots except between 9.0 and 10.0, when it was only one. *Neptune*, who at first had been doing over three, dropped to 1.4 after 9.0, and so continued. *Minotaur*, who had been doing 1.4, increased to 2 at 9.0. *Spartiate*, her second, did 2 throughout. *Dreadnought*, another slow three-decker, did only one knot till 10.0, when she increased up to 2 at noon. *Tonnant* did 2 and a little over, and 2.4 as she came into action. *Revenge*, a fast ship, increased from about 1½ to 2.4 and 3.4 as she came into action. *Defence*, a connecting ship, who had to run down from the northward on a wind, only did one. *Conqueror* did 2 throughout. *Swiftsure* at 11.0 increased from 2 to 3. *Victory* and *Royal Sovereign* apparently were doing 3 at the finish.
30. *Life of Codrington*, vol. ii. p. 60. Similarly *Defiance* enters in her Log simply "Standing for the enemy's fleet," without the usual specification of the actual course.
31. Some of the ships give their courses in detail. Of the lee division, *Tonnant's* was E. by S. all the time. *Revenge*, after her signal was made, shifted from E. by N. to E., and did not change again. *Swiftsure's* course was at 7.0 N.E.; at 8, N.E. by E.; at 10.0, E.N.E., and at 11.0, after Collingwood's last signal, E.S.E. *Defence* came down from the northward S.S.W., S. by W., and at 10.0 was going S.S.E. again. *Prince* did, E., E. by N., E.N.E, and at 10.0 turned E. *Dreadnought* did, at 7.0 E.N.E.; at 8.0 E. by N., and at 10.0 shifted to E. by S.¼ S., and kept it till she came into action. The ill-kept log of the *Royal Sovereign* gives her course as S. 80 E. throughout. In Nelson's division *Téméraire* only gives N. 34 E. *Neptune*, at 7.0 N.E. by E. and, after 8.0 E. ½ N.; *Conqueror*, E. ½ S. till noon; *Orion*, at 7.0 E. by N.; at 8.0, E.; at 9.0, E. by S., then for two hours E. by S. ½ S., and at noon E.S.E. *Spartiate* did, N.E. by E. till noon, and *Minotaur* must have done the same. *Britannia*, went E. till noon, and then turned E.S.E.
32. All the reports of the Allied centre, as well as the French official "Abstract," agree in this. Colonel Desbrière, however (*Trafalgar*, p. 208), thought the evidence on the whole shows that Nelson's division made as high as the vessel at the head of the allied line, and then filed off under the fire of the van on the opposite tack and at half gun-shot, till the moment he attacked the stern of the *Bucentaure*. But he only cites the reports of *Intrépide* and *Scipion*, and neither of these, if read in the light of Prigny's warning as to squadronal designations, appears to support his view. *Scipion* says Nelson's column "se portait sur le centre de l'avant-garde," by which may well be meant the centre of the van half of the line, that is, just ahead of the *S. Trinidad*. *Intrépide* says no more than that Nelson "manœuvrait pour couper en arrière du *Bucentaure*." Dumanoir, like the *Scipion*, says he made "sur le centre de notre avant-garde," and refers to a plan which shows the *Victory* steering to cut the line ahead of *S. Trinidad*. Of Nelson's alleged feint on the van of the line there is really no evidence except that of Codrington.
33. Vol. iii. 397.
34. See Blackwood to his wife: Nicolas, vii. 226. "Would to God he had lived to see his prizes and the Admirals he had taken — three in all — amongst them the French Commander-in-chief, who, I am sorry to say, is Villeneuve and not Decrès." An unpublished letter of Nelson's chaplain, Scott, confirms his preoccupation with the capture of the Commander-in-chief. "It was what he particularly aimed at," he says; but adds, "As, however, the Frenchman never hoisted his flag it was not yet known [*i.e.* when Nelson died] that the Admiral was taken." In this Scott was certainly mistaken. "I never went," he says, "higher than the middle deck. . . . I was quartered below with the Surgeon." He must, then, have gone

to his station before Villeneuve showed his flag. There can be no doubt it was shown, as the French and Spanish reports agree, or that it was seen by Nelson; for *Spartiate*, the last ship in the line, records: "12.59, *Victory* bearing down between a Spanish four-decker and a French two-decker with an Admiral's flag at the main" (Captains' Logs, P.R.O.). In her Master's Journal is the note: "The watch, the minutes of the action was taken by, appears to have been 34 minutes too fast." It was half-an-hour faster still by *Victory's* time, which makes *Spartiate's* 12.59 equal *Victory's* 11.55.

35. See Nicolas, vii. 154, *note*. The only other mention of Nelson's altering his course is when he altered it to starboard, *e.g. Thunderer's Log:* "Observed the *Victory* alter her course and lead . . . towards the enemy's centre "— *Ibid.*, 202, *note*.
36. The time here seems to be much the same as *Victory's*. *Euryalus* repeated, "England expects, &c." at 11.56. Pascoe says it was made about 11.45.
37. Vol. iii. p. 392.
38. The best contemporary French historian, a veteran of the older wars, had no doubt, after his careful and sagacious study of the battle, that this was what Nelson meant, though he naturally regarded it as a feint. "Nelson first made a feint of attacking the van and rear of the fleet. Then he reassembled his force on the centre and abandoned the fate of the action to the intelligence of his captains." — Mathieu Dumas, *Précis des Evénements Militaires*, xiv. 408.
39. Lieutenant G.L. Browne of the *Victory: Great Sea Fights* ii 196. He records it as made at 10.40. James says it was "a few minutes before the action commenced," but Browne says distinctly it was at 10.40 and he was assistant flag-lieutenant.
40. *Neptune* (Master's Log). "11.50, *Téméraire* took station astern of *Victory*, *Neptune* next." *Téméraire* (Captain's Log). "Noon *Victory* to *Téméraire*, 269, with *Victory's* pennants." *Téméraire*'s clock was 20 minutes ahead of *Victory s.* Captain Harvey says he had the signal about 15 minutes before the *Victory* opened fire. That would make it about 11 45.
41. *Neptune's* log puts it at 11.50: Nicolas, vii. 186. It was 7 minutes before *Royal Sovereign* opened fire, which *Victory* says was at 11.40.
42. Rapport du Capitaine de vaisseau Lucas (*Redoubtable*): Desbrière, *Trafalgar, App.*, 196.
43. The *Santisima Trinidad's* report (Desbrière, *Trafalgar, App.* 365) gives the situation thus: The *Victory* steered for the combined centre "formando con el Téméraire y el *Neptune* de tres pontes una linea casi paralela de la que formaban en acquella parte el *Bucentaure* por su proa el *Trinidad* y por la de este el *Hèros*." As these three ships had got into line of bearing the meaning seems to be that Nelson and his two consorts were also in a line of bearing or irregular line abreast, roughly parallel to that formed by *Trinidad* and her two seconds. *Cf.* Codrington: "Our line pressed so much upon each other as to be obliged to go bow and quarter line instead of ahead." — *Life*, i. 64.
44. She was first-rate of 112 guns, bearing the flag of Vice-Admiral de Alava, and according to Colonel Desbrière was thirteenth from the rear in actual line: *Trafalgar*, p. 207.
45. *Macmillans Magazine*, vol. lxxxi. 424.
46. *Orion's Journal:* Nicolas, vii. 192, *note*. What Codrington wrote at the time is of course good evidence, to be distinguished from the memories of his old age.
47. See the plan attached to Prigny's report. No. 4, Desbrière, *Trafalgar, App*. 142.
48. *Life of Codrington*, i. 61. Lord Northesk's part in battle is very obscure. He claims to have engaged ten minutes after Nelson, "three of the enemy's ships having opened their fire on us while edging (sic) down." — Log of *Britannia:* "At 3.0," it says, "passed through the line." This suggests he engaged for two hours at considerable range. Collingwood placed him last in his official list, but *Spartiate* and *Minotaur* were certainly astern of him. Magendie in the plan attached to his report places him fourth — possibly his real place in the order of battle. But the most authoritative lists and plans put him sixth, with *Ajax* and *Orion* following.
49. *Thunderer*, Captain's Log, P.R.O.
50. Collingwood's Journal: *Great Sea Fights*, ii. 203. He says he signalled after 3.30. See also Logs of *Minotaur* and *Spartiate*, *Ibid.*, 250 and 270. *Thunderer* says she got a verbal order after 3.30 (Nicolas, vii. 202). For

Dumanoir's account, see Desbrière: *Trafalgar, App*. 152. The signals at this interesting time unfortunately are missing from *Euryalus's* Log, and *Téméraire* ceased to record anything after 12.30.

51. *Log of the Dreadnought*. "At 4.5 made and repeated 101 general" (= about 3.35 *Victory's* time). *Phœbe* (frigate) says she repeated it from the *Victory* at 3.20 (= 3.40 *Victory's* time). *Victory* still had her mizzen standing at that time, and probably repeated the signal. The signification was: "Come to the wind in succession on the larboard tack after the leading ship, when arrived in the wake thereof." Read with the accompanying instruction, it was in effect an order for each division to re-form line by tacking or wearing as the circumstances required.
52. *Britannia* says she obeyed the signal at 4.30 (= 3.40 *Victory's* time).
53. *Diario del navio Principe de Asturias* (Gravina's flagship): Desbrière,(*Trafalgar, App*. 387. The passage is a note added subsequently.

CHAPTER XXV

1. Collingwood to Cornwallis, Oct. 26th: *Hist. MSS. Com*., *Various Collections*, vi. 412.
2. Nicolas, vii. 231: *Euryalus* off Cadiz, Oct. 24th.
3. *Hist. MSS. Com*., *Various Collections*, vi. 412, Oct. 26th.
4. Cornwallis to Marsden, October 29th, with report of Captain Rodd of the *Indefatigable*, 44: *In-letters*, 129. He had been sent to the westward of the Channel to cover the home-coming convoys, and on September 20th had sighted Allemand in latitude 48° 57′ and longitude 18° 19′. Having lost touch he ran back to inform Cornwallis, and meeting Strachan just as he was starting in search of Allemand, was detained by him and taken down to Vigo.
5. Captain Baker's Journal enclosed in Strachan's despatch: *Ibid*., Nov. 5th.
6. Strachan took these two vessels for part of the enemy's squadron. "We saw six sail," he wrote to Cornwallis, "and cannot conceive which way the other two went" — *Hist. MSS. Com*., *Var. Coll*., vi. 413.
7. Desbrière, *Projets et Tentatives*, v. 798-800.

CHAPTER XXVI

1. This famous corps, which served under the British flag with so much distinction all over Europe till the end of the war, consisted mainly of Hanoverian troops who, rather than submit to the French under the Convention of Suhlingen (June 3, 1803), escaped to England and remained in the king's service. See Beamish, *History of the King's German Legion*.
2. Harrowby's first despatch from Berlin, and Don's first from Cuxhaven, are dated November 17th. See Rose, *Third Coalition*, p. 222, and *War Office* (1) *In-letters*, 186.
3. Craig to Castlereagh, November 2nd and December 9th: *War Office* (1), 280.
4. Elliot to Mulgrave, Dec. 10th: Auriol. ii. 693. Napoleon to Prince Eugène, and Berthier to St. Cyr: *Ibid*., pp. 704-5.
5. Details of the whole episode are to be found in the despatches of Don, of Brigadier Decken (chief intelligence officer with Don), and of Lord Cathcart, the British, Commander-in-chief, all in *War Office* (1) *In-letters*, 186. Castlereagh's are in *Ibid*. (6), *Out-letters* (*Secretary of State*), 13, and in his *Correspondence, Second Series*, vol. ii. Harrowby's are in Rose, *Third Coalition*.
6. Elliot to Mulgrave, December 10th: Printed by Auriol, ii. 693.
7. A return, dated January 1806, gives the whole force as 27,000, of which the German Legion were 11,000. There were five British brigades under Dundas, Fraser, Wellesley. Shirbrook, and Hill. — *W.O*. (1), 186, January 2nd and 14th.
8. Cathcart to Castlereagh, December 25th (enclosing Harrowby to Cathcart, December 20th), and Cathcart to Castlereagh, January 1st: *W.O*. (1) 176.

9. Auriol, ii. 745: *Protocol of the Council of War.*
10. Elliot to Mulgrave, January 13th (Auriol, ii. 778) The reason for this order does not seem to be known, but it may be not unconnected with armistice and the fact that the remnants of the Russian army were permitted to retire without further molestation. Tolstoi appears to have told Cathcart the idea of Lacy's recall was to concentrate in Poland for an expected campaign in concert with Prussia. Cathcart to Castlereagh, December 25th: *W.O.* (1), 186.
11. Mrs. Nugent to Cornwallis, Jan. 23, 1806: *Hist. MSS. Com.*, *Various Collections*, vi. 417.
12. Barham lived in retirement nearly till the end of the war, dying on June 17, 1813, at the advanced age of eighty-seven. There was a rumour that he was to be succeeded by Lord St. Vincent "as Lord High Admiral at sea, to command from Cape Finisterre to John o' Groat's House in Scotland," but this was entirely contrary to the British tradition, and his place was given to a civilian, Charles Grey, the Earl Grey of the Reform Bill.
13. For these negotiations see the excellent monograph by Coquelle, *Napoléon et Angleterre*, part ii. Translation by G.D. Knox.

APPENDIX D

1. Paragraphing and punctuation are given as in the original. From the nature of Scott's amendments (printed in italics) it would seem as though he read the draft over to Nelson and suggested improvements in grammar, &c. as he went on.
2. Inserted by Scott.
3. Nelson first wrote here "in fact command his line and," but the words are deleted, presumably to make it clear he was not to have the direction of his line at first.
4. For the words "to windward in line of battle, and that the two lines," Nelson first wrote, "to windward, but in that position that the two lines."
5. Here are deleted the words, "I shall suppose them forty-six sail in the line of battle." The marginal note (see below, note 11.) was substituted.
6. "Your" deleted.
7. Deleted by Nelson.
8. "Fleet" inserted.
9. For "I will suppose" he first wrote "supposing."
10. "Enemy's" inserted.
11. Here Scott inserted an asterisk referring to a note which Nelson wrote in the upper margin, reversing the paper. It is as follows: "The enemy's fleet is supposed to consist of 46 sail of the line, British fleet 40. If either be less, only a proportionate number of enemy's ships are to be cut off. B. to be ¼ superior to the E. cut off."
12. "Friends" deleted and "rear" substituted.
13. The draft breaks off before this clause with a space. "Of the intended attack from to windward," occupies just one line, so that it may or may not have been intended as a heading to all that follows. The diagram is very roughly drawn. The lines are not straight or parallel, as in the illustration in this text, but their relative proportions and distances (half scale) are preserved.
14. "Then" inserted by Nelson.
15. In the upper margin is this note: "Vide instructions for signal, Yellow with blue fly. Page 17. Eighth flag, with reference to appendix." The "Appendix" was a small pamphlet of additional signals issued by the Admiralty in1804. This signal, however, is not in it. The presumption is that Nelson himself added it to the Appendix.
16. Inserted by Scott.
17. Scott suggested "are."
18. Here Nelson came to the extreme end of the second sheet of paper.

INDEX

B

C